Contextual Design

SECOND EDITION

Design for Life

CONTEXTUAL DESIGN

SECOND EDITION

Design for Life

KAREN HOLTZBLATT

HUGH BEYER

INCONTEXT DESIGN

ELSEVIER

AMSTERDAM • BOSTON • HEIDELBERG • LONDON • NEW YORK • OXFORD
PARIS • SAN DIEGO • SAN FRANCISCO • SINGAPORE • SYDNEY • TOKYO

Morgan Kaufmann is an imprint of Elsevier

Library of Congress Cataloging-in-Publication Data
A catalog record for this book is available from the Library of Congress

British Library Cataloguing-in-Publication Data
A catalogue record for this book is available from the British Library

ISBN: 978-0-12-800894-2

For information on all Elsevier publications
visit our website at https://www.elsevier.com/

Working together
to grow libraries in
developing countries

www.elsevier.com • www.bookaid.org

Publisher: Todd Green
Acquisition Editor: Todd Green
Editorial Project Manager: Anna Valutkevich
Production Project Manager: Punithavathy Govindaradjane
Designer: Greg Harris

Typeset by TNQ Books and Journals

Acclaim for *Contextual Design: Design for Life*

At GM, we are committed to putting the customer at the center of everything we do. By better understanding our customers, Contextual Design helps us drive innovation and design for their needs today.

—MIKE HICHME
Director, Vehicle User Interface

If you are going to the rainforest, you need a guide. Contextual Design has been that guide at Autodesk.

—AMAR HANSPAL
Senior Vice President, Products, Autodesk

At Wolters Kluwer, a global technology, software and professional information services company, one of our core values is to Focus on Customer Success. With customers at the center of what we do, we leverage Contextual Design as one of our core customer insight techniques. For years we've used Contextual Design as a best practice for driving innovation and designing award-winning products for our customers including professionals in the tax, accounting, audit, health, legal, regulatory, government, risk and compliance fields.

—KAREN ABRAMSON
Chief Executive Officer, Wolters Kluwer Tax and Accounting

For many years, Holtzblatt and Beyer have been pioneers in the field of human-computer interaction, showing how the context of computer use can be (and needs to be) the central focus of analysis and design. This book conveys the understanding and wisdom that they have gained from their experience in Contextual Design in a form that is accessible to students and design practitioners. It has been updated to reflect the new realities of interacting with computers, as people move to mobile and ubiquitous computing. It will serve as a guide and handbook for the next generation of interaction designers, and as a result we can expect the usability and appropriateness of computer systems to be continue improving.

—TERRY WINOGRAD
Professor Computer Science, Stanford University

To all the teams we have worked with – to all the employees of InContext – to all the professors who taught Contextual Design and all their students – to the industry for valuing user centered design.

Contents

Acknowledgments

When we first started our consulting business we said we'd run the company until we put ourselves out of business—until the industry come to accept the primacy of user data in the design process and indeed, the primacy of product design itself—deliberate design of the structure of the product and the user experience. Well, InContext is still in business today but our goals have largely been met—the field of user experience design is real and companies know they need this function. Not every company has the skill and not every product or IT organization knows the power of designing with data—but they know that it is now an expected part of product design. Much has happened in the last 19 years since the first book was printed.

This kind of industry change only results from a grassroot movement. We have provided an effective, repeatable process that works for teams. We have been spokespersons for user-centered design techniques and for our new techniques that help teams create a "cool" user experience. But our efforts and presentations alone would never have transformed the industry. We have been humbled and excited by the number of universities now using our books as core to their curriculum. We have been blessed by companies hiring us to help their teams learn the techniques. We have been honored with recognition of our contributions. But without the user researchers, user interface designers, marketers, product managers, directors, and all the rest taking up the methods and using them on real projects, little in the industry would have changed. We extend our deepest gratitude to the academics and practitioners who have helped to spread the word and used the processes in their own work. We know that you tune the process to your needs—that's to be expected—but you have taken on the core tenants of user-centered design, and we are thankful that you think that our techniques can help you deliver wonderful and successful products.

Our work would not be possible without a world ready to receive it—and professors ready to teach it. But the advances and changes in Contextual Design would also not have been possible without the wonderful work of every employee of InContext over the years. Together we worked with teams on their projects, and this work honed and challenged the process. The book you read today is a reflection of those learnings—what worked and didn't work in the original techniques, particularly as the type of people using the techniques went from developers to user experience experts working with cross-functional teams and the projects went from desktop software to consumer goods, vehicles, mobile apps, web applications and services, and more. The Contextual Design technique has been tuned over the years through this real-world experience. Thank you to our coaches and team members for making it a better process. A special thanks to Nancy Fike, Dave Flotree, Wendy Fritzke, Larry Marturano, David Rondeau, Kelley Wagg, Shelley Wood, Eli Wylen, and more for all their work tuning, teaching, and challenging the process with teams.

One of the greatest changes has been the introduction of the Cool Concepts and their implications for the design of the suite of products and applications that support people's lives across multiple platforms. The Cool Project was conducted by the InContext team and honed in partnership with them. Finalizing the concepts and the new techniques you see in this book was largely influenced by our collaboration with David Rondeau, our Director of Design for many years. Thank you David for your great work and collaboration—without you this would not have happened.

We also want to call out our special partnership with Carol Farnsworth and Daniel Rosenberg then at SAP for our collaboration bringing the Cool Concepts to enterprise work and developing the Cool Metric to show its validity and stability.

And we want to call out our special partnership with CMU who asked us to help them teach Contextual Design within a university context. They are not the only university we have collaborated with, but thanks to Bonnie John; they were one of the first to take up the method, and their commitment to teaching it well is commendable. This experience also taught us how the method was received by young emerging professionals and influenced its evolution.

We cannot even name all of the professors who have taken up Contextual Design—and all the other universities we have touched over the years—without you the word would not have spread so widely. Thank you so much for believing and teaching Contextual techniques.

Looking back at the origins of the work, we again want to thank:

John Whiteside who started Karen off in this industry and had the foresight to know that we needed to do something new to get real product transformation. And thanks to the whole SUE group at Digital Equipment Corporation, as well as Jonathan Grudin and Steve Poltrock, who took up the flag early on.

A special thanks to Sandy Jones in the SUE group, Karen's first partner in making the ideas about field data real.

John Bennett, Karen's first mentor, who pushed her into the CHI community and helped her write my first published words about a contextual perspective.

Lou Cohen, who introduced Karen to all the concepts and processes of quality—from which we stole shamelessly—and who nagged her into making the first Contextual Inquiry course.

Larry Constantaine, our consulting business mentor, who helped us learn to write, publish, and believe in our work.

Diane Cerra, our first editor, for her nagging and encouragement—and great dinners.

This book was written again as part of the authors' wonderful partnership and collaboration. Our shared voice is at the core of this work—a voice honed over 25 years together, to the point that we can write into each other's sentences and thoughts. But this book would not be as good as we hope you think it is without the hard work of those who have helped and contributed.

To Shelley Wood, who read every word and kept us clear and honest, along with Kelley Wagg and other readers from InContext.

To David Rondeau for helping us write the chapter on Interaction Patterns and cocreating our examples used in this book.

To Allison Druin from University Maryland and Jon Zimmerman from CMU for the pieces they wrote for this book.

To our current editors for helping us get the book out the door.

Finally, we thank our families for their support of our work and tolerance when they lost our attention when writing this book or honing our processes. We love and appreciate you always.

KAREN HOLTZBLATT AND HUGH BEYER

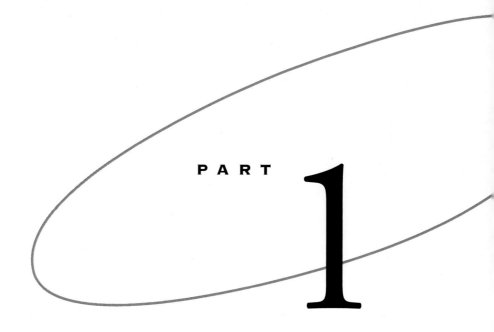

Gathering User Data

Introduction

1

Contextual Design is a user-centered design process built upon in-depth field research to drive innovative design. Contextual Design was first invented in 1988 and has since been used in a wide variety of industries and taught in universities all over the world. It is a complete front-end design process rooted in Contextual Inquiry, the widespread, industry-standard field data gathering technique. Contextual Design includes techniques to analyze and present user data, drive ideation from data, design specific product solutions, and iterate those solutions with users. In 2013, we redesigned the method to account for the way that technology has radically changed people's lives with the invention of the touch-screen phones and other always-on, always-connected, and always-carried devices. This book describes the current practices in Contextual Design, which has evolved to help teams design for the way technology now fits into peoples' lives. Twenty years ago we wrote:

> "Developing software has never been easy. But over the last 20 years the requirements on software development have gotten vastly more stringent. Whereas once computers were used by experts in glass rooms, now everyone on the street expects to use a computer to get their jobs done. Whereas once computer users knew and liked technology, now users want their computers to be as invisible as a ball–point pen so they can focus on their jobs. Whereas once applications supported a single, bounded task—compute compound interest for a bank's loans, perhaps—now they are expected

Contextual Design. http://dx.doi.org/10.1016/B978-0-12-800894-2.00001-6

to support the whole work of the business, from electronic funds transfers with the Federal Reserve to the company's Email system. It's no longer enough to be a good software engineer. To be successful in today's world, those who define and build hardware and software systems *must know how to fit them into the fabric of everyday life.*"

This is still true. But 20 years ago computers were not really mobile. Laptops were clunky and had limited use. Software applications required a person to sit at a desk, locked to a keyboard and screen, and a proprietary data source. There was no Internet back then, no possibility of streaming megabytes of data and video to a handheld device. There were no consumer applications to speak of. Supercomputers of that era couldn't match the cell phone of today. There was no online shopping, no social media, YouTube or streaming video at all, no search engine that could find anything instantly in a single request. We read paper books and newspapers. Games were locked in a box. So was business data. In other words, there was no possibility of real, on-the-go access—the technology didn't exist and the content was not available. Even the BlackBerry was a few years in the future. We had no access to all of our life's information, no support for work and life activities and no access to entertainment.

Real mobile computing radically altered how technology fits into life—so Contextual Design evolved

TERMS: PRODUCT VERSUS SYSTEM

We use the word "product" to refer to any technical system of support your team ships. This may be a new or enhancement of a commercial consumer or business product, a website, a mobile app, or suite of all these delivered on any platform. Or it may be an IT system, an enhancement or redesign of a function cluster within a larger system or a set of customized third-party products. So whatever your team is making, for the purpose of simplicity we will call a "product." When we are specifically talking to commercial versus IT professionals we will call it out.

So what did it mean to "fit systems into the fabric of everyday life," in that limited context? The history of user-centered design was a reaction to at least two things.

First, traditional product design was dominated by smart software engineers thinking up a bright idea, building it, and then trying to create a market for it. But even at that time our industry had moved away from green screens toward products that supported applications for regular people. Technology had become more sophisticated; user interfaces and interactions had gone beyond command lines. It had become critical to consider ordinary users—not specialists. Early usability professionals realized that fixing a product's problems by making better documentation made no sense. We knew we had to work with users. But usability testing, the hot new thing at the time, was and is not a way to invent a better product. Usability testing can fix 10–12% of the problems with an existing product or concept. It cannot reveal what will really enhance and transform people's lives.

Second, user-centered design[1] was driven by the need to create a space for design as an activity. A product or business system was defined as a set of requirements, a list of features that were parceled out to developers who did all the design. There was no concept at the time of design as a separate activity or of professionals who designed. A product was a list; requirement gathering was about what to put on the list. "Design," in software development, invariably and always meant design of the structure of the *code*. Even today, "design" usually means design of the look of the user interface only.

Design is its own activity and needs focused attention

As the industry moved to tools supporting everyday people, those of us leading the charge toward user-centered design recognized a need for a more systemic approach to product design. We realized that the way an engineer thinks about the world, the product, and the activity being supported is simply not the way ordinary people think and work.

---

[1] In the original book we referred to Contextual Design as a customer-centered design process. We used "customer" in the quality sense to emphasize supporting anyone using the product whether or not they were buyers. Over time the agreed-upon term became "user-centered design" and the word customer generally refers to buyers or the internal business requester for any IT system.

Witness an early word processor: Paragraphs, footnotes, headers and the like were implemented as "elements." A document was a collection of elements in a database. Behavior was coded as attributes on the elements. And so a footnote could float around the page, just by changing a few attributes! Not what any writer would expect.

Contextual Design helps teams figure out what to make to enhance life

For us, design has always meant figuring out what to make that will enhance life. Today the overarching concept of User Experience (UX) refers to a collection of activities—research, interaction design, and visual design—all of which work together to build the right thing for people. Product definition and specification are at the core of design.

Twenty years ago, the message of Contextual Design was: first understand your users, then design a coherent product that works for the task you want to support. Don't generate a list of features to achieve a preconceived purpose structured in a way that made sense to engineers. Fit to life meant design for a coherent task.

Contextual Design has been used to design business products and systems, websites, mobile devices, mobile apps, medical devices, consumer products and electronics, automotive electronics, business information products, CRM, manufacturing systems, and more. But none of these products radically altered the way people used technology in daily life. All these products could still be supported well with a task-focused design process. The activities they supported were all achieved sitting at a desk in front of a computer. Even as we moved to WYSIWYG, to the web, to online retail and social media, we were still sitting in front of a computer, doing a task, in a space which supported that task.

Then in 2007 and 2008, the iPhone and the Android put small computers into everyone's hands, and the role of technology in life radically changed. They supercharged a transformation that was already in progress: Google taught us that any question can be answered, in seconds, anywhere, without arcane query languages. Facebook and Twitter taught us that we can reach out and touch others any time we wish. Then iPhone, Android, and tablets gave us these and our whole world—our friends, shops, books, news, and pictures, the things we've created and the things we need for work—in our palms, on our wrists, always just a touch away. There's no boot time anymore—hardly any setup, login, or preparation. There's just me and my work, me and my life—and increasingly, not much distinction between them.

And, of course, how technology interacts with the people has radically changed. Technology is now an appendage—always available in every moment of time, anywhere. Now people get their whole life done by filling up every bit of time they have, anytime, anywhere, across multiple platforms. No longer can successful product teams focus only on individual tasks done in one stationary location. Now teams must *design for life*: how a product fits into all the contexts of everyday life.

The challenge: Move from designing tasks to Design for Life

Products must still fit *into the fabric of everyday life*, as we said in the first edition—but now they must understand the whole life. A simple focus on task is not enough. Today, users' activities are broken up into small bits of action strewn across time, space, location, and devices. So every task must be designed to ensure it doesn't slow people down as they barrel along, getting their whole life done.

To support design for life, Contextual Design had to change to help teams collect and use data about that larger life and how a target activity flows through daily life. This book reintroduces Contextual Design, building on the strength of its existing techniques; integrating lessons learned over the last 20 years; and incorporating new forms of data collection, analysis, ideation, and design so that product teams can more effectively design for life.

Contextual Design is a step-by-step process for collecting field data and using it to design any sort of product that includes a technical component. There are three phases to Contextual Design: First, the team immerses itself in the life of individual users through field visits and interprets the data using models to show a big picture of the whole

Contextual Design works for any product and with any development methodology

market. Second, the team uses that big picture to drive ideation, inventing new product concepts from the user data. Third, these product concepts are designed with concrete user interfaces and behavior, which are validated and iterated with users. Contextual Design can be used to create, refine, or extend existing products, design for new markets, or drive longer-term product roadmaps. It can drive coherent design to support a target activity across multiple platforms. It can be and has been used as part of many requirements and software development processes, including Agile. And because it addresses how to design for life it can help you deliver joy—or coolness—to your customers, as we explain later. Contextual Design is guided by three overarching principles and challenges which will recur throughout the book:

- *Design for life*, not just for individual task or activity;
- *Immersion* in the users' world to tune intuition and focus design thinking; and
- *Design in teams*, because in the real world, it's always a team of people that need to work together, design together, and come to agreement.

Here we describe these core principles and provide an overview of the Contextual Design techniques. Throughout the book we will refer to these principles and also introduce additional principles as relevant to the part of the process being discussed.

DESIGN FOR LIFE: THE COOL PROJECT

Contextual Design is driven by the realization that a product is always part of a larger practice, used in the context of other tools and manual processes to deliver value to the user's overall life and work. Product design is really about the redesign of the user's life and work, given technological possibilities—designing a new and better way for users to live their lives, achieve their goals, touch the people that matter to them, and perform their activities by introducing better products. The need for this deep understanding of users has only

Product design is about redesigning life and work with technology

become more compelling as touch phones, tablets, and other devices continue to infiltrate our lives.

Since at least the late 1980s, the basic idea that designers must understand the context of task activities has stood the test of time. Accordingly, Contextual Design introduced a set of models—diagrams and pictures, each showing one aspect of the users' life context. These original Contextual Design models successfully focused the design effort on understanding the context of task activity. They revealed the context of use, showed the structure of the users' activities, and revealed the key issues in a market.

These Traditional Contextual Design Models are still relevant; we describe the most important ones in Chapter 8. But to design for life, we must understand the whole of life as the context of use, which is very different from the context of use of the traditional products Contextual Design was designed to create. The wall of separation between home and work has broken down—torn down by people trying to make their whole life work. Work is done on the road, in the air, at tables in restaurants, and at Little League games. And personal life has filtered into work—tickets to the theater may be found at work between completing sections of writing or reading or filling out a form. They may be agreed on with text messages during a meeting, and bought later online while on hold during a phone call. A work task may be started over breakfast at home on a tablet, continued at traffic lights during the commute on a touch phone, and wrapped up in the office on a desktop machine. Today, the context of use for what used to be a single, coherent task includes all these places—flowing across place, time, and devices.

> *Transformative products must support activity across place, time, and devices*

Successful design now means going far beyond understanding the "cognitive load" or "steps of a task"—buzzwords from a previous generation of user-centered design. Transformative products help us get our life done, celebrate our accomplishments, connect to the people who matter to us, express the core elements of our identities, and create moments of surprise and sensory delight—all in a product that just works, like magic, with no hassle or learning required. That is a tall order, and means that designers must understand a much wider life context than they ever had to before.

When the iPhone and then Android phones came out, we at InContext noticed that the way ordinary, nontechnical, people felt about them had radically changed from older technology. The language people used was, "This is so *cool!*" We saw that something fundamental had changed in the way that people related to technology, and we wanted to understand it. So we started our Cool Project in hopes of uncovering the core of the cool user experience.

We went out in the field and talked with more than 60 consumers between 15 and 60 years old about what makes things cool for them. We asked people to show us products with some technical component that they experienced as cool.

The Cool Concepts show why people fall in love with their devices

Then we talked with them about their experience, watched them use the products, and discussed how they transformed their lives. We didn't try to define "cool" for them. Instead, we let them define it by showing us the products they thought were cool. We then turned to 30 enterprise workers to see if these same experiences were relevant for workers—and they were. The seven Cool Concepts, which guide the deliberate creation of a cool user experience, emerged from our analysis of this data.

To validate the concepts and create a metric, we partnered with SAP. The Cool Metric is a set of 40 questions that have been validated with over 2000 people worldwide[2]. The metric can differentiate coolness between different kinds of consumer and business software and between devices. It can be used to compare scores across competitors, or to focus an initial market study. It can be used in between rounds of iteration to see how the team is doing as it develops new product concepts and tests them with users. It works in the lab, in the field, and with a large population survey. Most importantly, this

---

[2] Holtzblatt, Karen, Farnsworth, Carol, Held, Theo, Held and Pai, Shantanu. Cool in Business: Measuring 'Cool'. Third International Conference, DUXU 2014, held as part of HCI International 2014. June 22–27, 2014, Proceedings, Part IV.

research provides quantitative validation of the Cool Concepts: that they indeed reflect key elements of the users' experience and identify the important design principles for the experience of cool. Armed with these tools, Contextual Design can help teams move the dial on their design's coolness.

So what makes things cool? The Cool Project revealed that successful products today deliver *joy in life*. Joy: not just satisfaction, not just a "good user experience." Joy: because cool products enhance our core human motivations in specific ways that

> *Successful products must produce joy in life and use*

we will explain. The Cool Concepts identify what is needed to design for life, and what is central to designing a product users will experience as transformative or "cool." We redesigned Contextual Design in light of the Cool Concepts to help teams design for joy and to collect the right data about human experience needed to manufacture joy.

The Cool Concepts are broken into two parts. The *Wheel of Joy in Life* (Fig. 1.1) organizes the four Cool Concepts that define how cool products touch our core human motives. The four Cool Concepts of the Wheel of Joy show how products enhance the *joy of life*, how they make our lives richer and more fulfilling.

FIGURE 1.1   The *Wheel of Joy in Life* describes how a product creates joy by enhancing users' lives.

Accomplishment: Empower users to achieve all the intents of their life, work, and personal, wherever they are in whatever amount of time they have, across place, time, and platform. Support the *unstoppable momentum of life* by helping users fill every moment of dead time with useful or amusing activities. Design with the expectation that users will be distracted, splitting their attention across multiple activities.

Accomplishment in life is the main driver of the cool experience in the Wheel of Joy in Life.

Connection: Increase the intimacy and collaboration of users' real relationships. Help them make frequent contact, have something of mutual interest to talk about and share, and find things to do together as everyone pursues their separate lives. Foster real connection in business relationships as well as personal relationships. Communities of interest—online or in person—will produce real relationships and a sense of connection if they support frequent contact, provide conversational content, and promote shared activities.

Each aspect of Joy in Life can be explicitly designed for

Connection is generally less important than accomplishment, unless the product's primary purpose is to connect people.

Identity: Support users' sense of core self and enable them to express that sense of self in what they do and how they show up to others. Identify the core identity elements associated with the activity being supported by a product and deliver products that increase the users' sense of being their best selves. If people are taking on a new identity, help them create that identity through examples of what others like them do and by checking with friends or trusted colleagues to determine if their behaviors, choices, and values are appropriate.

Features that support success in activities core to the person's identity increase the overall coolness of the product.

Sensation: Provide the user with pleasurable moments of sensual delight through color, sound, movement, and animation. Modern aesthetic design is expected by users today—use appropriate stimulation, graphics, and animation to enhance interaction and create products that evoke a smile. But don't add gratuitous or distracting graphics or animation—that just annoys users and actually reduces cool.

Sensation augments the coolness of any product but is not the main driver of coolness unless the product's value is delivering sensual delight, like games, entertainment products, and music.

The three Cool Concepts of the *Triangle of Joy in Use* (Fig. 1.2) show how the design of the product itself can enhance (or detract from) the *joy of use* by creating moments of "magic" or by eliminating the hassle people have come to expect from technology.

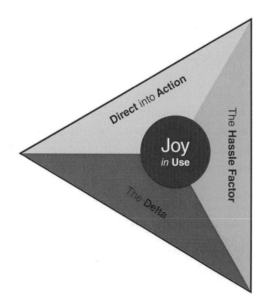

FIGURE 1.2 The *Triangle of Joy in Use* describes the impact of using the product itself.

Direct into Action: Provide immediate, simple fulfillment of core intents: I think of what I want and I get it—with no thought, no figuring, no deciding. It just happens like magic. Think for me— give me what I want without my having to ask for it, just as the Pandora service did for music when it first came out. Produce the desired result with little or no direction from me.

Of the Cool Concepts in the Triangle of Joy in Use, Direct into Action has the most impact on the user's joy in the use of the product. Direct into Action calls for much more than good usability and fewer clicks; it calls for true instant into action so that achieving an intent in moments is possible.

The Hassle Factor: Remove all inconveniences, setup, plugging in, logging in, boxes, customization and technology hassles from the product. Create joy by removing all the glitches and inconveniences that interrupt the flow of life. A "good enough" user experience is no longer good enough. Users no longer tolerate technical hassles and no longer value new function if it is not instant into action.

The Hassle Factor combines with Direct into Action in the Cool Metric to create one powerful design focus for creating joy in product use.

The Learning Delta: Reduce the time it takes to learn the tool as close as possible to zero by building on known interaction paradigms and natural interactions like touch and voice. Nudge the user into use with tiny hints. Reduce complexity; reduce the number of things the user has to know and places the user has to go to use the product. Avoid designing actions and options that increase complexity. Make product use so direct that there's nothing to learn.

Design for the way activities fit into the whole life—work and personal

The Cool Project revealed that good UX and user interface design are no longer just "nice to have"—they can determine whether a product is cool or not, valued or not, purchased or not. Even a product that is cool in concept can become uncool if its use is not Direct into Action.

The Cool Project taught us that the Cool Concepts are as true of business products or IT solutions as they are for commercial products for consumers. The term "the consumerization of business products" describes how users' expectations, driven by consumer products, are now creating demands on business products to measure up. Business products also must be designed for life: fit into the places and times life is lived, support connection to people that matter, enable users' professional identity, and provide appropriate sensory fun—and be direct into action without hassles. This is true even for highly technical products—everyone, no matter how technical, values and expects a cool user experience.

So what is design for life? We must design our target activity so it fits into life on the go: the unstoppable momentum of life. But design for life also means that we must design for a much wider spectrum of human experience if we want our product to be experienced as cool. Design for life means that we have to take a whole-life and a whole-person perspective when doing product design.

Experience Models help you design for core human motives

The insights from the Cool Project demanded changes to Contextual Design itself. A design team needs to recognize and collect new types of user data on core human motives and behaviors, on wider dimensions of life, and on how the whole of the user's integrated life fits together. So we extended Contextual Design to collect wider data about the whole of life experience, and have added new models to represent this wider view. We're calling these new models *Experience Models* to emphasize their role in highlighting life experience, and to distinguish them from the previous, *Traditional Contextual Design Models*. We also added design principles and ideation activities, all to ensure that the design thinking of the team is focused on the right dimensions of a product to ensure success.

IMMERSION: TUNING INTUITION AND DESIGN THINKING

Contextual Design is built around a series of *immersion experiences* for team members and stakeholders to continuously ground themselves in the lives of their users. Engineering-driven design, where technologists think up what *they* would like in a product, was typical 20 years ago—and sadly still is, in some companies today. These engineers had little contact with customers and little appreciation for the lives and challenges of the people who they were designing for. Engineers produced a list of features that they wanted or that came from marketing, and then structured the product however they thought best. Whether it's engineers, product managers, designers, or any other of the many job roles we have today, this process of figuring out what to build without really understanding the activities of the customers relies on faith in the individual and collective *intuition* of the people producing the product.

When a product is formed primarily from this inner gut feel we call it "Design from the I." You can tell if you and your teams are designing from the "I" because they will sound like this:

"I like this feature—it really works for me."

"Well I don't think it works best that way—I like it this way."

"We don't need that feature at all—I think we need to do it like this."

Design from the "I" focuses the team of what "feels right to me." When the team is isolated from the lives of users *they*

Don't design from the "I"—design from rich user data

only have access to their own personal experience to guide them. Without a user-centered design process, all teams have to draw on their own interactions with the tool, customer contacts, sales complaints, interactions with competitive products, and experience with their own favorite tools.

Without deep user data, teams default to designing solutions based on what seems reasonable to them—using their intuition to design for themselves. But no one on the product team is a good surrogate for the user. They know too much and love technology too much to design for the general public. And they know too little about specific work domains to get the details of a design right. Because of the way technology is thoroughly embedded in users' lives, because of the depth of knowledge needed to understand the interplay between technology and life, and because we must design holistically across platforms, it is more critical than ever to understand the whole lives and motives of users.

Nor can a product team create a holistic design by running down a checklist of parts. Engineers and product managers both love lists. Lists can be organized, checked off, and reviewed for completion—but they never lead to a holistic design. How much interruption can a driver tolerate before they are too distracted from the road? What quick questions does a medical practitioner need answered right away—and what questions merit in-depth research? What is the interplay between large applications with lots of function and related apps for monitoring, quick decisions, and in-the-moment information? The team needs to be immersed in the everyday details of their users' lives and respond with a coherent design if they are to get the right answers to questions mentioned earlier.

A holistic solution won't come from a list of features

To truly design for their customers, a team must be steeped in the life context of the users they are supporting. In this way, we deliberately tune the teams' intuition so it reflects the real life of their users. This combats "design from the I" and makes the team "get real." So Contextual Design includes a well-defined set of immersion activities.

This immersion recurs throughout the process. Contextual Design techniques immerse the team in the world of the user, give them an opportunity to reflect and respond—and then re-immerse them, and so keep the team grounded. The first of these immersion experiences is the Contextual Inquiry field interview, when the designer sits in the user's environment and finds out firsthand what the user's world is like. Later, other immersion experiences expose the team over and over to the relevant data, systematically tuning the intuition of the team and stakeholders. In the face of real data about a market, it is much harder to hang onto misconceptions about the customer or favorite features that match no actual user needs.

Immersion events put the team in the users' shoes

Explicit, articulated user data gathered through a well-defined public process ensures the data is trustworthy, avoiding arguments about what is best for the users. It's not a question of what I like versus what you like—two team members who disagree can go back to the user data and make arguments based on what they actually discovered. An initial design can be checked against the data to ensure it covers all the important points. When talking to stakeholders, design elements can be justified based on the observed user issues they address.

Data immersion guards against feature creep by tuning intuition

Immersion also guards against the almost inevitable tendency to add features that "might be useful" or that "make sense to me." And it ensures that when quick decisions must be made, the engineers' intuition has been tuned through repeated immersion to reflect the users' perspective. In this way Contextual Design supports tuning the collective intuition of the team. Together they can discuss and design from a deep understanding of users' lives.

But what about the belief held by some that good innovation never comes from talking to customers? Where does innovation come from anyway? We will talk more about innovation in Part 3, but at the core of any invention is the value a product brings to the people the invention is for. When a product delivers value that helps people live their lives and do their work better with more delight, it sweeps the market. So how do teams find that value? Contextual Design steeps inventors in the reality of the lives of potential customers. Then opportunities, delighters, tacit "needs," work-arounds, irritations, and potential transformations stand out in bold relief, inviting the team to be creative.

We have found that engineers, designers, user researchers—all members of a team—simply love to invent. If you've built your team well, they know what is technically possible and what great design looks like; they know the tools and principles of their trade. Then, when these people are steeped in the world of the user through field visits and through interaction with the resulting rich data, they naturally use their skills to reinvent the lives of their users.

So no, we don't ask the user what they need or want, as we discuss in Part 1. Users are not engineers and designers. Unlike the skilled team they don't know what is technically possible or what good design looks like. Often they say things like, "Make it work like my current tool," or "Make it faster," or "Fix this one little function that bugs me." Usability testing and rapid prototyping depend on users' tacit knowledge to tune an existing product or prototype but these tech-niques are not generative—they do not lead to new product directions.

Users may make feature requests, but they don't think of the product as a whole system supporting a coherent practice. If we only listen to these user requests, we will produce products that lack coherence, are over-featured, and are profoundly complex. As we discuss in Part 4, a product, or family of products, needs to be designed to hang together as a coherent system of support and to work smoothly in the context of the users' life. So don't ask your users what they want—understand the lives of your users so you can invent the product that will transform their lives. Contextual Design gives you a systematic way to do this.

> *Don't ask your users what they want. They can't tell you.*

Profound innovation emerges from the collective knowledge, insights, and intuition of the team who truly knows their customers. But therein is the third challenge that Contextual Design addresses, the challenge of working in teams.

DESIGN IN TEAMS

Contextual Design is team-based. It is designed to take advantage of a cross-functional team including such specialties as product man-agement, marketing, product architects, UX designers (user research and user interface), visual designers, developers, service designers, and more, each providing their unique skills and insights to help invent the right solution for users. Contextual Design builds in ways of involving stakeholders and other team members to assure buy-in from the business and ensure the solution is one the company can successfully deliver.

The reality of product creation is that it takes many people to make and ship a product. Commercial products, IT systems, cars, medical devices, games, even apps—all require the work of many coordinating people. And all these people contribute to defining requirements and translating those requirements into design, speci-fications, and implementation.

All these people need to have a shared understanding of both the user needs and the agreed product solution. Achieving a shared understanding isn't "nice to have"—achieving a shared understanding is at the center of shipping successful products in a reasonable timeframe. Products generally don't fail to ship because the technology doesn't work or because the people can't think up features. Products don't ship because people can't come to agreement.

No one person can design a whole product—so make the team work!

The challenge of a shared understanding doesn't go away with a small team or the "One Great Guru" theory of product development—the idea that you can hire one smart person and let him or her do it all. No "One Great Guru" can ever do it all. And as soon as multiple people are expected to coordinate to deliver, they must operate from a shared understanding to be effective. Product development is always about people acting together and in parallel based on a common understanding of the problem and the solution.

Unfortunately, people come with a host of idiosyncrasies, cognitive styles, cultures, interpersonal tendencies, and personality quirks. No organizational role definition, careful separation of the code into independent modules, management rules, organizational structures, or fun outings to build team spirit can eliminate the need to deal with the issues of getting people to work together well.

People come with a host of differences—Contextual Design helps manage them

One division manager addressed a particular thorny problem by booking rooms at a local hotel, sending his five senior architects there, and telling them they were fired if they didn't come up with a solution in a week. He got a result, but we find people are usually happier, more creative, and produce results more quickly if they have a reasonable process to work in. The typical response to having a process—even from people who say they hate process—is, "Thank you. Now I finally know what to do."

This organizational challenge—this need for a shared understanding and coordinated action—underlies many of the techniques used in Contextual Design. We don't address the whole of the product development life cycle, but we can get the team started by using clear, structured techniques for working together. Throughout the book we will describe techniques that are built around a set of principles that make creative face-to-face work. Here are some core considerations built into Contextual Design.

> **Use a cross-functional team:** Different perspectives on the problem lead to divergent, creative solutions. Including diverse job roles is one way to get different perspectives.
>
> **Manage interpersonal dynamics:** Divergent perspectives and interpersonal differences will deliver a more creative solution—but they will also create tension in the room. Structure the process to manage and direct that tension toward the design problem rather than the participants.
>
> **Create a creative team culture:** Articulate the process and the group norms to foster creativity. Group culture doesn't happen by itself—so Contextual Design includes elements to foster a productive team culture.

We explore these elements in detail in the Interpretation Session chapter, the first intensive design meeting in Contextual Design. But as you read the next sections, you'll see them start to emerge in the very first team activities.

CONTEXTUAL DESIGN V2

The first edition of this book introduced Contextual Design—a complete, user-centered front-end design process. This edition introduces Contextual Design V2.0—Contextual Design updated for modern technology, device use, and device capabilities. With Contextual Design 2.0 you can not only make your products useful and innovative—you can make them transformative and loved. When you find your users saying, "After using this product—I'd never go back!" you know you won.

Much of what we do in Contextual Design is to make explicit and public things which good designers do implicitly. Each part of

Contextual Design reflects an aspect of the design process which has to happen anyway—either informally in one person's head or publicly as an explicit design step. So Contextual Design explicitly defines how to gather, interpret, and model data about how people live and work, organizing it so that design teams can use it to drive ideation. It includes techniques which manage the interpersonal dimension of designing in cross-functional teams and keep designers focused on the implications of this data for redesigning life and work with new technology solutions. It organizes design thinking sessions to help teams structure the potential product and defines ways to validate that what is shipped is actually desired. With articulated, teachable technique teams are clear about what to do to achieve success—and how they may modify the techniques to better suit their specific needs.

Contextual Design externalizes good design practice for a team

In this book we introduce you to the techniques of Contextual Design in five parts. Each part starts with a chapter introducing the issues and principles of that part. Then it is followed by two or three chapters describing the techniques. We end with a chapter concluding the book.

PART 1: GATHERING USER DATA

Chapter 2: User data drives design.   User-centered design starts from the recognition that all innovation has to start with an understanding of the user—with a real-world problem to solve. And good design needs an in-depth understanding of users' tasks, motivations, intents, strategies, and detailed steps—as well as an overall grasp of how they go through their days, what technology they depend on, who is important to them, and their self-image. This depth of knowledge is best available through field research and has to be elicited through observation and inquiry—you can't just ask users what they want, and you can't just observe and know without talking to them. This chapter makes the argument for user-centered design and for field research as the essential starting point.

Chapter 3: Principles of Contextual Inquiry. Contextual Inquiry is the core field research process of Contextual Design. In this chapter we describe the four principles of Contextual Inquiry: Context, Partnership, Interpretation, and Focus. We talk about how the Cool Concepts affect the interview situation. We describe how to structure the interview itself and how to tailor the interview to different kinds of project. These field visits are our first immersion activity, putting designers out in the users' world.

Chapter 4: The Interpretation Session. Gathering data isn't enough—the insights need to be shared across the team so that everyone can see the issues and work toward a common goal. In Contextual Design, we make all design activities team-based so that everyone builds the insights and designs together. Every interview is captured and analyzed through an *Interpretation Session*, a team meeting where the whole team (or a representative subset) can see the data and pull out the implications. This is our next *immersion* activity, allowing the whole team to experience each interview.

In this chapter we describe the structure, roles, and process of the Interpretation Session. We also take the opportunity to discuss team-based design and how to use our understanding of working in teams to define a design process that works.

PART 2: REVEALING THE WORLD

Chapter 5: From data to insight: Contextual Design Models. Just asking designers to go out in the field and run inquiries is a big step forward. But it's still a challenge to see what matters when you're there. The user's world is complex, overwhelming, and full of a million details— some of which matter for any design problem and many of which don't. It has become a larger problem over the years to communicate insight from the user research to the whole product team, so that everyone can see what matters. Contextual Design has always used models of the user to communicate; with Contextual Design 2.0 we've expanded those models to communicate the aspects of design that matter for today's highly connected technology. In this chapter we discuss the problems of representing user data to reveal what is going on across an entire market.

Chapter 6: The Affinity Diagram.   Any type of ethnographic or qualitative data is hard to organize. It's complex and unstructured. The easiest methods of organizing the data, some sort of classification, tends to work against innovation—if you organize data into a classification you already know, how do you get new insight? The Affinity Diagram is an inductive process that bubbles structure up out of the details of the user data. It creates a single view of the market out of hundreds of individual data notes. Building it acts as another immersion activity, as the whole team comes together to organize the data. This chapter describes what an Affinity is and how to build one that will drive design insight. It also introduces *communication design* as an essential skill for organizing data to drive innovation.

Chapter 7: Building Experience Models.   Contextual Design 2.0 introduces a new set of models, the *Experience Models*, derived from the insights of the Cool Project. The Cool Project defined four ways that technology enhances life: accomplishment, connection, identity, and sensation. The Experience Models focus the team on these concepts to ensure that the team recognizes them when they see them, and captures the data in a way that enables the team to design for them. In this chapter we walk through each Experience Model, describing the model, how to collect data for it, how to use it in Interpretation Sessions, and how to consolidate the data into a view of the market based on the data of individual users. The models we cover are The Day-in-the-Life Model; the Identity Model; the Relationship Model; the Collaboration Model; and the Sensation Board.

Chapter 8: The Traditional Models.   The Traditional Contextual Design Models introduced in the first edition of this book are still viable and offer insight, but we have found that we rarely use some of them. In this chapter we discuss the Traditional Models that we do use regularly, and their variants: The Sequence Model; the Decision Point Model, derived from the Cultural Model; the Physical Model; and Personas.

Part 3: Reinventing life

Chapter 9: Inventing the next product concept.   More than ever, technology is inextricably integrated into daily life; designers today are truly reinventing daily life by creating a human–technical system, a way of living and working augmented by our products and systems. That product is no longer likely to be a large monolithic application but rather a constellation of products, apps, and platforms to help us get an activity done. Successful innovation results when a cross-functional team skilled in the modern materials of design is immersed in structured customer data. Then they naturally recombine elements of practice, technology, and design in new ways to create a vision of new product concepts. In this chapter we introduce the necessary ingredients and processes that help your team innovate consistently.

Chapter 10: From data to design—the Wall Walk.   At the core of innovation is immersion in the world of the user. Having produced the Affinity Diagram and consolidated models tuned to reveal insights and issues, the team is ready to use the models to drive design thinking. In this chapter, we describe the Wall Walk, a process whereby the team interacts with the consolidated data, letting it stimulate initial design ideas. The Wall Walk is a time-tested process for ensuring that the data collected drives invention.

Chapter 11: Ideation—Visioning and the Cool Drilldown.   Good product design ensures that the life of the user is enhanced, enlivened, and remains coherent. The best way to ensure a coherent life is to reinvent technology in the context of telling the story of the new ways that users' activities might be transformed by introducing technology. In this chapter we describe the Visioning workshop, a group storytelling process focused on reinventing life, not on technical solutions. This results in a set of visions implying new product concepts. Then, we describe the Cool Drilldown where the principles of the Cool Concepts are used to hone and enrich these new ideas.

Part 4: Defining the product

Chapter 12: The challenge of product design. Products aren't just standalone tools, particularly not in this day and age. Products—even cell phone apps—exist in a larger ecosystem of tools, processes, habits, and technology. Any new product has to fit into this ecosystem while simultaneously transforming the users' lives in desirable ways. The design team must not only think about the users' lives as a coherent whole, they must design a product that is also coherent, having the appropriate structure to best support the user. In this chapter, we lay out the challenges of detailed product design and introduce Contextual Design's techniques for helping teams see and define product structure in a way that keeps the user practice coherent.

Chapter 13: Storyboards. Telling stories of how people will work in the new system we're designing helps the team keep the user's life coherent. Storyboards are like freeze-frame movies representing to-be scenarios of the user's practice. These stories ensure that a task or activity works—the things the user wants to do are supported and that they can flow from step to step conveniently. Storyboards ensure that designers think through the different activities, strategies, and situations that have been revealed as important in the field data or are relevant to the Vision. In this chapter we describe storyboards and how to build them.

Chapter 14: The User Environment Design. Storyboards ensure the tasks and the flow of life are coherent, but they don't keep the system coherent and well-structured. The new product or feature set must have the appropriate function and structure to support a natural flow of interaction. For that, Contextual Design uses the User Environment Design. The User Environment Design is a floor plan of the new product showing the places in the product, the function in that place, and the links between one place and another. It shows the parts of the product from the user's point of view and helps the team think structurally about the product. In this chapter, we describe the User Environment Design, show how it is represented, and lay out the process for building one from the storyboards.

Chapter 15: Interaction Patterns. The User Environment Design lays out the structure of the new system. It doesn't define the look or layout. As with all aspects of design, Contextual Design gets the high-level structure right first, then designs the detail. Interaction Patterns help the team think structurally about the high-level structure of each page or screen in the User Environment Design. We give principles of design and layout to ensure this interface structure works for the user's activities and defines a user interface architecture that is both modern and ensures consistency across the product. We discuss the importance of having design-ers on the team and how to structure the interface but we do not cover detailed UI design—there are many other good books on this topic.

PART 5: MAKING IT REAL

Chapter 16: Making it real. In Contextual Design we drive product concept and structure from a deep understanding of the users' world. Once the User Environment Design and Interaction Patterns are defined we have a working hypothesis of what we think will deliver value to the target users. But we don't *know* if that is true—and we have a high-level design, but are likely missing lower-level details. All this is best tested and worked out with the user during paper prototype interviews. Furthermore, the result of any design process will likely generate more than a team can ship in a reasonable timeframe. In this chapter, we introduce the steps needed to make the product real and define a release that will deliver value. To do that the team needs to validate and iterate the design with users and then plan a rollout strategy that delivers the concept in useful, product-sized chunks. Last, we talk about how to set up and run the overall Contextual Design project providing practical advice and perspective.

Chapter 17: Validating the design. Testing is an important part of any product's development process, and it's generally accepted that the sooner problems are found, the less it costs to fix them. Rough paper prototypes of the product design test the structure and user interface ideas before anything is committed to code. Paper prototypes, now a well-known, documented practice, support continuous iteration of the new product, keeping it true to the user and giving designers a data-based way of resolving disagreements. In prototyping sessions, users and designers redesign the mock-up together to better fit the user's activities. In Contextual Design we use a combination of paper mock-ups, online mock-ups, and early versions of running code to get the right kind of feedback at each stage in the process. In this chapter, we introduce how to build a mock-up, run a paper prototype interview, interpret the data, and update the design for the next round of testing.

Chapter 18: Prioritization and rollout. Your Contextual Design project will produce a larger design than you can build in one version. That is a good thing because it helps you see where you are going next. So every Contextual Design project needs a prioritization step. Choosing what to put into each release is a design and communication challenge—the cross-functional team, including additional players from development and marketing, must come to a shared understanding of what to release. Prioritization works best when it is based on what is of true value to the customer, what will make enough splash to be worth shipping, and what is doable technically in the time available. In this chapter, we describe how to partition the validated User Environment Design into reasonable releases while keeping the user's practice, UI design, and overall system structure coherent. With an agreement in hand, the different organizational functions can work in parallel to ship the release.

Chapter 19: Project planning and execution. Having described the techniques of Contextual Design, we step back to talk about how to organize the team and the project for success. In this chapter, we describe how to set the project's scope and focus to map the business mission and willingness to innovate. We describe how to put your team together, considering both cross-functional roles and the leadership needed on the team to ensure success. We describe how to plan who and how many people to interview, how to gather data in challenging situations, and how to schedule the work. We end with a discussion of how to manage the team. This is a practical chapter to help you get your project started.

Chapter 20: Conclusion.   In this brief concluding chapter of the book we return to the core principles of Contextual Design: immersion, design for life, structural thinking, and team-based design. We wrap up insights and reflect on the future.

User Data Drives Design

2

The first phase of Contextual Design guides a team through gathering field data and interpreting it as a team. By capturing issues and modeling each individual's experience, the team records the data that will later be consolidated to build a coherent view of the practices and experiences of the whole user population. This part describes how to get the best design data while involving and immersing the team in the lives of their users. Here we will describe the Contextual Interview and the Interpretation Session. We will talk about the Contextual Design models in Part 2.

User-centered design recognizes that to create a successful design—to transform lives with technology—the product team must be grounded in the relevant details of their users' lives. Design for life tells us that understanding only the task is no longer enough, so the data we collect must include understanding core motives and a much wider range of life activities than before—even for a product that supports work. The sad news is that getting that detail is hard. It is best collected through field research: best for data quality and the best way to immerse the team in the users' lives. But going into the field is time consuming, takes coordination, and is expensive. Here we provide the motivation for gathering field data to drive design and show how the detailed observational data produced by field techniques such as Contextual Inquiry is vital to a good, innovative design.

> *Ground the team in the details of the user's work and life*

Contextual Design. http://dx.doi.org/10.1016/B978-0-12-800894-2.00002-8

THE CHALLENGE OF DESIGN DATA

Consider what it means for products to be integrated into users' lives as intimately as they are now. My phone plays my personal chime; I look and see it's telling me I should leave for my next appointment. I touch the screen to see the details. A quick swipe, and I can see the rest of my day. Touch again, and my phone dials the person I'm going to see. And that is just one app.

Every one of those interactions is a design decision, and every one changes my life to some degree. From the high level (Do I want

All design decisions make assumptions about the user's life

my phone to guess where I'll go next, estimate travel time, and tell me when to leave?) to the lowest level (Is that swipe a direct and easy way to see the rest of the day?), every design element is intimately tied to an aspect of my life and behavior. This raises the stakes for design: every one of those design elements

is an opportunity to enhance the user's life or to interfere with it, for a product to make itself loved or cause irritation.

And that is just the low-level design. How do we decide what products or apps to build in the first place? How can we find what adjacencies will expand our market? What are the best next feature sets to add to an existing product, website, or IT application? What will enhance human life—what will detract? What will create joy and relief from hassle? What product will be abandoned for lack of fit to life?

The same in-depth data informs both detailed design decisions and product innovation. It is very different from what marketing, usability, focus groups, and standard requirements-gathering techniques provide. The very language of "requirements" assumes that there is someone doing the requiring—that people are capable of knowing what technology will transform their lives, and that they are aware enough of their own behavior and experience that they can just tell teams where the problems and delighters lie.

Standard requirements techniques give teams a multitude of ways to ask their users what they need. But in today's world, design is invention. It's up to a product team to discover how their users work and live, and uncover opportunities for small and large life transformation. Looking for a "user need" is simply the wrong focus.

No one knew they needed a Walkman until the Walkman was invented; no one knew they would love music downloads until Napster made it cool and then iTunes made it legitimate; no one knew they wanted tailored music on demand until Pandora showed it was possible. Our experience of music has evolved with the introduction of products that met our unarticulated desire: instant, no hassle access to my music anytime, anywhere.

> *Don't look for user needs—look for unmet desires*

When the goal is innovation, whether in a wholly new product or even in the next version of your successful product, design methods must move beyond the idea of requirements, wish lists, pain points, and problem solving. These focus designers on solving specific problems rather than understanding the totality of the work and life context. Even thinking about user needs focuses the team on existing needs that can be articulated or recognized. But invention taps into our core unarticulated desires— so the data designers need is data that will lead them to identifying opportunities that even the users themselves don't recognize.

To design at this level, the team needs not just data but insight; not just facts, but understanding. So the first task of any user-centered methodology has to be to provide structured activities that guide a team through the process of gathering trustworthy, detailed user insight. This is the role that Contextual Inquiry plays in Contextual Design.

Contextual Inquiry helps answer the product team's most basic question: "What could I make that will enhance people's lives and enable them to do what they really want easily?" This question requires that designers understand what is really going on in the users' lives when they try to do the target task: What are you trying to accomplish? Is it so important that you need to do it immediately? Or is it a chore that you'd like accomplish during dead time? Where are you likely to be, and how much time and attention can you devote to the task? How do we give you an interface that lets you do what you need without forcing you to think about the tool?

Modern products impact work and life at a deep level, and speak to who we are as humans. To design for life not only requires a deep understanding of the whole work and life context but also of users' core motives as humans. Successful design means going far beyond understanding the "cognitive load" or "steps of a task," to quote two common concepts in the UX field.

Designers must learn to see how a product or device might enhance a user's sense of self, through function or look: I'm a salesperson—with my cell phone I can provide clients the 24×7 availability I always dreamed of. I'm a craftsperson—with my cell phone camera and my online community, I can share and receive kudos for my great projects. These issues are part of the context of use, and designers must learn to see them.

Designers must also learn to see how products can enhance people's relationship to their communities: I can connect quickly with a friend through text or Facebook, so I'm never out of touch. Even a quick touch counts—it reaffirms our relationship and keeps us in each others' thoughts. My sense of community—of being not alone—is part of what makes my life matter.

So as a discipline, UX design needs a new way of seeing this larger whole life context. We need to recognize and collect new types of user data on core human motives, on wider dimensions of life, on work, and on how the whole of the user's integrated life fits together. Designing for individual tasks is simply insufficient in this new world. Instead, we must understand the whole of how an activity fits into the structure and time of life and how it can enhance the wellbeing—the joy in living—of the person.

Products that impact us deeply touch core human motives while making life work

YOU CAN'T JUST ASK FOR DESIGN DATA

The challenge of user research is that many of the important aspects of work and life are invisible, not because they are hidden, but just because it doesn't occur to anyone to pay attention to them. These aspects of work and life practice cannot be discovered just by asking questions.

A group of friends on a multi-day bike trip send regular rude texts to the one member who stayed home. Do any of the participants realize how much these texts matter to his maintaining his sense of connectedness despite missing out on the trip?

A worker in accounting calls a friend in order processing to gossip and mentions that a rush order is on its way. Does his manager know this informal communication is the only thing enabling his company to fill rush orders on time?

A man gets alerts on his phone of transactions made against his account as they happen. Do we understand how this fits in with his overall desire to stay on top of his financial situation at all times?

Any method designers use must reveal *tacit data*—the aspects of users' life and work that are so habitual that there's no more need to think about them, or that are created in the moment so that no one did think about them.

In one health clinic, the request for a certain procedure is always on a green form. Not until looking at the actual forms did we realize the form isn't used at all—people simply wrote across the face of the form. The only thing that mattered is that it was paper, and it was green.

Traditional methods of gathering user data assume people will say what is important if asked. But people simply don't pay that much conscious attention to how they perform jobs they do well. Think about how difficult driving was when you were first learning—getting the steering coordinated with the accelerator and the clutch (if there was one) was awkward and jerky. With increasing skill came increased smoothness, and less attention to each detail, until at last the whole process became unconscious. Now, to teach someone else to drive, the teacher has to recover everything that is now autonomic. And driving is a simple, obvious

> *Users don't watch what they do—so they can't tell you!*

task—how is one to know what aspects of everyday work are important? Even the user doesn't consciously know what the questions are:[1]

> A new cell phone user discovered that her Bluetooth earpiece was the perfect solution to a problem that had been bugging her for a long time. She got very poor reception in her apartment—there was just one location where the signal was acceptable. With her Bluetooth earpiece, she could leave the phone there and walk around her apartment while on the phone, and never lose the connection. It certainly never occurred to her that this was one of her needs in buying an earpiece.

This is true in general with "wish lists" and other user requests; the user will focus on a narrow fix, whereas understanding the context of the work that drove the request will result in more insight and better solutions. The user acts as though the question were, "What simple tweak or addition to the product as it is will overcome the problem I'm having;" the designer wants to know "What new concepts or features would make the product radically more appropriate to the job at hand?" Answering this question requires an open-ended technique.

Users make their life work—they don't notice their own work arounds that fix product problems

Not only do users forget the details of the activities they do, when the products they use are broken, they figure out work arounds, get used to them, and then forget about what they did to overcome the product problem in the first place:

> Our user opened an online form requiring some numbers; but instead of using the facilities in the form to calculate the numbers, she opened a spreadsheet in another window and used the formulas there to do the calculation for her. When asked why, she said,

---

[1] Sommerville et al. 1993 describe the importance of understanding unarticulated procedures in the somewhat more critical domain of air traffic control; Goguen 1993 evaluates different techniques for the ability to reveal unarticulated needs.

"Oh, the online thing has never worked. We just use the spreadsheet. It's much simpler."

People always make their work work; they overcome technology to make their life work. Contextual Inquiry shows teams how to uncover all these tacit aspects of life so that they can be understood and designed for.

Gathering requirements for a product is not simply a matter of asking users what they need, like gathering pebbles from a beach. One cannot simply ask for design requirements, in part because people don't know what technology is capable of, but more because most people are not aware of what they really do. The everyday things people

Contextual Design helps you uncover the tacit practice that reveals innovation opportunity

do become habitual and unconscious, so they are usually unable to articulate their practices. People can say what they do in general terms and can identify critical problems; they can say what makes them angry with the tools they use. But they usually cannot provide day-to-day details about what they do. They cannot describe inner motivations such as the need to express a particular identity or to feel connected with people they care about. They are likely to forget about the work arounds they had to invent to overcome problems in their current products. This low-level detail of everyday practice is critical to design for life.

DEEP INSIGHT COMES FROM THE FIELD

If designers cannot just ask users for this detailed data about their lives, can they get it through traditional requirements elicitation techniques? After all, most companies do gather some level of user data in developing products. Developer Sue went to a user's group meeting and talked to people there; Marketing Director Joe showed a demo at an industry show; Project Manager Mary makes a point of meeting with internal users at least once a month. These are traditional and usual methods of maintaining user contact. And yet they do not result in the kind of design data discussed above. They do not generate real insight into the users' world and incorporate that insight into the design of a product. It's worth taking a few minutes to explain why that is so.

Marketing and design have different goals and need different data

Because marketing and design have different goals, techniques useful to marketing and product management tend not to be useful to designers. These techniques characterize and scope the market, rather than describing the structure of its practice. As a result, they tend to be quantitative. When you want to scope a market or apportion development resources, it may be useful to ask, "How much money do you expect to spend on equipment next year?" and average the results across all respondents. This is the kind of question you can answer with a survey. Designers must build on more qualitative data. "What does it mean to set up travel, and how do people do it?"—The answer to this is a description of practice, not any sort of number. Even if a question looks like it has a numeric answer—"How many times do you check email throughout a day?"—this is deceiving. For a designer, the true answer isn't a number, it's "Every free moment—I want my email at my fingertips and I want always to be plugged into my community."

Many traditional techniques assume you know what the questions are. For example, surveys and structured interviews both start

Contextual Design delivers an understanding of practice—not the answer to a preformed question

with a list of questions which explicitly or implicitly drive the interaction and define what is important. But as soon as design starts, no one knows what the questions are. No one knows what will turn out to be important. Perhaps customer satisfaction surveys (a marketing technique) report that installation is the #1 problem. But what is wrong with installation (a design question)? When do installations happen, and who does them? What information is available when they do them? Which of the many alternative fixes is the best?

None of this is to say that designers don't need to worry about what people will buy. It's only within the context of a market with needs to be met and money to spend that design makes sense.

Quantitative techniques using predefined questions can identify the market and show designers where it is interesting to explore. But once marketing techniques have identified a market and shown that there is money to be made there, designers must look in depth at the whole life and work context of people in the market to determine what to build.

Understanding a market requires a qualitative technique that explores the users' activities and makes new discoveries about what people do and what they might value. The discoveries may then lead to new strategies or product concepts for addressing the market and new market messages for

Qualitative and quantitative techniques build on each other

selling to it. They will confirm whether the identified market really has an opportunity given the mission of the company. Then, quantitative techniques may again be useful to show that the practice to be supported is sufficiently widespread to make a good business case. The two disciplines, marketing and design, build on each other with complementary goals and techniques, to result in a whole-product definition.[2]

Other traditional techniques have similar pitfalls. Two other common techniques are focus groups and hiring users to be in-house experts. But both approaches depend on the users to be able to articulate details of their work and life practice—which we already said is hard. Moreover, when the users are taken out of their daily context and put in a conference room with others, they lose the clues of daily life to help them remember what they really do—and they are overly swayed by the group dynamics in the room. Focus groups are great for getting a gut reaction to new product concepts, but they are not the way to find unarticulated opportunity. Similarly, putting an expert user on the design team immediately takes the expert out of doing the work she is now designing for. And since her practice was unconscious and her strategies uniquely her own, she can inadvertently narrow the team's focus as they defer to her knowledge, observations, and beliefs.

---

[2] Hansen 1997 reports on the effectiveness of different mechanisms for gathering customer feedback in a start-up.

Another popular approach to gathering user data is to start with an existing design: either build a prototype without user data or do "A/B" testing on a running system to evaluate alternatives. These techniques can improve a product incrementally once it has been invented, but they will rarely spark new invention. The users may be able to say they like something or do not, but they will have a much harder time saying why, what they are trying to accomplish, or what other features that the design team never considered would be more valuable to them. The team can tune their initial idea; they cannot discover what they don't know, which might lead to more innovative ideas.

Iterating an existing design can only tweak it—it can't generate a new innovation

Our job is to understand the detailed lives of our users as it pertains to the target activities we are trying to transform or improve. The problem is that everyone can tell you at a high level what they did and what they cared about, but no user, expert or not, can remember or even know the low-level details of their own behavior—or their underlying emotions, motives, and hidden intents. If innovation is your goal and not just incremental improvement, then the team must go to the field.

DEALING WITH THE DATA AS A TEAM

The team can only build from a deep understanding of the user's world if they experience and internalize that world. Going to the field is the first immersion experience—but only for the interviewer. How do we get this knowledge into the "gut" of the rest of the team? How do we make sure that the rich data collected isn't lost in a summary email, trip report, or list of key findings circumscribed by the point of view of a single interviewer? Without experiencing the users' world, the intuition of the team will not be tuned to reflect the reality of the users' lives. And without a way to quickly capture the detailed data of the field interview, the detail will be lost, or its significance overlooked.

When correlated with data from other interviews, data that may not seem immediately interesting can reveal transformative market issues and opportunities. Not only do we want to avoid "design from the I," from the designer's own point of view, we also want to avoid design for the issues of only one user. And for maximal market impact, we don't want designers to gener- ate new product concepts from only the one user they interviewed. When the team is immersed in

The team tunes their "gut feel" through interviews and Interpretation Sessions

the lives of the whole market, insight happens naturally. Our job is not just to get the best data for design but to capture and organize that data so that it can impact the final product design. This is the second challenge of design—making sure the whole team internal- izes the lives of the users at the market level.

In the last chapter of this part, we introduce the *Interpretation Session*, our first design meeting. The interviewer shares their experi- ence in the field with other team members, who capture the data into the affinity notes and models selected for the project. The Interpretation Session is also the first time we introduce the kind of design meeting structure that can help teams work together effec- tively in the face of their differing skills, job titles, and personali- ties. The Interpretation Session process lays the groundwork for later design meeting and teaches the team that they will go quickly, have fewer arguments, and be more focused and innovative if they work within a structured process.

Principles of Contextual Inquiry

3

The core premise of Contextual Inquiry is very simple: go to the user, watch them do the activities you care about, and talk with them about what they're doing right then. Do that, and you can't help but gain a better understanding of your user than ever (Fig. 3.1).

That is the basic idea, but we find people are generally happy to have a little more guidance. What should you do at the user's site? What should you pay attention to? How do you run the interview? Unless you're trained as a social scientist or anthropologist, running a field interview can be daunting. Contextual Design is structured so that product managers, engineers, user researchers, business analysts, and UX designers[1]—anyone on the product team—can be part of collecting user data.

The process used to conduct a field interview stood the test of time for 20 years, and the basic principles have not changed. But in this book, we expand the focus and scope of data collected to understand the users' wider life and core human motives. We'll introduce the interviewing process and explore the expanded focus in this chapter.

---

[1] Any of these roles may be conducting contextual interviews. We use the word "interviewer" to refer to them all—not just user researchers. It is much more effective to have the team in the field than to relegate all data collection to one person or job type. Immersion into the life the user is the best way to internalize their needs implicitly and explicitly.

Contextual Design. http://dx.doi.org/10.1016/B978-0-12-800894-2.00003-X

FIGURE 3.1   Contextual interviews in different life contexts: work, home, and car. Interviews are conducted wherever the activities of interest take place.

In Contextual Design, we always try to build on natural human ways of interacting. It is difficult and unnatural to act out of a long list of rules; instead we suggest a simple, familiar model of relationship. A list of rules says "do all these things"—you have to concentrate so much on following the rules you can't relate to the person being interviewed. A relationship model says "be like this"—if you can stay in the appropriate relationship, you will naturally act appropriately.[2]

Many different models of relationship are available to interviewers. A formal model might be scientist/subject: I am going to study you, so be helpful and answer my questions—it doesn't really matter whether you understand why I'm asking. A less formal model might be parent/child: I'll tell you what to do, and you'll do it because you want my approval (or else you'll rebel to show your independence). Each of these models brings with it a different set of attitudes and behaviors. A student telling a teacher he is wrong may be deferential or rebellious, but either way, it's a different situation than the teacher telling the student he's wrong. Relationship models have two sides, and playing one side tends to pull the other person into playing the other. Find a relationship model that is useful for gathering data, and as long as you play your role, you will pull the user into playing theirs. So what's a good relationship model for gathering design data?

Use natural ways of relating to people when interacting with the user

THE MASTER/APPRENTICE MODEL

The relationship we offer as a good model for a field interview is that between a master craftsman and apprentice. Overall, it embodies the attitudes and behaviors that will produce the highest quality data. Just as an apprentice learns through being immersed in the world of

---

[2] Goffman 1959 discusses how relationship models guide social interactions.

the master, interviewers can learn by immersion in the world of the user, discovering what's important from the people who know best.

The master/apprentice model creates an attitude of inquiry on the researcher's side and an attitude of disclosure and sharing on the user's side. So people with no special background in ethnography can rapidly learn to conduct effective interviews.

When you're watching users' activities as they unfold, learning is easy

In this situation, users, as the masters, don't need to be natural teachers; a master craftsman teaches while doing. This makes imparting knowledge simple. Users can talk about what they are doing as their activity unfolds, and the interviewer can ask a question or discuss the user's actions in the moment. Users don't have to develop a slide show to reveal the activities and emotions of their life. All they have to do is do their life, which reveals their motives and feelings. Consider this woman planning a vacation for her family:

> "I'm looking for something my husband and kids will both be happy with. Look, my husband would love this— a golf tour of Scotland. But what would we do with the kids? Here's a cruise—maybe that would work. Lots of kid activities, and my husband has always wanted to do a cruise…Getting it right really matters to me. I want everyone to have a great time!"

Seeing *what* people do is relatively straightforward. Understanding *why* they do what they do is harder. Some actions are the result of years of experience and have subtle motivations; other actions are habitual, and there is no longer a good reason for them. Like an apprentice, the best time to unravel the vital from the irrelevant and explain the difference is while in the middle of doing the activity.[3]

> A scientist came to the end of a painstaking series of mechanical calculations manipulating data from an experiment, turned to us, and said, "I guess you're surprised that I'm doing this." *He* was surprised at how inefficient he was, once he thought about it.

---

[3] Polanyi discusses what tacit knowledge people have available for discussion at different times in M. Polanyi, *Personal Knowledge*, Chicago: University of Chicago Press, 1958.

Because interviewers are present and immersed in the context of the user's life, they see the steps of an activity, and they see what matters to the user, including the emotion associated with it. They see the intensity when the user is invested or frustrated, the satisfaction when a product makes life easier to live, the pride of being a better professional, and the relief when technology or life hassles are removed. By being present, the interviewer can sense the user's emotional energy and start to understand it. This is how a team finds latent needs and delighters—the core opportunities for a product to transform life.

Inquiry uncovers why people do what they do by watching and talking about it

Because they talk about their activity while doing it, it's easy for users to see details that would otherwise be hard to discover. Every action they take and every object around them helps them talk about what they are doing. So users can describe the details of what they are doing, their motives, and even interesting stories of related things that happened.

Talking about what they are really doing keeps users from speaking in generalizations. And the interviewer watching what is happening can ask about what they see, rather than asking general questions that elicit generalizations.

> A doctor said he read journals outside his specialty because they often had information of interest to him. How did he decide what was of interest? "Oh, I just scan the article titles." That wasn't very specific. But when asked to do it, he was able to say, "Look, this article is about another use of a drug I prescribe. I'll read that. And here's an article about a procedure that uses a device I use a lot. There might be good stuff there…"

Sometimes users cannot describe an activity at all when they are not doing it. Their memory of how to do the task is partially incorporated into the objects they use, so without those objects and the context of the activity, they really don't know what they do.

A secretary was unable to describe how she made her monthly report. But when asked to create it, she brought up her last report and started filling in the parts—the old report was her reminder of how to produce the next one.

Contextual Inquiry is apprenticeship compressed in time

A product team can't spend weeks with a single user to learn what they do—and they don't need to. When grounded in the present activity, the user can tell stories about the last time something similar happened. Doing the activity naturally triggers memories of similar events from the recent past.[4]

A financial manager received a stock alert on his phone while we were talking. This reminded him about the time recently when he had gotten an alert of a PayPal transaction while he was watching a ballgame. But he knew he hadn't made any transactions—so he called, discovered it was fraudulent, and was able to resolve it immediately.

Together, user and researcher can walk through past events in detail, staying focused on what really happened. These *retrospective accounts* expand the time frame the field interview can cover.

Interviewers have the opportunity to observe the same set of behaviors across a number of users or across multiple instances by one user. What appears to be an idiosyncratic action when seen once, upon repetition reveals a pattern and suggests a strategy for getting things done—an unarticulated strategy which could be directly supported in a new product design. It is often hard to see these strategies precisely because the user's actions are everyday and ordinary. But by paying attention to repeating detail, the structure of daily life can be revealed.

Clues to design for people are hidden in the details of daily life

---

[4] Orr describes such storytelling to transmit knowledge among modern-day product managers for similar reasons in J. Orr, "Narratives at Work—Storytelling as Cooperative Diagnostic Activity" in *Proceedings of the Conference on Computer-Supported Cooperative Work*, December 3–5, 1986, Austin, Texas.

An enterprise worker used his smartphone at lunch to check and quickly answer emails, set up some appointments, and look up small bits of information. We learned he also did it at breakfast, and right before leaving work, and again last thing at night—and we saw other users do the same thing. Checking off small tasks and minor chores seemed to occur before getting on to the main activities of the workday or evening.

The design team named this strategy "clearing the decks," reflecting that people sweep away the little things they need to do to keep life going before entering a period of concentrated activity. Once the strategy was found and named, the team could design for it.

Taken together, the master/apprentice relationship makes the rich detail of everyday life available for observation and discussion. It steers the interviewer and user away from high-level abstract questions. It suggests an attitude of inquiry, attention to detail, and humility. And it recognizes that the user is the only true expert on their own activities. The interviewer acts like an apprentice, watching and probing and letting the users teach them about their lives. This relationship model allows users to shape the interviewer's understandings of their lives naturally, as they perform the activities of their day. And staying grounded in the real life of the user helps the interviewer let go of preconceived ideas that don't map to reality. Adopting the master/apprentice relationship model is the best starting point for an interviewer—if it is tuned as follows.

Find the strategies that make life work—then design for it

THE FOUR PRINCIPLES OF CONTEXTUAL INQUIRY

Apprenticeship is a good starting point, but it is only a starting point. Unlike apprentices, interviewers are not learning about the user's activities in order to do them, of course—they are immersing themselves in the user's world to transform it with technology. But apprenticeship is a good model for how to act when interviewing in the field. The attitude of inquiry and humility natural to apprenticeship when combined with the principles of Contextual Inquiry will allow you to collect high-quality data for your project.

In a Contextual Design project, a cross-functional team carries out the work. Individuals conduct one-on-one field interviews lasting 1½–2 hours with users wherever they live and work, focusing on the aspects of the practice that matter for the project scope. Four principles guide the Contextual Interview: *context*, *partnership*, *interpretation*, and *focus*. Each principle defines an aspect of the interaction. Together, they allow the basic apprenticeship model to be molded to the particular needs of a design problem. We will describe each principle and how to use it in turn.

Contextual Inquiry tailors apprenticeship to the needs of design teams

Context

The principle of *context* says to go wherever the user is and see what they do as they do it.[5] This is the first and most basic requirement of Contextual Inquiry. All the richness of real life is there with the user, available to jog the user's memory and for study and inquiry. The user makes a phone call in the middle of doing a task: Was she calling on an informal network of experts to get help in a task? Was she making a break from a heads-down stretch of work? Someone stops by to get a signature on a form. What is the user's role in this approval process?

Go into the user's world to get the best data

So get as close to the activity as possible. The ideal situation is to be physically present while the activity unfolds. Then interviewers can see how the target activities fit into the context of daily life. They will see how an activity fits into time and place, what platforms, products, or devices are used, how people collaborate or coordinate to get things done, and how policy or organizational structure affects what people are doing. And interviewers see the core motives driving the experience—the meaning of the activity within the person's life,

---

[5] Whiteside and Wixon 1988.

revealed verbally and nonverbally. But getting this rich data requires real, concrete instances of the activity as it plays out in people's lives.

Gathering field data in context results in this real-life, detailed data—*if* interviewers are mindful of three key distinctions. Our goal is to gather *ongoing experience* instead of *summary data*; *concrete data* rather than *abstract data*; and *experienced motives* rather than *reports*. We'll describe each of these distinctions in turn.

Summary data versus ongoing experience. People are taught from an early age to summarize. If you ask a friend about a movie she saw last week, she does not recount the entire plot. She gives overall impressions, one or two highlights, and the thing that most impressed or disgusted her. (Never ask a seven-year-old that question—they haven't yet learned to summarize and *will* tell you the entire plot of the movie in excruciating detail.) Ask people to tell you about their experience with a new product, and they will behave just the same way. They give their overall impressions and mention one or two things that were especially good or bad. After the fact, they have a hard time saying exactly why the good things were important, or why the bad things got in the way.

> *Avoid summary data by watching real activities unfold*

But if you're there to see the activity happen, you'll see all this detail and be able to talk to the user about what is really happening. Reality is never summarized.

Abstract versus concrete data. Humans love to abstract. It's much easier to lump a dozen similar events together than to get all the details of one specific instance really right. Because an abstraction groups similar events, it glosses over all the detail which makes an event unique. And since a product is built for many users, a product team already needs to abstract across all the users' experiences. If the product team starts from abstractions and then abstracts again to go across all users, there is little chance the resulting product will actually be useful to real people. So interviewers need to be aware of the signals that indicate the user is abstracting and should be brought back to the real instances of life.

If the user is leaning back and looking at the ceiling, he is almost always talking in the abstract. This is the position of someone who will not allow the reality all around him to disrupt the concept he is building in his brain. Someone talking about real experience leans forward, either working on or pointing to some representation of what he is talking about. Words indicating the user is generalizing are another signal. If the user says "generally," "we usually," "in our company," she is presenting an abstraction. Any statement in the present tense is usually an abstraction. "In our group we do…" introduces an abstraction; "that time we did…" introduces real experience. Instances described in detail from the near past are real—instances imagined about the future are not.

Avoid abstractions by returning to real artifacts and events

If the user starts to get lost in abstractions, just pull him back to real activity. "When was the last time you did that? Can you show me?" Every time you do this, you reinforce that concrete data matters, and you make it easier to get concrete data next time. If the user says, "I usually start the day by checking messages," ask, "What are you doing this morning? Can you start?"

If you can't be present while the user engages in the target activity, you have two other options for getting to concrete data. One is artifacts—the things the user creates and uses in doing the activity. If the user says, "We usually get reports by email," for example, ask, "Do you have one? May I see it?"

Your other option is a *retrospective account*. This recovers the full story of something that happened in the recent past. Retelling a past event is hard because so much of the context has been lost. People automatically summarize, omitting necessary detail. Most people will start telling a story in the middle, skipping over what went before. They will skip whole steps as they tell the story. The interviewer's job is to listen for what the user is leaving out and to ask questions which fill in the holes. Inquiry that focuses the user on their step-by-step action

Span time by replaying recent past events in detail

in order shows the user the level of detail we want. Going in order helps the user remember.

A car owner (U) talks to the interviewer (I) about how he handled a road trip to another city:

U: *I got in the car in the morning, and used the GPS to get me to my first appointment.*

I: *You entered in the address?*

U: *That's right.*

I: *Where did you get the address? Did you have it on your phone?*

U: *Yes, but I actually entered the address the night before.*

I: *The night before?*

U: *Right. Before I go on a trip, I enter all the places I'll go as destinations.*

I: *You mean you saved them as favorites?*

U: *No, I just entered them like I was going to go there, then I canceled. That's what I did the night before. Then, the day I left, they were all right there, easy to pick. [He shows the recent destinations list].*

I: *So you never have to delete them.*

U: *Right—they just disappear off the bottom of the list. I may never go to these places again, so If I entered them as favorites I'd have to delete them later.*

I: *Okay. So the night before, where did you get the address from?*

U: *My first address was a client we do business with all the time, so I got it from the contacts on my phone.*

I: *Can I see?*

At each point, the interviewer listens for steps that she thinks might have happened but the user skipped and then backs the user up to find out. In this process, the user walks through the steps in his mind, using available artifacts to stimulate memory. He recalls more, and is more accurate, than he would be if allowed to simply tell the story without interruptions or discussion. Using retrospective accounts, the interviewer can recover past events and can also learn more about events in progress.

Keep the user concrete by exploring ongoing activity

If the end of a story hasn't happened yet, the most reliable way to learn about that part of the activity is to pick up the retrospective account at that point in a previous occurrence which did complete. Asking "What would you do next?" forces the user to make something up; going to a past instance allows the user to stay concrete.

Retrospective accounts can be used to gather data on activities that happen over a longer stretch of time or to collect data on multiple instances of the same activity. These grounded, case-based retrospectives bring a richer view of how a target task may play out in a person's life.

Experienced motives versus reports.   Because researchers are with users in their real-life contexts, they can sense the user's feelings and emotional energy when talking about or doing the activities of their lives. If asked "How do you feel about this (product, activity, or event)," when out of context, users are prone to treat it like a report. They just tell what they thought they felt without any of the visceral response that is coupled with actions and thoughts when actually in situ. This emotional background is just as much concrete data as the user's specific actions, and it is important for collecting data relevant to the Cool Concepts. When people are experiencing something that matters to them because it's related to their identity, their words are accompanied by palpable pride or distain, for example. Data on sensation is present in the sensual delight they visibly experience. When Identity and Sensation

Emotion points to important stories and motives

meet, it might look like this immaculately dressed driver's reaction
to the lights on his Cadillac:

> He pointed out the vertical LEDs on the headlights of his
> new Cadillac: "They look really sharp. Other high-end cars
> have LEDs on their headlights, but they just look stupid."
> Reacting to the emotional charge in his voice, the inter-
> viewer said, "So the lights really matter to you—you seem
> sensitive to style." "Oh yes," said the user. "I care about the
> things I have around me and how I show up. I could never
> have something that looked so terrible as those other lights!
> I bought this car for the lights."

When you want to find the cool elements of a product, what
truly matters to the user is strongly connected to the user's sense of
self—so it is apparent in deeply felt emotions. Interviewers have to
be present in the moment the user is having these strong feelings
to uncover them. Then we can probe to understand what is driving
the feeling or to find a core motive. But if interviewers only collect
reports, another kind of summary, we will miss what really matters.

The principle of context is the key to getting good data: Go
where the target activity is happening, observe it, sense the user's feelings, and talk about it, all while it happens. Keep the user grounded
in concrete actions both by doing activities and by walking specific
recent incidents in the past—step by step. Probe emotional energy
and find its origin and motivations. Don't allow the user to summarize, abstract, or report on their world; it removes too much of the
real, important data. In this way, interviewers will have access to the
data they need to design for life.

PARTNERSHIP

The principle of *partnership* creates a collaboration between user and
interviewer to understand the user's life. The only person who really
knows everything about his or her life is the one
living it, so Contextual Inquiry creates a context
in which the user and the interviewer can explore
the user's activities together, both influencing the
direction of the exploration.

*Partnership creates a sense
of a shared quest*

John Kellerman
Attorney at Law

In an interview with a designer using page-layout software, the user was positioning text on the page, entering the text and moving it around. Then he created a box around a line of text, moved it down until the top of the box butted the bottom of the line of text, and moved another line of text up until it butted the bottom of the box. Then he deleted the box. Here is how we probed for insight:

Let the users lead you to insight about their world

Interviewer: *"Could I see that again?"*

User: *"What?"*

I: *"What you just did with the box."*

U: *"Oh, I'm just using it to position this text here. The box doesn't matter."*

I: *"But why are you using a box?"*

U: *"See, I want the white space to be exactly the same height as the lower-case letters in this line of text. So I draw the box to get the height." (He repeats the actions to illustrate, going more slowly.) "Then I drag it down, and it shows where the next line of text should go."*

I: *"Why do you want to get the spacing exact?"*

U: *"It's to make the appearance of the page more even. You want all the lines to have some regular relationship the other things on the page. It's always hard to know if it really makes any difference—you just hope the overall appearance will be cleaner if you get things like this right."*

I: *"It's like everything you put on the page defines a whole grid of appropriate places for the other things to go."*

U: *"That's right. Everything affects everything else—you can't reposition just one thing."*

We collected this data back in the 1990s, and this user was revealing a strategy for laying out a page which the actual page-layout tools wouldn't support directly for another 10 years. Now, the tools have features to help with this kind of positioning—but you'll still see users measuring distances on the screen. What are the tools missing?

Withdrawal and return.   The example above illustrates the pattern of interaction in a Contextual Inquiry. The user is engrossed in their activity; the interviewer is busy watching the detail, looking for pattern and structure, and thinking about the reasons behind the user's actions. At some point the interviewer sees something that doesn't fit or figures out the structure underlying an aspect of the activity and interrupts to talk about it. This causes a break in the action, and both user and interviewer *withdraw* from the activity to discuss what the interviewer saw. This break to reflect creates a separate space in time to think about the practice—right when it just happened. Users, interrupted in the moment of taking an action, can say what they are doing and why. The interviewer, looking from the outside, can point out behavior users might not notice or take for granted.

Alternate between watching and probing

When the conversation is over, the interviewer directs the user to *return* to the ongoing activity, and the interviewer returns to watching. This *withdrawal and return* is a basic pattern of Contextual Inquiry: periods of watching activities unfold interspersed with discussions of the events that just happened.

By paying attention to the details and pattern of the activity, the interviewer teaches the user to attend to detail and pattern also. Over the course of an interview, users become sensitized to their own actions. Questions reveal the structure of their own activity, and they start thinking about it themselves. Sometimes users then start interrupting themselves to reveal aspects of their activities that might otherwise have been missed by the interviewer. Because of the withdrawal and return over the course of the interview, a true partnership develops to inquire into the activities of the user's life.

Because interviewers are also product designers, they will naturally generate design ideas just by being immersed in the user's world.

The user is in the middle of doing the very activity the new idea is intended to support—there is no better time to get feedback on whether the idea works. If it does, the interviewer now both understands the needs of the activity and has a potential solution. If not, he finds out he did not really understand the issue after all. Sharing designers' first, unformed ideas with the user allows them to alter the team's initial thinking, opening the possibility of radical changes in product purpose and structure. In addition, the design idea suggests to the user what technology can do. Users can start to see how technology might be applied to their problem—and they may start inventing too. But watch out—a Contextual Inquiry should be an inquiry into the user's life. Return quickly to the activities important to the project focus, or you'll find yourself only discussing possible designs out of context.

Share emerging design ideas for immediate feedback

Avoiding other relationship models.   Adopting the attitudes and behaviors of the master/apprentice relationship model ensures the best data. But sometimes, interviewers fall back into more familiar models of relationship that get in the way. Here are some common pitfalls:

Interviewer/Interviewee: The interviewer and user start to act as though there were a questionnaire to be filled out. You ask a question which the user answers and then falls silent. You, anxious that the interview go well, ask another question, which the user answers and then falls silent again. This continues. The questions are no longer related to ongoing activities, because real activity has ceased. The best fix is to return to the action by asking the user to take their next step, which effectively cuts short this question/answer interaction.

You aren't there to get a list of questions answered

Expert/Novice: Like it or not, you start with the aura of the expert. You are the one designing the product, with all the technical knowledge. You have to work to get the user to treat you as an apprentice. So set the user's expectations correctly at the beginning of the interview. Explain that you are there to hear about and see their activities, because only they know their own practice. You aren't there to help them with problems or answer questions.

Then, if the user asks for help (or should you forget and volunteer help) step out of the expert role explicitly: "I'll never understand the problems with our product if I spend the whole time helping you. Why don't you go ahead and do what you would do if I weren't here, and at the end I'll answer any questions that remain." But if the user is so stuck that he cannot continue doing the activity you came to see, give them a hint to move them along.

You aren't there to help them learn the product

Guest/Host: Because it is the user's workplace and the user is a stranger, it is easy to act like a guest. A guest is polite and not too nosy. A host is considerate and tries to make the guest comfortable by seeing to his needs. You'll know this has happened because you find yourself feeling like a guest. Respond by moving quickly past the formal relationship to the role of partner in inquiry. This is where sensitivity to culture matters—if, as in some cultures, the user won't be comfortable until you've had a cup of coffee, then have it and move to observing their real life quickly, or you'll be wasting all your interview time.

It's a goal to be nosy

Being nosy is part of a good interview. A good field interview feels like the kind of intimacy people strike up on airplanes, where seatmates may tell each other very personal things. The user has already agreed to help by doing a field interview, so let them help. Move closer; look at what they are looking at; ask questions; be nosy. This way you create a real partnership in inquiry. Soon you'll have the user saying, "Come over here—you want to see this."

Partnership transforms the apprenticeship relationship into a mutual relationship of shared inquiry and discovery. It retains the close working relationship from apprenticeship while equalizing the power imbalance between a master and apprentice. It invites the user into co-inquiry. This results in an intimate relationship which allows for inquisitiveness, honesty, and good data.

INTERPRETATION

It is not enough only to observe and bring back observations. Interpretation is the assignment of meaning to the observation—what it implies about the behavior and experience of the user or how it reveals the structure of the activity. The typical language used to describe gathering data for design—data *gathering* or requirements *elicitation*—suggest that a researcher can go out in the field and pick up the nuggets of what to build next in the same way that one collects shells on the beach, as if they were just there for the taking. When we go out into the field, we are not just collecting the facts of what the people are doing—we must come back with an accurate interpretation of those facts. We must collect meaning. The principle of interpretation says that good facts are only the starting point; good product design is actually built on the designers' interpretation of those facts. Here's an illustration:

The "data" we bring home is always our view on what we saw

> The fact: A high-powered managing partner at an accounting firm has a client with a question about depreciation. The partner does some research into the issue using Google and their financial information tool, and then hands it off to a staff member to handle.

Why did she do some research herself before handing it off? Here are some interpretations of what that fact might mean.

1. She doesn't trust her staff. She wanted to get the right answer herself first, then lets her staff do the full research and write-up.

2. She plans to do the work herself, but finds it's more complicated than she expected and so she hands it off when it starts to become more than she wants to do.

3. She's curious; she wants to understand the issue rather than just passing the work off to her staff.

If (1) is correct, we might want better ways to do quality checks on staff work; (2) suggests building an easy way to package work in progress and hand it off to someone else; (3) suggests ways to get quick answers and do quick exploration without heavyweight tools for documentation and referencing sources.

Which of these designs is best? It depends on which interpretation is correct—the fact alone does not allow a designer to choose. (In fact, from discussion with the user, (3) turned out to be the right answer). But taking design action means choosing which interpretation to lay on the fact. It's the interpretation which drives the design decision.

Interpretation is the chain of reasoning that turns a fact into an action relevant to the designer's purpose. From the *fact*, the observable event, the designer makes a *hypothesis*, an initial interpretation about what the fact means or the intent behind the fact. This hypothesis has an *implication* for the design, which can be realized as a particular *design idea*. This entire chain of reasoning happens implicitly any time anyone suggests a design idea. Usually it happens so fast, only the final idea is made explicit. But the whole chain must be valid for the design idea to be put in the product.

Design ideas are the end product of a chain of reasoning stimulated by an observation

Design is built upon interpretation of facts—which may be observed behavior or observed emotion. For any fact, the interpretation must be right. Validation of the interpretation happens when you share it with the user.

Share your interpretations.   If the data that matters is your interpretation, you must make sure the interpretation is correct, and you can only do that by sharing it with the user. So share your hypotheses about the motives underlying the user's behavior, their apparent feelings, and any strategies you observe. Share what you think they are trying to accomplish and how you think they go about accomplishing it. Let them tune your understanding in the moment, when they can remember what they were just experiencing. Sharing your interpretations and asking users to tune those interpretations will get you very reliable data. In fact, it's the only way to get reliable data;

if you don't check with the user immediately, you'll take away an understanding which is at least partially made up.

Design is built on the interpretation of facts—so that interpretation had better be right

When exploring emotional energy and motives, the same process holds: sense the emotional energy; make a hypothesis about its origin; and share that hypothesis for the user to validate or provide you with a better explanation. Through this discussion you will understand the user's core motives and feelings about a product or situation. And if you listen for sources of joy, you will come to see the opportunity for building the cool user experience into the product.

Also share design ideas as you think of them, as we discussed in the section on Partnership. Sharing design ideas ensures that you come home with a well-founded understanding of the user's life by walking the chain of reasoning backwards—if the idea doesn't fit, some link in your reasoning was wrong. Probe and discuss why your idea doesn't work so as to discover what you misunderstood about their activity.

When it's the user coming to you with design ideas in the form of wish lists, treat them the same way—probe to find out the situation which gave rise to the wish. Understanding the underlying work and life context gives a design team much more flexibility to respond to the real problem instead of trying to implement hundreds of user requests. Often, a single solution will be able to deal with many apparently different requests, once you understand the motive behind them.

But won't sharing your interpretation bias the data? Can you really check an interpretation just by sharing it with the user? Won't users be prone to agree with whatever you say? No—in fact, it is quite hard to

Sharing interpretations with users won't bias the data

get people who are in the middle of living their lives to agree with a wrong interpretation. It's not at all hypothetical for them, because they are in the midst of the activity. This is an experience they are having *now*. The statement that doesn't fit is like an itch; they feel that the description doesn't fit their inner experience and so they rephrase it:

"It's like a traveling office," we said, looking at how a salesman has set up his car. "Well—like a traveling *desk*," he responded.

The difference between the two is small but real, and people will be uncomfortable until they get a characterization that fits exactly. We have had people run down the hallway after us as we were leaving to ensure that we had some minor point exactly right.

Finally, since users are not generally experts in seeing the structure of their own life, the interpretation you suggest shows them what to pay attention to. Open-ended questions give the user less guidance in thinking about their activity than an interpretation and result in less insight.

Sharing interpretations teaches users to see their own lives

Because users respond to the interpretation in the moment, they can fine-tune it quite precisely. Users commonly make slight changes in emphasis such as those above to make the interpretation exact. They can do this because they are given a starting point which they can compare with the experience they are actually having and adjust it, rather than having to start from scratch.

> "So you're acting like a master coder," we said to a development project manager. "Yeah," he said. "Except I wasn't looking at code. More like master QA."

Listen for the "no". An interviewer's assumptions can easily be wrong, their interpretations may be wrong—and so their goal must be to correct their understanding if they are to design something that responds to the real lives of users. Interviewers need to be committed to hearing what the user is really saying. The users may mean "no" but to be polite may not say "no" directly. Here are some indirect ways users say "no":

Users fine-tune interpretations

> "Huh?"—This means the interpretation was so far off that it had no apparent connection to what the user thought was going on.

> "Umm...could be."—This means "no." If the interpretation is close, the user will usually respond immediately. A pause for thought means that they are trying to make it fit their experience and cannot.

"Yes, but...", or "Yes, and..."—Listen carefully to what follows the "but" or "and." If it is a new thought, this is the right interpretation and yours was wrong. If it builds on yours, this is a confirmation with a twist adding *information.*

Users say "yes" by twinkling their eyes at you as they realize your words match their experience—or by saying "yes" flatly, as if the whole point was obvious. They will nearly always elaborate on what you said, even if all they do is put it in their own words.

All this means that, in a Contextual Inquiry, the interviewer needs to talk. They need to vocalize their interpretations, their design ideas, and their understanding of what the user is up to and feels. This may be uncomfortable to those trained in other data gathering methods, but it is necessary to be sure you have a credible interpretation.

In Contextual Inquiry, the interviewer needs to talk!

FOCUS

The project focus tells designers what to pay attention to—of all the overwhelming detail available, what matters for the design problem at hand. Before starting a project, the team defines the problem to be solved, the users who are affected, the users' activities and tasks that matter, and the situations and locations that are relevant. This project focus extends and refines the core focus on work and life practice given by Contextual Design and the Cool Concepts. It guides how the user interviews are set up and what the designers pay attention to during the interview.

The interview focus defines the point of view interviewers take during the interview. What should they pay attention to? Which aspects of the activity or its surrounding context matter and which don't? Without a list of questions, how can the interviewer steer the conversation at all? An apprentice learns whatever the master knows—the master decides what's important. But the interviewer needs data relevant to the project. The principle of *focus* gives the interviewer a way to keep the conversation on topics that are useful without taking control away from the user entirely. Focus steers the interview the same way that friends steer conversations with each other. The topics the friends care about—the topics in their focus—are what they spend time on. Anything one friend raises that the other doesn't care about is allowed to drop naturally. Similarly, an interviewer shares the project focus and then pays special attention to things related to that focus. The user picks up on this and the user and interviewer end up costeering the conversation naturally.

Taking a focus is unavoidable—everyone has an entering focus, a whole life history defining what they notice and what they don't. Their focus is formed by their personal and professional interests, by their initial understanding of what matters for the project, and what they think is true for the domain. Consider three interviewers talking to a homeowner about her TV and entertainment systems:

Clear focus steers the conversation

> One interviewer just bought a home theater setup and sees how the user has laid out her family room for watching TV and listening to music.
>
> Another interviewer is familiar with audio technology and notices the brands of speakers and amp and how she's gone about connecting them.
>
> The third interviewer is deep into mobile technology and notices how the user has workarounds for listening to music in different parts of the house and outside.

Each interviewer sees a different aspect of the entertainment systems, all of which are "true" in that they are all real. But each interviewer's different focus reveals different details. The third interviewer sees the larger context of entertainment in the home—but does he notice the connectivity issues? A focus gives the interviewer a framework for making sense of the user's life. Having multiple people with different job roles and experiences naturally builds in multiple entering focuses. Together, the team will see more than any one person could see alone.

Setting project focus.   To move the team forward in a shared inquiry, the team needs a shared understanding of what the project is about—a shared initial focus. The project focus guides how the user interviews are set up and what the designers pay attention to during the interview.

Focus reveals relevant detail

A project focus is defined explicitly. It tells the team what to pay attention to—of all the overwhelming detail available, what matters for the design problem at hand. Before starting a project, the team defines the problem to be solved, the users who are affected, the relevant activities and tasks, and the relevant situations and locations.

The project focus defines what a team *needs to find out* to design a particular product, solve a particular problem, understand a market from a particular point of view or redesign a service or process which includes technology. A project focus is not the same as project goal: "Port our product to our new platform," "Create a mobile app for our product," or "Define the next feature set." These may be the organizational statement of the project mission, but they don't say how to get the right data. The team needs to identify the behavior and experience that they must understand to accomplish that corporate mandate. The project focus clarifies what the project is about from the point of view of user behavior within the context of the corporate mission. A clear, articulated project scope and focus ensures that all interviewers are probing into the experience and activities relevant to the project. We talk more about project scope and focus in Chapter 19.

This project focus is extended and refined by the focus on work and life practice given by Contextual Design and the Cool Concepts.

Design for life broadens every project's focus

The Contextual Design models (described in the next section) broaden the team's focus beyond design for single tasks by revealing issues around design for life. To design for the Cool Concepts, it's not enough to focus on the steps of a task, the usability or problems of the current product, or current customer complaints. Accordingly, we will define *Experience Models* that express the issues of the Cool Concepts within the Wheel of Joy in Life. These models push the team to see the whole of how the target activity fits into life—both the structure of the life and users' core motives. They broaden the team's viewpoint and expand the data the team collects.

Experience Models are new to Contextual Design V2.0. The original Contextual Design models were *structural models*, focused on the details of task and practice—and those details still matter. They address the Cool Concepts in the Triangle of Joy in Use (Direct, Hassle, and the Learning Delta), and push the team to look at the low level detail of interaction and reaction to the tool itself. They do not help to reveal the concepts of the Wheel of Joy in Life.

So the project focus augmented by the Cool Concept focus becomes the initial lens that guides the interview. Depending on the project goals and the nature of the activity to be studied, the team picks a set of Contextual Design models appropriate to their problem. These models, both Experience Models and the older structural models, will then be the lens through which more specific data is collected.

But each interviewer also brings their personal focus—their beliefs about the target activity and users and their professional way of looking at things—both of which are likely to be unconscious. The actual interview focus taken by any team member will be an amalgamation of all these different focuses. Their job is then to let the participant and the facts of the interview to shape the focus so it reflects what really matters for the project.

Focus conceals the unexpected

Focus reveals and conceals.   If focus reveals detail within the area it covers, it tends to conceal other aspects of the user's world. Someone who notices physical room layout cannot help but notice when the home entertainment system has dictated the layout; someone who never thought about interior design cannot help but overlook it until his attention is drawn to it. Meanwhile, the first interviewer is ignoring how the family room is not the whole entertainment story—which may be equally important to the design problem. The first interviewer's focus has revealed rich detail in room layout; but how can he expand his focus and learn about the other aspects of life practice?

In Contextual Design, we seek to deliberately expand focus and break our entering assumptions. To expand focus during the interview, Contextual Design defines *intrapersonal triggers*, cues that help the interviewer recognize where their entering focus does not fit the reality of the user's life so they can probe to broaden their understanding. This encourages interviewers to deliberately create a paradigm shift rather than simply confirming their existing expectations.

Internal feelings guide how to interview

Intrapersonal triggers are flags alerting the interviewer when an opportunity for breaking a paradigm and expanding the entering focus exists. They work because your own feelings tell you what is happening in the interview and how to act to fix it.

Surprises and contradictions: The user says or does something that you know is "wrong." It's something, you think, no one else would do, something totally idiosyncratic. Or else it's just random—they had no particular reason for doing it. Any one of these reactions is a danger signal. It means that you are—right now—allowing your preexisting assumptions to override what the user is telling or showing you. The tendency is to let it pass as irrelevant; the solution is to do the opposite. Take the attitude that nothing any person does is done for no reason—if you think it's for no reason (even if they *tell* you it's for no reason), you don't yet understand the point of view from which it makes sense. Take the attitude that nothing any person does is unique to them—it always represents an important class of users whose needs will not be met if you don't figure out what's going on. Act like the apprentice, who always assumes a seemingly pointless action might hide a key secret of the trade. Probe the thing that is unexpected and see what you find.

Nods: The user says something that fits exactly with your assumptions, and you nod. This is the reverse of the first trigger, and it is tricky. What are you doing when you nod? Implicitly you are saying that what you hear in the user's words matches with your own experience, and so you assume that everything that happened to you and everything that you feel is also true for them. Is this a safe assumption? Instead, take the attitude that everything is new, as if you had never seen it before. The apprentice never assumes the master has no more to teach. Is the participant's experience *really* the same? Speak it back to them in an interpretation and find out.

Or make their world strange: Why would they do that? What's motivating them? Look for the paradigm shift—look for ways people are different from what you expect.

What you don't know: The user says something technical you didn't understand or is explaining something and you just aren't getting it. Now what? Are you going to admit your ignorance? Wouldn't it be easier to research the topic a bit back at the office? No. Admit your ignorance. Make the user go back and describe what they are doing step by step. Remember you are the apprentice—you don't need to have all the answers. Treat this as a good opportunity to step away from the expert role. You are there to learn—you might as well learn about the activities and technology you don't understand.

Don't ask a domain expert to explain what you saw—ask the user!

No one else will be able to tell you better what is going on with this person than the person themselves. Even if the user doesn't really understand it either, the extent of their knowledge and misinformation can be valuable for design. Furthermore, if you don't ask, you'll get more and more lost as the conversation continues.

Where the emotion is: When you feel emotional energy in the room, positive or negative, this is a signal to pay attention and probe more. The users' emotional reactions reveal what they truly care about—and so, what they will care about in a product you deliver. Don't assume that you understand the source of the emotion. Offer your interpretation to prompt a response and discover where it's actually coming from.

> **U:** *"Most reserved blocks are released a week out,"* said the nurse. *"Except for Dr. Smith's. His release the day before."* (Her face closed down and she compressed her lips.)
>
> **I:** *"Oh, he has a special deal?"*
>
> **U:** *"Yes. He's special."* (She tried to repress her disapproval.)
>
> **I:** *"So if a doctor is 'special' enough, they get their own rules?"*
>
> **U:** *"That's right."*
>
> **I:** *"I bet that makes it harder for you."*
>
> **U:** *"We live with it. It's our job to make everything work."*

Everyone has a set of assumptions about product value, usage, and what creates joy or coolness; treat these as what they are, entering assumptions. The Cool Concepts provide a structure for seeing emotions, but they also come with their assumptions—albeit widely validated ones. Although they provide a framework for understanding what might be happening in the user's experience, unless you validate your interpretation, you can't be sure. So if you see, hear, or feel emotion, probe to clarify the source, and use it to expand your focus.

It's easy to design a product from your own assumptions and prejudices. Breaking out of your preconceived notions of what the product should be and how it should work is one of your hardest design tasks. Allowing users to break your entering paradigm counterbalances the natural propensity to design from your own assumptions. The principle of Focus makes you aware of your assumptions. Paying attention to triggers to expand that focus reveals opportunities to probe and so widens your focus. This is how to find new delighters and opportunities for a product's design.

Commit to challenging your assumptions, not validating them

THE CONTEXTUAL INTERVIEW STRUCTURE

The principles of Contextual Inquiry and the Cool Concepts guide the design of the interview. The principles say what needs to happen to get good data, but the design problem and the nature of the activity being studied constrain the exact procedure to use. The most common structure for Contextual Inquiry is a contextual interview: a one-on-one interaction lasting 90 minutes to 2 hours, during which the user does his or her own activities wherever they naturally occur, while the interviewer engages them in discussion of what they are doing and why. During the interview, the interviewer gathers the additional data suggested by the Contextual Design models selected for the project. This structure has been used to study everything from office work to shopping, television use, vehicle driving, mobile device use, construction equipment, clean room chip fabrication, factory floors, medical devices, operating rooms, and real-time collaboration—to name just a few. It's all you need to collect field data for virtually any project type.

Take this basic interview structure and tune it for your particular project

Each interview has its own rhythm, set by the activity and the user. But they all share a structure which helps interviewer and user get through the time without losing track of what they are supposed to do. Every interview has four parts:

STARTING: GETTING AN OVERVIEW

You and the user need to get used to each other as people. Running the first part of the interview as a conventional interaction helps with that. You introduce yourself and your focus, so the user knows from the outset what matters and can participate in the inquiry. You promise confidentiality and get permission for any recording. Explain that the user and their actions are primary and that you depend on them to help you understand what they are doing and to correct your misinterpretations. Ask for opinions about the tools they have (if relevant) and get an overview of the larger context of their life as it pertains to the activity and what is to be done that day. Start the discussion about identity elements and see where it goes.

This is summary data, not concrete data, so don't pursue any issues in detail—instead, watch to see if they come up in the body of the interview and pursue them then, when they are in context.

Get enough of an overview to get started—move quickly to contextual data

Also get an overview of how the activity fits into the times and places of daily life. This may be a convenient time to start walking the day, looking at behaviors relevant to the target activity, including place, time, and platform used. This *Day-in-the-Life* data will feed the Cool Concept of Accomplishment later. This is just the beginning of collecting this type of data; you are about to make the transition to observing and discussing ongoing experience. But it's natural to backtrack and ask about the activities that occurred before the interview started.

The traditional interview step should last no more than 15–20 minutes. If you collect Day-in-the-Life data, it may be a bit longer but never extend beyond 30 minutes or you won't get to the contextual data you need.

THE TRANSITION

In the transition, lay out the new rules for the Contextual Interview: the user will do his or her activities while you watch; you will interrupt whenever you see something interesting; and they can tell you

Explain the new rules of a Contextual Interview

to hold off if it's a bad time to be interrupted. Anytime one wants to break social norms, it's best to define the new rules for social interaction explicitly so everyone knows how to behave appropriately. Here, you want to create the new rules for the Contextual Interview, so you say what they are.

This should take all of 30 seconds, but it's a crucial 30 seconds; if you don't do it, you run the risk of spending the entire time in a conventional interview.

THE CONTEXTUAL INTERVIEW PROPER

During the overview, you got an idea of the user's life and work and what is currently on their plate. At this point, suggest that the

Observe and probe the ongoing activity

user start doing one of his or her activities (relevant to the project focus) while you observe and interpret. This is the bulk of the interview. You are the apprentice, observing, asking questions, and suggesting interpretations of behavior. Analyze artifacts and elicit retrospective accounts. Keep the user concrete, getting back to real instances, using artifacts, and drawing on paper when the user draws in the air to describe something she doesn't have in front of her. Look for emotional energy and probe when you find it. Look for the ways tasks span time and space, and how the user's devices enable that. Look for connection and for moments of sensation. And take copious notes by hand the whole time—don't depend on a recording or a second person to catch everything.

Be nosy—after a phone conversation, ask what it was about. If the user goes to the files, look over her shoulder. If a text message comes in, ask about that. If she goes down the hall, tag along. If someone comes to the door and looks diffident about inter-

Bring back copies of used artifacts

rupting, tell them to come on in. And, of course, if the user says she needs a break, let her have one. The principles of context, partnership, interpretation, and focus guide your interaction during the interview.

STRUCTURE OF THE CONTEXTUAL INTERVIEW

Intro: Traditional interview steps
- Introduce yourself and reveal your focus
- Promise confidentiality
- Get an overview of their life vis-à-vis the target activity
- Explore Identity elements
- Start to walk the day looking at behaviors relevant to the target activity considering place, time, and platform used.
- Deal with opinions about tools

Switch to Contextual Interview
- Reset the rules to observation and discussion, not Q&A

Observe and co-interpret
- Take notes
- Follow your activity focus
- Follow your focus for selected models
- Look for Cool specifically
- Be nosy
- Interruptions are data too
- **Beware:** Cool data is more retrospective. Ground yourself in real story and detail!

Wrap-up
- Create a large interpretation of your learning about the activity in the context of life
- Share your rough model drawings and Cool takeaways
- Ask "pet" questions
- Thank the user

Cool Concepts in the Contextual Interview

The Cool Concepts augment the data to be collected during the interview. Above, we indicated the type of data needed and where in the interview to collect it. In Chapter 7, when we discuss the Experience Models, we will describe how to get data for the Experience Models in detail. Data for the concepts in the Triangle of Design are handled like any data on the use of a product. This data focuses the interviewer on the interaction design of the product and whether it supports a coherent intent with direct, hassle-free function that requires little to no learning.

Direct into Action:
- Can the user understand the overall interaction design immediately—no thinking?
- Can the product "Think for me"? "Bring everything together at the point of action?"

The Hassle Factor:
- How does the tool remove or reveal tool hassle?
- Are all inconveniences, set-up, plugging in, login, boxes, customization and technology hassles removed?

The Learning Delta:
- Is learning instant or nonexistent?
- Does the tool nudge into action and build on existing skill?
- Is there too much complexity that repels?
- Is there success with massively reduced complexity?

Probe for Joy in Use data as you observe product interactions

To get the right data for the Triangle requires continual attention to interaction throughout the interview. The interviewer watches tool interaction closely to identify issues of Direct into Action, Hassle, and the Learning Delta. See the box given above for reference. When observed we pause to discuss the impact of the interaction on the activity and tool experience. Look for examples of what works and what doesn't; what brings a smile and what irritates. Watch out for that joy in magic and surprise when something works so well. Notice where the user hesitates in confusion or smoothly glides through activity—all of this indicates their response to the tool's design.

Talk to the user about their reaction to the tool as it impacts the activities defined in the project focus. Take some time to observe them using consumer tools they love to get an idea of what brings them joy even when you are collecting data relevant to a business too.

Seeing the details of the interaction and the emotional response to it is hard—you may have to devote 15–20 minutes of the interview to focus on getting data for these Cool Concepts. You can do this at the end of the interview if it did not come out along the way.

THE WRAP-UP

At the end of the interview, you have a chance to wrap up your understanding of how the target activities play out in the user's overall life and motivations. Skim back over your notes and summarize what you learned. Don't repeat verbatim what happened; describe the patterns you saw in the activity you observed, what you thought was important, roles they play in collaboration, and identity elements you discovered. Share the drawing of the Relationship and Collaboration models you drew in your notebook, if you haven't already. Identify roles the person may play in their organization, describe the overarching strategies they use to get things done, and talk about what worked and what didn't. Review any Day-in-the-Life notes for emerging patterns. This is the user's last chance to correct and elaborate on your understanding, and they usually will—allow 15 minutes for the wrap-up.

Share your final interpretation of the user's life and work

DESIGN WITH AND FOR CHILDREN

Allison Druin, University of Maryland

Designers of new technologies for children (ages 0–13) often forget that young people are not *just short adults* but an entirely different user population who approach their experiences with abilities, norms, and complexities that differ from adults. Young people are growing physically, changing cognitively, and developing emotionally as they traverse the rules of their peer groups, parents, teachers, social workers, doctors, or other adults. Young people may not understand why they need to be kept safe in their virtual and physical worlds, when all they want to do is be given the freedom to explore. Designers must remember that there are big differences in what a 6-year old child needs, wants, or can accomplish as opposed to a child at 10 or 13. The idea of a K through 12 technology solution rarely exists, because children need such different tools as they grow older.

Even with these complex challenges in understanding the world of young people, designers still may believe that it's good enough to get an adult translation from other parents, teachers, and even themselves, rather than talk and design with children. Some designers may be parents, others may be teachers or know trusted teachers, and all designers were once children with memories of what the world was like in school, at play, and growing up. But no adult today can say they were a child in 2016 and know exactly what it feels like to crack the glass screen on their mobile phone for the third time because it fell out of their pocket while playing soccer. Adults today may not understand why it's so important to be on social media for their middle school friends' group chats. They may not get why children would rather follow a YouTube channel than watch broadcast TV. Children are actively mobile, social beings who want to control when they consume and create their information.

Designers need to learn more about today's children from children. Generally, young people are very willing to help and can be extremely honest in their ideas surrounding technology. However, depending on age, abilities, and communication preference, some young people may feel more comfortable sharing aspects of their lives and their preferences about technology more verbally, visually, and/or physically than adults. In our work, we engage children during user research and during the design process.

During research, children can play several roles, the most common being that of user. Children interact with technology, while adults may observe, videotape, or test for skills. Adult researchers may gather data on children's behavior and experience at school, at play, and at home within permission from parents. In these cases, adult researchers try to understand the child's world and the impact that existing or new technologies have on child users, so better technologies can be designed. In another role, the role of tester, children try out prototypes of technology that have not been released to the world by researchers or industry professionals. As a tester, children are again observed with the technology and/or asked for their direct comments concerning their experiences.

Children can also codesign or impact the design itself. Children who are informants may be asked for input on design sketches or low-tech prototypes. Children may share their observations and interpretations of their world and use of technology much like anthropologists solicit informants in cultures under study. And once the technology is developed, these children may again offer input and feedback. Finally, children can take on the role of design partner. They are equal stakeholders in the design of new technologies throughout the entire experience.

With adult facilitation, children create low-tech models of their emergent ideas, acting out the use of a possible new technology or drawing out an idea on big paper as a team.

Yes, if designers brainstorm with children it can lead to fanciful ideas—they regularly suggest magic sofas, interactive footsteps, superpower necklaces, and magic wands. But they can also expand a sometimes narrow adult vision to develop new technologies not just for work, but for play, creativity, communication, and mobility. But methods typically used with adults for design need to be adapted. Use more concrete, physical, prototyping tools which can be used as a bridge for communication and problem solving. These tools can include simple art supplies such as clay, string, paper, sticky notes, markers, and more. These tools can be combined with acting out the use of a new technology. These methods end awkward silences and transform boredom into active discussion including both adult and children's voices and ideas.

By including children in the research and design process, surprising and important uncharted territory can be coinvented.[6]

---

[6] For more see: Fails, J. A., Guha, M. L., & **Druin**, A. (2013). Methods and techniques for involving children in the design of new technology. *Foundations and Trends in Human-Computer Interaction, 6*(2), 85–166.
Druin, A. (2011). Children as co-designers of new technologies: Valuing the imagination to transform what is possible. *New directions in youth development: Theory, Practice, and Research: Youth as media creators, 128*, 35–44.
Druin, A. (2002). The role of children in the design of new technology. *Behaviour and Information Technology, 21*(1), 1–25.

TAILORING THE INTERVIEW

To get the appropriate data for task-focused activities, interviewers need just to observe people doing the task and discuss what is happening. Retrospective accounts let you find out about activities over a longer time than the 2 hours of the interview. If an activity is done by multiple people as part of a larger process, do interviews with the different people in the process to get a complete picture. Some activities have several stages—for example, first planning a vacation, then traveling to the location, and then doing things while there. In this case, interview people at each stage. And some activities, such as tax preparation, are seasonal—you have to gather the data at the right time. If you are designing a service, look beyond interaction with technology or activities where you plan to introduce technology—instead, look at all the players and the physical context involved in service delivery. To get the best data, make sure you are in the field with the right people at the right time while they are doing the right things.

Some project foci can present challenges that change the way you gather data. Typical software products supporting consumers or businesses can be studied easily with the observe-and-interpret structure outlined above. But other contexts require modifications. Here are some examples:

Where and how the activity happens affects where and how you run the interview

Travel: Plan interviews with people at each stage of travel: planning, getting to the location, and being at the location. Planning is regular research activity and traditional contextual interviews work well—but remember it's not just a heads-down, focused activity. It is likely to happen in small moments throughout the day, so use Day-in-the-Life retrospective accounts to see those small events. Plan to be with users at their vacation destination—try to find users who are vacationing where you are located. In addition, use retrospective accounts to gather similar data more easily. Unless there's a particular reason to go on the voyage itself, retrospective accounts of traveling to a destination are probably good enough.

Driving vehicles: Start at the user's home and get an overview of the experience of the car while standing next to it. Then get in and drive, talking about the aspect of the car you care about as you go. Plan for both long and short trips; you may need a chaser car to pick the interviewer up after 2 hours into a longer road trip.

Shopping: Start at the user's home looking at online shopping. Focus on the research or buying they are doing and do retrospective accounts of recent shopping from the last few days. Replay any online interactions to get the detail. Then go to an actual store to pick up an item. Alternatively, start in the store: meet them there to see what they do, their use of mobile information, and any communication. End the interview back at home if that is where they do most of their searching.

Group activities: (such as a meeting, a doctor appointment, surgery, or a teacher's class): These group events are hard to interrupt without disrupting the activity you came to see. So identify key individuals to shadow. Talk with them one-on-one first, then watch what goes on during the group activity. Write down your observations and interpretations but do not interrupt. Immediately afterward, debrief one-on-one with your user to go over what just happened.

Construction equipment: The problem here is there is often only one seat in the vehicle. For any activity where it is impossible to accompany the user, talk to them before they start their day to introduce the focus and do the traditional interview. Instrument the activity with a camera and capture about 30 minutes of videotape. Then watch the video with the user right after the event and talk about the experience. Do all this in a single 2–3 hour session.

Consumer electronics: When studying consumer electronics such as TV or music, go into the home and watch people use their products in the traditional way. But use of these devices often takes place all over the house, so also do a "room walk." Go from place to place in the house to talk about the experience within the context of each room and discuss how the experience changes as the family moves around. In each room, observe the family using the target products or replay what they did in the days before—asking them to do it again for you now. The room walk creates the opportunity to discuss the experience as families live their lives throughout the house.

Products for children: Working with children poses a new set of challenges for collecting data and doing design. We asked Allison Druin, an expert in the field, to share her thoughts on this. See the Box below.

The Contextual Interview structure forms the framework for designing any interview situation. Setting project focus so you know what you need to observe and discuss allows you to plan the data collection strategy so it ensures that you get the best data you can to drive your product design forward. There is *always* a way to get the data you need!

Gathering Data on your own

Gathering field data from real users is something you never want to trade off. There's simply no substitute for the real data, and it gives you instant credibility—especially if your organization isn't used to having it available.

If your organization is used to field visits, then you'll just plug into that mechanism. If not, do what you have to:

- Tag along with product managers when they visit customers. Work out the schedule with them so that while they are in "Very Important" meetings with management, you're doing user visits with the people who do the work.
- Work the support desk. Offer friendly and interested callers the opportunity to participate in the company's new "customer feedback program", which just so happens to involve onsite visits.
- Work through your business's user group or online forums.
- Find a supporter in the sales organization. In our experience, a broader plea to the sales team doesn't often yield results. They are focused on making their sales numbers and this is a distraction—and they are very concerned about disrupting a sale. But if you make friends with a given salesperson, he or she may be helpful. Look to go in after a sale is made; see the next point.
- Work with your implementation, onboarding, or professional services team. Many business systems have some sort of onboarding or implementation process to introduce the product or service to a new client. This is a good time to go in, help with the implementation, see the problems—and do some Contextual Inquiries as well.
- Work your personal network. Maybe a relative does the job you care about, or a friend of a friend. Put a plea on Facebook. Visit them where they do the activity if you can; meet them in a coffee shop if you can't.
- Advertise on Craigslist or any other communities where your user population hangs out. Offer a reasonable compensation for an interview.
- Work with a professional recruiter. You'll have to get agreement to pay the recruiters, and they'll expect you to compensate the users, but they can find people.

However you get to them, you want to run some interviews. If you're doing a small piece of a larger product, you'll likely find out about much more than you need—the overall practice, feedback on other parts of the system, and so forth. This is good—you don't want too narrow a focus. You'll be a better designer if you understand the whole context.

For the interpretation session, you can interpret on your own, but try not to. If your organization is starved for information about its users, there are people who are feeling the pain and who are desperate to know more. This is an opportunity to spread the knowledge and start building consensus. So look for others who can participate in an interpretation session: your product manager, another UX person on the same project, a friendly developer. (Developers, being engineers, like to see that a process is empirically based. They are likely to be quite receptive.) Don't look for a big commitment—just line up people to help interpret, one interview at a time. You'll develop a cadre of people who find value in the activity for itself.

The Interpretation Session

4

"I just talked to a potential customer at SXSW, and he said he wanted that feature we talked about—"

"But I just went along on a service call and that guy hated it—we should do this other thing—"

"No, I talked to a VP at one of our really big clients and she said—"

These are the voices of people who have talked to their users. Each one learned something valid. Now they are faced with the difficulty of communicating what they learned, reconciling the different messages from different people and coming to agreement on what the users really need. They have feedback of a sort; they do not have a shared understanding of what it means or what they should do about it.

The Contextual Interview is the first *immersion experience* into the world of the user—but only for the actual interviewer. The next challenge is to capture that data for use in such a way that it gets incorporated into the mindset of the team. Capturing the data is not the major problem for product teams—having a shared understanding of the world of the user is.

Interpretation Sessions let every team member experience multiple interviews

It's not enough for the members of a design team to understand the users they each visited and talked to themselves. If a team is to agree on what to deliver, all team members need to immerse themselves in the world of every user. It isn't a question of just communicating a few facts,

Contextual Design. http://dx.doi.org/10.1016/B978-0-12-800894-2.00004-1

as is typically done with a trip report. Team members need an appreciation of the user's world from the inside, as though they were there.

Interpretation Sessions are another immersive experience, providing a context for the team to understand the field interview data from a user interview in depth, listening to the details of the interview and capturing insights and learnings as they go, and also capturing the details of the user's practice for later use in design.

An Interpretation Session fosters this shared understanding through conversation and mutual inquiry into the meaning of the facts about the users' practice. Every team member learns about all the users, and they also learn each other's perspective, the unique focus each person brings to the problem. They can probe each other's understanding, learning from and teaching each other what to see. Together, the team generates a richer understanding of the user than one person alone would have been able to provide. Interpretation Sessions simultaneously immerse the team in the world of the users *and* create a shared understanding of the implications for the project.

BUILDING A SHARED UNDERSTANDING

An Interpretation Session is a structured group meeting consisting of the interviewer plus two to five team members. The interviewer talks through the events of a single interview. The rest of the team listens, asks questions, draws models, and records issues, interpretations, and design ideas. In their discussions of what to model and what to record, the team wrestles with the data and what it means, learns how each team member views the data, and develops a shared understanding of that user.

A shared understanding gives the team a common focus

The Interpretation Session is the first and prototypical Contextual Design meeting, so it's worth looking at the specific benefits it provides. Contextual Design is structured into a series of design meetings where the team engages with the data and invents the evolving design together. All Contextual Design meetings are based on techniques and approaches that make working in teams work. The Interpretation Session is the first of these design meetings and incorporates many of these techniques:

Better data: Because everyone asks questions of the interviewer, the interviewer remembers more than he would on his own. Walking the events in order, under questioning, prompts him to recall details he didn't know he remembered.

Written record of insights: One person acts as recorder and captures the key points as they occur. By the end of the Interpretation Session, the activities of this user have been characterized in models, and the team's insights, design ideas, and questions have been captured online. No one needs to take additional time to write up or analyze this user interview. People who weren't present can read the models and the notes to catch up on what was learned.

Effective cross-functional cooperation: The Interpretation Session is a forum in which diverse job functions cooperate, whether they be user researchers, UI designers, marketing, developers, testers, process or service designers, or anyone else. The Interpretation Session provides clear tasks and a clear set of roles for everyone in the meeting. It focuses the meeting not on the participants and their differences but on the data. Instead of arguing with each other, participants argue over whether a model or note accurately reflects the user. Instead of arguing about people's opinions, the only discussion is whether an interpretation can be justified based on the data. This makes a safe environment for a new team and people of diverse backgrounds to learn to work together. Learning to value the unique contribution of every participant happens almost by accident.

Multiple perspectives on the problem: Each team member brings their own focus to the problem, from their personal history, their current job function, and their understanding of the project focus. A cross-functional design team will always see more in an interview than any one person would alone. For this reason, the interviewer

A clear way of working together helps a diverse team listen, contribute, and learn

does not filter the information at all; something she dismissed as irrelevant may be picked up by someone else to reveal an insight of great importance. Any kind of predigested presentation of the interview—a report or presentation, for example—would limit the information that would be extracted from an interview to the point of view of one person.

Development of a shared perspective: The open discussion between team members helps them learn and take on each other's perspective. By hearing everyone's questions and insights on the data, every team member expands their own focus to include the concerns of others. The questions that people raise suggest new lines of inquiry and new directions to take future interviews. The team moves toward a common focus on the problem, which includes the particular issues of the team. Team members learn the new focus by participating in the interpretations; there is no need for an elaborate process to redefine the focus.

A well-structured meeting is an efficient way to generate insight

Immersion in the data: It is hard to process data—to think through what it means and might imply for design—when it is just presented. For a team member to truly make new information their own, so that it is part of their world view and can be used instinctually, they must be involved at a level you can't get from a report or presentation alone. An Interpretation Session reveals the data interactively through questioning and discussion. Team members immediately represent it in models, so they must internalize it to write the models and everyone else must internalize it to check them. And since everyone has a job, it's hard for attention to wander.

THE STRUCTURE OF AN INTERPRETATION SESSION

It's hard to do creative work in on-going, face-to-face meetings. Industry docs not provide many good models for face-to-face cooperation on the same project; it's easier and more common to split projects up into parts small enough for individuals to do independently. But there's no way to leverage multiple perspectives if everyone works independently. It's hard to develop a sense of common direction. Using structured meetings to interpret the data from a field study helps the team learn to work together. The Interpretation

Session is the first of such structured design meetings of Contextual Design.

In an Interpretation Session, the interviewer tells the story of the interview, using hand-written notes and memory. Team members ask questions about the interview, drawing out details that the interviewer might have overlooked, and offer insights from their own perspectives. One person acts as recorder, typing notes in a document. Other participants capture the selected Contextual Design models, representing the life and work context of the user. When the discussion sparks design ideas, they are captured in the notes.

Interpretation Sessions enable sharing that has to happen anyway

Here are the key elements of an Interpretation Session.

WHO PARTICIPATES

The whole product team (UX, marketing, product management, professional services, editors, content providers, developers, etc.) is generally too large for an Interpretation Session. But everyone should be in some Interpretation Sessions to share perspectives and create the shared understanding. For any Contextual Design project, define a core team, a subset of people responsible for moving the work forward. This core team should have diverse job functions so they share different points of view during an Interpretation Session. Involve the whole team by rotating other team members in and out as schedules permit. Often there's only one UX team member—when that's the case, create involve others on the product team in an ongoing way to simultaneously help the UX person and spread the immersion experience. Use the sessions to spread knowledge of the users and to forge relationships with the team.

Schedule all on the product team into at least one Interpretation Session

Productive Interpretation Sessions have between two to five people, depending on how many Contextual Design models are captured (two to three for notes plus one model; four to five for two to four models). But the first session often includes everyone on the design team, or at least the whole core team. A meeting this large is hard to manage just because there are so many people trying to be heard—and it's a waste of resources to have everyone in the same session. So after the initial session which gets everyone on the same page, it's more effective for large teams to interpret interviews in sub-teams and share the results with the larger team afterward. Mix job functions in each sub-team so diverse perspectives are brought to bear on every interview. In any case, never go above 12 in a meeting—it will be too chaotic.

ROLES

Any effective meeting needs clear roles to drive it forward. The Interpretation Session is supported by roles that give the meeting structure, so everyone knows what to do and what is appropriate.

Give everyone a job to keep them involved

The roles also give everyone in the meeting something concrete to do, which forces everyone to interact with and process the data. Everyone should have a defined role; double up on roles when you have fewer people.

The interviewer.   The *interviewer* is the one who interviewed the user. They are the team's informant, describing everything just as it happened, in the order that it happened. Just as we try to keep users from giving summary information, the interviewer does not summarize. Just as interviewers extract retrospective accounts from users, the team interrupts the interviewer every time they think she skipped a step or missed a detail. In many ways, it's as though the team interviews the interviewer to find out what she learned in her interaction with the user. For this reason we tell the interviewers not to discuss the interview before the Interpretation Session. This keeps them from creating summarizations of what happened. As long as you interpret within 24–48 hours you will be able to reconstruct the interview in detail—so don't wait!

It's easier for participants to visualize the interview when they see how the space is laid out. So even if the Physical Model is not one of the Contextual Design models to be consolidated, it's often best for the interviewer to start by drawing it. (We describe how in

Chapter 8.) The Physical Model (Fig. 4.1) is a simple line drawing which helps the team see what the interviewer saw, whether it's the inside of the user's car, a drawing of an office or home, or anyplace else the user was located. A high-level outline drawing of the space illustrating everything relevant to the story is better than photos, which include too much detail and don't reveal the structure of the place. Below is a classic office drawing from the 1990s and what it revealed to the team.

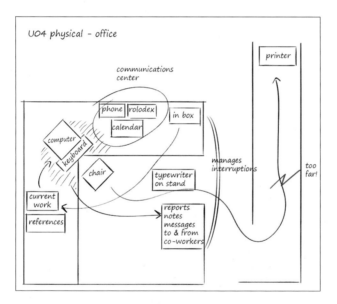

FIGURE 4.1 A classic Physical Model from the 1990s for an office, showing the workplace of one user. The model represents her cubicle and shows how she has structured her environment to help her get work done. The placement of her IBM Selectric in the doorway, the inbox next to the door, and the shelf used as a drop-off place all suggest a strategy to minimize interruptions caused by working in an open cubicle. The phone, rolodex, and calendar are all grouped together, suggesting that these tools work together to support communicating and coordinating with others. And the open space around her workstation suggests an intent to keep this area clear so she can lay out her next task. The team has annotated the model to reveal these distinctions and to show breakdowns, such as the printer being too far away. A photo would be too cluttered to reveal these distinctions clearly.

The recorder. The *recorder* keeps notes of the meeting online displayed, so everyone can see them using a monitor or projector. The notes capture the key observations, issues, and quotes the team deems important for moving the design forward. Notes record key practice issues, identity and cultural observations, tool and activity successes and breakdowns, task patterns, the use of time, place and different devices, design ideas, and any other issues that have relevance to the project. Later, these notes are transferred to sticky notes and used to build the Affinity Diagram.

The notes do not duplicate information from the Contextual Design models except for breakdowns or other insights important to understand the user's activities. Demographic information (e.g., the user's age, length of time on the job, skill level) does not go into the notes either. Demographics go in a profile describing the user (Fig. 4.2).

```
T05, editor for a medical information company: 32, female.
Travels most with her boyfriend, a web developer.
Has a Droid Incredible smartphone, iPad, iPod. Takes a work Windows
laptop between home and work. Uses gChat, gDocs, AutoEurope.com,
Delta.com,Google maps app on phone, Yelp app, AirBnB.com, Facebook
and Shutterfly.
```

FIGURE 4.2   A user profile. The team has assigned user code "T05" to this user—05 for the user number and "T" to indicate that this is a traveler, not an agent or any other role interviewed for this project.

Type while you listen—don't slow down the meeting to capture data

Teams often need help clarifying their points. The recorder may have to rephrase an idea which has only been expressed indirectly to capture it in a clear, succinct language. A good recorder hears the point the team is trying to express, states clearly what the insight or issue is, writes it, and moves the meeting on (Fig. 4.3). (Anyone else who hears what the underlying issue is can do the same—then they say it, someone says "capture that!", the recorder writes it and the meeting moves on).

```
T05-77 Kept prices of hotel and car options in a paper notebook.
       It took several weeks to get the best price.

T05-78 She knows prices change over time, so she searches at all
       different times of the day and days of the week looking for
       the best deal.

T05-79 She couldn't get both the cheapest price on airfare and the
       best price on cars--the cheaper places to fly to were more
       expensive places to return the car.

T05-80 Whenever she books a trip to a city where she knows
       someone, she emails them when she thinks she's found a good
       price. She figures locals will know if it's a good deal.

T05-81 Airline prices are not logical--not tied to distance. It
       takes specialized knowledge to know whether an itinerary is
       a good deal or if there are cheaper nearby alternatives.

T05-82 To her it's not a hassle to keep checking prices--she
       thinks travel planning is fun. "I do love it."

T05-83 DI: Capitalize on the competitive or fun aspect of travel
       planning--gamification, getting the best deal, using the
       best knowledge, sleuthing it out.
```

FIGURE 4.3 Extract from the online notes typed during an Interpretation Session. Each note is preceded by user code and note number. This section of the notes shows the development of an idea from a insight into the user's approach to an activity to a design idea (DI). These notes are displayed during the meeting so all can see and correct them. They are a permanent record of the design conversation, capturing the discussion and used to build the Affinity Diagram later.

Modelers. *Modelers* draw Contextual Design models on flip charts as they hear relevant data. When you start the project, decide which models will be most useful to your focus; these will be what you capture during the Interpretation Session (see Part 2). Each model captures its own kind of data from all the data of the interview. Modelers draw at the same time as everything else is happening. They do not stop the meeting to get agreement at each point; it's up to individual participants to raise an issue if they think the modeler got it wrong. Modelers have to be comfortable putting up one or two elements of a model as they hear them without waiting for the whole story to be complete—it's too slow to get the whole story, then stop the meeting and draw the model. Modelers do ask questions suggested by their models—if the sequence modeler can't write the trigger that started an activity because the interviewer never said it, he won't be able to record this and will ask. This is another way of improving the data from the interview. Give each type of model to a different person; let people double up if necessary. The notetaker can double up with the sequence model if you're short of people. Let people rotate through the different jobs.

Contextual Design models separate user data into different points of view

Capturing models improves the quality of the data recovered from an interview. The models capture what the interviewer saw or recovered in a retrospective account; they keep the team grounded in concrete, trustworthy data. Also the whole team can see what is being captured and whether it's complete.

Models separate the user's world into different points of view and so make it possible for the team to consider different aspects of experience clearly in a tangible, shared way. Building them during the Interpretation Session teaches the team to start thinking about the users' world more holistically—and this improves the quality of the data collected in subsequent interviews.

The moderator.   The *moderator* is the stage manager for the whole meeting. Any meeting has a *mainline conversation*—the discussion which is the primary purpose of the meeting. The moderator keeps the meeting focused on this conversation. In an Interpretation Session, the mainline conversation is: what happened in this interview and what do we learn from it? The moderator keeps the pace of the meeting brisk; ensures the interviewer doesn't lose his place with all the interruptions; ensures all the data is captured someplace; and makes sure everyone stays involved. The moderator has to stand outside the process enough so that they can see what is going on. Moderators who get too involved have to hand moderation over to someone else.

No meeting works without someone taking the role of moderator

Anytime you have more than three people in the Interpretation Session, you will benefit from declaring someone as the moderator. Do this explicitly and define the role, so that person has permission to guide the meeting—even when it's a manager departing from the mainline conversation!

Participants.   Every participant listens to the story of the interview, asks questions for understanding, and develops their own insight into the data. They propose interpretations, make observations, and suggest design ideas. The team's design ideas are captured at the same time as the data (clearly flagged as such) partly to encourage the team to think about the implications of the data, but primarily so the designer can stop thinking about the idea and go back to the data. (This is a useful technique for keeping a meeting moving forward: anytime someone gets stuck on a point, write it down in a form that won't be forgotten and will be used at the appropriate point in the process. Then the person can drop it and go on.) Finally, participants watch the models to make sure they are complete and watch the online notes to make sure they agree with the way they are written.

Manage people problems with meeting techniques to keep them on topic

Also, helping out the moderator, everyone acts as a *Rat hole Watcher*: recognizing when the conversation has wandered from the mainline conversation and needs to be brought back to the point. They then call "Rat hole!", and everyone returns to the interview. The idea of rat holes is part of managing the team.[1] By naming the concept, the team accepts that rat holes exist and waste time. Without realizing it, each person on the team has given everyone else permission to point out when he or she is off topic. Then, instead of getting defensive and angry, when someone calls "rat hole," people laugh sheepishly and get back to the subject of the meeting.

RUNNING THE SESSION

Interpretation Sessions are interleaved with interviews: interview a few people, interpret those interviews; interview a few more and interpret those. This way, you can always run the interpretation session soon after the interview so it's still fresh, and you can use your findings in future interviews.

---

[1] It has been brought to our attention that there is a community which considers these should be called "rabbit holes" rather than "rat holes" by analogy with the hole down which Alice fell. We do not traffic in such heresies.

If the session will happen the same day as the interview or the next, the interviewer can run the meeting from their hand-written notes. The best data is interpreted within 24 and at most 48 hours. Then memory will be good enough that, with the notes, the interviewer will remember enough of what happened. If the Interpretation Session does not happen until a day after that, the interviewer should annotate their notes from the audiotape of their interview. If they delay longer than 3 days, we suggest transcribing the notes to aid memory—but this is painful and not recommended, so do your interpretations right away, and life will be simpler.

Keep everyone engaged and on topic

Every user is assigned a user code. You promised the user con-fidentiality—this code protects the user's anonymity and is used in the notes, on all models, and in all discussions. It's recorded in a list of interviewees that the team keeps private.

The interviewer starts by giving a brief profile of the user—their job function or role, the type of organization, and any demo-graphic information. This profile is recorded in a separate file, so that later when someone asks "was U10 a secretary or a scientist?" the answer is easy to get. The interviewer draws a Physical Model of the place the interview happened to introduce the context. For the rest of the interview, he walks through the interview using his notes, line by line. Everyone listens and probes to develop new insights into the user's life, calling out "capture that!" whenever there is a suc-cinct insight, question, or design idea to capture.

Be nonjudgmental and keep a brisk pace

The tone of the meeting is active and involved, tending to be slightly chaotic: the interviewer is trying to tell the story, every-one is asking him questions, two or three people are drawing models, the recorder is typing away, and the moderator is advis-ing people all at the same time. The tone of the meeting is also open and trusting; everyone is expected to share insights and design ideas without stopping to think whether they are going to look stupid or whether the design idea is any good. No evalua-tion happens at this point—only capturing people's thoughts and insights. If one person thinks a point is important and another doesn't, don't get sucked into an argument about it—just record it. It's just another note. Arguing over whether a note is a duplicate or already captured wastes more time than writing it again. It will be sorted out in the Affinity Diagram process.

An Interpretation Session usually lasts as long as the interview, about 2 hours. The first interpretation in a project will be longer, and later interviews on very focused tasks may be shorter.

Models, insights, and design ideas are the first deliverables

At the end of the interview, the team takes a few minutes to clean up. They capture *insights*, the key learnings from this user. They note *vignettes*, insightful, characteristic stories from this user that give a good flavor of the data. And they flesh out the models to ensure that no important points were missed. Insights are captured online and on a flip chart; vignettes to be written are just captured in one place online. Together, insights and vignettes make it easier to talk about what the team learned while interviews are going on, giving a quick answer to a skeptical manager who asks, "So what did you learn from all these expensive field visits?"

In a productive Interpretation Session, everyone in the room has a job to do, so everyone has to process the data and think about its implications. This combination of listening, inquiring, thinking, and drawing or writing the implications creates the immersion in the data that results in real understanding and insight. By the end of the Interpretation Session, all participants "own" the data and have incorporated it into their view of the user and the project. Interpretation Sessions save time—there's nothing more to be done or shared with others after the Interpretation Session to handle the data from this user.

There's a culture in our industry that says real work doesn't happen in meetings. "Another time-wasting meeting!" we say to each other. Yet it's through the stimulus of bouncing ideas off each other that people work most creatively. It's through the cross-check of several people looking at the same user data that people work with the highest quality. The Interpretation Session is a working meeting that allows for creativity and quality. It brings together activities that might otherwise happen individually and sequentially and allows them to happen simultaneously in a team process. It's an efficient way of turning an interview into data useful to a project, recorded in a form that can be saved, communicated, and used to drive design. You'll know your Interpretation Sessions are working when people start clamoring to get in, because they know that's where the creative design work starts.

REMOTE AND ONLINE INTERPRETATION SESSIONS

It's often not convenient for a team to be all in one room for an Interpretation Session. Collaboration tools make distributed Interpretation Sessions feasible and no less productive than face-to-face meetings. But make sure the core team did a few sessions together first to familiarize them with the process and each other. Then they can work remotely or have adjunct team members or stakeholders remote into the meeting. To be effective:

- Make sure everyone has a job to do, especially people who are alone at their location. This helps keep them tied into the conversation.
- Use online meeting tools or phone conferencing to share the conversation. Use online meeting tools to share documents or a collaborative document tool such as Google Docs.
- Capture Affinity notes and some models online, updating them during the session. Once the team knows what to capture, you can keep these models online: Identity, Relationship, Day-in-the-Life, Sequence, and Decision Point Models.
- Some models must still be captured in paper but can be mailed back and forth, or use a camera to share. Collaboration and Physical Models should be drawn by someone who is *not* alone. Ideally, they are drawn at the interviewer's location, where the interviewer can check them for accuracy.

WORKING IN TEAMS

The Interpretation Session is the first intensive design meeting in Contextual Design, so this is a convenient time to discuss how to design a meeting that works. Much of design work happens in teams, which means meetings; how good your design process is, depends to a great degree on how good your meetings are. With that in mind, here are the principles we use for designing effective meetings.

Real work and creativity happen in meetings if they are well structured

USE A CROSS-FUNCTIONAL TEAM

Every person involved in product development comes to the job with his or her own personal experiences. We each naturally see the product from our own point of view. Marketing sees trends and motivations. Developers see the possibility of function ("fix this") and data structures. Usability testers tend to see problems. UX designers see the interaction, page layout, and graphic design. Data modelers see data. Business people see business problems. And so it goes.

The people who need to coordinate to get the work done don't actually live in the same world of experience. And yet all these points of view matter to the ultimate success of the product.

Design with a cross-functional team working together face-to-face

Inspired by Deming,[2] Contextual Design starts with a cross-functional team. The team's job is not to oversee the project or simply review direction, but to do the real work of requirements and product definition, together, face to face. Over the years, we have learned that a robust shared understanding comes from doing real work together in situations where individual expertise informs the joint work but does not divide responsibility by job role. Everybody works together as an equal participating in all aspects of Contextual Design. Because they are all immersed in the same user data and work out product direction through structured activities, they automatically take on each other's point of view while collectively

---

[2] Deming, Edwards, *Out of the Crisis,* MIT Press, 2000.

developing a shared understanding of the user, the opportunity, and the direction for the product. Then, armed with a common direction, they can act independently to guide the work of their independent job roles, guided by the same user and product assumptions. Contextual Design builds in buy-in and creates a well-functioning team naturally. We talk about how to form your team in Chapter 19.

STRUCTURE DESIGN MEETINGS FOR CREATIVITY

Companies know that to produce products, people need to be able to effectively collaborate. At the very core of product design is the ability to get along and work with others. More than any other profession, engineering and product design is about a team coming together to get the work done every day of the week. But how can we make sure that creative collaboration happens consistently, particularly when the popular conception of meetings is that they are a waste of time?

In our experience, the fastest and best way to achieve a shared understanding of the user and a unified product direction is to bring the responsible people together in creative face-to-face meetings. In Contextual Design, time together is where all the real work happens—not alone at your desk. Contextual Design is a collection of creative meetings which combine to produce a successful design, while managing the process of doing the work with people. In Contextual Design, each working session has a defined procedure and clear rules of engagement. People of any background and skill can participate because they know how to move the work forward productively. Structure does not limit creativity—on the contrary, it frees people to be creative because they don't spend emotional time figuring out how to run the process, how to deal with the people in the room, and how to influence the outcome.

Contextual Design is a series of meetings to drive invention

Here are some of the basic principles that structure all our creative meetings.

Pick a process and stick to it. Typical corporate methodologies for product development provide general outlines about what to do to move from requirements to shipping but few communicate what teams ought to be doing on a daily basis to get the work done. Even with more structured processes such as Agile, the requirements and design part of the process is left undefined and unclear. Contextual Design defines structure for these looser parts of the process, so it can fit any method. It provides a backbone structure to guide teams.

It's Monday morning—what's the first thing you do? If there's no clear process, each person on the team, with their separate skills and history of doing work, begins a process of influence, talking, designing meeting structures, and sometimes trying them out to varying degrees of success. People can waste a lot of time storming, forming, norming[3] and second-guessing what they are doing—and repeating the whole process over and over again each time a new person joins the team. Knowing what to do to get the work done cuts through much confusion, friction, and argument, and opens the way for creative, efficient design action. Whether the people are experienced or new members, with a defined procedure they know what is expected and how to work together for success.

> *Continuously discussing process wastes time— choose it in advance*

Contextual Design structures front-end design with a set of creative meetings, each with their own structure. Central to each meeting is a defined procedure, clear roles, and clear rules of engagement. Meeting structure includes who does what, how long a process should take, when and how decisions are made, what quality work looks like—and who gets to decide. It builds in techniques to resolve differences of opinion and to work with differences of style.

Know and articulate the purpose of the meeting. This is a simple meeting principle, but it's at the center of any successful creative meeting. In Contextual Design, each creative session is convened for a specific purpose. It is structured to achieve only that purpose. For example, the Interpretation Session brings people together to hear the story of one user's data and capture what is relevant—and that's all. The affinity building session brings people together to take hundreds of individual notes from the research and structure them into themes. The visioning session is designed to help

---

[3] Tuckman, Bruce W. "Developmental sequence in small groups", *Psychological Bulletin*, Vol 63(6), Jun 1965, 384-399.

a team use the data to generate new product concepts. Everyone knows why they are there and the expected outcome.

We help this process by defining the *mainline conversation* for each meeting, as we did for the Interpretation Session. When people know what is on topic and what is not, it's easier to stay focused and easier to call people back to the topic when they wander.

Without clear purpose or roles the team will flounder

Assign roles, responsibilities, and articulate expectations of participation.   Depending on the purpose of the meeting, we define appropriate roles, responsibilities, and procedures. When any meeting seems to have no discernible structure, people think that no one is "running things." So they either check out mentally or take over and try to drive the meeting. But with a clear understanding of what to do, everyone gets down to doing the work.

In Contextual Design, every meeting defines the roles needed to get the work done. These are not job roles—they are meeting roles which can be played by anyone. Often we rotate who plays the roles. In the Interpretation Session, the roles are notetaker, modeler, interviewer, participant, etc. Everyone knows what they are doing so the meeting stays focused and the work gets done. Moreover, when a new person joins a meeting or participates intermittently, the team can tell them the rules, and they can join in smoothly.

Externalize conversations.   Many years ago, Lucy Suchman[4] discovered that when product teams think together, they hover over some external representation— often a picture or abstract model of concepts. It's a cliché that great ideas start out on the back of a napkin—they are written down, externalized as a drawing on the napkin. To help a group of people stay focused on the work of the meeting, we borrow this natural technique. So in an Interpretation Session the data is displayed for

Let a design artifact focus the team conversation

---

[4] Suchman, L. *Plans and Situated Actions: The Problem of Human-Machine Communication*. Cambridge University Press, 1987.

all to see, the Affinity Diagram is built on the wall, the vision is captured on a flip chart, and so on.

Particularly when working with a team, having a representation of the product concept as it emerges is essential to avoid "talk in the air"—where misunderstandings are so prevalent. The artifacts of Contextual Design capture the findings and represent the ideas of the team; anything not captured is not part of the design considerations going forward. When the team understands this, they realize that general talk or side conversations not only get in the way of a shared understanding but also won't matter in the long run. So team members start to care that their thoughts are captured in the artifacts produced by each meeting.

Taken together, meeting artifacts represent both the conversation and the result of the meeting. Meeting artifacts, publicly displayed, pull the attention of meeting participants back on topic. They focus the direction and the action of the meeting. Moreover, when ideas are physical, they can be left and returned to with context preserved. When ideas are physical, they are no longer owned by an individual; they belong to the team. The artifact, not interpersonal dynamics, becomes the focal point of the meeting, keeping everyone productive and on track. When data and ideas are physical, they are the living representation of the emergent shared understanding. Look for the way we use physical artifacts to support creative meetings throughout Contextual Design.

Moderate and self-monitor. Any creative meeting can get off track. Sometimes, after we have taught clients how to run Contextual Design meeting, they call for advice because their meetings aren't smooth, people are arguing, taking too long, and so forth. The first thing we ask is, "Did you assign a moderator?" Usually, the answer is, "No." Anytime people come together—especially in groups larger than three to four—the work works best when someone is watching the process. A moderator makes sure people are operating by the rules of engagement, they make sure people are listening and heard, and they remind everyone of the process. The job of the moderator is to keep the meeting on track. Anyone can be a moderator, because everyone should know what to do. But in the heat of the moment, people don't watch themselves—so we assign a moderator to do it for them.

Self-moderate and address all issues in Process Checks

Moreover, roles and procedures may need to be tuned given the people, the company, and the needs of the project. To make any process work, you have to design and iterate that process given the context. So we define a Process Check which can be done daily if needed but should be done at least weekly. Even seasoned teams may recognize that they have become too chaotic and call for a Process Check. A Process Check is simply a time to list what is working and what is not with that meeting for those people—and to generate design ideas to improve it without losing the core purpose of the meeting. Then the team chooses to try something new and continues tuning the process.

Have a space.   "Working as a team" traditionally means breaking the design problem into small bits and assigning it to individuals working in cubes. Then members review each other's work, make suggestions, and return the problem to the "owner" to fix. Today, remote teams reinforce this separation with geographic barriers. This can lead to overfeatured products, as each engineer expands his part because it is all he has to focus on. The result is incoherent products—often hung together by a menu bar linking together components representing each department that produced a subsystem.

A team room acknowledges that team work is continuous

Organizational architecture also reflects this way of working—where can people work together? Individuals have a space—but not the team or the product. The most common work environment for a developer is the cubicle—an area big enough for one person to work in, containing a laptop and a desk. But it is not big enough for several people to work together comfortably, and it has not got the wall space to support group work.

Some companies eliminate the walls and cubes and put everyone in one open area. The lack of walls, close proximity of people, and whiteboard walls may facilitate an easier flow of conversation. But because it's all open and people need to focus, chatting by a desk is discouraged—and a creative group meeting would disrupt the whole space.

Meeting rooms do exist, but a meeting room's key characteristic is that it is shared and booked by the hour. So the only work that it supports is that which can be completed in a short time—a half day at most—and nothing can be left in the room. Every conversation has to restart from scratch, and every meeting has to start with spreading out all the design diagrams again.

In the end, if we want to work together—at least for the key period of building a shared understanding of the user and shared design response—we recommend that the team have a room that they don't have to clean up and that they can keep coming back to. Then the process, rules of engagement, and the space help the team work well together.

Manage interpersonal dynamics

Working together is a new skill for most people. Collaboration in teams is not explicitly taught in schools and is rarely taught on the job. Working together effectively means understanding how to keep a design conversation on track; how to focus on the work issue, not each other; how to manage everyone's personal idiosyncrasies; and how to uncover and address the root causes of disagreements. Unless teams learn to do this their designs suffer, because the models people

We may call ourselves a team but we rarely work continuously face-to-face

have for handling disagreements trade off coherence of the design for keeping people happy.

One primary model people have for handling disagreement is horse-trading: "I think you're wrong on that. But I'll let you have it if you'll give me this other thing that is really important to me." Horse-trading leads to a product which is a patchwork of features, with no coherent theme. And horse-trading causes everyone on the team to disinvest from the design, because everyone has had to agree with at least one decision they thought was fundamentally wrong.

Other models for handling disagreement exist, but most don't work any better. There's the compromise model, which says, "You say we should design everything as dialog boxes. I think everything should be buttons. So we'll implement both and make everyone happy." Everyone is happy except the user, who has a dozen ways of doing each function, and no clear reason why one rather than another. Or there is the guru model, which says, "The guru is smart and knows everything. We'll all do what the guru says." Except that the population of gurus who are infallible on technical architecture, GUI design, user work practice, marketing, project planning, and the host of other skills necessary to get a product out is vanishingly small.

Well-structured design sessions manage the interpersonal by eliminating the jockeying that goes on when people try to figure out how to move forward productively. The purpose of the meeting is clear, each person knows what is expected of them, and conversations are externalized. All this ensures the team is focused on the work of the session. Add a moderator watching the process, and much of the interpersonal friction disappears.

But even with all this, interpersonal differences and personalities will still play out and can get in the way of moving the work forward.

Plan to manage problem interpersonal dynamics such as disagreements

So Contextual Design defines techniques which help manage the interpersonal. It defines procedures for deciding among design alternatives based on data, not arguments or horse-trading. It helps people accept each other's differences by raising awareness of how such differences can both help and get in the way of the work. It includes ways that everyone can be heard and valued irrespective of personal style, gender, or culture. These interpersonal techniques are introduced along with the roles and procedures as relevant to each design session.

Here are a few core principles guiding the process. But the most basic principle is *make interpersonal dynamics that might get in the way explicit in advance.* Then everyone is on the lookout for it—and when it happens, people interpret it as a known event to be managed, not an interpersonal blowup.

Name behavior to raise awareness.   A concept like "mainline conversation" is introduced to the team so they know what they

With awareness of interpersonal differences, people can self-monitor and accept

are supposed to be talking about. Mainline conversation is a good example of naming behavior to help people manage their behavior. Any behavior that can get in the way of smooth communication can be named. In Contextual Design sessions, we routinely define and name cognitive styles and how they play out in different design sessions, participation tendencies (too little or too much), team-leading skills, and expectations about interruption (when it's ok and when it isn't), for example. We discuss interpersonal styles by giving examples of the behavior with both its positive and negative attributes—revealing the value the style has for the time in the right circumstances, as well as discussing how it can get in the way. When the concept defines personal attributes such as cognitive style or participation tendencies, it allows people to self-recognize. We then provide ways people can both value and manage their own behavior and that of others in a nonconfrontational way: "Dan, you're doing your 'diver' thing again. We don't need to figure out every detail right now. Do you agree with the concept?"

Make sure people are heard.   The single biggest complaint in design meetings is people feeling unheard. People who feel unheard either keep raising the issue over and over—annoying everybody— or checks out of the meeting altogether. So Contextual Design builds in lots of ways to make sure what people say is heard—most often by capturing the thought physically. We capture thoughts in an interpretation note, on a model, as a design idea or question associated with multiple design artifacts, on a product vision, or in a "parking lot" for issues to be addressed later. This is another example of

> *To move fast, write down people's issues so they are heard*

externalizing conversation—making thought concrete both captures it for productive use and deals with one of the most difficult interpersonal issues to manage. Everyone wants to be heard— Contextual Design builds in productive ways to listen.

Provide a way to handle problem behaviors.   Problem behaviors are rarely caused by people trying to make trouble. Usually, they are just people being their normal, unmoderated selves. Contextual Design introduces ways to recognize, name, and handle these behaviors. For example, in the Interpretation Session we introduce the role of the *Rat-hole Watcher* (which everyone plays). A rat hole is anything that is off the mainline conversation. The explicit, shared role of the Rat-hole Watcher communicates the expectation that everyone should look for rat holes and point them out—and simultaneously reminds everyone to stay on point. And because it is humorous, it simultaneously softens and legitimates the previously socially unacceptable behavior of publicly calling out people for nonproductive behavior. We encourage people who interrupt too much to ask the team to let them know so they can build self-awareness—this encourages the team to work together to self-moderate. Quiet people are sometimes given flags or whistles so they can again humorously have a prop to help them participate. We have developed a bag of interpersonal tricks we developed to handle disruptions, many of which are described in this book. But don't stop there—start looking out for these issues and develop your own tricks!

Keep people engaged.   People can't stand being bored or sitting around waiting for their turn to participate. If there is not enough air time because there are too many people in the room, if the process demands that they just sit and listen, if they have nothing to do, or if the task they are given doesn't match their interest and skills, they naturally zone out. When a person checks out mentally, they won't buy in to the data or the design—and they are more prone to disruptive behavior. Contextual Design meetings give everyone in the session a job and a voice. We make sure that the group size is small enough for everyone to be needed. Often, we'll deal with

Fun techniques and lots of jobs help people engage and grow past natural tendencies

a large team by breaking it up into small teams of two to four people, all working simultaneously in the same room. Each person is engaged, and there's enough happening that everyone can be given a role that matches their skill set.

Contextual Design creates a culture within the team in which everyone makes the design session work by focusing on defined purpose, roles, and procedures—and by being aware of and helpful in managing natural differences between people.

DESIGN A CREATIVE TEAM CULTURE

Contextual Design is about innovation—the creation of new products or new product features that serve users' needs in ways no one thought of before. But no matter how good the process, innovation depends on the people in the team. They have to be given the tools and the freedom to think creatively, despite organizational, interpersonal, and procedural roadblocks thrown in their way.

At the core of Contextual Design is the deliberate creation of an articulated team culture designed for creativity. Contextual Design provides a base process for requirements and design. Contextual Design provides a structure so everyone knows

Create an explicit team culture that manages diverse skill and style

what to do on Monday morning, how to work with each other, and how to modulate interpersonal dynamics. Then it puts process and team management tools in the hands of the team so they can adapt and improve from there. In this context, it does not matter what national or group culture, gender or interpersonal characteristics individuals have—the culture of the work sessions guides all members into effective participation. (And, a clear structure makes it easier to work remotely).

The other aspect of supporting a creative team, mentioned above, is to give the team a room. They need a place they can come together for extended periods of time, which they can mess up with their design artifacts. There's a reason a space for creativity gets called a "sandbox"—creativity needs a place.

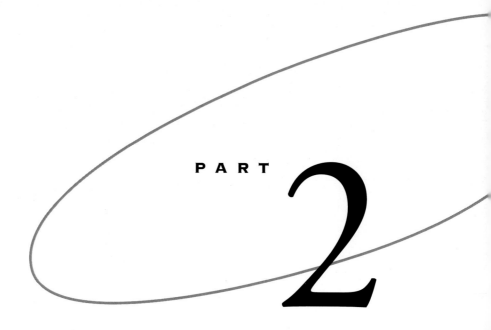

PART 2

Revealing the World

5

From Data to Insight: Contextual Design Models

In the first part of Contextual Design, teams collect in-depth field data about relevant parts of their user's lives. In the interpretation session the team captures the data of one interview in notes and in the Contextual Design Models. In this Part we introduce the Experience Models developed to represent data needed to design for life and the Traditional Contextual Design Models representing task context. We discuss their power to communicate the world of the users to teams. The Affinity Diagram and Contextual Design models are your best tool for bridging from data to design.

Lives are complex and detailed, full of people, places, activities, and products all woven into the seamless whole of the user's life. What are the boundaries of the activity being supported? What parts of life matter for design—and what parts don't? Does it matter if the surgeon checks texts between surgeries, when your product provides content to doctors? If a financial advisor goes home to meet a delivery person, is it relevant to your design? Should you understand people's shopping companions at the store if you're designing for shopping online? Do you focus on tool hassles or will you then miss the transformative product possibilities? Should you look at the consumer apps a user loves when you are building a business tool? If you want to design for life, what do you pay attention to?

Contextual Design. http://dx.doi.org/10.1016/B978-0-12-800894-2.00005-3

MODELS REVEAL WHAT MATTERS

All the Contextual Design models help the team see what matters—and then design solutions that impact lives. If I ask you for a cup you can pick it up and hand it to me. But if I ask you for your understanding of the users' life—what can you point to? Life is not tangible. Seeing an activity within the context of life is hard. Walking through the user's world on a field visit bombards you with many disconnected stimuli. You may try to simplify this complexity for your team by producing a list of "needs," but that list is not a view of their activities within life; a feature list of design ideas is certainly not the life practice. Simplifying complexity may reduce overwhelm but it also hides what we need to know to drive transformative design thinking.

Models focus our attention on significant aspects of life

Hidden in the details of real life is the structure of the day and how activities play out within it, why we do what we do, who we do it with, how we feel about ourselves when we are doing it, the culture we are operating in, and more. Dealing with this complexity to help a team see a big picture of their users' lives is our challenge. If we do it well, we will reveal their challenges and potential delighters, failed communications and collaboration patterns, invisible yearnings, and core motivators. Now you have the context you need to reinvent their lives with technology.

So how do we make the complex approachable? Remember the human anatomy books many of us had as kids? First, you see an outline of the person; then successive transparencies overlay the skeleton, then the blood, then the nervous system, and so forth. Understanding the person as a physical organism is complex and messy, but those books broke it down into meaningful subsystems—the skeletal system, neurological system, and cardiovascular system—which encourage thinking about one system at a time. By looking across all the systems, we have a shot at understanding the whole body and the interaction between the parts (Fig. 5.1).

FIGURE 5.1   An anatomy book with transparent overlays. Each overlay focuses
the reader one of the body's systems—but shows it in the context of the whole body.

Identifying the body's systems led to whole professions surrounding each system. Researchers were able to pay attention to each system,
find its structure and rules, see how it interacted with other systems,
develop hypotheses about how it worked, investigate chemical interaction, and so forth. A whole professional language developed to describe
what was going on—that's what medical jargon is. A specialized language of this sort creates a focus—a set of things to pay attention to.
Once you know how the pulse sounds in the ventricles of the heart, you
can start to make sense of the noises a body makes. The medical language gives doctors a way to see—a way to interpret what is observed
and a structure of understanding they can elaborate as they learn more.

Because a language creates a focus, it is not neutral. It directs
your thought. Any language is designed to say certain things easily—the things for which it provides concepts. Artists have a language of color, shape, and shade to talk about the sky; meteorologists
have a language for talking about the sky too, but it is very different

from the artist's language. Which language is better depends on whether your current concern is aesthetics or weather. So language reveals and conceals—meteorologists have many words for clouds, enabling them to see more when they look at the sky and to draw more meaningful implications for the weather. But do they forget to appreciate a sunset? In this way, language structures thought—which can be constraining. We must be able to use the point of view it offers but deliberately break it when we find the data doesn't fit.[1]

Just as language helps you see more, models help you see more

Complexity is simplified and made actionable through frameworks such as the physiological systems of the body. Similarly, Contextual Design models provide a framework for understanding human behavior and experience *for the purpose of design action*. Any practice has structure—it hangs together to achieve work and life intents. But that structure has many aspects. People take on roles and responsibilities, collaborate with others, act out of core values and identity, and are influenced by culture, organizations, physical location, and space. So to see life we need to look at it from multiple points of view. We need multiple models, each focusing the team on a different aspect of work and life.

Each model expands the team's entering focus, enabling them to see more details when they interview. This is a starting point—team members can expand on this focus, creating new concepts and distinctions unique to the domain they are designing for. The Traditional Contextual Design Models we introduced 20 years ago represented the core dimensions of practice for designing task support:

- The *Flow Model* represents the roles and responsibilities multiple people take on while they coordinate within a work process to be supported by a product;
- The *Cultural Model* represents the influences on a person, a group, or an organization revealing the cultural milieu in which the product will have to succeed;

---

[1] Contextual Design is built upon a commitment to deliberate paradigm shift—looking for ways to break our assumptions about the users, and the frameworks we use to help us see more of their world. This is how Contextual Design itself grows and changes. See The Structure of Scientific Revolutions Thomas S. Kuhn for discussion of paradigm shifts.

- The *Physical Model* represents the structure and flow of activity as it is manifest in space, including layout, things used for an activity, and footsteps taken in service of the activity;
- The *Sequence Model* represents the steps and intents of the activities to be supported equivalent to a task analysis;
- And the *Artifact Model* represents the structure and usage pattern of an artifact used during the activity which will be put on line or eliminated.

Along with the issues captured in the Affinity Diagram, these models provide a 360-degree view of the context of the target task. These models are our first framework for understanding the users' lives. And these models were sufficient for any project we encountered for over 20 years.

But then came the radical transformation of life introduced by truly mobile touch-screen devices. Technology now touches more of life—and the worlds of work and personal life are being merged. The Cool Concepts expanded the framework needed to understand our users. To support inquiry into these areas of life, we developed new data collection techniques, new models, and new design practices. To help teams characterize life as represented in the Wheel of Joy in Life, we created the Experience Models:

Experience Models reveal new aspects of life that influence core motivations

- Accomplishment: The *Day-in-the-Life Model* shows how the behaviors of the target activity play out in the different places in the user's life, what is done in each different place, the devices which support the activities, and the content accessed in each place;
- Connection: The *Relationship Model* shows the important relationships in the user's life and how the target activity plays out within those relationships bringing people closer to each other—or not;
- Connection: The *Collaboration Model*, a variant of the Flow Model, shows each type of collaboration discovered during the interview, including who interacted with

whom, what they were trying to achieve, and what was shared, done, or discussed;

- Identity: The *Identity Model* shows the core identity elements relevant to the target activity, including sources of pride, self-esteem, and value that emerged during the interview;

- Sensation: The *Sensation Board* shows the key visceral experience the new product should manifest, based on data collected from the interviews, in a pictorial representation with key messages to help industrial and visual designers.

These models reveal human behavior and experience. They show what people are doing to get the activity done, their responsibilities, and their motives. They reveal the activity within the context of the larger physical and emotional life.

With all 10 models, our view of the world of the user is greatly expanded. Each model brings its own point of view into focus and challenges the team to think from that point of view. But we have learned that in practice, not every model is necessary for every project—and 10 points of view is too many for a team to use productively. Today, when we plan a project, we pick only the models most relevant to the problem.

Because of changes in the nature of technology and practice, many of the Traditional Contextual Design Models are relevant in only a handful of projects. Mobile apps have a narrow focus on a single core intent; large enterprise applications supporting huge corporate processes are giving way to suites of focused function sets with additional

Use only the models that are right for your project

apps to fill the gaps. New functions in these enterprise systems are chunked into "products" organized by target activities. IT is building less and buying more. As a result, the Flow Model, which focused on process and complex collaborations, is often not needed. Most artifacts are already online these days, so the artifact model gets much less use. The physical environment is no longer a single place—an activity is continued throughout the day, wherever the user is, so there's not one physical environment that matters. And in a world that is increasingly multicultural and characterized by remote work, cultural influences are diffuse—more easily represented within the Affinity Diagram. All of the Traditional

Contextual Design Models can be useful depending on the project. And for some we have developed variants which we have found useful. But in our projects now, our focus has shifted largely to the newer models, the Affinity, and the Sequence Model.

We discuss the Affinity Diagram in Chapter 6, Experience Models in Chapter 7, and the Traditional Contextual Design Models in Chapter 8. We introduce each model, how to collect data, interpret it, and consolidate the data to build the model. We also discuss when each model is most useful.

To see the longer discussion of the original Contextual Design Models go to http://booksite.elsevier.com/9780128008942 where text from the first book is available for reference.

GRAPHICAL REPRESENTATIONS GIVE THE BIG PICTURE

All Contextual Design models are graphical diagrams that represent the structure, behavior, and experiences of human activities in a tangible way. Diagrams are a familiar part of a developer's world. Whether it is a data model, an object model, a process diagram, or any of a 1000 other modeling techniques, developers have been using drawings to show different aspects of a system since programming became its own discipline. Making the abstract tangible is a natural part of everyday team design. As we said in the last chapter, having an artifact to represent the team's conversation helps externalize the concepts and facilitates clear interaction. If you watch teams at work, you will

Graphical models show the practice as a coherent whole

see that teamwork is naturally supported by these artifacts—people hang over them and focus their talk by looking at them, updating them, and pointing at them. But data models represent data—they don't represent human behavior and experience as Contextual Design models do.

Why do *graphical* representations work? Unlike a textual language, graphical representations let you take in a whole picture at once. A textual language must be read and parsed; this is not only a difficult chore, but the information has to be taken in sequentially, one idea at a time. Given reasonable methods for handling complexity, a picture can be scanned and taken in as a whole. A picture is a better external representation than a page of text—it's easier to see what you are talking about. A picture reveals overall pattern and structure by showing each part in relationship to the whole. This is critical to creative work and design. Once a team understands the target activity in the context of life, they can identify inventions and interventions that make sense for the people and the project goals. Without a coherent understanding of the practice, each need or problem stands alone and can only drive single-feature solutions. It's hard to see when a solution to one problem creates new problems elsewhere—just as automated phone systems solve the problem of giving quick answers to standard questions but make it difficult to get to a live person to deal with nonstandard situations. A diagram supports systemic thought and makes it possible to create a coherent design response.

Each Contextual Design model represents one face of the practice in a coherent graphic. Multiple models allow the team to synthesize the whole practice by systematically looking across multiple models. This reveals the entire practice in an organized way. People won't overfocus on the Sequence Model's steps when they have the Day-in-the-Life model showing the whole life context. They won't worry only about supporting the tasks of the activity when they have the Identity Model reminding them of core motives and attitudes. They won't forget that the activity is embedded in real relationships and collaborations when they have the Relationship and Collaboration model. Multiple models provide a digestible view of the complexity of the user's world.

Multiple models give multiple perspectives on the user

For these reasons, we use graphical models to capture knowledge about the users' life and practice. They provide a shared focus on an activity which gives the team an external, concrete form to record and communicate what they saw on user visits. As long as users' practice remains insubstantial and invisible, there's no good way to share what you learned or to check that your design really accounts for the practice you discovered. Models make concepts concrete, creating a physical artifact the team can talk about and touch. Teams can use them to share with stakeholders, other interested teams, and each other as a record of what was learned and as a way to focus design thinking.

By providing a coherent, synthetic view of the practice, Contextual Design models give design teams effective ways to handle qualitative data. Any qualitative technique such as Contextual Inquiry produces huge amounts of detailed knowledge about the user. This knowledge is critical to product design but isn't amenable to reductive statistical techniques: you can't take the average of 20 interviews to identify the "typical" user. Graphical models provide a coherent way of structuring all this detailed data, revealing the underlying structure and experience, eliminating irrelevant detail, and bringing important aspects into focus.

Consolidated models make sense of qualitative data

In themselves, the models represent a significant deliverable for user researchers, UX designers, and product teams. They remind the team of what they saw in the field; they evoke users' practice and help team members who were not present envision users doing the activities; they are the source of any needs analysis, the origin of new design ideas, and a statement of the real world of the users. As such they are the arbitrator of argument about what the users are or are not doing or feeling.

But most importantly, because they are physical, able to be interacted with, they drive design thinking. They are the way teams move toward a more transformative, more systemic product concept. Insight comes when brilliant designers are *immersed* in the world of the users as represented by the models. *Design for life* is easier with the life represented physically. And *team buy-in* is helped when the team builds the data themselves and uses it to drive design.

CONSOLIDATION THINKING: INDUCTION

It's remarkable that products and systems can be built to support large numbers of people at all. People don't coordinate across industries to make sure they work in consistent ways. Families and consumers don't agree on how to live their lives. Yet we take it for granted that products can be built and will be successful with all their disparate users. Products are not designed for individuals; they are designed for whole *user populations*—intended users doing the target activities within the target market or an internal organization of a business. Just as we can buy clothes from department stores that fit, products can be shipped that work for business people and consumers alike—even across industries and cultures.

So if a product can address the needs and delight a whole user population, it's because aspects of the activity are similar across all users: common structure, strategy, and intent; common motives, values, and experiences. A design responds to the common approach associated with the target activity while allowing for individual variation among people. But how can we discover these common aspects? How do we recognize them among all the surface differences in how people act and feel? And how do we represent the common aspects of life so a design team can respond to them?

We do it with data consolidation, but people often have a hard time believing it works. It is common, for example, to hear vendors of the productivity tools we all use say, "We have millions of users, and they all use our product differently. There is no one office user." They put themselves at a standstill—there's no way to go on to understand those aspects of the activity which are common. There's no way to find the common tasks and motives which, if they were better supported, would give a product a market advantage. There's no way to see the common flow of activity which a suite of products and apps could successfully support.

No person is as unique as they like to think they are. Neither are markets.

It isn't just vendors who say that all their users are different. People are invested in being unique, and the first thing that users often say is how different they are from everyone else. But much of the detail that makes people different is not relevant to designing a product for a market—the common pattern, structure, and experience related to a target activity; it is this common pattern, structure, and experience that make generic software possible.

For example, when we first studied configuration management, we found that some companies made it a very formal process, with people who have the job title "Configuration Manager," who decided what went into a configuration and made sure it got built and tested. These days, small companies value minimal process, continuous integration, and frequent release. In a startup company with web-delivered software, we found the engineering manager walking around to people saying, "Remember we go live with the new features tonight! Lisa, make sure your stuff is integrated. Anil is testing now. Joe, keep your stuff on its own branch—we'll integrate it tomorrow."

The first organization recognized the role and formalized it as a job; the second didn't recognize the role formally but made sure someone was responsible for performing it informally. The role is part of the common work structure of the market; the different ways of assigning the role as a job are

> *If your data doesn't consolidate, you have more than one market*

differences of detail. A product could be structured to support both types of organizations, though it might have to be packaged and marketed differently to deal with the customers' different attitudes. Whether we like it or not, given any target activity for workers or consumers, the variation in how and why people do things the way they do, the technology they use, the concepts they operate from, the things they manipulate to get things done, simply doesn't vary all that much. This is at the root of why a small population of well-selected users can characterize markets of millions.

And what if the data can't be consolidated?[2] Contextual Design models show teams how to address a market strategically, segmenting the market based on similar practice. If the practice and experience is common, it can be represented in a single set of consolidated models. Where the models identify differences—such as different cultures—they show how the product must be packaged or sold differently to different groups of people. But when one set of models cannot represent all users, it shows that there is not one market. It shows that the structure of the activity in the two contexts is likely too different for a single product to address.

---

[2] Over the last 20+ years only one project's data only failed to consolidate. This client insisted that they could make the same product for consumers and people who worked out of their homes. We didn't think the markets were the same, and that is exactly what showed up in the data—all the consumer data consolidated together and all the small home business data consolidated together. Their two markets were there, hanging on the wall separately.

Data consolidation and the thinking process behind it are the key to getting a reliable, actionable view of the market. Products serve whole markets, but we can only find out about users by talking to them one on one. Consolidation brings the data from all users together into a single, coherent view, showing common patterns without losing the key variation across users. The challenge of consolidation is to do explicitly, on purpose, and externally what is usually tacit, haphazard, and internal: develop a sense for a whole target population from particular instances and events.

All consolidation is the result of *induction*, reasoning "from the particular to the general, from the known to the unknown."[3] The goal of consolidation is to generate new insights about users, their behavior, and their experience. You can't develop new insight by applying existing rules and concepts to the data—all you'll ever discover is more detail about the things you already know. The consolidations we build in Contextual Design use induction to bring together many instances from individual interviews, discovering structure hidden in detailed observations. In this way we can reveal new concepts, patterns, and insight relevant to characterizing the market for a target activity.

> *You can't create new insight with existing concepts. You have to create new ones.*

Quantitative techniques make data manageable through *data reduction*—for example, by looking just for the top findings—which hides the richness of the actual data. Contextual Design doesn't reduce the findings—it synthesizes the individual observations into higher-order insights. Synthesis through inductive reasoning simplifies the complexity of the data and makes it approachable. To get this insight we start by consolidating data from multiple users at the same time. This ensures that the team is faced with enough data to see patterns and develop new insight. The volume of data forces the need for structure and challenges the team's entering assumptions about what the themes are. If we organize the data by a priori assumptions and categories, we will not

---

[3] T. Fowler, The Elements of Inductive Logic, 3rd edition, Clarendon Press, Oxford, 1876.

discover insights we haven't already thought of. This is the power of inductive reasoning: to group instances together into meaningful elements to reveal core elements, experiences, and patterns. This creates new insight.

Because the structure is built up out of detailed observations, consolidations naturally accommodate variation among users. Examining users one by one, designers might have seen only random differences; but bringing many users together through inductive reasoning reveals how differences may be variations on a theme. If one person prefers to write an outline before starting a paper and another just talks out her ideas, we can understand that these are different ways of clarifying thought before starting to write. New variants in user data can be recognized and positioned within the consolidation structure—so someone who wrote lots of different rough paragraphs and then went back to rewrite them can be recognized as achieving the same intent of clarifying his thoughts but in yet another way. Variations exist within a larger structure of understanding. Consolidation through inductive reasoning provides a way to help the team think about complex data *without* tossing out the complexity.

Consolidation reveals common patterns within a market without losing important variation

Consolidation is a process of inquiry: looking at details from specific users and asking how each detail has meaning for the project and fits with observations from other users. When the key insights bubble up from individual observations, we then label the groupings in the voice of the user. Though it's applied differently for each kind of model, this same thinking process is used in all model consolidations. When done as a team, a consolidation design meeting acts as an *immersion* experience: team members who participate in consolidating the data interact with it intimately and learn the user's world.

Contextual Design's consolidated models synthesize the complexity of qualitative data into a set of graphical representations revealing a big picture of the target market. The consolidated models focus and drive design action through ideation, by communicating the insight to a team tasked with invention.

Design communication: using data to drive design

We have been watching teams interact with the Traditional Contextual Design Models and the Affinity Diagram for years. When we set out to design representations of the new data for life, we took a step back to use what we learned. All the models presented here—the new ones and new variants—emerged from this reflection and iteration with our client teams. What did we learn?

In the days when developers were the primary team members, they were the source of insight and had to do their own synthesis. They loved the Traditional Contextual Design Models because all the detail was available, unfiltered but organized into models

> *Communicating the implications of data for design is a core skill for UX professionals*

similar to those they used for data representation. They did not want—and often did not trust—the emerging user researchers to do this for them. The Affinity, which everyone loves, is a simple hierarchy, organizing the actual data points into a structure that gives access to the detail. The Flow Model looks like the bubbles and arrows of data-flow diagrams; developers could transfer their inquiry skills from data modeling directly into understanding people. The Sequence Model focuses on specific tasks; task analysis and flowcharts were also known forms. Once they were into the idea of models of human behavior, it was easy for them to use the models to organize user data. Gleaning the meaning of the models was their job.

But the user experience field has grown into a profession with university degrees and many user-facing job types. Technology has changed so that products support less technical users. Consumer products and websites have technology built into them. As a result, teams doing requirements and design now tend to be composed of content experts, UI designers, user researchers, information architects, product managers, marketers, editors, and more. Developers and technical architects are less often a primary part of the team collecting and organizing data. They may be part of ideation based on the data, but they no longer dominate ideation.

This new population of designers is not used to complex data representations such as dataflow diagrams. They looked to us to simplify and focus the findings. And this is true for managers as well. The desire to see and manipulate all the data gave way to the need to structure the data to reveal in a single glance the most important patterns and insights of the data collection team. The Decision Point Model, a variant of the Cultural Model, grew out of that effort; it shows the influences on people when making decisions for purchase or in life. Data captured in the Flow Model evolved to focus more on work groups, core roles, and discrete process—eventually emerging anew as the Collaboration Model. The Physical Model, when used to represent cars and homes, became enriched in layout, color, and story content. Over time, we began changing the original models to better match the needs of modern cross-functional design teams.

When setting out to design the models needed for the Cool Concepts, we also looked at which models best stimulate design thinking. This was easy to do because during the Wall Walk (described in Part 3), designers write ideas on sticky notes and put them on the model that sparked the idea. If a model collected few ideas, it was clearly not getting into the minds of the designers and was not driving product concepts. So our measure of success of any model became the number of design ideas it collected. The Affinity Diagram has always collected the most design ideas so we looked at its attributes to get insight when designing the new models. Other models, though still beloved by many developers and designers, did not pass the design idea test. This included many of our original Contextual Design models, including the Sequence Model. People value it for guiding scenarios, but it rarely stimulates new product concepts.[4] When Personas[5] become popular and we added them into our processes, we noticed that although they provide stories which helped

Intentionally design how you communicate the data to encourage innovation

---

[4] Sequence Models are most useful to guide detailed design: to ensure that the steps of a task and their intents are dealt with. The design thinking they stimulate tends toward low-level fixes, not large product concepts or new direction. They are important for detailed design but rarely collect many design ideas unless we force the team to walk through them step by step—which is considered tedious.

[5] Cooper, Alan (1999), *The Inmates are Running the Asylum*, SAMS, ISBN 0-672-31,649-8.

focus the team, they too failed the design idea test. And the Flow Model was simply too complex for many people to approach. So our goal was to create models that were so approachable that they would naturally drive design thinking.

We designed and redesigned the new models, iterating them with teams until they stimulated design ideas in good numbers. By introducing these new models and the new approach to building them, we saw a huge change in the quality and scope of the design concepts that teams generated. The new consolidated models when used during visioning pushed teams to consider the whole life in the way we intended. Teams naturally generated design concepts to deal with the user's whole life and motives.

This evolution revealed the absolute necessity for and power of *communication design*. Effective design depends on the UX professional's ability to communicate the user data and insights in a way that is comprehensible by the people in the design process. Communication design, the intentional creation of artifacts that communicate user data, is a necessary design step and an important skill for all UX professionals.

At this writing, Contextual Inquiry has been taught in universities for well over two decades. UX groups are now a standard part of technology companies. But the creation of UX groups tasked with research means that all the insight and deep knowledge about users tend to be locked in that group. Transferring not just knowledge but insight, understanding, and a feel for the user's world is the first step in creating a bridge between data and design. One of the greatest challenges for UX professionals is how to drive data into the ideation process; how to ensure that the lives of the users actually impact design thinking in the large. This is the single biggest question we get from UX professionals—how to get the product team to design from the user data.

Use principles of communication design to create representations of your user data

The consolidated models of Contextual Design V2 are designed to help teams internalize the world of their users. The principles of good communication design are built into the model consolidations so that you can implement them easily. Designing the communication is critical to successful ideation because it is at the center of the bridge from data to design action. Communication design has its own set of principles that make it work; we'll illustrate these as we discuss the consolidation process. Here is an overview:

- **Meaningful structure**: Design the structure of the graphic so that layout and color highlight the structure of the practice; organize and simplify the data into bite-sized chunks.
- **Story language**: Use short direct stories of the users' experience, including real-life detail to illustrate key points; use direct language with real incidents to hook the designer emotionally as well as intellectually; do not generalize or abstract.
- **Way in**: Use the layout of the graphic to draw the reader's eye—and so the mind—through the story; use design questions and example ideas to suggest key issues to the reader.
- **Interaction**: Use the graphic within a process that makes the designer manipulate the data so they engage with it; don't depend on passive reading only.

The new Experience Models were designed with these principles in mind and include guidelines on color, whitespace, number of graphical elements, text length, and writing voice. Feel free to copy and use what we have done with your design teams. The Traditional Contextual Design Models have also been adapted to communicate more powerfully. The Journey Map[6] that we and many people use is an example of communication design.

PUTTING MODELS INTO ACTION

During project planning the team determines which models will be used for the project. All projects will capture notes for the affinity. Most projects won't need more than the Day-in-the-Life, Identity, and Sequence Models plus one of the Relationship or Collaboration Models. These are enough to support all the design conversations

---

[6] S Moritz., Service Design: Practical access to an evolving field. 2005.

of a team. Which models are best depends on the product being designed and the focus of the project, and that may lead you to add a model or two. For example, the physical model becomes important to show drivers' behavior and experience inside an automobile; the Sensation Board brings insight to industrial designers of vehicles and appliances; the Decision Point model reveals thought processes of shoppers. Choosing the models to use affects the data collected and the scope of the design—the team can only consider aspect of the users' world they have characterized.

Modeling happens during data collection and interpretation—it's not a separate process

Each model implies that certain type of data must be collected at the field interview and captured during the interpretation session. We will introduce these processes as we describe the models. But note that modeling is integrated with data collection and interpretation—it's not a separate process done on its own. Models are initially created during the interpretation session. As the interviewer retells the story, modelers listen for the relevant data elements and capture them in the model.

Capturing models in the interpretation session make it possible for the team to describe and analyze aspects of the user practice in a concrete, shared, tangible way. They also automatically teach the design team how to see more when in the field.

Once the team has conducted 12–16 interviews do a preliminary consolidation. Build the Affinity Diagram and whichever Contextual Design models you select. If the project plan calls for 16 interviews or less, this consolidation is final. Otherwise, this preliminary consolidation lets the team reset focus for the remaining interviews and dive deeper into areas that look weak. After interpreting the remaining interviews, the team rolls the data into the existing models, makes appropriate changes, and prepares the final graphical representation. All graphical models and the affinity are put online and printed in large format so that they can be hung on the wall for ideation.

In the modeling chapters we describe the data collection, interpretation, consolidation, and communication design practice for each model. But first let's look at building the Affinity Diagram.

The Affinity Diagram

6

The Affinity Diagram is the simplest way to organize field data. It arranges the notes from Interpretation Sessions into a hierarchy that reveals common issues and themes across all users. The Affinity shows the scope of the problem: it reveals in one place all the issues, worries, and key elements of the users' lives relevant to the team's focus. It also helps define the key quality requirements on the system: reliability, performance, hardware support, and so forth. The Affinity Diagram should be built for every project. It is the first model consolidated, allowing it to be used to harvest data that might be needed for other models and also to teach the consolidation thought process (Fig. 6.1).

To build the Affinity, all Interpretation Session notes from all users are printed on sticky notes in random order. Then the team arranges the notes into a hierarchy, using a facilitated process. An Affinity takes 1.5–2 days to build, depending on the number of notes and the size of the team building the Affinity. The notes are grouped on a wall to reveal distinctions relevant to the design problem; each group describes a single issue or a point. Groups are kept small, four to six notes in a group. Keeping groups small forces the team to make more groups when there is a lot of data on a point, pushing them to find more issues and more insights. Groups are not predefined—they emerge from the data and are specific to the data. Finally, the groups

Bring all the issues and opportunities of the market into one place

Contextual Design. http://dx.doi.org/10.1016/B978-0-12-800894-2.00006-5

are labeled with blue sticky notes[1] to characterize the point made by the group. The blue labels are then organized into larger areas of interest under pink labels, and the pink labels are grouped under green labels to show whole themes.

The Affinity or "K-J" process was introduced as one of the "seven quality processes" from Japan[2] back in the 1970s. It has since then become a widely used tool. We have optimized the process to handle much larger affinities, typically about 1500 notes—though we recommend not more than about 500 notes in your first Affinity. We build the Affinity after a good cross-section of users has been interviewed. This usually means between 12 and 16 users covering all target roles in three to five work or life contexts, assuming 50–100 notes per user. We always prefer to finish the Affinity in a single day, or at worst time-box it to 2 or 3 focused days. We can do this if we have one person per 80 notes or better. If the project plan is to collect more data than this, first do a preliminary consolidation, which you finish. This allows the team to refocus and clarify the most important data to collect in the remaining interviews. Then do the remaining interviews and roll in the data in all at once in another 1–3 day session.

The Affinity is a quick way to organize a lot of unstructured data

Building the Affinity is a managed team meeting with a process that ensures it gets done in the time designated. Letting the process drag on drains the team. If your team is small and you don't have enough people, invite others who are interested in the design to participate. Order pizza! Do whatever you have to do to get them into the room. Remember managers and team members alike experience elapsed time, not man-hours. Ten people working together for a day or two looks short. Two people working for a week looks long, even though it's fewer hours—you don't get the immersion, buy-in, and range of perspectives you would with a wider group. This is also

---

[1] When we started the process, there were only blue, green, and pink sticky notes. While working with teams, the colors took on meaning relative to the level of abstraction or the part of the model, so we keep these colors. Whatever you do have a consistent color associated with one of the three levels of the Affinity.

[2] M. Brassard, *Memory Jogger Plus*, GOAL/QPC, Methuen, MA, 1989.

why we don't build affinities in an online document—it's too much data, too much manipulation, and not enough team interaction to achieve a high-quality result, either for the Affinity or for buy-in and immersion.[3]

FIGURE 6.1   An Affinity Diagram during construction, showing how notes and pictures from individual interviews (*the yellow notes*) are grouped into a hierarchical structure (*the blue, pink, and green labels*). Photos taken during interviews are integrated into the Affinity wherever appropriate.

BUILDING THE AFFINITY DIAGRAM

The Affinity is built bottom-up. We don't start with known categories such as "Usability issues" or "Quality." That would reduce building an Affinity to a sorting task; each note goes in its own bucket, and at the end you know no more than you did before. Instead, we allow the individual notes to suggest grouping they might belong to. We intentionally resist using categories that might be familiar to the team, suggested by their experience instead of by the user data. We even ban words the team is too familiar with—one configuration

---

[3] One day we may have real digital walls all over a room—then we can do it without the paper! But the team will still have a shared experience in the room.

management group was not allowed to use the word "version." Banning the term forces the team to say how the concept is relevant to the project focus and helps them to come at their problem with a fresh perspective (Fig. 6.2).

Ban jargon and specialized words to force rethinking old concepts

Building an Affinity is inductive reasoning at its purest. The basic process is to put up one note, then for everyone to look at the notes in their hand for others that seem to go with it. When found, additional notes are added to the group. There's no need to justify *why* they go together. But we do push for a certain kind of "affinity": Two notes have an affinity if they are saying similar things about

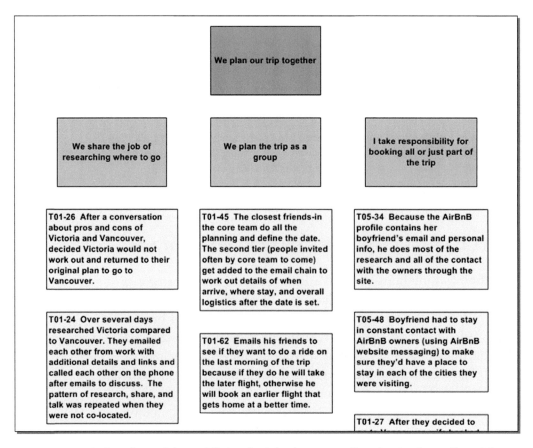

FIGURE 6.2   A slice of a much larger Affinity after it has been put online, showing how yellow sticky notes from individual interviews group into blues and pinks revealing issues and themes. Note that the blues and pinks are written in the voice of the user.

the user's life as it relates to the design focus of the team—the notes express a similar intent, problem, or issue. So deciding if notes go together is the result of an inquiry into the meaning of the words on the note to understand the practice issue they represent. When it's not clear how to interpret the words, the team can appeal to the interviewer to check whether an interpretation is valid.

Inquire into the design significance of each note

Here are some examples of using the data captured on a note to infer meaning for the practice. Each example gives some of the context (which the team would be aware of) and shows how to look at the data from a particular focus and see implications for redesigning the practice and technology. If these insights occurred to team members during the Interpretation Session, they would be captured in separate notes; otherwise the Affinity process gives the opportunity to consider the data again. These notes are all taken from interviews with people planning vacations.

```
U07-39 She likes Orbitz because their dates were flexible—
she sees a matrix with departure and return dates. She
can see each price and pick the best one.
```

This note discusses a particular feature of a travel site's UI (Orbitz), but it's hiding an implication about travel planning. When thinking about her vacation, the user isn't committed to a particular departure and return date. Those might change depending on the trip, the price, and other factors. And in fact, many decisions in vacation planning are tentative, dependent on other aspects of the vacation working out. Any tool we build needs to take this flexible, uncommitted attitude toward planning into account.

```
T05-90 She says her mom never traveled much, and her mom
was proud of U5 when U5 started traveling a lot: "you do
it all, you see it all."
```

This note suggests values and experiences associated with identity—the mother's attitude and by implication the traveler's own. The notes in an Affinity relevant to values and how we see ourselves will group together to reveal themes. This section of the wall will both reveal these values and will also be relevant data to create identity elements, described in Chapter 7. Here it suggests that being adventurous is valued by both mother and daughter—and it reveals that the mother would like to encourage the daughter to do what she could not. As the team looks for the meaning and key ideas in the notes, they can group like notes together. The meaning a team reads in a note and the way they group them are driven by the project focus. The above notes could be taken in different directions—features in cars, finding restaurants, providing search functionality. But put together, they point toward one of the Cool Concepts (in fact, they are where the concept came from). Together, they suggest "Think for me"—give me what I'm looking for *without* asking me, without search, and without setup. Grouping them this way across domains reveals the higher-level principle.

> *Notes will represent and enrich the meaning of the Cool Concepts*

```
I love getting local results immediately, without having
to ask
```

```
U6-40 She likes that Google gives you local listings first
for restaurants and stores nearby
```

```
U5-58 Likes using the built-in Zagat feature in his car
to find good restaurants in the area.
```

```
U4-60 He uses the icon feature of the map in his car to
help him find gas stations nearby.
```

Now we collect notes with similar themes together and give them a *label* representing the insight suggested by the group. A good group label states the issue that holds all the individual notes together. It is a succinct phrase that summarizes the content of the group. "Different ways of finding nearby things" would not summarize the content in the above example; it would just say what you could learn by reading the content. Including "without having to ask" states the key principle; the individual notes give examples of this general statement. The data in the individual notes below the label supports the statement in the label. If the label is good, it reveals the distinction important for design. The label is the synthesis of the detailed data—now there is no need to read the notes. The label is sufficient. So a good label matters.

Labels are the user's voice speaking from the wall—succinctly

A good group label is written as though the user was talking to the designer; direct, immediate language has more impact than third-person language. The label is not a sentence; it is succinct declarative personal message from the user. When the labels use the user's voice, the whole wall speaks directly to the design team—the labels are a central communication device. Here are some examples of good first-level labels, all revealing how travel planning supports relationship between people:

```
Planning the trip is another opportunity to connect and
have fun
```

```
The closer I am to a person, the more ways I have to
                communicate with them
```

```
It's important to plan regular trips so we can get
                together
```

First-level groupings such as the above are themselves collected into higher-order groups. The result is a hierarchical structure that breaks the data about the user into manageable chunks. We use green sticky notes at the highest level, which describe a whole area of concern. Under this, pink labels describe the specific issues which define that area of concern. Blue labels describe each aspect of the issue. And the individual notes under the blue labels describe the instances illustrating the blue label. When well written, the labels tell a story about the user, structuring the problem, identifying specific issues, and organizing everything known about that issue. The labels represent the new information in an Affinity. All labels are written in the voice of the user.

Labels are the synthesis of the data revealing meaning

We limit each first-level group to four to six notes to force the team to look deeply and make more distinctions than they would otherwise be inclined to. It pushes more of the knowledge up into the group labels. Remember your findings are in the labels—they are what will drive design thinking. A pink label can contain up to eight blue labels, and a green label might have six to eight pink labels. Bigger groups than that mean there's not enough structure to see what's going on quickly.

When complete, each green section tells a story about the users' life. It raises the distinctions relevant for the project focus, revealing what matters. In this way, the labels synthesize the findings and drive design thinking. For example, here is a section of an Affinity describing how travel supports the Cool Concept of

METRICS FOR AFFINITY BUILDING

Start when you have multiple users to organize.
- About half the users or at least 300 notes from four to five users

Groupings start with observation notes
- Not design ideas or questions—the first note frames the group meaning

Number of notes below the blue (1st level) labels is based on the size of the Affinity:
- Less than 1000 notes: two to four in a grouping
- 1000–1800 notes: four to six in a grouping
- More than 1800 notes: 6–10 in a grouping *if* there is a lot of real duplication

Notes under higher-level labels:
- Pink (2nd level) six to eight blues under a pink
- Green (3rd top level) 4–10 pinks under a green

Build a preliminary Affinity if there will be more than 20 user interviews:
- Build preliminary Affinity after 10–16 interviews—or about half
- Preliminary Affinity should be complete but broad and shallow: only one to three individual notes beneath each blue label
- Later interviews will deepen the groups and create new labels

Accomplishment. (Individual notes have been skipped for brevity—colored triangles map to colored notes in the Affinity):

▶ Challenge is a part of task accomplishment

   ▷ Travel provides an opportunity to pursue personal goals

      ▷ Travel is an opportunity to continue working on things I or my family do at home

      ▷ Travel is an opportunity and inspiration for me to improve myself

      ▷ I look for apps to help me connect my interests (such as food) to travel

      ▷ I want to learn new things, and travel/travel planning helps me do that

   ▷ Travel itself gives me a sense of accomplishment

      ▷ Getting a good deal makes me feel good

      ▷ I enjoy and take pride in planning travel

      ▷ Figuring out the best deal, route, etc. is fun

   ▷ I care about keeping track of my accomplishments

      ▷ I keep track of the places I've traveled

      ▷ I want to have a full collection of all my travel photos

      ▷ I like getting feedback about how I'm doing

This section of the Affinity brings together data from many users and many situations to tell the story of travel and the experience of challenge. When sharing the data or reviewing the wall yourself, you might read it like a story: "People see travel as a challenge, and that's a good thing. It gives them a sense of accomplishing personal goals, furthering their interests, and growing as a person. And overcoming the challenges of travel is fun and meaningful in itself. I'm proud of what I did and want to share it with my world." Each pink label names an issue which is described by the blue labels underneath it, so that each section of the Affinity tells a coherent story about part of the practice, and the whole wall brings together all issues and observations to tell a single story about the user population.

The Affinity tells a story of the user's life

Labels in the Affinity bubble up from the data. Together they tell the story of the practice and life of people in the market. The data, as always, represents detailed information about the target activity. But with the introduction of the Cool Concepts, the data now also represents detailed data about the life, use of mobile devices, identity, and motives of people. And the Cool Concepts also focus the team in

LABEL GUIDELINES

Labels should enable the reader to:
- Read blue labels to see themes without reading individual notes
- Read quickly without having to parse any sentences
- Focus on generating design ideas, not figuring out language

Blue label guidelines:
- Represent the data to highlight the key point
  - There should be one key point
  - If the group hangs together this is easy—if it doesn't, break it up
- Use direct language summarizing an observation, not a category
  - Good: "I don't choose a destination until I check out available accommodations"
  - Bad: "How I choose accommodations"—forcing review of individual notes for the point
- Written from the user's point of view, talking to the team
- Use short succinct "Hemingway-type" statements—simple, direct, unadorned prose and no long sentences with clauses
  - Does not need to be a complete sentence
  - No more than two to three handwritten lines long on the Post-it
  - Not design ideas
    - "Booking accommodations is too complicated" not "I want an easy way to book accommodations"

Pink and green labels organize sections.
- They reflect a theme/category of findings, but still use "I" language
- For example, "I use multiple strategies to decide where to go"

new ways on details of sensation, direct tool interaction, tool hassles, and learning. Because this is not traditional task-oriented data, it's easy to miss during consolidation.

So to be sure that the team pulls together the data needed for the Contextual Design Experience Models and ideation techniques, we need to raise up issues of design for life. To do this, before build-ing the Affinity, we suggest the team start with

Cool Concepts change classic Affinity building

a set of preliminary green labels related to Cool Concepts. These are placeholders which can be changed later by looking at the data grouped into that section. All of the green labels talking about the target task bubble up naturally. We do not recommend predefining green labels for the primary task—that won't help the team break their preliminary assumptions. But by using initial labels associated with the Cool Concepts, we help the team recognize this important data and bring it together. Below are the green labels we suggest to ensure a design for life focus.

- My on-the-go life

- I connect to people that matter

- I define myself personally and professionally

- My tools are a sensual delight

- My tools are Direct into Action

- My tools are a hassle

- I have to learn how to use my tools

These *placeholder* labels allow the related data to find their way together more easily. A team might not have all Cool Concepts in their project focus; if so, they will only use the preliminary green labels that are relevant for them.

Affinity building reveals the core process of consolidation: look at individual observations and group like data from different users. Bubble up key distinctions relevant for design. Label the distinc-tions at multiple levels of abstraction—in the Affinity, the blue labels reveal detailed distinctions, and the pinks show key aspects of one overall theme or story area represented by the green label. Let the groupings emerge through inductive reasoning to reveal

> *Building an Affinity teaches inductive reasoning to find important themes*

new themes, aspects, and distinctions. Present the whole in a structure that's easy to understand and walk. For the Affinity, this structure is a simple hierarchy.

You can read a good Affinity from beginning to end to see every issue in the practice and everything the team has learned so far, all tied to real instances. There's no better way to see the broad scope of the problem quickly. And it's also the first example of the process of consolidation.

BUILDING THE AFFINITY AS A TEAM

Building the Affinity is a group process. Building the data into a consolidation with multiple people is critical because it ensures that the lapsed time is reasonable. But more importantly, building the Affinity together is another immersion experience for those who did not go to the field to collect data. It exposes people to the users' lives and naturally expands their understanding of that life. And through manipulating the data and building into a structure that all share, they buy into the implications of the data.

For any group process, people need to know the rules of engagement; they benefit from a clear structure to guide getting the collaborative work done. We saw how Contextual Design provides such a structure for the Interpretation Session; we also provide a clear structure for the Affinity and other team tasks as well. Here are the basic steps to building the Affinity.[4]

During Affinity building we encourage quiet, one-on-one discussion between team members. This process is an opportunity to explore the data together and bounce ideas for labels off each other. Working in

---

[4] See **Holtzblatt et al. (December 28, 2004)** for more detailed step-by-step description of Affinity building.

STEPS TO BUILD THE AFFINITY DIAGRAM

Prep work

1. Print the notes captured during Interpretation Sessions on printable sticky notes or in a 3″ × 5″ grid, cut apart so each is on its own label-sized slip of paper. Preferably mix up the notes so different user's notes are interleaved.
2. Print all notes of all users in order, just as a list, for reference.
3. Prepare a room with bare walls. Hang good-quality butcher paper one the walls (floor to ceiling). Build your Affinity on this.

The morning

4. Give everyone building the Affinity a set of notes to start—8 to 10 per person
5. Put notes up on the wall one at a time as a group. Read out the note. After each note goes up, others add notes that go with it. Don't discuss the positioning—anyone can put a note anywhere.
6. Continue this formal process until a bunch of groupings, about 20, are up on the wall.
7. Now everyone works individually putting up notes until the stack of notes is all up on the wall without labels. People get more notes as they need them.
8. People will naturally put groups together that are variations on a theme. While working, they will announce where things are.
9. Remember everyone can move any note to create and recreate groupings as they accommodate new data.

The afternoon (and following days if needed)

10. Before starting formal labeling, put rough "type" labels using any other color over these rough groups so you know what is where. (We keep them at an angle so we know they are not real and don't need review.)
11. Collect similar together based on the rough labels.
12. Introduce labeling and start labeling together, breaking down long groups and writing real blue labels; pink labels will naturally emerge.
13. Assign pairs to each section of the wall, dealing with priority areas first. Each pair writes labels for their own part of the wall, relocating notes that don't belong to their area.
14. As groups continue to add individual notes, break them down so there are no more than four notes in a group, or the number appropriate for your Affinity size.
15. Add pink and green level notes to collect groups and keep the structure tight.
16. Check all sections and labels for quality and that key distinctions have bubbled up, and that labels are in the correct language at every level.

pairs, people can discuss their insights and get someone else to check their thinking. Writing the labels reveals what you're thinking; if someone disagrees with the grouping structure, they may move notes and rewrite the label. Adding notes to a group will naturally change what its label needs to say. All the data instances are there to support one interpretation or another, so it's easy to change your emphasis or split a group to show several distinctions.

There is no need for consensus before creating or changing a label or grouping. But if a pair gets stuck on their part of the wall,

Use the minds of the whole team—everyone works the whole Affinity

they can ask others to come in to help. Never stop and have a whole-team discussion on any part of the wall! Let two or three people make a quick decision and move on. Working in parallel, the wall will naturally shift to better reflect the themes that matter for your project. Green label sections become separate areas of work; move people around the sections so multiple minds consider each part. Ownership of a part is a problem, not a goal.

Doing the work in pairs helps move people from thinking in buckets (all notes with the term "hotel" on them get tossed in one group) to thinking about the practice. Moving from section to section to stay fresh lets people review each other's notes and labels for clarity, rightness for that group, and to see that a story is being created. When people can't agree on where a note should go, they talk about what underlying issues they see. When people don't under-

Use the Affinity process to think in new ways about the practice

stand a note, they go back to the list of notes from that Interpretation Session or to the interviewer to ask what happened in the interview. If a note seems to have two points, cut it in half or write a second note. Remember the Affinity will never be "perfect." Perfection is not a goal; structuring the data so it is useful to drive design thinking is. Everyone should be able to look at the resulting wall and see how it addresses the project focus and any business issues.

To help manage the team we put strict boundaries on disagreement, just as we did in the Interpretation Session. Team members may draw different meanings from the same note. A note might fit into an existing blue group or might be used to create a new one. In that case, create a new group and a new distinction. More insight is better. Rarely do you need the note in both places; if you already have two good notes in a group you don't need a third—use it elsewhere to push new insight. A note might fit into several existing groups—in that case, just pick the weakest grouping and beef it up by adding the note to it. If a team member has an insight from the Interpretation Sessions but doesn't have the notes to support it, it's up to them to find the supporting data first (the notes

Manage disagreements within the rules of the process

may have been buried in other categories) and then write the label to support it. But most of all, remember that no one note is critical.

Building the Affinity in a few days creates a team event that binds the team together and is also important for creating new insight. Building smaller Affinities more quickly or building up one Affinity over time lets team members incorporate each piece of data into an already existing structure of understanding before having to deal with the next; this leads to assimilation of each point instead of promoting a paradigm shift. With the above process, in a single day the team has to face a whole new way of looking at the users' world.

Building a 1500-note Affinity is exhausting, so knowing how to handle disagreements and individual differences is key. It's an entire day of reading and conceptualizing hundreds of separate bits of data and matching them with other bits of data. It's like a combination of Concentration, the memory game, and translating Shakespeare into Latin: the words on a note have to be interpreted to translate them into the underlying practice issue; then the note has to be matched with the note you saw 5 minutes ago and you know is on the wall somewhere. Everyone's working at once, moving back and forth along the wall, discussing notes with each other, and yelling general questions to the group at large ("Who interviewed U4?").[5]

Organize hundreds of observations into a coherent story in a single day

Some people will be overwhelmed when the first notes are going up with no labels, and others will love it. But the people who hate it find that their overwhelm evaporates when they have one piece of the wall to label. Now the task is bounded, and they can focus on putting in

---

[5] See a real time Affinity being built here: https://goo.gl/a4zvm4.

structure. Some people will be great labelers and others will be able to find groups but won't write good labels. Working as a group means the team can lean on the strengths and work around the weaknesses of individuals. No process will feel comfortable to everyone all the time. But if people know what to expect and what to do, we find they can deal with it.

When the team is done, they have a single structure representing all their user data, which organizes their knowledge and insight and gives them a basis for design. And when they see it finished—then everyone gets excited!

MANAGING PEOPLE DURING AFFINITY BUILDING

Building an Affinity is not an easy process for some and people will react to the process in different ways. Here are some guidelines.

People's response	Advice
The number of Affinity notes and the lack of structure are overwhelming. These people can organize a limited part of the Affinity but find it hard to put up the original groups.	Talk about this before starting so people who get overwhelmed will know it is normal to feel this way. Reassure them that they will find it easier later in the process and that at the end when the wall is organized they will have the structure they need. Explain that building the Affinity this way is the quickest way to get the Affinity notes up and organized, while taking advantage of multiple perspectives.
Some get concerned about creating the "right" Affinity.	Help them see that there are many ways to put an Affinity together and you will produce only one. This is okay—the purpose is to push your understanding of the users by revealing key distinctions. As long as your Affinity makes you think new design thoughts, it is good for your purposes.
Some people need to clear out distractions and focus on just a part of the problem.	They may not be able to deal with working with someone else because talking and thinking is too hard. If you have two people such as these, suggest that they pair up because they will work in parallel but engage in some discussion.
Some will get frustrated trying to track "their" section of the wall when others add to their groups or move their notes somewhere else.	Coach people to be comfortable with multiple people creating the diagram, without anyone keeping the whole thing coherent. Tell them to trust that something good will come out. This is how to move quickly.

DESIGN COMMUNICATION AND THE AFFINITY DIAGRAM

Once the Affinity is built, structured, and labeled, it is time to ensure it is really ready to be used in an ideation session. Because teams always love the Affinity, it is our gold standard for learning what really works for communication design. So let's look at its attributes. Just as the Affinity teaches the inductive thinking process needed for any consolidation, it illustrates principles of good communication design.

The Affinity illustrates principles of good communication design

Meaningful structure: A meaningful structure is one that can be used, understood, and consumed quickly by anyone walking up to the model. A hierarchy such as the Affinity presents is the most familiar structure for information across all professions. How you organize that hierarchy is critical for success. The Affinity structure contains the overall story of the practice and life of the target population. Read top-down, it presents the story in sections, or chapters, denoted by the green labels. So the Affinity presents the key issues of the market in digestible chunks. A person can read through one green label grouping and only focus on what that group is trying to say. This helps focus design thinking and generates targeted design ideas. The green label says "Look here, think about this—now what will you invent to deal with my issues?"

Each green is composed of chunks too—the pink groups—and so on. Each chunk is a call for design thinking. When information is chunked well within an overall framework (like the Affinity hierarchy), people know how to approach complex data without overwhelm. The green labels lead the reader through the data, creating natural stopping points such as "chapters" in a story. It invites but circumscribes the design problem to something manageable. Any good communication design must have a recognizable structure that chunks information while it moves a reader systematically and naturally through the full story represented in the whole model.

The structure of your communication makes it overwhelming or consumable

So what makes a good Affinity? We provide metrics on size so that the chunks don't get too big. We put the greens in a sensible order so people can move through them without disrupting their understanding of the big picture. To use it, anyone can start anywhere—but no matter where they start, the flow from panel to panel will end up telling the whole story.

The labels, and language of the labels, are critical too. If they are too long, people have to stop to parse them, disrupting their flow. If they are too categorical, they force the reader into the notes, again disrupting the flow. If there are just too many words on a label, they can't be easily and quickly scanned. To simultaneously get the big picture and the detail, the data must be read like a novel, moving through it quickly so that the mind can be free to generate ideas while reading. Anything in the way of fluid movement through the data gets in the way of design thinking.

The last step in creating the Affinity is to check that the size and order of groupings are correct, that the most important themes are revealed, and that the labels are short, succinct, and invite immediate understanding.

Story language: People are wired to tell and consume stories. We write our stories on steles, on cave walls, in novels, in newspapers. We share stories as examples of larger principles. Although we can abstract, we naturally know how to consume content in the form of a story. And when we see an abstract concept, we naturally generate stories (or examples which are themselves stories) to tell ourselves what the abstraction means. So if we want people to internalize the data easily, we'd better use story language.

People know how to absorb a story—so give them one

A framework for understanding provides a set of abstract concepts which organize understanding. But without story examples—real-life examples of how that concept plays out in life—abstract concepts alone will not drive design thinking. Or worse—the concept, without story, invites us to make up stories to fill in the blank. This drives designers to lean on their own life experience, not the market data. The most powerful way to drive data into the mind of designers is to find the organizing concepts through inductive reasoning and then illustrate them—tell their tale in story form.

The labels in the Affinity simultaneously organize and name the core concepts and tell their story. They are constructed in first-person language expressing the users' experience. Because they are deliberately short, declarative, and succinct, they are easily consumed. In this way the designers learn the core concepts through story language in the voice of the market. And it's all tied to the actual data, available to flesh out the concept.

The story language used in the Affinity Diagram invites design thinking and drives designers away from design from the "I." It provides a way for readers to quickly immerse themselves in the life of the users just by "walking the wall" as we will discuss in Part 3.

A Way In: A wall-size graphic of complex data can be overwhelming. Since our goal is to invite the readers to engage with the data, we need to build a "way in" right into the structure of the graphic. Every consolidated model must guide the reader through the data by its structure and layout. Every consolidated model provides a big picture of one aspect of the users' lives. But we cannot swallow it whole—we must move through it linearly, or at least one piece at a time.

Help everyone know how to approach your data representation—by its structure

The Affinity Diagram provides a natural Way In through its groupings. Every green label defines a coherent part to be dealt with. The hierarchical structure tells people that blue labels define pink labels and pink labels define green labels. The flow from one green to the next guides movement through the model—and lets those who are looking for one favorite part to find it at the green level. The way in is clear.

The Way In is not defined by structure alone. The story language also invites inquiry and pulls the reader through the story. The Affinity hierarchy—well designed and labeled—is a great way to represent discrete observations in an accessible way. But other models show other views of the practice. The structure of a practice is not best represented in a hierarchy. In the next chapters we will talk about each model's structure and how to create a Way In for them.

Interaction: Even the best designed graphical representation of data doesn't communicate by itself. If passed around as a big document, readers might glance over it or think it looks cool—but will they really engage with the data? Will they use it? Will it drive design thinking? To be sure that the data get into the design, you

Give people something to do while interacting with the data

must push designers to interact with the data—to think about it, manipulate it, dialog with it, and respond to it. So support for this interaction must be built into the communication design of any model.

The Wall Walk described in Part 3 is the step where we ask people to engage with the data by giving them an activity to do while they move through the model. Reading alone does not ensure they are using the data for design. We must create a link between the data and design to be sure that it gets in to the mind of designers.

If designers are asked to write design ideas in response to the labels in the Affinity, they naturally start designing from data. If we tell them that a more systemic, better, idea is one that responds to a pink or green label, addressing a whole theme, they naturally move away from one-off ideas responding to individual notes. And it doesn't hurt if it creates a little competition to get the most, and most systemic, notes up.

People need something to do besides read when they engage with data. We build engagement into the process and into the structure of the model for all the consolidated models, as we describe below. But there are lots of ways to create interactive activities that drive designers into the data.

Communication design is at the core of bridging the gap between data and design thinking. So create a meaningful structure, use story

Communication design bridges the gap between data and design

language, define an obvious way in and a process for interaction. Once you have done that you are ready for ideation.

The Affinity Diagram is a fabulous teaching tool for your team. It teaches induction, how to structure information, how to raise up distinctions, and how to manage complex information. And when done well, it is an excellent communication design. Now we turn to the other models to learn how to build them and how they also can drive design thinking.

Building Experience Models

7

The Contextual Design Experience Models were created to help teams collect, incorporate, and use data related to the Cool Concepts. They show the structure of users' lives from the multiple points of view of the Wheel of Joy in Life. (The data for the Triangle of Design is collected as notes and consolidated into the Affinity Diagram.) Each model communicates the data and highlights the team's insights. They are built upon principles of communication design to provide one coherent picture of the users' life experience. We discuss each Experience Model in turn, including when each should be used. Each model helps focus the team on one of the Cool Concepts.

Nearly every project benefits from one or two Experience Models

Day-in-the-Life Model: This model collects data in support of Accomplishment. It shows how a target activity is accomplished as people move through their world; what they do in the different places; and the devices they use to get things done and access content in that place. It shows how we interleave home and work while on the go.

Identity Model: This model reflects data relevant to Identity. It reveals the key identity elements in the target population that a product might touch. It shows sources of pride, self-esteem, and value.

Contextual Design. http://dx.doi.org/10.1016/B978-0-12-800894-2.00007-7

Relationship and Collaboration Models: These models represent Connection. They show how people connect to others who matter in their world, at work, and at home, as relevant to the target activity. Relationship Models show how closeness is affected through the activity; Collaboration Models show how collaboration fosters both positive relationship and accomplishment.

Sensation Board: This model reveals the aesthetic and emotional experience that would hook people, based on the data. It identifies the list of keywords and images that industrial and visual designers can use for their work.

Contextual Design Experience Models are guided by the same principles as the Affinity Diagram:

1. Collect the appropriate data for the model in the field interview;

2. In the Interpretation Session, capture the key story points relevant to the model in a preliminary model structure;

3. Put the data into an appropriate and easy-to-understand structure for communication;

4. Collect like observations into groupings through induction;

5. Label the groupings with a summary and, for some models, a tagline;

6. Design a *Way In*;

7. Tune the final presentation using principles of communication design.

Finally, like the Affinity, work in teams with rules of engagement to guide quick decision-making and teamwork. In this way create an *immersion* experience and buy-in. The data itself is key to *design for life*.

We look at each model in turn discussing what data to collect, how to interpret the data, how to consolidate it and how to present it graphically. See http://booksite.elsevier.com/ 9780128008942 for Illustrator files you may use as a starter for your own models.

THE DAY-IN-THE-LIFE MODEL

The Cool Concept of Accomplishment focuses us on collecting data about how the target activity fits into the structure of the day—how tasks get done in small and large chunks of time, interleaving life and work activities across place, time, and platforms. People seek to fill every piece of dead time with productive or fun activities and by frequently checking in to their worlds.

To see this view of the users' world, we created the *Day-in-the-Life Model*. This model (Fig. 7.1) shows the overall structure of users' days and how their activities fit into time throughout the day, supported by technology. Since any life or work task can be pursued anywhere and anytime, designers need to see how technology is used to support the target activities in all the contexts of life. That's the job of the Day-in-the-Life model.

> *The Day-in-the-Life model shows how the activity fits into the whole life.*

We recommend the Day-in-the-Life Model be built for every project. It is a basic model like the Affinity Diagram.

COLLECTING THE DATA IN THE FIELD

The data needed for the Day-in-the-Life Model is a combination of a retrospective account of the past several days as well as the observed actions during the interview. To get this life context, listen to what the user says and does from the point of view of Accomplishment (see box). Listen for how tasks are split across time, place, and device. If a task is done at the office, is any part of it ever done elsewhere? Is research done at home? Coordination via calls from the car, bus, plane, doctor's office? Do users interrupt themselves at points in the task to get a mental break? Designers can no longer assume that any task is done in one sit-down, focused session.

Unstoppable Momentum of Life: Going on a trip

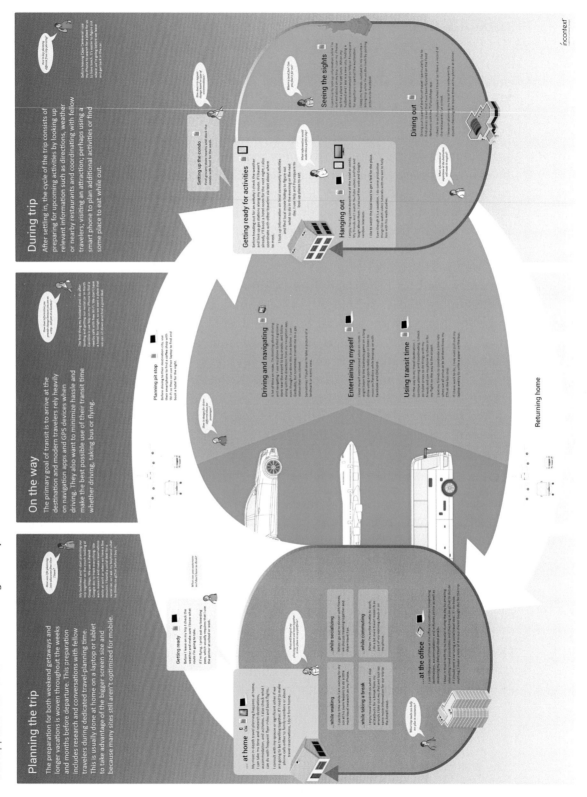

FIGURE 7.1 A full Day-in-the-Life model for travel. This model shows the three primary areas of interest for travel—at home and work prior to the trip, getting to the vacation location, and activities during the trip itself. Activities, issues, content accessed, and device use are shown in each location.

ACCOMPLISHMENT IN A CONTEXTUAL INTERVIEW

Start the interview with a global overview of the activity in life. Then walk through the day understanding how the activity played out. Observe and discuss the following:
- What they did and how they did it
- Where (what physical location) it took place
- At what time of day it was done
- How long it lasted (moments, minutes, longer)
- How people use dead time—or whether they devote prime, focused time to it
- How much attention is given to the task; how much is demanded or desired
- What device and app was used
- What information was accessed, correlated with different time chunks and locations
- Who they did the activity with and why with that person

At some point in the interview, walk the user through one or more specific past days, discussing what happened at each point in the day and how the user's technology enabled (or inhibited) doing the tasks of work and life. Use calendars, email, texts, or other trails to ground the discussion in the real day. Pay special attention to how activities are broken up into chunks of time and across platforms and with mobile devices, when the user's attention is split between activities, and the content they access at each point.

Get data for the Day-in-the-Life Model with detailed retrospective accounts of the past few days

Long periods of heads-down work hardly ever happen anymore—if they ever did. Probe for interruptions and self-created breaks during long activities such as office work. Look for how activities considered to be chores or side jobs get done in bits and pieces of time throughout the day. Technology often takes up the job of supporting chore tasks—short tasks which must be done but aren't valued in themselves (paying bills, time cards, travel receipts, etc.). If your target task is not a chore watch how it is interleaved with these activities.

Whenever possible, have the user recreate the events on the device or application being discussed. Combined with the techniques for eliciting a retrospective account, this results in a story of technology use throughout the day, grounded in the particulars of real instances of the target activity. Capture this data by writing it all down in order in your notebook, annotating it with relative time of day and platform used. For example, the data captured in the interaction below will directly feed the Day-in-the-Life Model, as well as creating other notes and models. So use the Day-in-the-Life retrospective account to enrich all your data.

> **User (U):** *I was doing the research for a family trip to Canada yesterday.*
>
> *Interviewer (I): So where were you, alone? On your computer? Tell me about it.*
>
> **U:** *I was sitting on the couch having morning coffee in the living room so I looked at the Web site for possible locations on my laptop—we've been wanting to go to Alberta.*
>
> **I:** *Did you discuss it with your wife?*
>
> **U:** *I sent her some of the links and pictures right then, but I had to go off to work. Here are some of the links…*
>
> **I:** *Did you do anything at work about the trip?*
>
> **U:** *She wrote back with her own links so I looked at those on my phone after a meeting and we texted about what looked good. We really need a family-friendly place.*
>
> **I:** *Anything else you did that day about the trip?*
>
> **U:** *Yes—after the kids were in bed we sat on the couch with our two tablets. We were each looking on our own but trading back and forth to share what we found—like, she found pictures of a cool park she wanted to show me. Then we started looking together for programs for the kids.*

Eliciting Day-in-the-Life information from a user requires a particular focus on when and where things happened, and the mix of personal and work activities throughout the day. When you collect this type of data from multiple users you will be able to see the pattern of how the target activity fits into the daily life of your users.

Collect data on how users accomplish your target activity across place, time, and device

Capturing during
the Interpretation Session

Use a skeleton model to collect relevant observations

The Day-in-the-Life Model represents how people do an activity while moving through their places in the world. So the typical Day-in-the-Life Model has a core structure composed of those places relevant to the target task. Nearly all projects will have anchor places like home, work, and commute. Additional anchor places may be added—for example, if the project focus is shopping you might need to add the physical store. You can start with a basic skeleton model like the one in Fig. 7.2 and write observations on it. Observations should be succinct, user-oriented language similar to Affinity notes. Put the model on a flip chart and write directly on

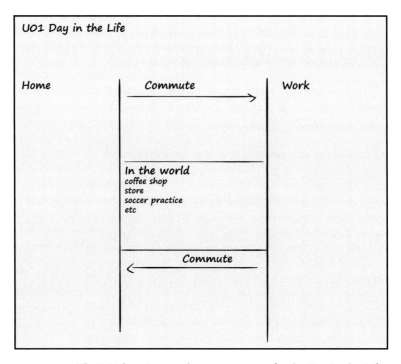

FIGURE 7.2 The initial sections used to capture notes for the Day-in-the-Life Model.

it, as in Fig. 7.3. Or keep a file online in a table with the different sections. As the data emerges in the Interpretation Session, new locations within places may need to be added—which means the models from different users may have different places on them. These differences across users will be normalized and organized in the consolidation process.

During the Interpretation Session, maintain a focus on how content and devices are used throughout the day. Look for moments of connection with others and how information is shared. Look for the moments when the device comes out. The Day-in-the-Life retrospective will focus the Interpretation Session so the data can be captured. More Day-in-the-Life data will come out throughout the session so keep listening for information to add to the model.

Capture little life stories—real instances not abstractions

Data in the individual model includes every instance of device use and every act related to the target activity. If travel research happened in the morning write it higher in the home section; if places like coffee shops become locations for the activity, add it as a section to "in the world." For each instance, capture where the user was, what they were doing, what content they accessed, how much of their attention it required, and what device they used.

These little stories of use will be important for the final consolidated model, so don't abstract or summarize—put in detail. A line or two is sufficient to capture a small story and its meaning.

CONSOLIDATING THE DAY-IN-THE-LIFE MODEL

The Day-in-the-Life Model is a graphical rendering showing the way technology is used for the target activity, highlighting the team's collective insight. The team selects the best stories from the Day-in-the-Life Models captured in the Interpretation Session. These stories make the life of the user real. When complete, the Day-in-the-Life Model

Reveal the team's insight— select the best real user stories for the model

communicates the world of the user and what they are doing across place, time, and platform in one large printed drawing. Let's look

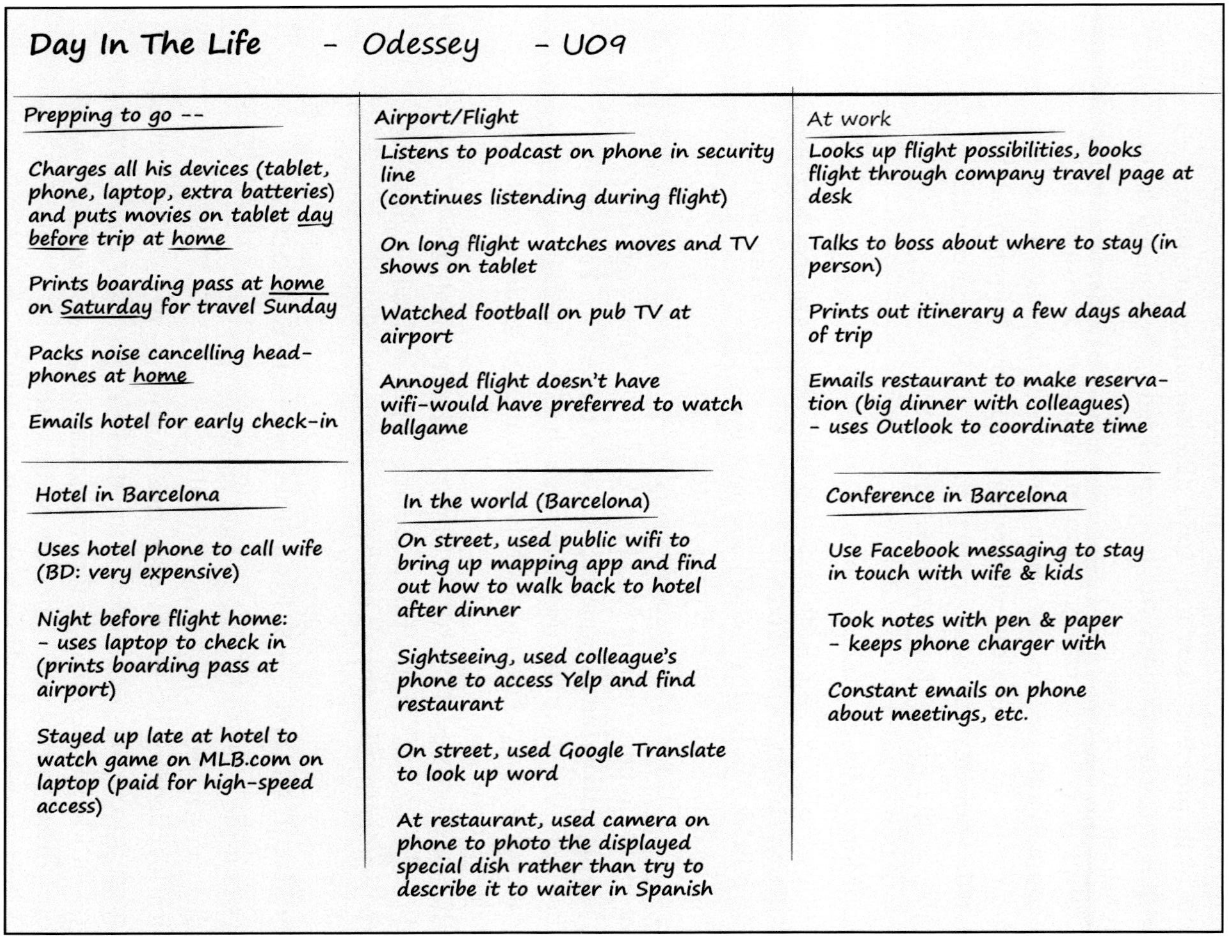

Day In The Life — Odessey — U09

Prepping to go --

Charges all his devices (tablet, phone, laptop, extra batteries) and puts movies on tablet day before trip at home

Prints boarding pass at home on Saturday for travel Sunday

Packs noise cancelling head-phones at home

Emails hotel for early check-in

Hotel in Barcelona

Uses hotel phone to call wife (BD: very expensive)

Night before flight home:
- uses laptop to check in (prints boarding pass at airport)

Stayed up late at hotel to watch game on MLB.com on laptop (paid for high-speed access)

Airport/Flight

Listens to podcast on phone in security line (continues listening during flight)

On long flight watches moves and TV shows on tablet

Watched football on pub TV at airport

Annoyed flight doesn't have wifi—would have preferred to watch ballgame

In the world (Barcelona)

On street, used public wifi to bring up mapping app and find out how to walk back to hotel after dinner

Sightseeing, used colleague's phone to access Yelp and find restaurant

On street, used Google Translate to look up word

At restaurant, used camera on phone to photo the displayed special dish rather than try to describe it to waiter in Spanish

At work

Looks up flight possibilities, books flight through company travel page at desk

Talks to boss about where to stay (in person)

Prints out itinerary a few days ahead of trip

Emails restaurant to make reserva-tion (big dinner with colleagues) - uses Outlook to coordinate time

Conference in Barcelona

Use Facebook messaging to stay in touch with wife & kids

Took notes with pen & paper - keeps phone charger with

Constant emails on phone about meetings, etc.

FIGURE 7.3 Notes for the Day-in-the-Life Model captured from one interview.

the Travel Project Day-in-the-Life Model as an example (Fig. 7.1). This is a more complex model than you may have for your project, but it illustrates the same key principles. (See a blank background for typical enterprise or consumer work in Fig. 7.7).

The model is organized at the high level into the main contexts of life that are relevant to the travel activity. Looking at the gray rectangles structuring the drawing you can see three big phases in the practice: Planning, On the Way, and During the trip. Note that most other Day-in-the-Life Models will not have phases like this! It happened to be useful to think of travel planning this way. Most projects aren't so dominated by a time sequence, but they are still likely to have three to four main locations laid out across the page.

One of the insights of the team is that travel planning is never over—even while the trip is happening the travelers are planning that evening's meal and the next day's activities. The large white arrows in the model show the flow of the trip: there and back again. People travel in different vehicles so we showed these between the arrows to tell the story of activities done on the way.

Within each gray section the graphic tells the story of what happens in that place or during that time. Travel planning at home, the orange bubble, contains text chunks describing what people did at home. Similarly, the other gray sections tell the story of important travel activity on the way and during the trip.

Every large graphic element tells a coherent story about the user's life

So just like an Affinity, the Day-in-the-Life Model has layers of structure. Instead of a hierarchy the graphic is a framework for understanding the practice. The gray rectangles provide the primary structure, breaking the model into three parts. Each part has a unique graphical representation—for example, the orange bubble as shown in Fig. 7.4. The graphic in turn contains story elements chunked into rectangles necessary for understanding the issues in that section. The labels on each text chunk focus the reader on what matters. The text stories are structured in paragraphs revealing each key point the team wants to highlight.

The question bubbles scattered across the graphic are stimulus devices to provide a Way In to the model.

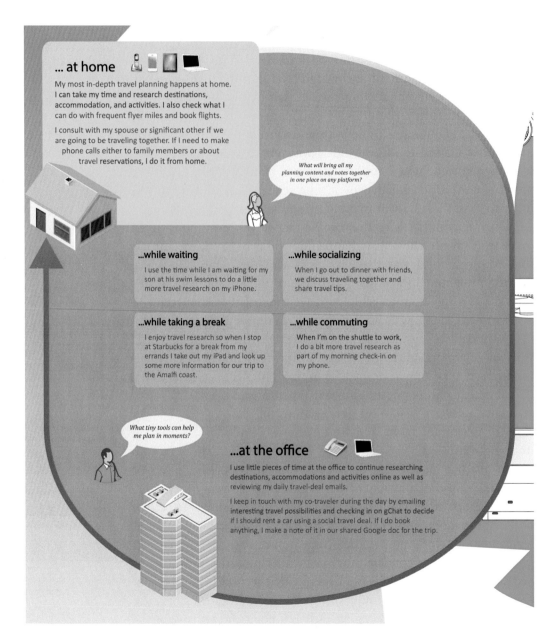

FIGURE 7.4   A portion of a Day-in-the-Life Model showing how travel planning fits into life, in different locations and on a range of devices.

The power of the Day-in-the-Life Model is that the structure and layout of the graphic itself allows the reader to take in the life practice in one sweeping view—then with that framework, they can drill down into the detailed stories. Now let's discuss how to build it.

Create the graphic framework.   The first step in consolidation is to identity the best framework to use to collect individual data stories. The internal elements of the framework naturally bubble up during interpretation and consolidation. Pick a starting structure for your Interpretation Session and let it evolve as you interpret. When you consolidate, look across your individual models to quickly identify key large organizing contexts (home, commute, work) and get a hint of the internal elements (time of day, location, meeting type) that might be relevant within the larger context. This is your entering framework for consolidation.

The graphic layout will either help or hinder design thinking

The exact structure of the graphic will either help or hinder design thinking so it is important to get it right. The overall form of the model above was developed through exhaustive iterations with our teams, so please copy it! Then, if all your data fits into the home–commute–work skeleton we provided, you are done.

Collect observations into the framework.   Once you have a workable framework, start consolidating your individual data onto it. In the Affinity, the individual data was the observations on sticky notes; in the Day-in-the-Life Model, the data are the small, focused activities which occur throughout the day in different places, at different times, on different platforms. For example, when studying travel planning, we saw a user pass the time waiting for her son's swim lesson by researching possible destinations on her iPhone. This is a small, self-contained activity, easy to interrupt and easy to pick up again, which might happen at many points throughout the day. These are the type of activity stories you wrote into your individual interpretation models.

Look for the best stories by selecting six individual models with the greatest ink density—the most observations and the most written into each section. Include those that cover all the sections relevant for your framework. Then, working in a small team, collect the observations section by section. Write a few words about the story and where to find it on a sticky note and put it on the relevant part of the framework. Walk the individual models in turn, collecting observations, writing them down, and posting them on the framework. Or work in parallel: assign two to three people to each large section and have everyone collect stories simultaneously.

Start with six individual models with the most detail and observations

You may find that stories group together, creating possible subgroups within one area of the framework. In home, for example, several stories might happen first thing in the morning. Collect these together in the Home section. Physical places like the coffee shop may have multiple stories, so collect them into a coffee shop place in In-the-World. Be literal with place—don't create a "leisure place" that groups coffee shop stories with those at the gym. The Day-in-the-Life Model needs to evoke real life, and in real life, no abstract "leisure place" exists! These subgroups might represent physical place, time of day, and type of thing the user is doing.

Once you have collected and roughly grouped your stories, check the rest of the individual models and harvest any other good stories. Look for new internal groupings. When you are done, you will have collected all the stories which are now contenders to be included in the model—but more importantly, you will have found the key distinctions you need to raise up within the large framework. Now you can really tell the story of daily life and your target activity.

What are your key insights? Intentionally choose the message to communicate.

Choose the message and the stories. Once you have collected the key observations, you have to decide what message you want to communicate. What does the data tell you? What are the key chunks needed to tell the stories that the team must consider? What are the best stories? Go place by place (Home, Work, Commute, In-the-World) and decide what story you want to tell in each place. You won't keep all the data—look at each piece and decide if it's worth telling. Is it new and unknown? Is it insightful? Does it tell about a unique aspect of the activity? Is it especially characteristic? Is there no place else to show the information? Is it a good example of a key strategy? Will it drive design thinking? You are using the model to tell a story, and any story is defined as much by what you leave out as what you keep in.

Bring your insights together, defining the sub-structure of each key place and the story you want to tell about it. Write a text block to tell each piece of the story. Decide on its location and how to graphically represent it. Label each section with the key distinction you are highlighting. This helps to define the structure of the model and provides the information in bite-sized chunks. In our travel model, we collected observations of quick research done to fill up time while waiting. This insight (Fig. 7.4) is represented as a rectangle within the orange home bubble labeled "*...while waiting.*" We chose the story about doing research during a child's swim lesson as a characteristic example. The label focuses the reader on the need to design for dead time; the story of a specific activity suggests a class of activities that might be supported. We did not attempt to abstract or cover all instances we observed— instead, we provided a characteristic example to communicate the behavior in a lively way designers can connect with viscerally.

Pick and choose—don't try to put every detail on the model.

Once the insights are identified and written as stories, organize them into the full Day-in-the-Life Model by sticking them onto a wall-size skeleton. Now you are ready for final communication design.

Communication design.   Using a variant of our Day-in-the-Life Model templates, tune it for your stories and framework. Remember, the fundamentals of communication design are built into our graphics, which have been iterated with design teams. We honed the layout, structure, color, text size, graphic elements illustrating places, and everything else to drive design thinking.[1] We use bold colors (never pastels), white space, limited story chunks in sections, and short word counts to ensure that readers can move

---

[1] The Day-in-the-Life is structured left to right typically from home through commute to work or another context. Left to right and clockwise movement is normal reading flow for North America and many countries. If this is not true for your region create a variant guided by the principles.

through the model easily. Everything is designed to easily engage the team who will use the data in ideation.

In communication design, less is more. Force yourselves to hone your message, to pick the best stories. Don't try to tell everything just because it happened. You are designing with the design relevance of the data in mind. Crowded information is overwhelming. If your model's structure is unclear, it likely has no real framework. This will not help the team engage with the data or stimulate design thinking. If you vary the layout to modify core places be sure that you don't add too many and that they are key for the target activity.

> *In communication design, less is more. Choose your data and be succinct*

Introductory text is written at the top of each gray rectangle to provide an overview and the key insights related to that section (Fig. 7.5). Similarly the dominant graphic in a section like the orange home bubble has introductory text to focus the reader. Keep the stories

Planning the trip

The preparation for both weekend getaways and longer vacations is woven throughout the weeks and months before departure. This preparation includes research and conversations with fellow travelers during dedicated travel-planning time. This is usually done at home on a laptop or tablet to take advantage of the bigger screen size and because many sites still aren't optimized for mobile.

... at home

My most in-depth travel planning happens at home. I can take my time and research destinations, accommodation, and activities. I also check what I can do with frequent flyer miles and book flights.

I consult with my spouse or significant other if we are going to be traveling together. If I need to make phone calls either to family members or about travel reservations, I do it from home.

FIGURE 7.5   Introductory text makes it easy to see at a glance what a section of the model is about.

short, pithy, and to the point. Be ruthless about eliminating stories that may be interesting in themselves but do not drive design action.

Now design the *Way In*. Like the Affinity, the Day-in-the-Life Model graphic structure draws the readers through the diagram allowing them to absorb the story in a flow. But to help the reader engage and bridge from data to design we include design questions throughout the diagram. See the examples in our models. To create these, look at each part of the model and ask yourself: What are the design issues here? What does the team need to consider? Write questions that will provoke answers to these questions. Remember these are not design ideas—they are challenge questions for the team (Fig. 7.6).

These questions give designers an initial focus when looking at the model—an entry point for thinking about the implications of the data, highlighting what the team thinks matters to the design. From there, designers can jump off to think about other implications—and they can ignore the questions entirely if they wish. The question bubbles stand as an example of how to use the data. We have found

> *Designing question bubbles help the reader find a way to engage the data.*

that the simple addition of these questions has dramatically increased the number of design ideas generated for each model.[2]

The questions also support *interaction* with the data. They give the readers a challenge while walking the data that will help them generate design ideas for the Wall Walk (Fig. 7.7).

FIGURE 7.6 A question placed on the model to spur design thinking.

---

[2] The final design of each of the graphics for the Contextual Design models was iterated with users in Visioning Sessions. After their early use we talked about what worked and didn't, where participants were confused, and what models prompted the most design ideas. The structures of the models we present as a standard part of Contextual Design have stood the test of successful use.

Unstoppable Momentum of Life: My work day

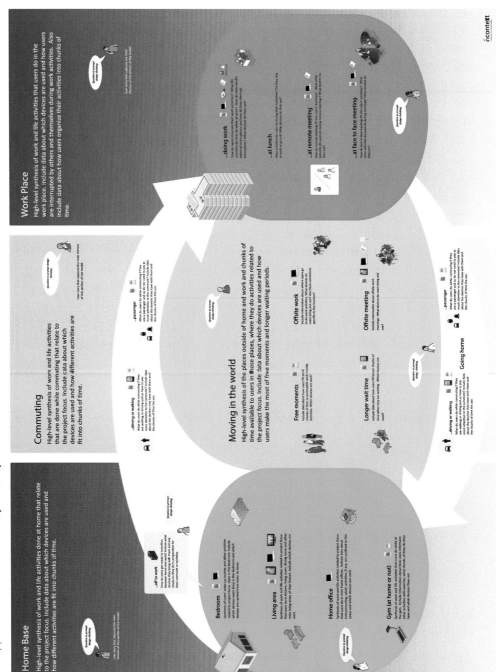

FIGURE 7.7 A blank template suitable for many business products.

Working in teams

As with the Affinity Diagram, consolidating the Day-in-the-Life Model and all other Contextual Design Experience models is best done in a set of small groups working in the same space. This facilitates communication about the data—at least in the beginning. Manipulating the data and structuring it for insight creates an immersion experience for those who did not go on interviews, so it's a good opportunity for them. Sub-teams of two to three people can be assigned to each model to do the first layer of work. Or the team can work simultaneously on one model, the Day-in-the-Life Model for example, assigning the work of collecting instances for the key places to sub-teams. In either event all work is shared in a review with others to tune ideas and how the model is presented.

Work together in parallel on multiple models to facilitate data sharing

This pattern of breaking the work into sub-teams, whose work is later reviewed, is standard for Contextual Design. Often we also mix up members of the sub-teams so everyone feels ownership for the whole result. Working together in a room in parallel creates a feeling of teamwork and allows for easy conversation to answer questions and get feedback. Once the basic framework and insight for any model is established, two-person teams can finish on their own, So sub-teams can be in different locations and, depending on the stage of consolidation collaboration, may be remote even within the sub-team.

The work goes smoothly when everyone knows what to do, what constitutes a good job, can reference examples, are guided by metrics for the work, and feel that what they are doing is important. Though some people may be better at writing, others at labeling, and others at identifying insight, this won't matter if the team pulls together to get the work done. Leaning on everyone's strengths while working in a well-defined process is a core tenant of Contextual Design. If you put everyone to work on a model in parallel, a first-cut consolidation can be ready within a few hours. Then it can be handed off to one sub-team to finish.

Breaking up the work to lean on everyone's strengths creates quality

We will note how sub-teams work together as we describe each model.

THE IDENTITY MODEL

The Cool Concept of Identity focuses us on collecting data that uncovers the sources of pride, self-expression, and core values. These reveal the person's core identity elements associated with the target activity. When a product reflects and enhances one's sense of identity we found that people experience it as cooler and more essential. When a product undermines identity, which always includes the feeling of competency, the product is very uncool. Knowing the identity elements lets us design user experience that touches people's core motives and will be profoundly valued.

To see this view of the users' world, we created the *Identity Model*. This model (Fig. 7.8) shows the identity elements of the market as relevant to your target activity. These are the aspects of users' personal identity that matter to your design. So a doctor takes pride in being knowledgeable, but a shopper may value himself for getting the best deal, a travel planner defines success creating the best trip for everyone in the family, and a sales person is doing the job right if they are available 24/7. Each activity in life comes with its own set of identity elements.

Find your identity elements—the source of pride, self-expression, and value

When we depend on technology as a partner in getting our lives done, how the product affects our sense of self is core to the overall experience. The Identity Model reveals these aspects of self so that designers can build to them explicitly. We typically identify 8–12 identity elements that characterize a market. No one will manifest them all; most people will be dominated by only a few. But taken together they describe the core elements the team should focus on.

We recommend the Identity Model be considered for every project. Like the Day-in-the-Life Model, it is a basic big-picture model that aids design and market positioning and messaging. Anytime a project has a branding goal or wants to characterize the people in the market this is the best model to use. Our teams have been loving it.

Identity Model

FIGURE 7.8   A full Identity Model for travel showing the three sections "I am," "I plan," and "I like."

"If I'm going shopping, I find my husband a museum nearby—and everyone has a good time."

Master Planner

I love to plan trips for my family and friends. I like the challenge of managing our schedule and budget to get the very best travel experience possible. I get emails about travel and bookmark a bunch of great sites for travel information, but I'm always looking for new sources of travel tips and info. It's really important to me that everyone has a good time and gets to do the things they really want to do.

Give Me

- Allow me to create multiple "what-if" variations of a trip so I can experiment with different options for flights, accommodations, etc. for my traveling companions and myself.
- Allow me to search based on location and time – so if I'm here at this time, what's nearby and available

"If I can't find a good deal then I'm not doing it."

Deal Hunter

I know that there are good deals out there. It just makes sense to plan my trips around deals, special offers and using travel points. I like the challenge of getting the best deal and have lots of ways to find out what's available. Subscribing to deal emails for interesting places helps me learn about fun things to see and do, AND I always know I'm getting the most bang for my travel buck. If I feel like I haven't gotten a good price it ruins the trip for me.

Give Me

- Show the average price paid for this type of service to show what I'm saving compared to others
- Show my all time best deals so I can relive the thrill and so I have something to "beat". Give "awards" or "trophies" to people who get the best deal on a flight, hotel, activity, etc.
- Show me a running total for the cost of my trip as I try out different configurations for flights, hotels, dates, etc. Alert me when I have gotten to a great price.

"I'm not a tourist."

Culture Sponge

When I travel I want to have authentic experiences, I didn't come all this way to eat at a McDonald's. I decide on travel destinations and accommodations based on what will allow me to really be part of the place I'm visiting. I love just walking around a city and soaking up all the sights and sounds. I don't do guided tours, I'd much rather just explore the place myself. I'll get a guidebook if I want to find out more.

Give Me

- Tell me about locals-only hangouts and places that are off the beaten path
- Help me visit the main sights without feeling like a tourist. Suggest a cultural twist or unique local perspective to enhance the experience
- For any street or location, give me a cultural overview of the immediate surroundings that includes history, recent mentions in local media, and events happening here

"I'm a beach person."
"I have to get out of the cold."
"It's all about comfort – we don't camp."

My Kinda Place

I know what I like. If I'm going to go some place, I want to be comfortable and be able to do the kinds of things that I like doing. There are certain things that are just non-negotiable when I'm choosing a destination. I don't mind going to the same place every year if it's got what I'm looking for.

Give Me

- Let me set acceptable thresholds for criteria that matter to me: Comfort, destination climate, travel distance/time, and only show me trips meeting my criteria
- Let me read other people's Trip Advisor reviews and then give them the thumbs up or thumbs down – like Pandora – to zero in on what I like

"I want to have my own experience."

Me, Myself and I

Travel is a personal experience. There is so much to take-in; I don't want to be distracted by other people. Museums are the worst when you feel like you have to look at each piece for the same amount of time as the person you are there with – I'd so much rather go alone. It's also just easier. I only have to worry about me.

Give Me

- Focus on the "single traveler" experience when making suggestions – beyond helping me meet other travelers. Anticipate what will enrich my experience.
- Show me deals, ticket to events, and reservations at popular restaurants that wouldn't be available to a group, but have space for an individual.

I like

(Characterizing what I like when engaging in this activity)

FIGURE 7.8 Cont'd

COLLECTING THE DATA

Identity focuses the interviewer on uncovering how a product enhances or detracts from a person's sense of self. In many activities, aspects of the user's sense of self get bound up in the things they do and use: I don't just do surgery—I'm a healer. Her first flat screen TV was cool because: "I bought it with my own money!" She was proud of her emerging adulthood. A librarian loved Amazon because it enhanced her competence as a librarian: "I can find any out-of-print book the professional staff wants."

Start the user thinking with you about identity from the start of the interview

For any activity, people have a set of identity elements which bolster their sense of self. The interviewer's job is to find those elements and raise them to awareness. Understanding the elements of identity for a user population allows designers to generate product ideas that are not just accepted but loved.

To find out about identity, introduce the idea of identity elements right at the beginning of the interview. Don't worry if the user has difficulty articulating anything clear at this point. Most of the real data will emerge later, as users do the target activity, especially on seeing their emotional reactions. This initial conversation will sensitize the users to the concept so they can recognize it when it shows up. You are looking for indications of pride, of feeling good about oneself generally, or of how they feel the product fits their unique self. These reactions can be blatant or mild, but they all indicate where the user is personally invested.

A good stimulus to find identity elements during the traditional interview step in the Contextual Interview might be something such as the following:

General: "We all have different aspects of self and feel god about ourselves when we feel like our best possible self—and we don't like it when things prevent us from being our best. Our tools can help us be our best self. Tell me how you think of yourself when doing this activity."

Travel: "We all have 'who we are' as a traveler. A trip is comfortable if we can plan it and do it the way that feels right for us. Some people are always looking for an adventure—others like everything planned to a 'T.' Do you have a feel for how you think of yourself when traveling or doing travel planning?"

Automobile: "Cars are kind of like clothes—we know when we put something on if just feels like me—and other clothes aren't like me. Tell me about how your car reveals who you are."

Shopping: "Everyone orients to shopping differently. Some people are deal hunters, almost like it's a game; others just want to get what they want and be done. How do you feel about shopping?"

It helps when you have a few examples or a metaphor to get the user going. Once users figure out what you mean by "identity element," they can talk about it. When you see their excitement, personal investment, or disgust during the interview, you'll know you have hit on one of these identity elements. At that point, share

GATHERING IDENTITY DATA IN A CONTEXTUAL INTERVIEW

In the introduction, stimulate awareness of identity elements with words such as the following:
- We all have different aspects of self. We feel good when we feel we are our best possible self—and we don't like it when tools make us feel bad about ourselves!
- We have different identity elements for different activities. For example, while planning vacations we might see ourselves as the Master Planner or the Deal Maker. How you orient to_____? (target activity)

During the interview:
- Look for sources of pride.
- Listen for how products increase or decrease the sense of pride, competency, or well-being.
- See how a product helps the person be their best selves by fulfilling core values and roles.
- Try to name the identity element.
- Discuss your interpretation as you go.

your interpretation, try to name the identity element, and see how the user responds. Let them tune the name. For example here is a woman talking about her vacation.

> **U:** *"I'm not a tourist." "I want to go somewhere off the beaten path and interact with the locals. I want to know the particular history of the place and see sights others don't know exist."*

> **I:** *"It's like you want to immerse yourself in the local culture." "Like you're an anthropologist."*

> **U:** *"That's too analytical." "I just want to be in there, soaking up the culture."*

> **I:** *"Like a cultural sponge."*

> **U:** *"Yeah, just like that."*

We have many identity elements—find the ones relevant to your target activity

We all have many identity elements: Mom, Dad, Grandma, Teacher, Developer, Manager—the ones we are aware of. But we also have a set of identity elements associated with driving, shopping, doing taxes, our professional self, and more. When you collect this type of data from multiple users you will be able to see the identity elements that characterize your market and show you the experience you want to enhance.

Capturing during the Interpretation Session

The Identity Model represents a set of identity elements. We have found that these elements will generally fall into three groups: I do, I am, and one or two others specific to the people being characterized (Fig. 7.9).

- *I do* refers to identity elements related to doing the work of the target activity. You may rename this to be more specific to your topic—so "I plan" is related to travel, but "I audit" might appear in an auditing project or "I drive" for an auto project.

- *I am* refers to how the person approaches the activity. "I am adventurous," for example, in travel; but "I am an expert juggler" of tasks for audit. These identity elements are more likely to transcend the target activity, reflecting attributes of the person in many walks of life.

- The identity group specific to the project will bubble up out of the data. "I like" bubbled up for the travel project because people were attached at their core to the kind of things they liked to do. "In my organization" was better for auditing, because identity elements appeared that had to do with their larger role within the company; and for auto "The car is me" worked better.

At the beginning of the Interpretation Session, put a framework up on a flip chart dividing the Identity Model into possible sections, leaving space for things to emerge. If you have a guess at a third one put it up as a place holder.

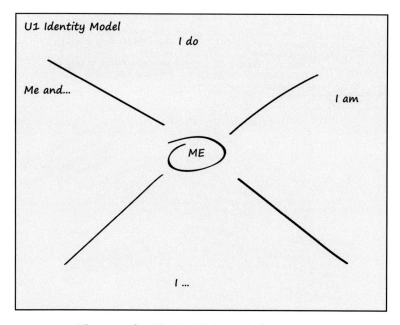

FIGURE 7.9 The parts of an Identity Model, ready for an Interpretation Session to capture the data.

When data comes out that speaks to identity, write it up on the model in whichever section feels best. Write phrases; include quotes and points of pride. Include enough context about the situation so the underlying story is clear—*this is critical for later consolidation*:

• "It's up to me to make sure everything in the trip goes smoothly—then when it does, I feel great!"

• "I'd never have a car with those silly LED headlights. That's just not me."

• "Two days before the surgery, I check to make sure everything's ready and accounted for. I know other people are checking, and I looked last week myself. I check again anyway. That's because I'm responsible."

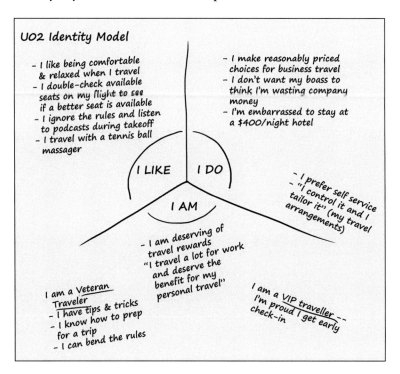

FIGURE 7.10   An Identity Model as captured for one user during the Interpretation Session.

• "If the numbers aren't right I'm not doing my job, so I check and double check—I'm not letting something out the door that's wrong!"

Write it in such a way that it sounds like you are talking about identity, not about an action they took. If it's apparent that there's an identity element and you can name it easily, write the name. But don't struggle—if you feel that the data speaks to identity write it down even if you're not yet ready to identify the identity element. That will happen later. And remember everyone is acting out of their identity—there is no such thing as a person having no identity elements. Either you didn't collect the data or you didn't listen closely to their experience (Fig. 7.10).

Capture feeling phrases not actions—identity reveals emotional investment

CONSOLIDATING THE IDENTITY MODEL

The Identity Model is a graphical rendering of the identity elements the team identified. They emerge from the grouping of the phrases collected and recorded during the Interpretation Session. Let's look the Travel Identity Model for an example.

As we already discussed, the model is broken into three or four sections, which are the top-level structure of the model. Within each section, the next level of structure is the *identity elements* themselves.

We show these as bubbles describing the identity elements as small stories. The identity element name—the most important focusing element of the model—evokes the experience of the users. The tagline spoken by the head on each bubble is the "elevator pitch" for immediate recognition of the core of the identity element by the reader. In this model, we use design ideas, "Give Me's," as the Way In. See Fig. 7.11.

FIGURE 7.11   One identity element from the travel Identity Model. The "Give Me" design ideas act as starting points for the team's own design thinking. Note how they respond directly to the special concerns of the Cultural Sponge.

Collect observation into potential identity elements.   The job of consolidation is to find the aspects of self which go together to create an identity element. As always the process is bottom-up, grouping sets of observations that go together thematically and experientially among those captured during Interpretation Sessions. During interpretation you may have already been sorting observations into potential elements; you may have candidate names. Also, possible new sections may have emerged. So the team has a lot to go on once all interviews are interpreted.

To do the consolidation, start with six of the most detailed models as we did for Day-in-the-Life Model. Break into groups of two to three people each with a few of the models. Walk the statements of identity from the individual models you were assigned, looking across each section for common statements. Group similar statements together and give them a name. As you group them, keep in mind that these are aspects of self, not behaviors. They should complete the sentence of the potential sections, "I *am* a…" without sounding trivial: "I *am*… someone who stands up in the plane when I travel." Nope, that's a behavior, not a core aspect of self. "I *am*… someone who is embarrassed to spend $400 a night for a hotel on a business trip. I don't waste corporate money." That might work.

Identity Model consolidation is a process of collecting like phrases and naming the element

Once the sub-teams have contender identity elements with preliminary names put them on sticky notes and post them on a flip chart. Now as a team, step back and review them. Combine those that are really the same and eliminate the ones that are trivial to produce a reasonable, manageable set. You shouldn't have more than 6–12 in all, and they should both characterize the market and challenge design thinking.

Name the identity element. Now the team must choose the names for the elements. Getting the name right is the hardest part. The name must evoke the inner experience in someone who did not collect the data. If the name evokes the wrong experience—something other than what the data says—then it is not a good name. Remember this is not about logic. The name carries meaning and feeling, and no reading of the text below it will undo the impact of the name if it's wrong. So getting the name right is a key challenge.

The name must naturally evoke the feelings and values described in the text

Look at the statements that make up an identity element grouping. Think about the best name to focus people on the real experience of pride, competency, and value that you felt during interviews. Read the observations over and over until the right words jump out. Brainstorm a list of possible names together. When the right one emerges you will know; it will feel like it fits the actual people you interviewed who manifest that identity element.

Good names sound a bit like titles. For example, "Cultural Sponge," rather than a verb phrase like, "Loves to Visit Other Cultures." Here's a list of observations coming from multiple users in the travel project. What's the best name for this identity element?

- I love to plan

- Planning is like a hobby—figuring it out is fun!

- I make a spreadsheet of everything we should do to figure out the days

- I collect great ideas of where to go on trips over the year

- I figure out the best ways to get there and best places to eat and stay

- I organize trips for my group of friends

"Trip Planner" describes the behavior but not the feeling behind it.[3] "Grand Organizer" overemphasizes the organization part. "Trip Wizard" demotes the planning behavior too much. "Hobby Travel Agent" suggests an element of service that is not quite right. We picked "Master Planner." It has the planning which evokes organizational skill, but the word "master" connotes pride in being that wizard with trips, but brings along the sense of the in-charge person for the trip. It raises up the person as a *master*—like a martial arts black belt. The word "master" communicates the pride element of this identity element.

Pick your names with care. The words you use are powerful communicators of implied feeling and values. They resonate with the inner experience of the reader calling up their own interpretation. Be sure that the words you use evoke the understanding and feeling you intend.

Put the elements in the background sections. Try different groupings of the identity elements to decide on how to place them the background. Like collecting blue sticky notes under

---

[3] For those who read the first edition of this book, this is a good example of the difference between a role name on the Flow Model and an identity element. "Trip Planner" would be a fine role name.

pinks, the identity elements must fit sensibly into their sections. "I am" and "I do" will always be there, but you will have to discover what additional sections might be useful and what to name them. You want at least two identity elements in each section.

Put like elements within each section with an eye toward balance—two to five in each

In the travel example, "I am" connotes self-image: I can pick up and go to Macchu Picchu on a moment's notice; or, I travel for the adventure others can't handle; or, I create mind-broadening experiences for my whole family.

"I do" is tied to the target activity directly. For travel, "I plan" connotes how I approach the planning. Like a Master Planner, on top of every detail and option, loving the fun of investigating. Or the people who are driven to get the absolute most from every penny—"Europe on $5 a Day has nothing on me." That's the Deal Hunter and it would go under "I do" as well.

The other sections emerge when you find elements that don't fit "I am" or "I do." In the Travel Project, we had the "Cultural Sponge" element. Is it really expressing an element of self, like the other "I am" elements do? It's certainly not an "I do" element, but it is tied to the target activity. It says what kind of trip fits with the person's sense of self—with what they value. So we combined it with two other elements that had to do with the kind of trip—"My Kinda Place" and "Me, Myself, and I"—and created an "I like" section of the model to talk about how the sense of identity affects the kind of vacation a person looks for.

Now you are ready to draw your sections and lay out the identity elements each in the appropriate section.

Communication design. Communication design of the graphic for the Identity Model is easy. Just put your elements and other parts of the graphic into our templates, changing the number and placement of bubbles as you need to. The hard part is writing the story text and tagline to evoke the desired experience and to draw the reader in.

The narrative should reflect the core motives, values, and specific details of how the identity element drives behaviors and choices.

Specifics are combined from the multiple users that were the source for the element. Fig. 7.11 shows an example.

Create a short direct narrative describing core motives, values, and related actions

Use direct, personal language written from the point of view of the user, and speak directly to the reader. "I want authentic experiences." Incorporate users' actual words into the narrative: "I didn't come all this way to eat at McDonald's." Use emotional language that is true to the users' experience: I love this, I'd never do that, I find this tremendous, exciting, exhilarating. Avoid neutral, "objective" bureaucratese: "User finds diverse experiences preferable." Such language does not communicate the feeling of users' lives.

With a name and a narrative, you now need a catchphrase. The catchphrase is the team's key insight about this identity element. It is written as though spoken by the user, summarizing the user's emotion around the identity element. The catchphrase frames the reading of the story focusing the designers on the most relevant aspect of the emotional experience. For the Cultural Sponge:

"I'm not a tourist."

It's hard to design for feelings—"Give Me's" are examples to get you started

Finally, add a Way In. Other models use design questions but the Identity Model is more abstract and we find direct suggestions more useful: Give me this. Do that for me. Write two or three such design suggestions for each identity element. They don't have to be great ideas—they just have to respond to the actual data. The design team may love them or hate them but either way, they'll think about how they relate to the narrative and that will start the wheels turning. Note in Fig. 7.12, how the ideas on the model directly address the desire to immerse in local culture.

MODELING CONNECTION

Almost any activity involves other people. The Cool Concept of Connection says that feeling close to the people who matter, being able to touch them easily, gives people joy. We found two aspects of Connection that shouldn't be conflated: the real relationships in the user's world, and the collaboration between people to get things done. Tools can enhance or detract from both kinds of connection. They can enhance the joy of living in the world with others as well.

The initial concept of connection emerged from interviews with consumers, during life outside of work. We found that cool tools help people feel connected to the people that matter to them in three important ways: *frequent contact*, *things to talk about*, and *things to do together*. These three dimensions of connection help us feel known and a part of the lives of friends, family, and coworkers. To support this aspect of life we created *The Relationship Model*.

The Relationship Model shows how close relationships are woven into life

But when we studied enterprise workers the power of smooth collaboration emerged as a second factor in a product's coolness. Communicating and coordinating with others at work, or during any complex activity involving multiple people, affects the feeling of being in the world with other people successfully, being up to something together. Smooth communication and coordination, easy checking in on how a team or coworker is doing, feeling professional on the team—these all contribute to the feeling of connection, and to the successful achievement of the joint activity of the team. We created the Collaboration Model to reveal these additional aspects of Connection.

The Collaboration Model shows how people stay in touch and coordinate to increase involvement

Taken together, both models help teams enhance the feeling of being in the world with others. Depending on the project, one or both models may be used. Nearly any business tool has dimensions of collaboration to be supported. Nearly any consumer tool plays a role in enhancing involvement with the core people in one's life. Online communities focused explicitly on connection like

Facebook and Pinterest will benefit from both models. Some projects may not need either model. For example, interactions with others are simply not dominant for drivers and the important points about connection can be captured in the Affinity Diagram.

Depending on the project focus, one or both of the connection models may be appropriate, but often we can't tell which is most important until we collect the data. So listen for relationship and collaboration—in the end they will both broaden your focus and yield the data you need to find the connection delighters. We will deal with each model in turn.

THE RELATIONSHIP MODEL

COLLECTING THE DATA

To design for the real relationships in a person's life, we have to find them first. For the Relationship Model, listen for how other people play a part in the user's life and the level of emotional connection the user has with them. Listen for both personal and professional relationships as they participate in and influence the target activity. Once you've heard enough to know some of the people important to the target activities, chart out those relationships with the user (see Fig. 7.12). Get the user to talk about how close they feel to each person and what their role is in the activity; let them add more people as prompted by the discussion. In the remainder of the interview, still more people may be added as they come up. Pay attention to who is central to the activity and why—what does the user do with them, and why are they important emotionally? Note the conversational content, the topics they discuss, and information they exchange. Note the activities they do together. Note whether interaction is face-to-face or remote. And try to find out why some are felt to be closer than others.

Pay attention to who is central to the activity and why—what increases connection?

COLLECTING DATA FOR THE RELATIONSHIP MODEL IN A CONTEXTUAL INTERVIEW

Listen for other people involved in the activity.
- Who that person is and their role
- How often that person is touched as part of the activity
- What information or conversational content is shared as part of the activity
- How decision-making is impacted
- How the activity promotes doing things together

Look at the level of intimacy or importance of the person.
- Both relative to the activity and in life
- How the interactions of the activity promote or damage the relationship
- Note what contributes to closeness (history, frequency, multiple shared interests)

Draw a preliminary relationship model as you go.

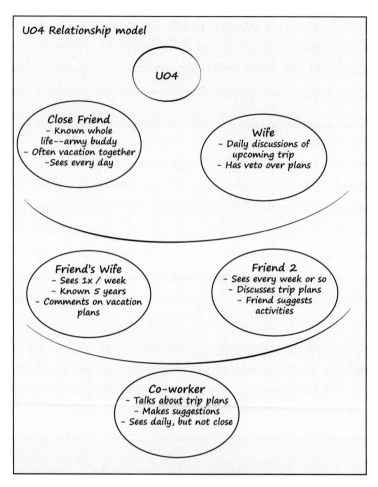

FIGURE 7.12   Relationship information captured during an interview. Farther from the user implies more emotional distance. The interviewer and user worked together to decide where the various people in the user's life should go to illustrate closeness. Activities and feelings about that person relative to the activity are captured in the bubble.

The Relationship Model shows who is important in the user's world from the point of view of the activity to be supported. People build up networks of relationships and depend on them for support, advice, and assistance throughout their lives. The Relationship Model reveals this support network. The core background structure reflects the experience of connection and is used during the interview, the Interpretation Session, and for consolidation.

CAPTURING DURING THE INTERPRETATION SESSION

Whether or not you captured a Relationship Model during the interview, you want to record the model full-size on a flip chart sheet. That way all models look the same—easier for consolidation—and the process of writing the model will lead to more inquiry and more data being captured than if you just accept the interviewer's model with no real interpretation.[4]

If data on relationship doesn't come up naturally during the Interpretation Session, just capture it at the end. Talk back over the user's relationships—all the people who came up in the story—and write them up in different levels of closeness to the user. Be guided by the interviewer here—they talked to the user and have the best idea of how close the different people are (Fig. 7.13).

Seek relationship data—if it doesn't emerge naturally probe at the end of the interview

CONSOLIDATING THE RELATIONSHIP MODEL

The Relationship Model is a graphical rendering of the layers of relationship, showing how frequency, conversational content, and doing things together play out to create connection. The core organizing structure is three levels of relationship organizing the main relationships and illustrative stories at each level. Individuals from the actual models are grouped into similar kinds of relationship, named, and given a focusing tagline.

Clear structure, sections, and elements make consolidation easy

On the left, overview text introduces the issues, activities, and sources of closeness for each level of relationship. The triangular strip to the far right defines the aspects of closeness that influence the feeling of connection at each level. Question bubbles

---

[4] If you are a very distributed team you may choose to capture this data online in a document structured into the levels of connection. Then you will need to print these with very big font to consolidate. If only one person is remoting in, we recommend capturing data in paper where the rest of the team can watch for quality. It's hard to monitor multiple online models and the Affinity notes.

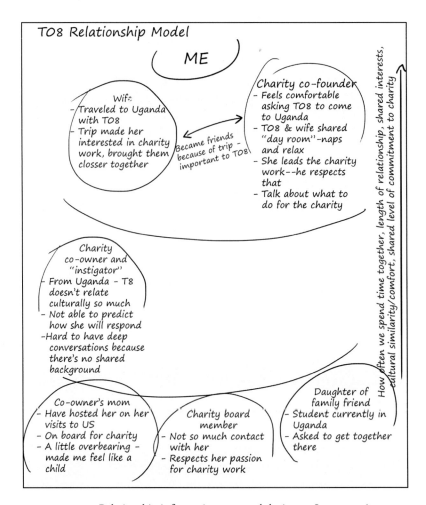

FIGURE 7.13   Relationship information captured during an Interpretation Session. Activities and feelings about that person represented in the bubble are captured along with drivers of intimacy up the side.

throughout provide the Way In. See Fig. 7.14 for the travel relationship model.

Design from this model pushes the team to learn about the players in the activities, and how to better involve and support them so as to increase the feeling of connection in the context of the activity.

As always, small teams start with about six dense, interesting individual relationship models from the interviews. Separate the

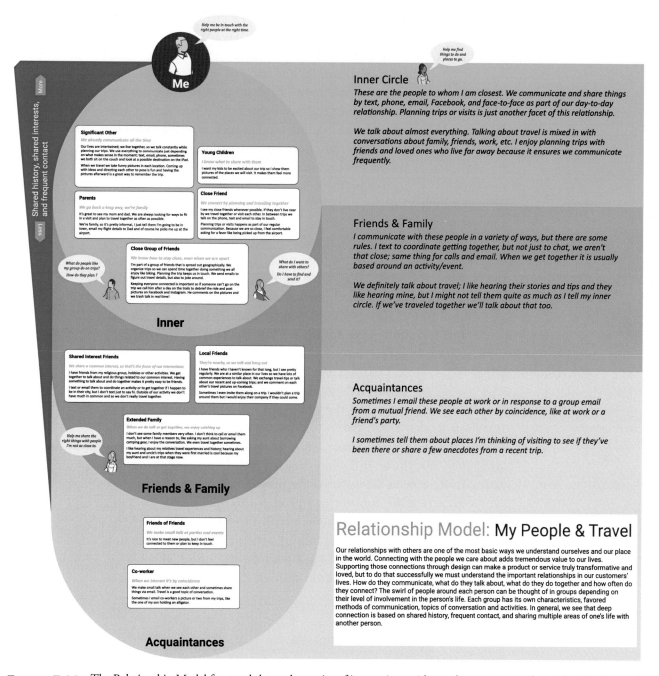

FIGURE 7.14 The Relationship Model for travel shows the stories of interactions with people most intimately involved in the travel planning. The triangle on the side denotes the reasons people feel closer in this context.

people on the models into three levels—intimates, friends, and acquaintances. Very occasionally there will be one outer level for people who are just providers—there's no real long-term relationship, but you may want to show them as part of the story. Often companies think they are central to an activity—this helps them see they are not. The individual models may not have all three levels, or might have more depending on what happened in the interview. You will consolidate it all into these three levels.

Identify the important relationships relevant to the task within each level of intimacy

Then look across the models and identify bubbles (people or groups) who can be consolidated. Because you are representing the relationship, do not consolidate different types of relationship—so even if I go to my spouse for the same type of advice as I get from my childhood friend, keep those bubbles separate on the model. You might, however, consolidate a childhood friend with an army buddy, if both suggest a deep level of intimacy and provide advice. Then the bubble could be called long-term friends.

Collect the best stories into each relationship bubble

Collect stories into each bubble on the developing consolidated model showing what the nature of the relationship is. Show what leads to intimacy in this relationship, or not; show how often they connect and how they connect (face-to-face, email, phone); show what they talk about and what they do together—always emphasizing those aspects relevant to the project focus.

Look across all bubbles from individual models at the same level and write story text characterizing the relationship at that level—writing like the user is talking about their own life including example detail to make that relationship come alive. Then write a tagline for each bubble and introductory text for each level (Fig. 7.15).

FIGURE 7.15   What creates intimacy in this domain? Look at the data and collect the key elements on the left of the model.

Create insights from individual models that will inform the intimacy triangle strip on the far left—what pushes the closeness and differentiates the levels. Identify factors such as frequency of doing this activity with the person, trusted family member, etc. that distinguish why relationships differentiate by level. Put those keywords in the strip along the left.

Add questions to stimulate design thinking—that's your "Way In"

Finally, write your design questions. One or two per level is enough. When you are done, share, review, and update. Then, using this template, put the model online and your communication design is complete (Fig. 7.16).

FIGURE 7.16   One "Way In" question from the Relationship Model.

THE COLLABORATION MODEL

COLLECTING THE DATA

The Collaboration Model reveals how the people in the user's world communicate and coordinate to get activities done, often using technology. The Connection concept also highlights the transformation of life when this coordination can happen with necessary information ready to hand and when people can coordinate instantly to get things done when on the go.

If the project focus involves significant collaboration, build a Collaboration Model. This representation is important when interactions and information must be shared and activities coordinated

Show the communication and coordination between multiple people working together to get something done

among three or more people. If all of the interactions just involve two people, with simple, point-to-point interaction, you only need the Relationship Model. And even if sharing is between the user and a few others, if they are not really working together to get something done the data is best handled in the Relationship Model. The Collaboration Model reveals what is going on when coordination gets more complex—when groups of people come together to plan or do shared activities.[5] Most such projects should choose one of the Connection Models as the best representation of their users' practice.

If you have an activity with a lot of collaboration, users will tell stories of who does what, who called or emailed whom, who shared what with whom, and how they felt about it all. Leaders in the group will want to know the status of other people's assigned tasks—even if it is for an informal activity (like vacation travel). Leisure activities or volunteering in an organization can start to look like real work collaborations. People prepare things for the group to use, lay out schedules and deadlines, and check in with each other as they go along. All of this is core data on collaboration to be collected.

The best data is in the details—so collect anything that might help or hinder collaboration

For the travel project focus, people talked about who they coordinated with and how exploring locations and logistics became a fun and necessary activity that they could do together. We noticed how people took on different roles in planning. Some took over the whole task, collaborating with the other travelers; others continuously consulted with a single partner. Prompt users to talk about the role of technology in making it easy or hard to share important information or coordinate logistics. This is the data you need to better support collaboration—anytime, anywhere, with information at your users' fingertips. If you hear this kind of data, collect it—later you can decide if it will become part of a Collaboration Model or rolled into the stories on the Relationship Model.

---

[5] The Collaboration Model is a variant of the original Flow Model but focused more narrowly on a work group, or small group of people doing something together. If you are familiar with Flow Model consolidation you may apply that thinking here.

COLLECTING COLLABORATION DATA IN A CONTEXTUAL INTERVIEW

Anytime the user interacts with a person for the target activity:

- Discover the communication and coordination between people, identifying the intent of the interaction
- Capture who does what, shares what, and needs what or needs to know information as they go about getting their joint activity done
- Capture what device supports the interactions and where they are when collaborating
- Pay attention to what body of information supports the collaboration, whether shared, co-produced, or used by individuals
- Note what role each person plays in the process—both formal and informal—in helping the collaboration work
- Everyone in the Collaboration Model should also be in the Relationship Model if you are doing both, but not vice versa—the user may be close to a set of people they don't collaborate with in a more complex task.

CAPTURING DURING THE INTERPRETATION SESSION

Instances of collaboration will come up throughout the Interpretation Session. Capture collaborations that are relevant to the project focus and have some complexity. Early on, you won't know about complexity, so just capture all collaborations as they come up. Later you can decide if the complexity or insight is sufficient to warrant creating a real consolidated Collaboration Model.

The format is simple: Each person in the interaction gets a bubble. All communication between people goes on arrows between bubbles. Write what the communication is on the arrows. Make a note of the tool used (email, cell phone, etc.). Write what the people are doing in the bubbles as you go along. Keep each model to a single collaboration surrounding a core intent—the collaboration may have been spread out over days, but it is still a single task or problem being solved with others. The Collaboration Model does not care about time—just who interacted with whom. So you will have more than one collaboration

Draw a different little model for each collaboration that has a different intent

instance if you have multiple intents or different groups of people collaborating for different parts of the activity.

If you get comfortable with this way of representing collaboration, you can use them in the field interview. Capture small drawings of the interaction in your notebook, and use these to talk to the user in more detail about who did what and how well it worked. Let the user correct and extend them with you (Fig. 7.17).

CONSOLIDATING THE COLLABORATION MODEL

Having captured multiple mini-collaboration diagrams you need to decide if they warrant consolidation. If collaboration is central to the design problem and reasonably complex, it's worth building a Collaboration Model. Look across the mini diagrams created in the Interpretation Session. If all interactions are between the interviewee and one other person, collaboration is not complex. Simple collaboration can be captured well enough on the Relationship Model, Day-in-the-Life Model, or on the Affinity. In this case, just use the mini diagrams a source of stories for these other representations.

Look at the complexity of the interactions, then decide whether to build a Collaboration Model

Having determined that building a Collaboration Model makes sense, the first step (and most difficult) is to figure out the key insight the team wants to communicate. Unlike the other models we discussed, the Collaboration Model does not have a consistent, defined structure that works for all projects. Instead, the structure must be designed to fit the message. So first figure out the insights, then design the background structure that communicates them. You may produce one or several (1–4) models to communicate the key messages.

Find the key collaboration activities and generate insight. Start by grouping your mini diagrams into the primary collaboration activities based on core intent. It's possible that during interpretation you captured interactions about more than one intent on the same model; if so, split them up now. Identify each primary collaboration activity and decide which are core to the message. Examples are: plan travel, manage customer relationship, create and

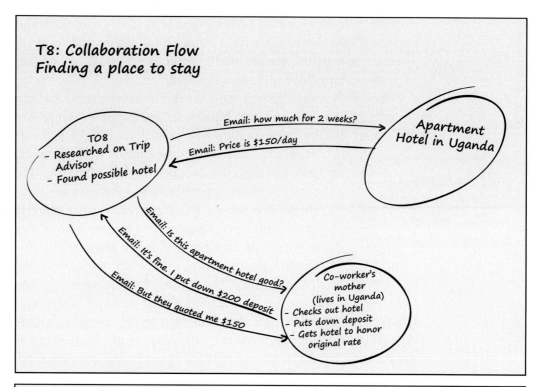

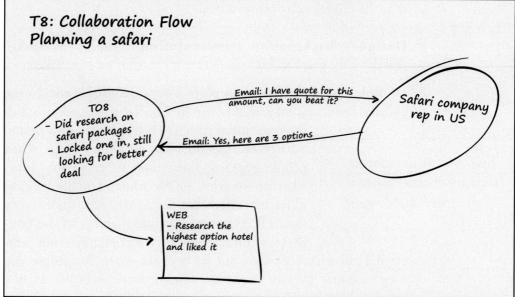

FIGURE 7.17 Small Collaboration Models from the same interviewee captured during Interpretation Session separately to show interaction around two intents. They would look much the same had they been captured during the interview.

close sales deals, oversee a project, deal with client questions and problems, buy electronics with a lot of consultation, and so forth. These are all activities that involve multiple people working together to get something done or make a decision.

Now within each group, look across the interactions and ask yourself, "What is going on? What roles are people playing? Are there a set of core roles to support—is that an insight to communicate? What are the interactions between people—are they smooth or full of hassle? Do they represent opportunities to improve relationships? Are people talking to each other directly or through text, email, pictures, or communities to help make a decision? Is the topic of the discussion the big insight? Is better content needed to support the shared activity? Do you need to automate sharing to help coordination? Or do the people who are supposed to collaborate fail to do so—are they simply nagging, begging, ordering, and beseeching each other?" Only the team, by looking at the detailed data, can see what is going on in the relationships. Write down the main learning and insight—this is your message that the model must communicate.

Find the insight that drives the message represented in the Communication Model

Design a background representation. The main message will drive the graphic. Here are some approaches we have taken.

Role-centered: If the user plays a key, identifiable role in the collaboration, this may be the best option. Roles are collections of responsibilities which, when executed by a person on a team, help the team get things done. When people organize themselves to get a job done, whether for work or life, they naturally take on different roles. "You write the first draft," they say, "I'll review it." Or one member of the family takes on the role of travel planner—the others tell her what they like, but let her take over. The people you interview may play an important role, in work or in life. In life, roles such as "travel planner" are key parts in getting the activity done. When studying work, you may have interviewed people in

Your message determines the background structure of the consolidated model.

the same organizational role—but that doesn't mean they all do the work the same way. Also, they may take on roles that are not part of their formal job description to get the work done. Look for the formal or informal role which is key to accomplishing the target activity. In every case, the user has a story to tell about how collaboration takes place relative to their role. This is the story you want to tell in the model.

Typically, you'll have one to four core roles worth representing. Fig. 7.18 shows the graphic we designed for a Project Overseer, who works to ensure all aspects of a project go forward in sync. The main message is about what it means to oversee. The graphic represents the inner experience and core motives of the overseer wanting to know all things all the time about his team while simultaneously providing air cover to the team and status to the organization. Interactions with others are shown but this graphic is telling the story of the role as the dominant message.

Interaction-centered. The interaction-centered Collaboration Model may include a concept of role but sees the specific interactions with others—and the roles those others play—to be an important part of the message. An interaction-centered model highlights the meaning of the interaction between roles, the content supporting the interaction, and what works and what doesn't.

For example, the team creating the travel Collaboration Model found the role of designated trip planner to be a dominant role: the person or people who do the legwork of planning a vacation and works with family members on plans and preferences. The key finding is that this role can be shared, so the team was challenged to show the two strategies people used. But they also realized that there was an additional message—that planning does not happen in vacuum. Travel planning involves continuous coordination with people in other roles: trusted advisors, fellow travelers, and people being visited.

Highlight the strategies, shared content, and interactions between roles to drive redesign

These insights led the team to the model shown in Fig. 7.19. It characterizes the two role behaviors and experiences in the colored rectangles, placing those they coordinate with in the middle. Labeled areas and text chunks organize the communication and talk bubbles to

Project Overseer: I'm always in touch with my teams

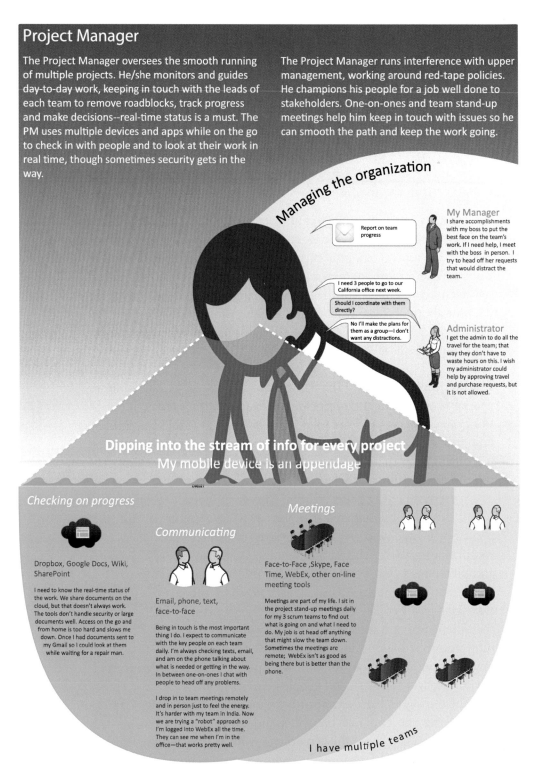

FIGURE 7.18 Collaboration among enterprise workers, showing how individual mobile devices and apps support them. The Project Overseer is one key role that a company might support.

provide specifics from the data. When the structure of the interaction, the nature of the interaction, the content of the interaction, or the difficulties of the interaction are the key insights, choose a variant of this format to represent your consolidation. If there are also two strategies for fulfilling a role—as in the travel data—the insights can be combined.

Story-based consolidation.   Models show the structure of how things are done, how roles and interactions are organized, and strategies associated with collaboration. But what if the insight of the collaboration issue is that the collaboration at its core doesn't work. Sometimes the insight is about how non-collaborative the interactions are.

If the collaborations are fundamentally broken find a compelling way to tell the story

Our Audit team kept expecting real collaboration between auditors and their clients. Certainly people passed documents back and forth, made calls, and wanted status. People interacted with each other, but these interactions were so frustrating and difficult that we decided the best way to communicate the impact of this insight was to do it in a cartoon. A cartoon can communicate pain lovingly, with humor. It can use real instances and focus the reader. Here the purpose of the "model" was to highlight the relationships' dysfunction. The impact of this message would be lost by simply showing interactions that were continuously broken—the insight wasn't in any one interaction—it was in the overall way work was done in that profession. We wanted to challenge the design team to invent how the players could start to enjoy working together instead of living in a culture of nagging. You can see one of the cartoons in Fig. 7.20. Note the Way In is still there, but for humor we made it come from a dog.

Model Completion: Once the team determines their message and approach, the right background structure will become clear—though it may well take several iterations. Knowing the structure, the process of consolidation proceeds as usual: collect relevant observations from individual models, group observations into meaningful sub-areas, name the sub-area and write story text, or provide examples for each area. Create taglines, overview text, and questions for a Way In. Apply good graphical design and you have told the story.

The consolidation process is fundamentally the same across all models

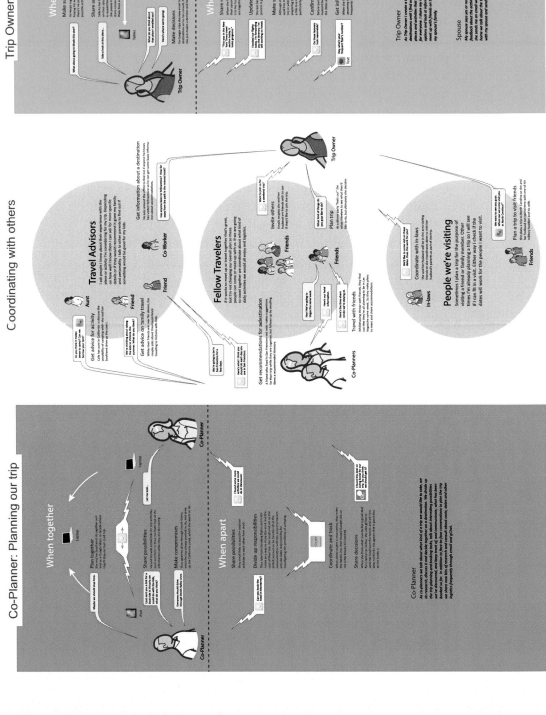

FIGURE 7.19 The consolidated travel Collaboration Model shows two primary strategies for fulfilling the planner role—trip owner and coplanner. But because success in the role depends completely on communicating and coordinating with others we chose an interaction style for the Collaboration Model. Here the key players in travel planning are in the central panel.

Request List

The Torture of Gathering Info for the Audit (Dragging Data from the client)

We don't really collaborate with the client- We just nag them to give us information that they may not have or know how to get. We just try to train our clients to get organized, and it's an endless battle. There must be a better way...

Before we go...

We've been auditing this client for 10 years... What could be new? I feel like I've done this a million times...

I'm going to pretty much just go with what we just asked the client for last year... but I guess I should just check...

Better start rounding up what's new!

2014

Where's the Risk...

Maybe there's a new risky area this year...

Hey- I had lunch with the client yesterday. They just took out a new loan for an expansion, so make sure you get everything you need for that.

Got it. I'll add it to the request list!

FIGURE 7.20 A cartoon describing the broken coordination between auditor and client.

SENSATION BOARDS

The Cool Concept of Sensation highlights that we are sensual creatures and we love products that deliver stimulation: color, motion, texture, and good aesthetic design. Trends and practices continuously redefine modern aesthetics—any product must live up to these trends to be considered cool.

Help graphics, visual and industrial designs drive their work from data too!

Most of the data collected on sensation for business and consumer products can be organized into the Affinity Diagram. But when a product's core value is to deliver sensation—surround-sound TV, music, automobile design, video games—sensation is central to the value delivered. Then observations on sensation will be more extensive and the Affinity Diagram will have a large section devoted to the aesthetic and visceral experience of the product. The industrial design and visual design team will benefit from creating a Sensation Board.

COLLECTING, INTERPRETING, AND USING THE DATA IN THE AFFINITY

When a large part of the product's mission is to deliver sensory delight, the sensual experience will appear like a strong emotion, easy to probe:

> The user grinned a bit when he started his Cadillac and the car played a little fanfare. "Don't you find that annoying after a while?" asked the interviewer, who found it annoying. "Not at all," said the user. "Every morning, it's a celebration."

Watch for the smile and the eye-twinkle to find sensation data

But for most products Sensation shows up like a fleeting smile or grimace. The joy of sensation reveals as an emotional response—a spark of delight or fun or a pause to enjoy an interaction. We have even observed users unconsciously stroking their devices as an expression of their attachment to it. When you see this kind of emotional response to an aspect of the product, talk about it and let the user respond.

FINDING SENSATION IN A CONTEXTUAL INTERVIEW—IT'S SUBTLE

Pay attention to the smile
- Look for fun and delighters
- Or a grimace denoting annoyance

Look for reactions to
- Color, sound, movement, and animation supporting a purpose
- Is the animation gratuitous? Does it add visual complexity? Why not?

Does the aesthetic design enhance or detract?
- Listen for negative comments or expressions

Sensation data for typical consumer and business products can be hard to recognize—people focus on getting their lives done with the products, not on the aesthetic experience. But poor aesthetics, too much animation, a clunky interface, visual complexity, or jarring colors all undermine love of the product. So look for these small reactions to see what doesn't work.

If you haven't collected enough sensation data during the interview and especially when sensation really matters to the project, save 15 minutes at the end of the interview to focus on it.

Then during the Interpretation Session, share what you found and capture notes as you would any other data. These notes are now ready to be built into the Affinity Diagram and will likely fall into their own Green section.

CREATING THE SENSATION BOARD

Building a Sensation Board is a powerful way to focus industrial designers and visual designers on the importance of user data and team insights. Most inspiration boards used by these designers are created from their preexisting assumptions, open brainstorms, the brand message from marketing, and other means—not including customer data. But what if their inspiration boards could be customer-driven?

The Sensation Board builds on the known practice of inspiration boards

The practice of visual and industrial designers is to hone a list of words and collect materials and pictures meant to guide their design thinking. This list defines the inner human experience they want the product to evoke during any encounter. The Sensation Board is a customer-driven inspiration board embodying the list of words the team believes are the best to drive the design in a direction the customer will value.[6]

Walk the Affinity collecting quotes and insights explicitly to drive aesthetic design

Fig. 7.21 shows the Travel Sensation Board. Like all our consolidated models it is separated into chunks of insight with top-level labels. Lower level words in a section call out the experiential meaning of the larger section. Instead of textual stories, however, the team collects pictures that elicit the emotional experience behind the words, reflecting the customers' experience and desires. These are selected to stimulate the desired emotion and communicate it to the designers. The Sensation Board focuses the design team on the aesthetic and emotional message they must communicate with their design.

Sensation Boards are created by walking the whole Affinity Diagram looking for emotional themes implied in all the data—this includes the section where sensation data was collected. As they walk, they jot down phrases and themes which they can share and discuss. Together, they agree on four to eight sections that will challenge the design team to invent visceral pleasure for the customers.

Just like naming identity elements, the labels of the sections must evoke the feelings the team wants the product to produce. So the words matter—choose them carefully. Then pick the pictures to match and begin the layout. For industrial and visual designers, the Way In is the list and board itself. It is a known tool in their profession.

---

[6] To develop the Sensation Board we collaborated with our wonderful team from GM using data and the same principles of for design communication we have been discussing.

FIGURE 7.21 The travel Sensation Board communicates the key phrases and visual inspiration needed to help visual and industrial designers create the emotional experience desired by the customer population.

CONCLUSION

All the Contextual Design Experience Models help the team focus on the data and points of view they need to design for life. They define a way to pay attention to the Cool Concepts in the Wheel of Joy in Life. With them the team will immerse themselves in the whole life experience of their user population as it pertains to the target activity. This tunes their personal gut feel—and gets them ready to design transformative products. In Part 3 we will talk about how to use these and the Contextual Design Traditional Models in ideation.

Experience Models deliver data in a compelling and consumable form

In the next chapter we turn to consolidating the Traditional Contextual Design Models.

MODELING ON YOUR OWN

So you don't have a big team to help you with all the models, and in smaller or more agile organizations spending the time to do a highly polished presentation may not be worth it. But the activity of modeling is valuable whatever your team situation is. Look over your problem and decide which models you want.

The Affinity is always desirable, and it's the most difficult to do alone. But building it can be timeboxed—invite the people with the best reason to be interested for a specific period of time. Offer them pizza and other goodies and make it fun. Then, if they get into it and want to stay they can. Even 2 hours of help at a time is valuable.

For the other models, sketch them on flip charts and whiteboards. Sketch them during interpretation, as described in the text, if you have an interpretation partner. If not, sketch them while describing the user practice to a coworker; or sketch them on your own and then have a brown-bag lunch and walk through them with the group. When you present them, have a pen in your hand, and as people ask questions or as you find yourself saying things that aren't on the models, write on the models right then.

Think of this as an internal discussion more than a formal presentation. You get as much credibility with your coworkers—rough work in progress has its own authenticity. Marking up the models in the moment demonstrates that you're listening and invites everyone into a collaborative discussion about the user practice. If people start telling you how users work, capture it—but use a different color or a different part of the model. Talk about the difference between field data and the background information that floats around an organization, and talk about how you'll use this as a focus for future interviews. You're not just sharing the data—you're also eliciting knowledge from the team and introducing a shared value around trusting field data.

But draw the models, even if—especially if—you don't find it a natural way of thinking. It will force you to think about the user practice in an organized way, separate from the implications of design.

8

Traditional Contextual Design Models

The Traditional Contextual Design Models were introduced in the first version of this book. As we said in Chapter 5, they were designed when teams were composed primarily of developers to help them understand the human context of a task, generally for business. The models use a visual language borrowed from modeling approaches familiar to developers and so were easily adopted by them. Developers liked the detail of the users' world and wanted to dialogue with it through their own inquiry—not the summary of a UX professional.

But the field of UX grew, and teams and communication styles have changed dramatically since then. Products and the scope of products have also changed. Our use of these models has changed too. Some we have honed to make them more accessible and focused. Some we use rarely—but they are still useful for some projects. And some we still use regularly. Here we touch on some of the traditional models and their use. For more detail on the original models and their consolidation, see this website: http://booksite.elsevier.com/9780128008942. The Traditional Contextual Design Models are:

The project focus always determines which models to choose.

The Sequence Model is the basis of task analysis. It captures the triggers, intents, and steps of users' activities, with technology and without. These are needed to drive detailed design, so we still use it regularly.

Contextual Design. http://dx.doi.org/10.1016/B978-0-12-800894-2.00008-9

The Cultural Model captures the cultural influences within a population which affect the target activity: formal and informal policy, business and legal influencers, interpersonal friction, and values which affect choices. It reflects the constraints and support people feel while doing the activity. The Cultural Model is valued by teams representing their internal organizations for IT system projects. Today we usually represent cultural aspects that the team must consider in notes in the affinity or with the *Decision Point Model*. We won't describe the classic Cultural Model here.

The Decision Point Model looks at the influences that affect a key decision. Where the decision is critical to the project focus, it provides a good summary of the factors that must be considered.

The Physical Model captures the structure, use, and particular insights about the environment within which the activity takes place. It is important when the product is a physical environment such as a vehicle, when it lives in and interacts with the physical environment such as a device or appliance for a home, or when designing a service or technology which lives in real space, for example, a retail environment.

The Flow Model is used to represent complex processes such as those within enterprises. It highlights the roles and responsibilities multiple people take on while they coordinate within a work process. It is still relevant for complex processes and brings insight when collaborating with process reengineering efforts. But the Collaboration Model discussed in the previous chapter has replaced it as the representation of choice for revealing communication and coordination of a target activity. We won't describe the Flow Model here.

The Artifact Model is used to represent the structure and usage of a physical artifact, such as a form. Since most artifacts are already online we rarely use this model anymore, but if you must move a paper artifact into a product, consider it. We won't describe the Artifact Model here.

Personas were not one of the original Contextual Design Models but have become popular. They are used to characterize the behavior, values, and attitudes of the target population as a set of archetype characters. We describe how to create them from rich field data in detail in Rapid Contextual Design.[1] We'll touch on them below.

Traditional Contextual Design Model techniques for consolidation are guided by the same principles as the Affinity Diagram and the Experience Models: use induction, label groupings to evoke story thinking, consolidate into a background structure, and create a graphic guided by principles of communication design. You will see, however, that as a consequence of when they were designed and who they were to be used by, the communication design element is much more basic than the new Experience Models. Feel free to apply a more exciting graphical treatment when they are important to helping your designers understand the data. We discuss the traditional models we use now below.

THE SEQUENCE MODEL

The Sequence Model is a basic task analysis, capturing users' actions while doing a task. Many teams create these models to guide detailed design. Sequences help define the scenarios of use that the product must support and identify lower-level

Sequence Models define as-is scenarios of use

usability issues. They are not "big picture" models that help open up innovative thinking, the way the affinity and experience models do.

Sequences represent the way people do a task or accomplish an intent. Activities are ordered; they unfold over time. The steps people take aren't random—they happen the way they do because of an underlying intent or habit of the user. They start because something in the user's environment or inner experience triggers them to act.

---

[1] Rapid Contextual Design—pg x for personas.

A commuter pulls into the parking lot at his office, but he doesn't get out of the car right away. Instead, he pulls out his phone and spends a few minutes checking messages and Facebook. It's a break, a quick check-in, before diving into the business of the work day. And it helps him clear away any quick requests.

Watching the detailed actions people take in doing a task reveals their strategies, their intent, and how tools help or hinder. Understanding the real intent is key to improving any practice—you can redesign, modify, and remove steps as long as the user can still achieve their underlying intent. An intent is stable: people have had the intent of communicating over a distance for ages. The steps, the way that intent has been achieved, have changed over time—from hand-written messages to email, the telephone to mobile phones, videoconferencing to Skype, instant messaging, and so on. Our inquiry when collecting, interpreting, and consolidating sequences is to find the core intents implied in the steps.

Understanding the users' intent is the key to design

Our design challenge is to help the user achieve the intent more directly and recognize how technology might help or get in the way. If doctors look at their email and calendar in the parking lot to see what is coming up in their day but the electronic medical system won't let them see it directly, an opportunity to delight the user will be missed.

COLLECTING THE DATA

Collecting the data for a sequence is easy. Just watch the activities targeted in your project focus and write each step down in order as they unfold. Or during a retrospective account, write the steps as you hear them—leaving space to write in steps you find out about later, because you'll get them out of order. Remember to pay attention to the overall intent of the task and the intent of each step. See if you can find the trigger—what got the user started doing the task. If you see breakdowns in the practice, put in a lightning bolt breakdown sign.

Remember, in real life people do things in liner order—no looping, no alternative strategies. These will come out in consolidation. So write it all in order. If you hear about alternative ways to do the same things, just note it in the margin of the page.

Look for the triggers, the intents, and breakdowns in the steps

Sequences may be studied at any level of detail, from the high-level activities to accomplish an overall task, to the detailed interaction steps with a particular user interface. For new product concepts or feature sets, capture steps at the level of the action. Only capture observations at the level of the clicks for a project focused on usability fixes.

CAPTURING DURING THE INTERPRETATION SESSION

Sequence Model capture during the Interpretation Session is straightforward: Capture every step as it happened just as you did during the interview, putting it on a flip chart or into a document. Don't just write up your notes in advance—capture the steps while speaking them to the team. Their questioning will trigger more memory, identify more intents and breakdowns, and truly share the events with them. See the example sequence (Fig. 8.1) from the Travel Project.

Remember the steps don't usually come out in perfect order, particularly with retrospective accounts. Triggers and intents may require some discussion to identify. If the interviewer discussed intents with the user, it's easy—just capture them. Otherwise, the team may identify intents which are clear from context even though they weren't captured in the interview. The interviewer is the last word on whether an intent really was experienced by the user.

U06 Sequence 1: Plan family trip

1. Trigger: Decided to give wife a family trip for her birthday
2. Ask wife about going somewhere new (agree with wife to find a new destination)
3. Open home/work desktop
4. Research a place using Google Maps
5. Start search at Rockaway (their usual place)
6. Intent: Find hotel, places of interest
7. See a place that's a condo, not a hotel
8. Decide to search for condos in Rockaway
9. Find a place that looks good
10. Email link to wife
11. BD: Link didn't work and had to send again
12. Once finally received, wife confirms that it looks good
13. Discuss more in email and text
14. Have face to face discussion to commit to the place
15. Intent: Don't commit until we're sure we agree
16. Decide the website is not trustworthy
17. Call the condo rental place
18. Book the condo
19. Night before the trip:
20. Research travel route in Google Maps
21. Intent: See if anything new to see or a new way to go
22. Decide to take their regular route
23. Print directions

FIGURE 8.1   Here is a sequence of activities captured at a high level showing what a husband did to plan a trip for his wife. You can capture this on a flip chart or in a document displayed for all to see. "BD" in step 11 stands for "breakdown"—a problem or issue getting in the user's way.

CONSOLIDATING THE DATA

As we have been discussing, every Contextual Design model represents the structure of the practice from its own point of view. Fig. 8.2 is a partial consolidated sequence to illustrate the idea. It's enough to show how the structure is revealed in the levels and colors.

- The *Title* of the sequence tells us what it is addressing. Most projects benefit from 2–8 sequences defining the things people do in service of the target overall activity.

- The green bar denotes an *activity* chunk within the overall activity—a set of steps that hang together to achieve a coherent intent. The first activity section—"Have idea for trip" in this case—shows the triggers for the sequence as a whole.

- The blue steps are consolidated step (or trigger) descriptions. These step labels are generated by collecting similar observations from across all users doing that same activity, just like bringing notes together under a blue label in the Affinity.

- The pink notes are the intents, placed next to the step that achieves that intent. Intents can also go with the activity—put those right below the green bar.

- The notes with lightning bolts are breakdowns.

The process of consolidating a Sequence Model is much like the Affinity Diagram. Analysis of the specific sequences reveals the activities that comprise the action of the sequence (Fig. 8.3). So if we look at our captured sequence above, we can see the activities within it:

It is helpful to consolidate 4–6 sequences on the wall to get the basic structure and then check the rest for additions. Once you find all the activities by looking at these sequences, put them in a reasonable order that reflects the data. Now you are ready to consolidate steps into them.

Collect like observations and name the step—then put it in order

Working with one activity at a time, look across the individual sequences and group the specific steps into abstract steps. Write the abstract step to describe what people are doing, as in Fig. 8.4.

Planning a Trip

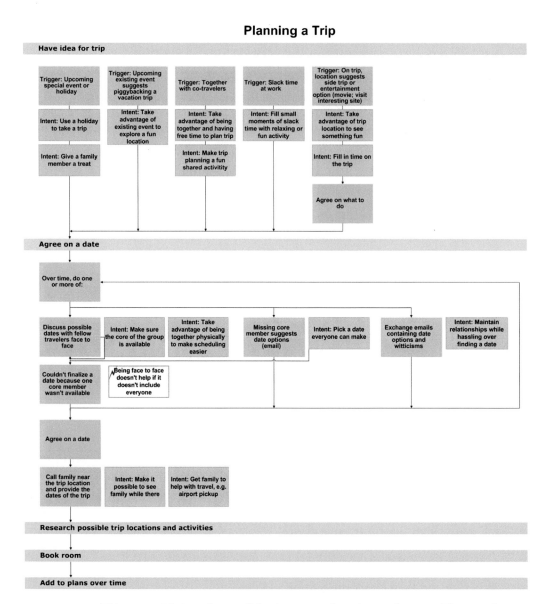

FIGURE 8.2   This is a partial view of a consolidated sequence from the travel project. The green bars mark off activity chunks; they contain blue consolidated steps with their associated pink intents and red breakdowns. Backing up the blues are the actual steps from individual Sequence Models which defined that step.

```
U06 Sequence 1: Plan family trip
    Trigger of this sequence
        Give wife a family trip for her birthday
    Activity: Get agreement on trip
        Ask wife about going somewhere new (agree with wife to do that)
    Activity: Research usual location for a place to stay
        Open home/work desktop
        Research a place using Google Maps
        Start search at Rockaway (their normal place)
        Intent: Find hotel, places of interest
        See a place that's a condo, not a hotel
        Decide to search for condos in Rockaway
        Find a place that looks good
    Activity: Confirm choice with travel partner
        Email link to wife
        BD: Link didn't work and had to send again
        Once finally received wife confirms that it looks good
        Discuss more in email and text
        Have face to face discussion to commit to the place
        Intent: Don't commit until we're sure we agree
    Activity: Make sure travel resource is reliable
        Decide the website is not trustworthy
        Call the condo rental place
    Activity: Book desired place to stay
        Book the condo
    Activity: Research travel route
        Night before the trip:
        Research travel route in Google Maps
        Intent: See if anything new to see or a new way to go
        Decide to take their regular route
        Print directions
```

FIGURE 8.3 The actual sequence model from U06 with activity chunks identified, ready for consolidation.

Consolidate the abstract steps in each green activity, including their intents and breakdowns, and add them to your emerging model. When there is more than one way to do the same thing, you have found a branch. Branches may indicate that different users have different strategies, they may be options based on intent, or they may simply reflect different situations (Fig. 8.5).

Strategies emerge when looking across different people

Repeat for the other activities, check the other individual models and add additional data, and you are done!

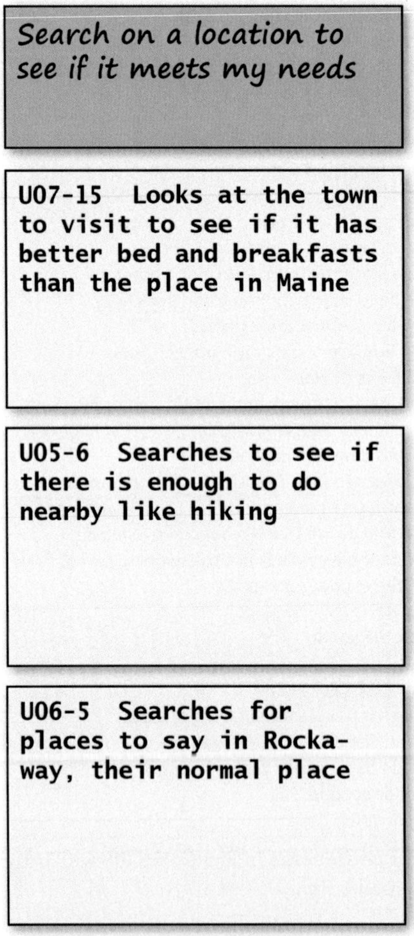

Search on a location to see if it meets my needs

U07-15 Looks at the town to visit to see if it has better bed and breakfasts than the place in Maine

U05-6 Searches to see if there is enough to do nearby like hiking

U06-5 Searches for places to say in Rocka-way, their normal place

FIGURE 8.4   A set of steps from different sequences all doing essentially the same thing being consolidated together, and the consolidated step written from them.

If a small teams work on parallel sequence, consolidations in the same room they will be available to each other for consultation and sharing the data while they work.

COMMUNICATION DESIGN

Sequences are steps of an action in order; designing for a Sequence Model means changing the steps and giving people better ways to achieve their intents. So put your consolidated sequences in a graphic tool such as Visio. You may show only the abstract steps or you may

Search on the location	BD: Trip planning app kept crashing so went back to Google
Strategy 1: Enter search string, identifying location and activity	Intent: Find out when the event is happening
Strategy 2: Go to travel site (TripAdvisor)	Intent: Find out general information about a location from a tourist perspective
Strategy 3: Go to review site (Yelp)	Intent: Find out what others think from a trusted source
Strategy 4: Go to tickets site (Orbitz)	Intent: Find the most accurate price for hotel rooms

FIGURE 8.5 Consolidating a branch. Here, we're using a spreadsheet so the different strategies are laid out vertically. On the wall, we'd be using sticky notes, and they'd be laid out horizontally.

pick representative observations for each step to bring home the real experience and keep the sequence grounded.

For the most part Sequence Models are a tool for design, rather than something that inspires new product concepts. The detail, the intents, and the strategies in a Sequence Model are a good guide for storyboarding and detailed design: don't design out things that work and do overcome things that don't. Support every intent, even if it is in a new way or with new technology.

Sequence Models guide lower-level design to get the details right

The level of detail in a Sequence Model can sometimes overwhelm the team—but they are great for making sure that the I's are dotted and T's crossed when you are doing detailed interaction design.

DECISION POINT MODELS

Cultural and Decision Point Models show feelings and values like the Experience Models

The Decision Point Model has superseded the Cultural Model we introduced in the first edition of Contextual Design. The Cultural Model reveals values, standards, constraints, emotional and power relationships between people and groups, and how they all intermix. It is the only Traditional Contextual Design Model that concentrates on feelings and how different people and groups influence each other. The influencers in culture must be taken into consideration when designing.

For example, in one profession we studied the people said they never worked at home—that they worked so hard during busy season that they actively avoided work at home. This was their cultural value. But a close look at their life revealed that, nevertheless, they did check email, respond to critical requests, and prepared for the day using their mobile devices—they just thought they did nothing! Knowing this helps our clients think about market messages and what kind of mobile support will be accepted by a culture that denies its use.

In the past, we would have captured this data in a Cultural Model, but because we are now designing for life this data is naturally captured in the Affinity Diagram, in the Day-in-the-Life Model, and as Identity Elements. Since the new models are capturing feelings, values, motives, and their impact on behavior the Cultural Model is redundant.

Today, we do not use the Cultural Model very often,[2] but we do use a variant: the Decision Point Model. Companies want to know what influences choices—to buy a product or service, to stay in school or leave, or to choose one delivery option over another. It can be interesting to see all the influences on a choice brought together in one diagram.

Decision Point Models show what influences choice

The Decision Point Model is a very simple model with a simple structure. At the top is the decision to be made. Influences on the left of a center line push the person positively toward making the choice; influences to the right of the line push the person away from that choice. Once a company sees what is influencing the decision they can decide how to design their product, service, or market message (Fig. 8.6).

---

[2] Internal IT teams often like the cultural model because it shows the internal power struggles, policies, and other issues their users need to deal with. Also when working with a marketing team the Cultural Model helps with the market message. Consider your project focus to determine what is right for you. See http://booksite.elsevier.com/9780128008942 for excerpts from the first version of the book.

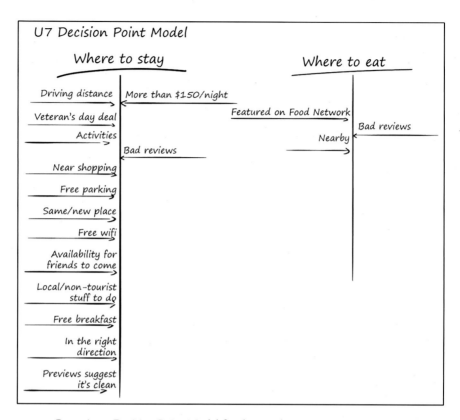

FIGURE 8.6   Capturing a Decision Point Model for the travel project.

The Decision Point Model is easy to build and consolidate. In the interview, collect data about what influences a choice. In the Interpretation Session, capture the influences as they appear over the course of the story. Then consolidate the influences, bringing together the ones that go together. Write a phrase that summarizes the influence in the language of the user, in the same way as a blue label in an Affinity. Finally, choose which influences are most important to raise up to the team if there are too many. Put it online and you are done (Fig. 8.7).

Collect the influences, name them, and pick the most important

Decision Point | **Buy or Shop Around**

Decision Point

Decide to buy without shopping around   Decide to shop around before buying

Money

Decide to buy without shopping around	Decide to shop around before buying
I don't want to think about it – the price isn't that high	I know I can get cheaper
It's not worth the effort to shop, this price is good enough	The price increase broke the next $100 level
My time's too valuable to worry about a $20-40 difference	I think I can get better value somewhere else
I think my price is good based on word of mouth	

Service

Decide to buy without shopping around	Decide to shop around before buying
It would require too much time and effort to shop – even though I'm not happy	I'm irritated with the customer support - they aren't responding to my complaints
The price is low even though I'm not happy with the service	They aren't providing the service features I want
I've received great service so far	

Life Changes

Decide to buy without shopping around	Decide to shop around before buying
I've been with this company for many years	I need to adjust my plan, which will increase my cost
I know someone who found a cheaper price and a year later the price went up	Life circumstances have changed - time to see if there's a better fit

FIGURE 8.7 A consolidated Decision Point from a project focused on how people choose insurance. (The decisions we observed in the travel project weren't compelling enough to warrant doing a full consolidation; we just allowed the Affinity to hold the decision point data.)

THE PHYSICAL MODEL

Life happens in a physical environment which either supports and enables activities or gets in their way. Luckily people are adaptive. As they live their lives within a car, when they shop in stores, when they work in their office space, they tailor how they do an activity to fit the space and they rearrange their spaces to best suit themselves. So you want to understand how people use their space; and if you are doing service design you need to understand how the space, the service providers, the layout of items, and more affect the customer. When this is your project focus, use the Physical Model.

Think of the idiosyncratic ways in which people arrange their cars: cell phones are stored in cup holders, on passenger seats, and in other slots; wires are draped this way and that to get a charge; the cell phone used as a navigator obscures the car's built-in navigator—which becomes a great place to lean the phone.

Your project focus determines what you represent in the Physical Model

In grocery stores people only use the aisles they need, based on their shopping strategy, values, and intent on each shopping excursion. And then they adapt their use to the environment. For example, "I'm a perimeter shopper. I go around the outside to the fresh vegetables, meats, and bakery—no unhealthy packaged goods for me." Or they let the environment help their process—so they hang out in the spaghetti aisle thinking about what to make for dinner and what else they might need if they make pasta. And now, more of the outside world is available in the store. People can take and send pictures ("Is this the pizza sauce you're talking about?") or make calls to significant others ("How do you feel about pasta tonight?"), and get information from Google ("Is this brand really organic?").

If you are studying service workers or the role of kiosks, then you will need to interview the service workers directly and also watch people by stationing yourself at the kiosk. Then use your Physical Model to show activity around the kiosk, and the presence of store workers affects the shoppers (Fig. 8.8).

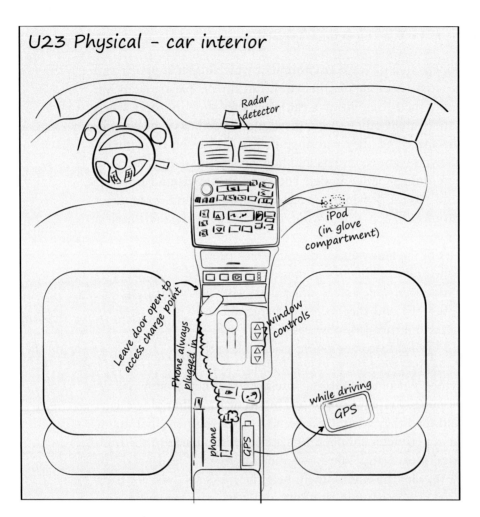

FIGURE 8.8 A Physical Model showing the interior of a car and how all the things people use fit into the space.

When the design and use of space is central to the product or service, we create a Physical Model. Studying the users' space ensures that the product accounts for their behaviors, work-arounds, and intents. Studying the way users organize and cluster their space tells you how to improve the space—and how to cluster things online if you are creating a parallel online space.

Studying the movement and actions of attendants, the reaction to displays and in-store information, and any technology in the space gives you an overall picture of the real customer experience from a service perspective.

The Physical Model is essential for retail service design

The Physical Model captures this information and is easy to build and consolidate. In the interview, collect data on how space is used—just draw a picture mirroring the physical environment they are in. Write down where the user puts things, moves them around, organizes them, and how she moves through the space. Look for intents and note them.

In the Interpretation Session, start with a drawing of the user's environment as we described in Chapter 4 on Interpretation Sessions. Add detail as it unfolds in the interview and check that it's complete at the end.

The layout of the space is your background structure for consolidation of the key stories

Now you have a set of individual models to consolidate. As always, pick the six most detailed to start with. To consolidate, look for the structure of the space. There is always a natural structure: the dashboard, seats and center stack of a car, the aisles and special sections of a grocery store, or the rooms and furniture in a home or office. These are your physical spatial areas. Lay them out as a background, mimicking the real space.

Then review, select, and clarify the insights by looking at all the individual observations within each area. Create one or two descriptive statements as an overview to that area and include stories to illustrate what happens in each one. (This is most like consolidating the DIL.) Finally, step back and look at the whole model. Clarify your insights and the message you want your model to show. Represent the stories as you would in a DIL—add color, small pictures, and challenge questions. Put it online and you are done (Figs. 8.9 and 8.10).

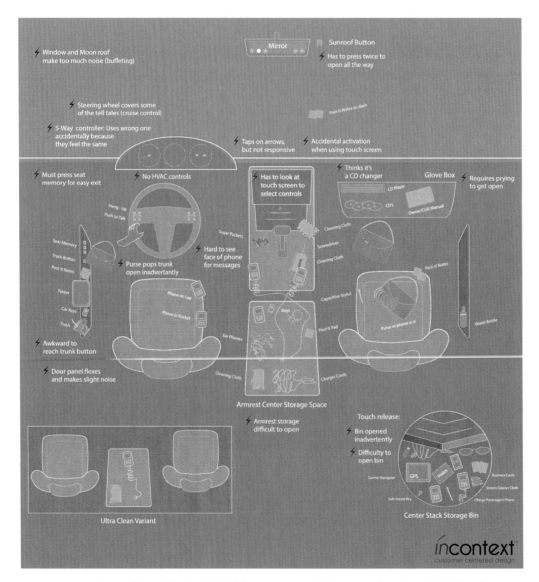

FIGURE 8.9   A consolidated Physical Model from an automobile project showing only the break-downs—the team wanted to highlight how problematic the design of the internal space was for the driver.

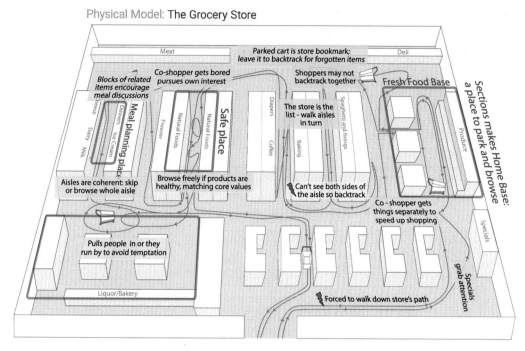

Physical Model: The Grocery Store

FIGURE 8.10 A Physical Model from a shopping project. Both this and the automobile model were constructed before we started putting story-based communication design in each model, but they are all amenable to that approach. Try it out and see what works for your team.

PERSONAS

Personas[3] are a way of communicating who your users are in a way that is familiar and easy to understand. Personas provide a quick introduction to your users that is easy to share outside the team. They help the team have a character to think about when they are designing and can help target market messages. Our teams have found them valuable over the years. We review our process for creating and using personas briefly here; see *Rapid Contextual Design*[4] for more detail.

---

[3] Cooper, Alan, *The Inmates are Running the Asylum*. Sams—Pearson Education, 2004.

[4] Holtzblatt, K Et El Rapid Contextual Design 2005 Morgan Kaufman pg 181.

Emma: The Emerging Professional Adult

Emma sees herself as "cool, connected, creative, hip, up on fashion, health conscious, having depth and opinions." Emma knows who she is and is trying to stay authentic to herself as she moves into the professional world. Emma also realizes that part of becoming an adult is moving toward buying things of quality, rather just what's cheapest.

"The coolest people I know don't need to flaunt anything."

Emma is actively engaged in deliberately creating a public image of herself, so she carefully considers the devices she uses. She says, "It's not just if you have an iPod or any one thing. It's the whole package." Emma is struggling with how to maintain her unique identity while adjusting to the new corporate world she's part of now.

The phone Emma uses perfectly embodies this struggle. She carries a Blackberry, which they gave her at work. But the two-tone color is too industrial and the overall image is too corporate. Emma covered the phone with a black neoprene case to try to reconcile its appearance with her image. But a case only goes so far. Emma would strongly prefer using an iPhone, its appearance and streamlined interface better reflects her image. The functionality of the iPhone feels immediate—"boop, I've done it"—whereas with the Blackberry she feels like she's tediously "loading and pressing," even when using the same "cool" app, like Facebook. The Blackberry's clunky interaction doesn't represent Emma.

Nonetheless, there are certain gadgets that Emma loves, though they don't fit her public image, so she uses them in private. For example, her Bluetooth headset gives her freedom to move around her apartment, where the cell phone reception is spotty. To Emma, the headset is "super cool and cute." But Emma would never be caught using the headset out of her home. She says, "People who use a Bluetooth are trying to project an image of importance that ends up working against them."

Part of being an adult to Emma is making careful, higher quality purchases. Her proudest "adult" purchase was a 42" flat-screen TV. She did research and asked her friends for recommendations to make sure she was getting a good deal and a good product. This careful consideration before purchasing has changed the way Emma now purchases almost everything. For example, rather than buying "cheap, junky" clothes, she researches and gets a good price on good clothes. Emma says, "My new TV is the electronic version of a cute new outfit."

Cool Characterization
- Sleek design
- Immediate interaction
- Things that portray self image

Life Tasks
- Work, commute to work
- Keep up with current events
- Stay in touch/socialize

Devices/Technology
- Blackberry
- Flat-screen TV
- Digital camera
- iPod
- Bluetooth headset
- Windows laptop (not MacBook)
- Nice car when commuting

Demographics
- Female or male
- Mid-20's
- Single
- Rents in city or suburbs
- Middle class

FIGURE 8.11   This persona from The Cool Project exemplifies the attitudes, values, and behaviors of young people relative to their cool tools.

A persona describes typical users of a product as though they were real people. They are presented on no more than a page, so they are easy to scan in a single pass. A persona has a name, description, and photo to make them real for the team. They emphasize goals and key tasks, so the team can see what motivates each type of user. And they have a narrative which provides some of the key details about how the user approaches the task. See Fig. 8.11 for an example from The Cool Project. We chose not to build personas for the travel project as we find the Identity Model to be better at helping teams focus explicitly on aspects of character that matter for design. Doing both the Identity Model and Personas is a way to get the best of both approaches.

Personas introduce the wider design and marketing team to their users

In Contextual Design, personas are built from the interview data. This gives them unmatched depth and richness—you have plenty of stories and examples to draw from as you build your personas. This is critical for personas to be useful in the design process—a common complaint of personas is that they simply are too sketchy to drive action. All the data you collect in a Contextual Design project is present for you to incorporate when building your personas.

Consolidating data for personas

As with all models, in Contextual Design, we build personas bottom-up. Start by walking through your users and identifying the job role and key distinguishing features of each person. The key distinguishing features should be related to your project—e.g., they use a device, site, or product you care about. Your personas should not be overly driven by demographics, but note demographic information—you want to show the range of people who fall into each persona. If you have a lot of users, flag the most interesting ones—the ones where it was a rich interview, the user is important to your project focus, and provides a unique perspective. This will let you focus on the most useful interviews first and then you can add the rest.

A good Persona set should map to all the people you interviewed cleanly

Now group the users into potential personas. Users should group together if they do the same job, have similar attitudes toward it, and similar strategies for getting it done.

Expect to have four to eight personas for a project—more than that is rarely helpful to focus design. Each persona should be obviously distinct from the rest. You should be able to identify one primary persona for each person you interviewed. If personas start to fragment people, you are probably identifying identity elements, not personas. So don't try to make fine distinctions—you can show minor variations in the same persona. Do not allow yourself to be driven by demographics and market segmentation—it may be useful to show how a persona cuts across segmentation types.

Shuffle the groupings, clarifying core attributes of each persona until you have a clean set of personas. Give each one a title which captures the key differentiators of that character type. (The person planning travel might fall into "Hobby Planner" and "Just-Enough Organizer" personas, for example.) If you can't come up with a clean title, or if you can't say that each user in the persona could be given that title, your persona thinking probably isn't clean. In that case go back and look at your groupings.

Use details from the data to make rich personas

Then collect the detail for each persona. Walk through the data from the interviews of each user in that persona and pull out key data: Strategies, intents, tasks, quotes, and characteristic stories. This will be the raw data for your narrative.

List the key goals, tasks, and demographics from each user in a persona. For consumer products you may want to show attitudes and values as well; you may want to track devices they use. This will be winnowed down in the next step so don't worry about keeping the lists short for now. Just be sure to keep the distinctions clear: A goal states what the user is trying to achieve. A task is a specific action they take to achieve some goal.

It's often easiest to base your persona off one main user. You'll use this user as the basis for your descriptions, adding details from others and leaving out anything especially idiosyncratic. The main user should be one of the rich interviews that cover much of what the persona is to reveal. Choose your base user at this point.

You're finally ready to do the actual writing. First decide what sex to make the persona and give it a name. Choose a sex based on the users—if all the users were female, don't make the persona male. For a name, just choose something unobtrusive. We often go for alliteration so they are easier to remember: Harriet the Hobby Planner; Joe the Just-Enough Organizer.

Start with the narrative, taking 3–4 paragraphs to summarize the key information about the persona, writing as though the persona was a real person. Use specific stories to add color. Once the narrative is written, it's easy to come up with a 1–2 sentence summary and a characteristic user quote. The quote doesn't have to have been literally said by a user, but it should capture what they would say if they were talking straight. For example, for an operating room nurse: "The patient is in the doctor's hands—but the doctor is in my hands." The writing is much like that we discussed for the Identity Model.

Personas should be broad—they are not identity elements

Finally choose a photo and clean up your lists of goals, tasks, attitudes, and demographics. Choose the most important 3–5 of each. For demographics, just show the range of age, job title, and anything else you care to track that you saw in the user population. The photo should be characteristic of the users you saw.

Remember, a persona is characterizing the whole person's life—they are not single identity elements. In our experience, although they help focus ideation, personas do not generate many design ideas in a Wall Walk. But when coupled with the other models, they are a powerful way to introduce the type of person the team will design for.

THE POWER OF MODELS

Graphical models depicting the life and stories of the users in your population are powerful drivers of insight and ideation. Each model presented in this part—Affinity Diagram, Experience Models, and Traditional Models—reveal a different perspective on the users' lives. Taken together, these perspectives provide a full view of the world your users are living in while doing the target activity you want to support.

Models help focus design thinking on one aspect of the user's world at a time

The more you know the better you can design—you can see opportunity for new products, challenges for new technologies, constraints you must consider, practices that already work and that you do not want to break, and how technology is infused into users' lives now. Stepping back and looking at the models together reveals all the different aspects of the practice of life and how they relate to each other. They communicate the whole world of your users to anyone who engages with the data. They can be revisited time and time again, added to for updates, and most importantly be the living representation of your users' world. They expose the team and stakeholders to the realities of life in your users' world. So they are the best way to drive data into design.

In Part 3, we'll see how to use these models to drive ideation.

CONTEXTUAL DESIGN AND JOURNEY MAPS

Customer journey maps are a convenient and popular way of communicating a lot of information about the user experience in a single diagram. They are similar to sequence models, in that they lay out a process, but generally at a much higher level—they usually cover the whole journey from initial awareness through completion of the customer engagement.

Build customer journey maps when the whole engagement matters for your design. Often, this will be a sales engagement, such as a customer at a shopping site, but that's not the only use. When designing services, or systems where service is an important component, a journey map may make sense. When users interact with your system intensely, as with tax preparation software which gets heavily used during tax season, a journey map can tell the story of the season or of using the system for one client within the season.

Build a journey map in the same way as other models. Collect information from all your interviews showing points of engagement with the system or activity you care about. Look across them to identify the key phases or milestones along the journey. Lay out the engagement points in a linear fashion, with loops and exit points if they occurred.

Finally, apply our principles of design communication. Decide what the main messages of the model are. Lay out a few primary chunks to organize the display of information (these will probably be the phases or milestones you identified). Within these large divisions, chunk the information into 3- to 5-bite-sized pieces using story language and user vignettes to illustrate the points. And design a Way In with pointed questions or suggestions. A journey map is just another kind of model—base it on real user data, consolidate it, and present it using the same principles as the Experience Models.

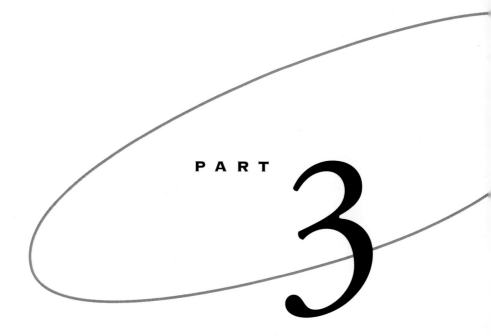

PART 3

Reinventing Life: Ideation with User Data

Inventing the Next Product Concept

9

In Parts 1 and 2 you collected the field data, consolidated it to see patterns across your market, and prepared it, guided by communication design, for use. In Part 3 we introduce techniques for creating new product concepts from this deep understanding of the users. Contextual Design's group ideation process, built on immersion in user data, is the best way to stimulate innovative ideas and build a shared understanding of what to build.

When a design team invents a product, they aren't just putting bits of software and hardware together to make a neat gadget. The real invention of a design team is a new way for people to do things. If you're building a commercial product, you want to make a splash in the market by offering a new, attractive way to work or live. If you're building an internal system, you're looking to transform the business through the appropriate use of technology. Even the smallest app with the most limited effect must fit into the user's larger life.

Today more than ever, technology is inextricably integrated into daily life; we can hardly do anything without support by some technology or continuous reference to some product. Designers today are truly reinventing life by creating a *human-technical system*, a way of living and working augmented by our products and systems. And that product is no longer likely to be a large monolithic application but rather a constellation of products, apps, and platforms to help us get an activity done. And users expect you to build in the cool

Contextual Design. http://dx.doi.org/10.1016/B978-0-12-800894-2.00009-0

experience, as defined by the Cool Concepts. So how can we do all this within our companies?

Corporations split up the job of delivering a product across multiple roles, each role focusing on its own part of the problem. Engineers care about the hardware and software technology; user experience professionals care about good data and interaction design; industrial design cares about the physical container and visual design about the software aesthetic. Product management thinks about function, rollout, and pricing. Marketing cares about how to message to a market. And then the company duplicates it all over again when they assign a different team to develop the mobile versions for each platform!

Teams invent new ways of living—not just products

Of course, these are important aspects of delivering a product, but with so many people and organizational functions involved, it is easy to undermine the total end-to-end user experience. So successful innovation is not just about redesigning the practice well or creating a beautiful product. At its core, it's an organizational problem: how to generate a shared understanding of what to build.

IT departments, supporting a single business, have the advantage of a closer relationship with their users. But employees' expectations are set by their consumer devices—company tools have to measure up to that standard. Most companies have customer-facing websites and apps; they have their own user experience and design groups. So even for IT applications, the same challenges of generating a shared understanding of what to build must be addressed.

Successful innovation requires multiple people to agree on what to make

Any design team must come to an understanding of users' world; see the opportunities to transform it; invent a new human-technical practice which users will want; and design a solution which all parts of the organization agree to and can deliver within their corporate culture.

But just any product won't do. We might get the different people to agree to a direction but is it the right direction for the customer, for the business, and as a market direction? Today's business puts a premium on thinking "out of the box"—coming up with the creative product concept that no one else has thought of. For a commercial product, this can be the competitive edge that makes it possible to dominate a market. Internal systems are looking for the innovative work practice that will transform the business. The word innovation is used everywhere—but what does it mean?

PRACTICAL INNOVATION

When the iPhone shipped, it was a game-changing product. Everybody was talking about it, gathering around the phone just to watch the pinch, the swivel, the pictures, and the games. The technology companies reacted as well; they wanted to create a game changer for their niche too. And businesses worried what changed consumer expectations meant for business tools—they wanted their business products to be "cool." Every client we talk with wants to create a "WOW!" experience. It was like they thought that Apple woke up one day and said, let's make an iPhone—and a few months later it shipped.

Let's look at what really happened. We have found certain prerequisites to be essential for any innovation to ship from a company. No company is consistently innovative. Even Apple has had flops: the Newton, the Lisa, and MobileMe, to name a few. But the real question is, what do we mean when we say innovation? Do we mean developing a new technology such as the ARPAnet, which kicked off massive change over time and eventually resulted in today's internet—but didn't produce useful and profitable products or services for years?

> *Transformative innovation comes after years of technology maturity*

Now there is a buzz about the "internet of things," including the Smart Grid, creating a language for things to talk to each other. The ARPAnet, the Smart Grid, digital paper, voice recognition, self-driving cars, and such are what we call *foundational innovations*. Everything on this list takes 20 or more years until they are ready for regular use. Foundational innovations are new core technologies which ultimately create new *materials* which, when stable, design teams can use in products for people. Not until they are really reliable, easy to implement, free of hassles, and impose little to no burden on users, can they be used to invent new useful products—what we call *practical innovation*. Once foundational innovation has done its work, designers can figure out the best way to infuse them into people's lives appropriately. No one actually wants the electric company to turn off their freezer every 10 minutes out of an hour to save energy, as was suggested in one Smart Grid conference—so what is the right use of that technology? It took years for voice input to be viable, but now it is amazing. There is a lot of work that needs to be done before a team can use a technology as part of a practical innovation that transforms lives.

So transformative innovation takes time and patience. Apple shipped the iPhone in 2007—but registered the URL iPhone.org in 1999. It might have *seemed* like the iPhone leapt into being, but in reality it was a long process of corporate focus, design, iteration, and a lot of waiting for the conditions for its success to be ready. What kind of readiness?

Real innovation takes years. Don't expect it to happen overnight.

The iPhone waited for *technology readiness*. By 2007, wireless networks became available everywhere; smartphones were widely adopted; 3G networks had 295 million subscribers worldwide; and touch screen technology, introduced in 1971, had matured and was reliably used in kiosks, PDAs, grocery stores, GPS devices, and games. Without the maturity and widespread use of these foundational technologies, the iPhone just wouldn't work.

But the consumers needed to be ready too. *Consumer readiness* grew until in 2007 most people were using cell phones for email and text (many with the Blackberry); people were used to accessing information and services from the internet on desktops; and real online content from retail, travel, social media, location services, music, and streaming video became part of normal life. Without any content and services, the iPhone would have been just a pretty box.

Technology and content availability had to mature for it to become accessible with a hand-held computer such as an iPhone.

But Apple also needed a way to distribute the product and a business model to sell it; they needed *distribution and business model readiness*. To get there, Apple built on its already successful processes (Fig. 9.1) to design and sell desktop computers, its developer's network for apps, and the Apple Store; it created a relationship with ATT to distribute the phone and provide the network; and it leveraged its existing iTunes store to sell apps and music. Apple had the corporate knowledge and processes to make roll out of the iPhone real—but this took years to put in place.

Innovation can only happen when technology, the consumer, and the business model is really ready

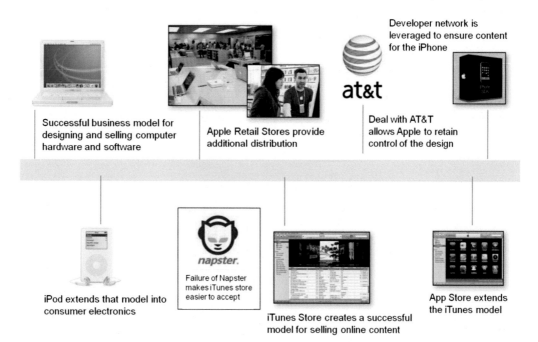

FIGURE 9.1 Apple created distribution technology and relationships critical to making the iPhone successful.

But perhaps most importantly the iPhone fit with Apple's already existing mission and skill. For Apple the iPhone didn't grow up from nothing. It was simply *the next right thing for that company* (Fig. 9.1). To reach the goal, Apple had to maintain a corporate focus and commitment to the vision—and they did. They conceived of the product and then started putting everything they could in place while they waited and nudged technology and content along. They tried out different products in the small, mobile space—failing with the Newton and ROKR but succeeding with the iPod. They perfected, learned, and borrowed from the practices of their music products. They already had the iTunes store where customers could buy music—it was simple to add apps to the store. They already had a way to work with developers to build software—apps were just different software to make. For Apple, the iPhone fit with their core competencies. Their vision didn't require radical change for them—it was just the next right thing (Fig. 9.2).

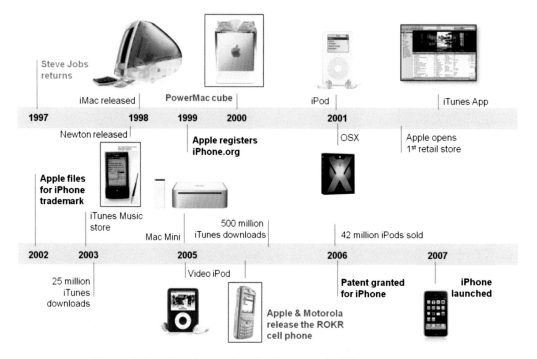

FIGURE 9.2   The evolution of Apple's products leading up to the iPhone.

So what does it take for a company to produce a game-changing product? Technology, market, distribution, and business model readiness (Fig. 9.3) are all prerequisites. But there is one more critical factor—they need to introduce a transformation in user practice. A transformative product delivers a dynamic change in people's life or work practice. (There may be useful, eye-catching features such as the iPhone's pinch and swivel but those are add-ons. By themselves, they do not create transformative innovation.) Given that the foundational elements are in place, user-centered

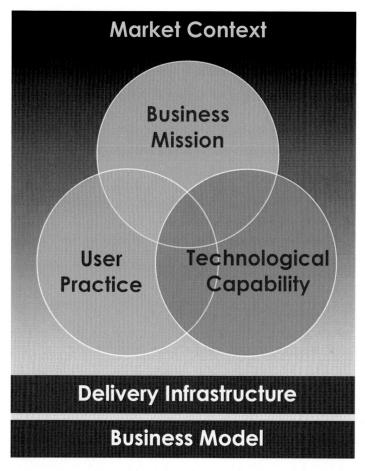

FIGURE 9.3   Practical innovation brings together the user voice, business mission, and technology to create transformative solutions.

design informed by principles such as the Cool Concepts determines ultimate success.

Practical innovation is the sum of all these elements. It speaks to the culture and practices of the whole corporation, not just the work of the design team. Too often a company talks about innovation, they want to ship a game changer, but they don't have everything in place. No matter what good intentions they may have, they simply cannot deliver on the promise.

We have watched teams generate truly transformative ideas— only to see them buried by short-term fire drills and more important priorities of the core mission of their company. One enterprise company we worked with, for example, hired us to help them understand business to business relationships. Well before WebEx, SharePoint, Dropbox, Skype, or any other collaborative technologies more complex than email, we and the team envisioned all those technologies in support of business collaboration. In the years since they've all been shipped—but not by our client. Why not? Their corporate focus was managing enterprise data. All these elements were too far outside their focus, required too much new technology, and demanded new business and sales models. So innovation is not just about coming up with a great idea—it's about coming up with a great idea the company can ship given the mission and skills of the people in that organization.

Any innovation must fit the business's core mission— or it won't ship

Practical innovation rests on technology, market, corporate, and business readiness. These are the larger conditions needed for intentional innovation. But then with the right user data, the right skill on your team, and a process for ideation, you can make innovation and coolness happen on purpose.

STORY: WINNING THE MARKET WITH PLANNING

A large publishing company delivered very large paper reports. These reports compiled the findings of professional researchers and included opinions for a very key business issue. The Web was encouraging publishers to provide paper products online. But these reports were enormous—hundreds of pages. "Would our customers want something online?" they asked. Could they be wooed away from paper and accept an electronic solution? What would it take to put it online? It is so big—could it even go online? This company began by asking some good questions—before they acted.

The company's enlightened VP knew where she wanted to take the company and knew that she had to build a software organization and competency to get there. They started by going to focus groups showing some initial mockups based on what they thought customers had told them they wanted. But the customers said "No—this is all wrong." Then they came to us.

In 2003 no competitor had anything online. Our work with the team revealed that delivering on paper had real problems that an online report could address: finding information in the report fast; bringing the most desired information to the top; designing the content layout for simplified scanning; and providing highlighting and tagging tools. Reinventing the product using Contextual Design enabled the company to deliver on the promise—and took the market by storm. Not because they were first (which they were) but because they designed their solution to directly overcome the known problems of paper. But simultaneously they developed new business models, a new brand presence, and a new software delivery organization. They delivered an organizational solution—because they were committed to this new direction and planned for it. Having the right design was critical—but aligning the organization made it possible.

USER DATA DRIVES INNOVATION

Contrary to what Apple actually did, the cultural myth about how innovation happens is that some brilliant person goes up a mountain, or into a garage, and invents something new out of whole cloth. We've even heard that one company kept their engineers away from customers intentionally because they didn't want to stifle innovation. But an examination of where brilliant ideas have actually come from suggests the opposite is true—not only does working with users not stifle innovation, but it is the most basic prerequisite.

Dan Bricklin designed VisiCalc, the first spreadsheet, while he was taking accounting classes in business school.[1] He saw the

---

[1] As described in H. Beyer, "Calling Down the Lightning," in *IEEE Software*. September 1994, Vol. 11 No 5, p. 106.

tedious and mechanical work required to manage a paper spreadsheet and realized that with his knowledge of computer systems,
he could automate the calculations while maintaining the spreadsheet metaphor in the user interface.
WordPerfect, one of the first of the modern word
processors, was invented when Alan Ashton and
Bruce Bastian were working downstairs from the
secretaries who were their customers. They would
bring new ideas and new code upstairs on a daily
basis for the secretaries to try and comment on.

Successful innovators immerse themselves in users' practice

These people did not innovate by doing what their users asked
for—no one was asking for an electronic spreadsheet, and word processors were dedicated machines. As we discussed in Part 1, the section
on interviewing, users don't have a good, articulated understanding
of their own practice. They are focused on the day-to-day issues of
doing their jobs. What's more, they have only a limited understanding of what technology might do for
them. Rather than responding to explicit requests,
we find classic innovators immersed in the culture of
their prospective users. Innovators observe problems
first-hand and use their technical knowledge to recognize opportunities for using technology in ways
users themselves may not see. By talking with people immersed in the
activities, building prototypes, and testing them out with users in situ,
innovators turn these ideas into real products. (We'll talk more about
the role of prototyping in Part 5).

No innovation is ever totally disconnected from what went before

The spreadsheet and WordPerfect show that no innovation is ever
totally disconnected from what went before. Paper spreadsheets already
existed for VisiCalc to model; editors and word processors existed before
WordPerfect. The physical "face book"—yearbook—existed at col-
leges before Facebook; music was carried around in
a Walkman before the iPod—and the portable radio
preceded that. Uber opened up the model of the taxi
company to the public and made it work with a great
interface building on known GPS technology and
reasonable security measures. And the list goes on.
Steeped in the world of the user, with the skill to see the possible and
realize it, inventers create practical transformative innovation.

Users reimagine products through their daily use

Innovation that creates a new class of product and captures (for a time) a new market fulfills the core intents, motives, challenges, and longings already present in the lives of people. But once in the hands of users, that new technology reinvents their lives again in ways no one foresaw. Spreadsheets have grown beyond anything accountants envisioned in the 1980s. Word processing today has very little in common with the creation of documents with typewriters. Uber created the sharing economy—not just rides in automobiles. As people adopt a new invention and begin to explore its possibilities, others see the invention as a model for other inventions, and new market and life transformations emerge.[2] New practices become a part of daily life and can now stimulate and challenge the next generation of designers.

Practical innovation is absolutely dependent on having a deep understanding of people's lives. The spark which ignites brilliant design ideas, the niggle in the back of your mind, the flash that excites, happens when designers are steeped in the real lives of the target population. In Contextual Design we create this immersion experience on purpose. Once you collect the field data, interpret, model and consolidate it you are ready for a formal immersion process. Each type of consolidated model puts a specific aspect of the users' lives into focus. Probing into one model after another in quick succession, leads naturally to a synthesis of the issues across models. The team absorbs one coherent aspect

Immerse your team in rich field data to create transformative products

of users' lives at a time, making the complexity of people's lives manageable. Discussing each model in turn begins a dialogue about the data, stimulates design ideas, and simultaneously fosters a shared understanding of the data and initial direction for the design.

With a set of models tuned to communicate insight for the purpose of design, the team can hook into the data quickly. Seeing the life as a whole, what delights and what challenges users, naturally stimulates new possibilities in the mind of people with the skill to realize it.

---

[2] It's through this process that products take over markets. The early adopters show how the product might be used; then as the product matures it becomes easier for the larger market to adopt it. Through continuing innovation which fits the product to the market, the product becomes more likely to succeed. [ref. *Crossing the Chasm*].

People are part of the secret sauce

Good inventors also naturally follow the chain of reasoning outlined in our discussion of interpretation in Chapter 4: see a fact about the user; see why the fact matters for people in the world; recognize the implications for bringing technology to bear on the situation; and turn the opportunity into a concrete design idea. The design isn't explicit in the data. This is often a stumbling block for those new to user-centered design, who sometimes expect the data to tell them what to do. It doesn't work that way. Specific design ideas are rarely in the data; they are inventions created by the team in response to the data.

But this is only true if the designers know what technology can do. They need to be masters of the *materials of design* for their domain.

The team must know modern materials of design to create innovative products

User data may provide the inspiration, but it is the materials of design that are used and recombined to create something transformative. The materials of design include everything that can be brought to bear on the problem: knowledge of apps, responsive design for different screen sizes, appropriate paradigms for presenting information and functions on different devices, use of location information, tracking user actions, active learning, machine learning, accessing cloud data to make the users' data available, UI layouts and graphic design trends, and foundational innovations ready for prime time—these are just some of the materials of design necessary for successful products today.

When technology changes—as it did with the introduction of the window/mouse interface, and again with the web, again with touchscreens on smartphones, and will again when the internet of things becomes a reality—the materials of design change too. Designers have to relearn the materials to stay current. As a community, we also invent new expectations for what is modern. Whereas once a tree structure UI was innovative, it became dated and old. Whereas users once expected to fill out forms to tell applications their preferences, today they expect products to figure out what they want through their actions. Without a thorough grounding in the materials of design at every level, designers cannot create appropriate products for their markets; they must have these ideas and concepts at their fingertips while they are immersed in the users' world so that they can respond creatively with invention, while building on modern standards or creating new ones.

At its core, innovation is a recombination of known parts with a twist: Putting together elements of known practices, technologies, design approaches in new ways to realize a vision of the possible.[3] Good designers steal and twist concepts from one practice and apply it to another. The iPod is just a USB storage stick, already widely used to

> *Innovation is a recombination of known parts—with a twist!*

transfer files but now made beautiful and given an easy interface. Gaming principles are being applied to nongame applications. One successful design for a network management tool borrowed UI concepts from a video game. If the team doesn't know its material, then they can't do a good job. We have seen this over and over with our clients—you can't have a good interaction design if you don't have a trained interaction designer knowledgeable in modern approaches on the team; you can't get a great technology solution with no technologists on the team. A cross-functional innovation team is essential.

This is why in Contextual Design we design in cross-functional teams. When people are immersed in the user data they see it from the vantage point of their own field, skill, and experience. The different perspectives of a cross-functional team determine what kind of product concept they imagine. So the more different perspectives available to the team, the more design options the team can consider. *What* you invent is dependent on *who* is doing the inventing.

The materials that are important to the team are more than the hardware and software possibilities. Product management thinks whole product, shipping, and pricing. Marketing has materials and principles of packaging, product structure, and how to talk to a market. Manufacturing has materials of how to build and deliver the physical product.

> *Apply diverse knowledge and skill sets for a creative response*

Business analysts or process designers bring a way of thinking about how work is done. Service designers or process reengineering professionals have their own perspective and materials to bring to bear

---

[3] Temple Grandin gives an excellent description of this recombination for invention in her book *Thinking in Pictures*.

on the overall solution, beyond a technology-only focus. So what marketing sees isn't the same as what development sees; each profession brings its own perspective and its own materials. Successful innovation requires a command of the materials of design needed to support the project focus.

DIVERSITY ON TEAMS MEANS BETTER DESIGN

Using cross-functional teams has been a cornerstone of Contextual Design from its inception. We've seen for many years how this leads to better designs and innovation.

But what about having teams with a mix of gender, race, sexual orientation, and culture? What impact does that have, especially since at this writing high-tech companies are striving—and struggling—to have more diverse workforces?

There's an abundance of evidence we can point to that positively correlated diversity with innovation and financial success. If you are working with an executive in business, academia, or government who cares about numbers—and they all care about numbers—here are a few examples you can use to support the importance of having diverse teams.

- A McKinsey & Company study found that organizations in the top quartile for gender and racial diversity have better financial returns when compared to their industry medians. Companies in the bottom quartile are statistically less likely to achieve above-average returns. In other words, diversity is a competitive differentiator. The natural extension of this finding is that other forms of diversity such as age, sexual orientation, and culture could also bring an advantage.[1]

- A National Center for Women & Information (NCWIT) analysis of IT patents found the US patents produced by mixed gender teams were cited 30–40% more than other similar patents. This analysis has been done twice—2007 and 2012—with very similar results.[1]

- The London Business School studied the impact of women in professional working teams and found that the optimal gender representation on teams is 50:50. The study concluded that when innovation is crucial, companies should construct teams with equal proportions of men and women. Note the emphasis on equal. In their words, "tokenism" had negative results on both the women and the team's performance.[1]

- In a study by Ernst & Young, researchers demonstrated that diverse groups almost always outperformed homogenous one—and by a substantial margin. This held true even when the members of the homogenous group were individually more capable.[1]

Nothing in this research says that it's easy for these diverse groups to work together. Rather, at times what makes them so effective—a variety of perspectives, experiences, and attitudes—make working together challenging. So we're back to another cornerstone of Contextual Design. It's comprised of a series of techniques designed to help people work together as a team.

Beside these functional roles we now know that women, men, and other diverse groups have different points of view on life and product. Inclusion of underrepresented groups such as women on a design team leads to more creative results.[4] It's hard to imagine any woman inventing such a painful and awkward procedure as mammogram—and no woman did.[5] But we are stuck with as the only way to get a clear picture until someone replaces it!

Each person on the team brings their own skills and perspectives, which impact what is ultimately conceived and delivered. Creative design comes from immersing the right people with the right skill into the data in the context of a process that helps them invent a coherent response together. Through their discussions, team members learn each other's perspectives while they use the skills and technical knowledge they bring to the table. As the whole team dialogues with the data, they reassemble the whole user context in their minds and respond to it from their individual points of view. Then when they participate in a group visioning process, each of their voices can help reinvent the way technology will enhance life.

THE CHALLENGE OF DESIGN FOR LIFE

The Cool Concepts reveal the scope of design that a team must consider—and they provide their own new perspective on the design challenge. As directors moved from stage to movies and now to motion-capture technology, the old way of telling, visualizing, and creating a story had to change. Early movies did little more than put a camera in front of a stage;

Design for life requires that we think about what we are making differently

the practice evolved as directors explored the possibilities of the new technology. Now scenes are filmed bit by bit and often in conjunction with graphic rendering.

---

[4] Vivian Hunt, Dennis Layton, and Sara Prince. Why Diversity Matters. McKinsey & Company. January 2015.
Catherine Ashcroft and Anthony Breitzman. Who Invents IT? Women's Participation in Information Technology Patenting. National Center for Women & Information. 2012 Update.
[5] In 1986 Patrick Panetta and Jack Wennet invented the decompression unit at the core of mammography today.

In the same way, continuing to conceive of products as feature lists or task support tools will not result in products that support the Cool Concepts and will not redesign life. Design for life does not mean just designing for more tasks, or for a different type of task. It does not mean having a product on every platform, or putting bits and pieces of function in a phone but leaving the real work on a big computer. Design for life calls for a new way of thinking than the one the User Experience field (ourselves included!) has been promoting since the 90's.

Focus on delivering value in moments—design for time!

Design for life recognizes the unstructured nature of peoples' activities as they do bits and pieces of work and home tasks on multiple platforms throughout the day. Design for life also introduces a focus on design for time—providing value in moments of dead time, time between activities, and break time. And people care about their important people, community, and their identity. They like tools that provide visual interest and fun. Designers who think only about activities and cognition miss much of what causes people to love a product "Task-oriented design," though better than feature-oriented design, now misses the mark.

But design for the Wheel of Joy in life is also not enough. Joy in use is essential: the magic of getting things done in moments, the disappearance of every technical hassle, and tools that deliver instant into action use with no learning. A "good enough" user interface is no longer an acceptable user experience for any kind of application. If the product does not deliver value at first glance and interaction, if it holds life hostage with its complexity and confusion, if it expects any learning—well, it simply won't be adopted.

Invent new user experience approaches—good enough isn't enough

The time of huge monolithic applications or websites is waning. No more locking the user to their chair inside your application, hoarding users' data and not sharing with other applications, adding more function and complexity but adding little value, clinging to old style interfaces. Design for life means direct support for users' intents in small chunks when needed, accessible across multiple platforms in the smoothest, smartest interfaces you can imagine. This is the challenge faced by teams today. Your market may not yet be clamoring for this but it will—and if you are the first to deliver, you will claim the market.

To make this happen, designers need explicit support in using the Cool Concepts and Experience Models to guide design. We have found that, when immersed in this data with a design process that makes use of it, a team's way of thinking magically moves in the direction of design for life.

A DESIGN PROCESS FOR INVENTION

The single biggest challenge we hear from design teams is how to use the data they collect to drive new product concepts. People get caught up in their personal hot ideas, what the last big customer said, the enhancement database, and of course longing to be the next transformative product. Some want the data to tell them directly what to do—others fear that user data will constrain them too much. As we have said, data is a tool; it does not direct or constrain. It creates a context for invention. Any product must fit

Data is a tool; it does not dictate design

into people's life structure, improving life activities while juggling life's demands. The life of the people you are designing for is the water in which your product must swim. A design process needs to guide you in looking at the data so you can see what's needed to enhance the journey.

At the same time, since product development requires multiple people with multiple organizational functions to collaborate, any ideation process must help people work together to generate product ideas. Discussion and synthesis, in a group, without argument, within a reasonable timeframe depends on a clear process—a set of concrete actions to take. That's what Contextual Design provides.

In this Part we introduce an ideation process that has been used and honed over the last 20 years. It is built on the principles of immersion, team design, and ensuring the team produces a result that is both impactful and keeps the users' lives coherent. Successful ideation focuses first on

A good ideation process starts wide, then works out details

generating wide-ranging impactful ideas and then honing these to something workable—always guided by data. In Part 3 we will walk through the steps of ideation that drive overall concept and direction: the *Wall Walk*, *Visioning*, and the *Cool Drilldown*. In 2–5 days, depending on the scope of the project, the team can generate a set of high-level product concepts stimulated by the team's dialogue with the data and honed by the Cool Concepts.

In Chapter 10 we describe the *Wall Walk* where the team immerses themselves in the consolidated data and generate initial design ideas in response to it. The Wall Walk is a prerequisite to participation in Visioning. It is also a great way to share data with stakeholders and other groups who might benefit from the data but may not be on the Visioning team. The result of the Wall Walk is an initial set of issues the Visioning team must address and the first "hot ideas" which can be used to start off ideation.

In Chapter 11 we describe *Visioning* where the team tells the story of the new life of the user if technology solutions were applied to their activities. In a series of visions the team addresses the issues they saw. Creative design is hampered by agreeing too quickly. It's important that the design team think widely and consider several alternatives, including radical solutions, before converging on a single approach. The team develops multiple solutions, pulling out different aspects of the users' situation to address. These different solutions are consolidated into a set of high-level product concepts that the team determines is best to take forward.

A good ideation process explores multiple divergent ideas before converging on one

With a set of concepts in hand, we next discuss the *Cool Drilldown*. This facilitated process focuses on enriching those product concepts using the principles of the Cool Concepts. Addressing one Cool Concept at a time, the teams deepen the design, adding detail focused on supporting each concept in turn—based on the data. The result is a set of high-level product concepts tuned for cool and fitting the user's world.

Contextual Design ideation techniques focus the team on imagining technology in the world of the user—not on generating a list of possible features. This ensures that the technology fits life. It's important that the design process make these steps explicit. Much of the argument within a team at this point looks like arguments about features: Sue wants to implement a shared online place where everyone traveling can share ideas. Bob thinks that wastes time and that they can just use email, text, and maybe a Google Doc. Joe wants to give the main planner full control, with everyone else just making suggestions. This isn't just an argument about features—it's a disagreement about what the most natural and successful travel planning process is, and what people will value. It's asking which human-technical system is best. So trying to settle the argument by talking about technology or features is futile.

Reduce interpersonal friction through explicit process

Instead, Contextual Design immerses the team in the actual data together. Contextual Design guides them to consider all the technology available to them to use and ensures they understand the basic intents and motives of the travelers. As a result, those arguments evaporate—the data and Cool Concepts reveal what makes sense for the users. Giving the team time to think about the different aspects of travel planning and the implications for design both makes it easier for the team to have the design conversation together and makes the team more creative.

This is the goal of the Contextual Design innovation steps: to look across the different Experience Models and see a unified picture of the practice; to use the team's perspectives and skills to reveal the issues; to widely explore multiple possibilities to open up the team's collective mind; to apply the Cool Concepts to ensure joy is built in; and then the team will be ready to hone the detail so it works for people, the team, and the business. This is how creative solutions that work can be consistently generated. With the right data, the right people, and the right process, practical innovation can be baked into your organization.

The Bridge From Data to Design: The Wall Walk

10

The Wall Walk is designed to help the team explore the data and its implications for the design. It is the immersion step prior to ideation and occurs right before Visioning. It is Contextual Design's formal process for drawing the product team into the world of the user. The Wall Walk is the bridge from data to design; it solves the problem of how to ensure that the team will design from the users' world as a lived experience.

Getting designers to invent from data is not actually the hard problem. Any engineer, designer, product manager, or content creator—anyone tasked with creating new offerings—naturally starts inventing design ideas once they actually see the challenges and opportunities in the users' world.

> The Wall Walk is the bridge immersing the extended team in data

This is the very essence of being a designer: you are always looking at the world and are driven to improve, enhance, and enliven lives with new inventions and technology. Inventors will invent. The hard part is getting the whole team to engage with the data and respond to it creatively together.

Our challenge is to engage the team so that they take the data in—own it—and want to come back to it time and time again. That is why we spent so much time getting our consolidated data well-designed for communication. The Wall Walk is what you have been getting ready for—it is the debut of the data. Now you will find out

Contextual Design. http://dx.doi.org/10.1016/B978-0-12-800894-2.00010-7

how well your communication design efforts on the Affinity and consolidated models will stimulate design thinking. But communication design has one last principle to complete the bridge to design: *interaction with the data.*

Reading the data will not ensure it gets into the mind of designers, that it is internalized and tunes the inner gut feel to align with the world of the user. It is too easy to skim; it is too easy to space out; it is too easy to not engage with reports, slideshows, and white papers. The principle of interaction calls upon us to stimulate the team to really engage the data—to think of ways to draw them into the data so they will process it and see its implications. This is what walking the data and posting design ideas is all about.

When people actively interact with the data they internalize it

The Wall Walk is an opportunity for individuals to privately engage the data using the writing of design ideas as a way to stimulate their thinking. Much of Contextual Design happens in group meetings which keep people active and engaged. By contrast, the Wall Walk allows for individual thinking and reflection in preparation for the group experience. Any individual activity benefits from having a clear purpose with expectations. Having something specific to do while reviewing the large amount of information in the Affinity and Experience Models helps team members focus. Without that, they might just skim the surface or become overwhelmed. But with a coherent task focusing them on thinking about the data, they can systematically engage with it. This is the purpose of both writing design ideas in response to the data and the challenge questions on the models. Then the team can let their minds react from the perspective of their experience and their skill. It is in this moment that insight and invention happens—in the encounter with the users' world. Rather than wandering the world for real until a great idea hits, we have assembled structured user data into an immersion experience to deliberately create the conditions for initial idea stimulation.

Getting the team immersed and engaged with the users' world is the necessary first step for our ideation processes. No one gets to vision who has not been steeped in the data—it's the immersion that ensures people design for the target market and not from "The I."

The Wall Walk takes anywhere from 2 to 6 hours depending on the number of models and the extent of data you have prepared. The Affinity and all the models are printed in large format and hung on the walls of a large conference room. The Visioning team and any stakeholders you invite will now walk the data, sticking design ideas up on the wall right next to the data that stimulated the thought. This interactive process focuses team members on how their design ideas respond to the data they are looking at. Walking the data in a facilitated group process creates a time-bound, interactive event producing a tangible result focused on creating new product concepts.

Anyone who visions must first be steeped in the user data

During the Wall Walk we aren't looking for full-blown design solutions; we just want team members to think about the data in detail and start to envision all the different ways they might respond to it. Just as we set focus before going on an interview so people know what to look at, we use these activities to get the team's ideation juices going. Then, through discussion, we start to build a shared focus for Visioning a solution. When the user data is understood and internalized, team members will find it natural to design solutions which respond to the primary issues it raises.

This is a good point to include others in the process, whether or not they gathered data and whether or not they will participate in Visioning. Consider inviting your other key stakeholders such as managers and adjacent groups who will benefit from seeing the data. External groups can walk the wall, take away insights for their own problems, and also contribute to both teams' thinking. When your data collection and synthesis team did not include engineers, product managers, or interaction designers or other critical skill sets, this is the point to invite the larger team into the design process. They can walk the data and participate in the vision. This is the best way to develop a shared direction between those who will be responsible for creating the product.

Invite anyone invested in the product to the Wall Walk

For example, one automotive team collected such extensive data about everything that happened within the vehicle that it was relevant for industrial design, storage, interior layout, marketing, and more. So they ran multiple Wall Walks, inviting different groups to see and learn about their customers. This built buy-in across the organization and exposed everyone to the richness of field data. The depth of knowledge represented gave the team credibility with other internal groups. Never forget, product development is about managing the organization, and the Wall Walk is a great technique.

The Wall Walk is a facilitated meeting introducing the process and guiding the people to use their time efficiently. It starts by introducing the group to the focus of the project and the kind of people interviewed. If you have personas, present them here. Then the group walks the Affinity Diagram, putting up design ideas. This is followed by making lists of what the team learned and their key design ideas. Then we apply the same process to each consolidated model: introducing the model, putting up design ideas, and adding to the lists.

> *The Wall Walk facilitates a dialogue between people, the data, and each other*

Taken together, the Wall Walk creates a structured dialogue between people, the data, and each other. Everyone can discover what matters in the users' world and what initial design directions were stimulated. It is a great way for everyone to get a high-level feel for the team's initial design thinking without discussing anything in detail or committing to any one direction. Working out more detail and coming to a shared direction is the job of Visioning and the Cool Drilldown covered in Chapter 11. Doing the Wall Walk together creates a buzz in the room—and lots of side conversations—all of which contribute to getting the group moving in the same direction.

WALKING THE AFFINITY

The Affinity Diagram is structured to tell the story of how users do the target activity while living their lives. During consolidation you arranged all the individual notes to present their activities and issues coherently in a hierarchical structure. Walking the Affinity gives the team a chance to review and think about what this story means for the product they hope to design. It's the team's first chance to see the whole scope of data together, and consider how to respond with a coherent design solution.

The Wall Walk is managed like a visit to an art museum—each person experiences the data silently, having their own experience with it, and writing up design ideas as they go. After introducing the process, the facilitator acts as the guard reminding people to be quiet so that everyone can explore the data on their own. The Affinity panels are placed in a natural order for telling the story, but it need not be walked in that order. People can spread out to find a green section that draws them in and then proceed around the room. We do recommend that no one start with tool problems—that will focus you on small, one-off tool fixes. It's better to start with the meat of the practice. Participants from other groups can be directed to those parts of the Affinity most immediately relevant to them, and they can work from there to the rest of the wall. Seeing the part they care about gets them interested; from there, they can see how it hooks into the larger life context.

The Affinity presents the story of the users' world

Participants read the story top-down, starting from the green label, then the pinks, and then the blues, so they start with the high-level statement of an issue and work down to the specifics. They read the individual notes as necessary to get examples and details summarized in the blues. Each person follows his or her own thread, building their own understanding of the data, and exploring the design consequences in their mind. So loud discussion is disruptive. If participants feel a need to talk, the facilitator directs them into the hall until they are ready to continue the walk.

Each participant is given a pad of 3 × 5 stickies and a blue Sharpie pen. When a design idea strikes them, they write it on a sticky note and post it at the label that generated the idea. They may also record "holes" in the data with a green Sharpie. Holes record additional information and questions the participant would like answered, and that might be answered in future interviews. By writing them down, participants get them off their mind so they can go back to reading the wall and generating ideas. This is how we make sure that individual concerns about the data are captured without disrupting the overall process.

For some people, design ideas may start small and vague, responding to a blue label here or there. But as they see more and more of the whole practice revealed by the Affinity, they naturally start to weave together themes and develop ideas which address larger aspects of the users' world expressed in the pink and green labels. Eventually they may see a coherent product concept addressing much of the wall. These are convergent thinkers. They build up multiple small ideas into something larger—but only from the thematic point of view they see. Other people will see each chunk of data as a separate challenge creating more divergent design ideas—several for each label. They don't see the links between the ideas; they just see lots of possibilities. You need both kinds of inventers on your team to ultimately envision something coherent that addresses the full scope of the design challenge.

We also try to encourage everyone to be strategic in their thinking. We strongly discourage design ideas that address the individual notes. These would be tiny fixes, not a source of significant new value or market transformation. And we create a game—we challenge the team to push themselves to generate design ideas that will address the issues in whole blues, whole pinks, and whole greens, pushing the scope of their ideas wider. Out-of-the-box reasoning is naturally facilitated by trying to think of something at the green level. And we give them a place for ideas that address the whole Affinity—as an ultimate challenge! We find that everyone likes this little bit of competition and self-challenge. In the end it serves to drive them deeply into the data—again forming that bridge from the data to design.

The challenge is to address the whole wall of issues with a single design idea

Finally, we discourage people from reading each other's notes on the first pass over the wall. We don't want them to get stuck in thinking about each other's ideas. But if they have time, on a second pass people can read each other's notes and see how others are responding to the data—and this may stimulate more design thinking.

Writing design ideas on the wall is a great way of interacting with the data. It provides a way to stimulate initial design thinking from data, helps everyone feel that they contributed something to the design, and brings everyone in the room into contact with the same expression of the users' world. In this way everyone ends up on the same page automatically, without need for discussion or resolving differences. The data is the final word on who the user is and what the user is doing. Once you walk it, you know their world too.

The Wall Walk brings everyone into a shared understanding of the user

The Affinity Diagram is the centerpiece of Contextual Design's bridge to design thinking. Every project should have one. It is the first step before Visioning and later it is a key reference to find and remember the data to guide detailed design.

MAKING LISTS: CREATING A FOCUS FOR CREATIVITY

After the team walks the Affinity we want to capture our learnings and our ideas. Having just immersed in the data the team knows what stood out and what ideas they are excited about. If we wait any length of time, people forget their gut feel of what matters and what to do about it. So after we walk the Affinity, and again after each model, we capture what the group saw.

We create two lists. The first is a list of *issues*. Issues are observations you made about the nature of the practice, what is broken, what is surprising, and what might be an opportunity. The issues list answers the question, "If this is the world of the user what must we address, support, or solve to add value and improve their world?" An issue is not a design idea or solution. It is the practice that we must consider when creating a design. We avoid talking about "user needs" because a user may never feel like they "need" anything—instead an issue is the team's perception of what matters in the data to address.

Walking the data creates a team focus for the vision

To create the list a facilitator stands up at the flipchart and writes down whatever the team who walked the wall yells out to them. Everything is written down in the order it arises, unless it is actually a solution. For example, "Travelers need a single location to store all their travel ideas" is not an issue or user need. It is a design idea. In such cases the facilitator pushes the team to identify the issue behind the design idea, such as: "Travelers keep sending each other tons of links in email and text and lose track of them." This is the practice issue that any number of design ideas could address.

By recording everything the team lists until they run out of issues, we harvest the group's thoughts and share them aloud so that all can hear what others think matter from their individual perspectives. This is the simplest and fastest way to get a shared focus for Visioning. Everyone has been heard, everything has been recorded, and now we can use this list to guide Visioning and to communicate insights to others. The lists are produced quickly, in about 15 minutes each, because everyone walked the wall and understands the context.

After making your list of issues, make a list of *Hot Ideas* in the same way. This is a list of specific design ideas. It isn't simply rewriting every design idea the team put on the Affinity and models; those were uncommitted, spur-of-the-moment ideas—they may not even be good ideas. Small ideas may have built up during the Wall Walk into bigger, more strategic ideas. Contextual Design encourages the team not to get overly attached to every design idea on the wall; don't treat them as an enhancement database.

Design ideas on the wall are to feed creativity only—not a commitment to implement

Instead, see them as the residual notes of creative thought—good ideas won't be forgotten in the Visioning process.

But we do need good starting points for our visions—Hot Ideas that will stimulate creative design thinking. So we write a list of the most strategic, wide-ranging design ideas that have captured the imagination of team members. Hot Ideas can be contradictory. They can be extreme, more extreme than the company is likely to accept—but even these ideas can push a new way of thinking. Each of these ideas is a seed, a starting point for the team to elaborate into a whole approach to a design problem. A hot idea may be:

- A *slogan* that the team wants to commit to. For example, here's a goal for the installation of a new mainframe computer system, "Be up and running in 24 hours."

- A *metaphor* for what the practice is, such as: "The lab should be like Federal Express tracking packages—you always know the state of every experiment," or "Make travel planning like a game."

- A *technology challenge*: "Automate everything; never ask the client for a single document" the insurance department needs.

- A *user experience challenge*: "Put the manager's whole job on the phone."

- A *business challenge*: For a retail firm, "Eliminate channel silos! No matter where the customer starts, online, in the store, or on the phone, they have one coherent experience end to end."

- A *data challenge*: "Bring all information about every customer from every system into one coherent page for the agent."

Capturing the broadest, most systemic ideas in a list is an easy way for the team to share the ideas that excited them without committing to building anything and without having to argue about whose idea is best. During the process, people will be tempted to elaborate on the ideas when they come out. Discourage that. The time for elaborating is the vision. Now, just capture a list and don't worry how things might overlap or could be grouped. Some team members tend to offer small, one-off ideas as Hot Ideas. Don't shut them down, but where you can build up their ideas into large, systemic ideas. For example: "You want to let people mark favorite places? That's a good idea, but it's a single feature—let's make it part of a whole facility where the system knows the user, tracks their preferences and offers them options that match what they like–like Pandora." This lets the individual be heard and teaches the team how to think systemically.

Hot Ideas provide a seed to start the vision

The Hot Ideas list lets everyone hear where others are coming from, and lets everyone voice what they are excited about. In this way all start to consider what these ideas might mean; the team chats informally, exploring the possibilities—all with no commitment and no need for formal agreement. This helps prepare the team for Visioning.

The bridge from data to design has to work not just for individual designers, but to bring the whole team together in a shared direction, without overly constraining design thinking or converging on a single solution too quickly. List-making after data immersion is a great way for the team to share thoughts and create focus without engaging in a long, contentious dialogue about the most important thing to do. Because it is just a step in a process of moving from immersion to design, it does the job quickly. When done you have a set of the issues and Hot Ideas that you can reference to help focus and direct the vision, and that you can return to for later detailed design.

Having a clear process to engage with data helps everyone be creative

WALKING THE EXPERIENCE MODELS

After walking the Affinity and making lists, the team walks each of the Contextual Design Models—the Experience and Traditional Models—in a similar way. The basic rules of interaction are the same but since models are not as big, introduce one or two models at a time and then assign small groups to each model. If you have a lot of people, it's helpful to make two copies of the models so several small groups can look at the same model at the same time.

Each model represents a different point of view, a different dimension of practice. When people walk one after another, they naturally synthesize all the different dimensions into a single three-dimensional picture of the user. Our communication design presents information in a guiding structure and self-contained story chunks, leading participants to respond to each chunk as a whole but with the larger context in mind. All this helps participants respond with ideas that are relevant to the whole problem, not just point solutions to particular problems. In addition, the questions and "Give Me's" on models present challenges readers can respond to—providing a Way In for the participant.

Each model helps keep the practice coherent—so design ideas are broader

At this initial stage, when the team is still deciding on a design direction, you are looking for high-level, "what matters" issues that will affect overall direction. As participants read and discuss each Contextual Design model, they naturally bring in issues from the other models and from the Affinity. What started as point solutions to individual problems weave together into a synthetic response to the whole user situation over the course of the Wall Walk experience.

Look for high-level issues and opportunities first

When the small groups have had enough time on each model, make lists of issues and Hot Ideas model by model. Each model raises a different set of issues and drives design thinking in a different way. Here we look at the unique perspective of each of the Contextual Design Models.

DAY-IN-THE-LIFE: FIT TECHNOLOGY WITH THE PLACE, TIME, AND SITUATIONS OF LIFE

The Day-in-the-Life model drives the team to think about how their solution fits into life. It reveals all the times and places throughout the day that users think about the activity the design needs to support, and shows all the technology and connectivity available to the user at that moment. It helps the team get out of the box of thinking of their product as supporting a person sitting in a chair in an office using the product in a focused interaction with no interruptions. It helps them deal with the reality of mobile, always-connected lives.

A look at the consolidated travel model (Fig. 7.1) shows how travel planning happens on multiple platforms in spare moments throughout the day, with par- 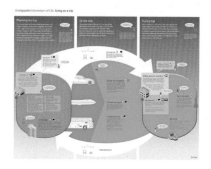 tial attention, and may be interrupted at any time. A key take away is that time that would otherwise be wasted dead time is now useful. Also we see that planning happens during the trip itself—it is not a process of creating a plan and then executing the plan. Rather, travel involves evolving, continuous decision making. Any design should support this context of use by being quick to pick up and get into, simple enough to work despite partial attention, and hold the user's place when they are interrupted.

Introduce each model and its core focus so people know what to look for

Every Day-in-the-Life model tells the story of how your activity is accomplished while moving through all the activities of life. So while walking this model for insight, ask yourself about these things:

- Where are the activities happening? Can your activity be done *anytime, anywhere*? What is the overall context you have to consider when supporting this?

- How is *time* used? What happens in moments versus longer periods of more concentration? How could you support making meaningful decisions, making some progress, or really doing a step of an activity in moments?

- How long does the user have and does that lead to split *attention*? Is the activity in each place prone to random interruptions? Can your design let users pick up the activity quickly enough and be interrupted without losing progress?

- What are the *smaller intents* the person has as they move through their day? How can they be supported in chunks of action and information?

- What *devices* support the activities? Are they connected? How big is the screen? Do they have a keyboard? How can you overcome the constraints of the device available? How can you leverage unique features of the devices—e.g., the camera on cell phones?

- What *information* do they need? What will keep their life or work moving? What real-time data can move decisions and actions forward? What review and signoff can occur on the go?

Identity Model: enhance the expression of self

The Identity Model tells the team how users see themselves: what characteristics they are invested in, their source of pride, and self-value. Users approach any activity from the point of view of their perceived self as relevant to the target task. The Identity Model characterizes the market as a whole; any single user will manifest no more than a few identity elements. But if you design for them all, you will cover the market.

The *Cultural Sponge* from our travel example will enjoy immersing herself in local culture, in the details a mere tourist wouldn't know about—she will love quick, easy, and locally relevant access to those details. But *Family Travelers* won't care about that—they'll want to hear about how the local hotel will cater to their children and how to get to child-centered activities easily. The

The Identity Model invites design ideas for each identity element

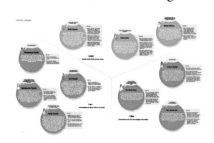

Master Planner will love help getting and staying organized, and finding just the right things for the travelers to do—because part of their self-value comes from

Your project focus determines the type of design ideas you generate

giving the other travelers a great experience.

During the Wall Walk, challenge the team to put design ideas on every identity element. Let the Give Me's suggest a focus but everyone should come up with their own ideas. For people who manifest these identity elements, ask yourself:

- What *function or information* can the product or service provide that will help the user achieve the core driver of that aspect of self? How can your product help them be their best selves?

- Alternatively, what in the current user experience *undermines self esteem*? What undercuts the sense of pride, competency, and being knowledgeable? How can you change it?

- What *market messages* will appeal to this identity element? What do you have to deliver and highlight to attract their attention?

- How can you help people *celebrate* their accomplishments— or anything they are proud of? How does the culture of the profession or people determine what's appropriate—so the celebration is professional and doesn't feel like bragging? Remember, sharing doesn't have to be solely through existing social media forums. One team invented personal scrapbooks for medical professionals who collected their achievements but didn't want to go public or brag.

- Will *sharing* enhance this aspect of self? What forums, if any, make sense? What content might be shared as part of manifesting this aspect of self? Who would users be sharing with, and why do they matter? Are they professional colleagues, communities of interest, friends?

- Is *competition or games* appropriate for this character type? If so, what are others like them doing? How can you provide games to spur involvement and excitement?

In addition, your product may be supporting emerging aspects of identity. Identity elements form over time and become stable but people look for help during the formation phase. Young people and people new to an activity or role must form their own sense of self relative to that activity or role. For example, young people care

Emerging adults and professionals need a different design response

about what it means to be an adult and want to make adult decisions so they look for role models. New parents want to know the latest parenting techniques among those most like them. Online resources help support these decisions providing example actions and values. Finding and sharing experience with people "like me" for this aspect of self supports these emerging aspects of identity.

Forming a unique identity really means forming something that feels right for the self and also fits with those in my community that I identify with. If your population contains people who are taking on new roles or forming who they want to be when performing the target activity, consider the above questions from that point of view. And ask how you can provide content about what others like them think, choose, and do. How can you help them be confident that their decisions are right? And how can you help them get quick feedback on their choices from friends and family that matter?

THE RELATIONSHIP MODEL: SUPPORT REAL RELATIONSHIPS

People depend on their relationships to inform and guide what they do. The Relationship Model describes who is involved in an activity and how they contribute to the sense of connection and relationship. And it tells you who is *not* someone who matters—or who is not close and so is in a less impactful relationship. In our travel example, the important relationships to enhance are those in the inner circle—spouse, close friends, children, and parents. Notice that communities of interest don't even make it on to the model— for travel planning, they may be resources but they are not real relationships.

The Relationship Model focuses you on increasing the intimacy between people

The Cool Concept of Connection taught us that we can deliberately enhance relationships. So while walking this model for insight, ask:

- Who are the *people that matter*? What is their core role in the target activity? How can you better support that interaction? How can you enhance being a part of a family, friends, or work group?

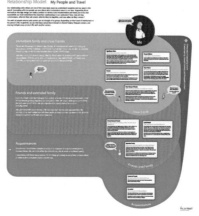

- How can you help people *connect frequently*? How can they share easily about things relevant to the target task—no matter where they are and what device they use?

- How can you help people *connect positively*? How can you reduce friction? How can you provide information that reduces the need to nag? How can you increase the value people provide each other?

- What *conversational content* will enhance the relationship? What information or content can you provide that promotes conversation, face to face or remote? Can you remove hassle in the way of sharing this content? Can you support quick, informed conversation between team members?

- Can you help people *do things together*? Can you help people find things to do relevant to your target activity? Can you make doing the activity more fun?

- Can you help people *celebrate the relationship* and what they did together? Can you help collect and share pictures, documents, memories of shared activities—and so create more conversations?

- Who is giving *advice and support*? What are their values and messages? If the users' parents are emphasizing responsibility and diligence, that becomes a focus for the user too. If there are go-to experts such as a mechanic, a knowledgeable uncle, or other informed person in the users' circles, can your product deliver value those experts will recognize? Win over the influencers!

- Can you help *expand their network* of relationships? When the user doesn't have the relationships they need, offering an online or real community of trusted people with a shared interest can be valuable. But if people already have enough resources and friends, don't try to force a community on them! It won't be used.

Make sure users want a community that helps the business before you invent one

It's the job of the Relationship Model to show what community means and what will be valued by your population. If it makes sense for you to create a community of users, it will be apparent in the data. But don't assume this is always needed. Professionals already have their trusted communities, and shoppers already have their trusted friends and family. Master Planners find their trusted sites—but for information, not for relationship. On the other hand, far-flung hobbyists love to share their creations and love to trade tips on their hobby. When the community they need doesn't exist, this is the time to think about creating one.

COLLABORATION MODEL: SUPPORT THE DAILY COLLABORATION OF WORK AND LIFE

The Collaboration Model matters especially for professional or volunteer work groups collaborating to get something done. When the work activity calls for more organized, cooperative behavior and when your

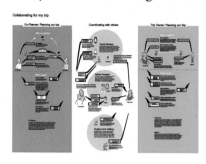

product can help smooth that cooperation, you deliver value. Family or personal activities may also need this level of collaboration for complex tasks—and usually have inadequate tools to help. With the on-the-go, connected life people are living now, it's natural to depend a lot on remote and mobile devices for coordinating.

Effective collaboration requires that people be able to interact. Videoconferencing tools such as Skype, real-time messaging, photo sharing, and good old email all have become technologies you may need to integrate. And effective collaboration always means exchanging information and progress updates—while getting rid of bottlenecks in the work. The roles people play when doing an activity imply what information they need, what will move the activity along, and the kind of updates they need. In our travel Collaboration Model (Fig. 7.19), the challenge is to support a smooth back-and-forth exchange of travel choices between the planners, their advisors, and other travelers. Can we infuse fun into considering all the choices while making the planning decisions easy for all travelers involved?

These considerations are added to those of the Relationship Model. It's still critical to provide frequent contact, conversational content, and things to do together. But now we also consider:

Effective instant communication and collaboration is the design goal

- Can you help people *contact each other in a positive way* to check in, discuss decisions, and conduct meetings? Can you make project information available so status and progress is always known—so nagging and helicopter oversight are minimized?

- Are you supporting the *roles* people are playing with the right information and easy exchange between collaborating players?

- Do you help people share *real-time project information* and find out what is happening—anytime, anywhere? Provide in-the-moment status, identify bottlenecks, and support quick sign-off to keep tasks moving along.

- Does everyone have access to the *background project information* such as a history of what has been done, a collection of reference material, and other useful resources? Remember that resources can be people as well as documents and websites.

- Do people have the *artifacts* they are collaborating over available to them: the document they are creating, their spreadsheets, or their plans? There's always some created artifact to make the conversation concrete.

- Can you help people manage work relationships so they show up *professionally*? Particularly when remote, professional presentation can be a challenge.

- Can you help people *connect personally* so they have non-verbal cues of what is happening or personal stories to make work relationships more real?

Both the Relationship Model and Collaboration Model help people interact and stay in touch with each other in ways that enhance the feeling of connection. But in today's world, this is often centered on keeping the relationships and project work going while remote or on the go. So keep the Day-in-the-Life model handy so you can design mobile support for moments of collaboration interspersed throughout a users' life.

SENSATION BOARD: CREATE SENSUAL DELIGHT

The Sensation Board is an inspirational list of words, phrases, and pictures that represent the experiences of the people interviewed—what they feel now and what they would like to feel. It evokes the sensual and emotional experience that the team wants to evoke in the market—based on the data. It provides visual and industrial designers with a user-centered emotional focus for their work. This emotional focus is also useful for products with a primary focus on delivering an emotional experience, such as game designers.

"Inspiration boards" are already a part of the work of these professionals, so the Sensation Board is familiar to them—it's just an inspiration board developed from user data and focused on the aesthetic or sensation aspect of design. When visual and industrial designers are part of the team we invite them to interact with the Sensation Board by putting up design ideas—but using drawings, sketches, colors, animation ideas, cartoons, and other visual representations of their initial design thinking.

The Experience Models are built to drive design thinking. Like the Affinity Diagram, they are big picture models that reveal the whole scope of the users' world. Walking the wall interactively opens up the thinking of the design team as they progressively take in one perspective on the users' world after another. The data characterizes the large issues and the primary practices of the market. They encourage the team to integrate all the models into a deep, 360-degree view of the life of the users. This big picture helps the team uncover the large strategic possibilities for this market.

WALKING THE TRADITIONAL CONTEXTUAL DESIGN MODELS

The Traditional Contextual Design Models are detailed models. They focus the team down into the detail of what is happening in the steps of a task, decision making, or interaction with space. They generate more targeted, lower-level design ideas than the Experience Models. Walk these after the other models, so the team has the big picture view already. These models provide an immersion experience akin to looking at life through a magnifying glass, as opposed to the sweeping view of the big picture models.

The process for walking the Traditional Contextual Design Models is the same as for the Experience Models: introduce them, walk them, and put up design ideas as you go. Then, as before, make issues and hot idea lists recording only the new ideas and issues. We'll discuss how to derive design implications from the models we have found most useful—the other models are treated similarly.

SEQUENCE MODELS: IMPROVE THE STEPS OF A TASK

Sequence Models make the detailed structure of a task explicit. They show how the task is broken into activities, the intents that people are

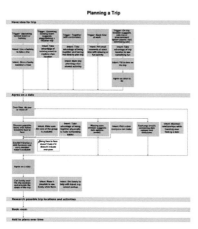

trying to accomplish in doing the task, the different strategies people use, and the individual steps which make up the task. Sequences are your best guide to structuring a product to match and extend the way people approach a task.

A Sequence Model describes how a particular task is done. It is composed of the activities, their steps, the associated intents and breakdowns. Each of these elements are natural chunks inviting design ideas. Just as with the Affinity, design ideas at the whole sequence or activity level are larger ideas than those at the step level. Remember that the core challenge of the Sequence Model is to design a better way to fulfill the intents of the sequence—or to eliminate the need for that intent altogether. Breakdowns naturally invite solutions, but don't think just at this level. If all your designing is too low level, you will solve all the small problems and miss the opportunity to redesign the task as a whole. While walking the Sequence Model for insight, ask yourself:

- What is the user trying to accomplish? Every consolidated sequence has a *primary intent*—the reason why the task was worth doing in the first place. Can you simplify life by helping to achieve intent of the sequence in a radically more direct way?

- Can you *automate the whole process*? Could the primary intent be supported instantly through machine learning, smart algorithms, data integration, or other ways of getting the job done for the user? Or do you need to invent a combination of automation and user interaction to support all the intents of that sequence?

- How can you support the *multiple strategies* that people use to get the task done? Strategies emerge from the needs of different roles, work styles, intents, and circumstances. There are usually two to four in any market, and each usually represents a significant part of the market. So good design doesn't choose between them. How can you support them all or introduce a new way of working that supplants them?

- Can you improve the flow between activities and steps? Why is there a separation between activities—are they a change of intent, a hand-off to another person, or driven by technology? Is the transition a necessary aspect of practice that you should enable or a problem you should overcome?

- Are there *wasted steps*? What steps can be eliminated, partially automated, or made simpler? How can the pain and tedium of the task be eliminated? Does your existing product require steps that overcomplicate the activity?

THE DECISION POINT MODEL:
SUPPORTING CHOICES

Decision Point Models reveal what influences important decisions. If the team knows what influences a critical choice—such as what store to shop in or what brand of product to buy—they can redesign market messages to emphasize their real value or reinvent the product to meet the important needs.

Because the team is cross-disciplinary, people with different jobs naturally generate different kinds of design ideas to fix the conditions pushing customers away from a choice. They are made aware of what influences pushing customers toward a choice. During the Wall Walk simply encourage people to create design ideas that include messaging, content, and key features that win the decision. Each influence becomes an opportunity for design thinking.

If key influencers such as family, friends, or known experts contribute to the choice then the connection models become important opportunities for redesigning impact on these influencers. And if trusted information sites or reviews are critical to choice then your social media and marketing teams have their work cut out for them—invite them to the Wall Walk so their thinking can be added to the overall mix driving invention.

THE PHYSICAL MODEL: REDESIGNING AND
LEARNING FROM SPACE

Consolidated Physical Models reveal how a physical product such as a television, sound system, or refrigerator are placed and used in the home. They also show how people set up an internal space like a car to support their daily life. They reveal the interaction between the activity and the environment—e.g., for a car, the model reveals the lack of space for phones and handbags, what is in or out of reach, what's visible and not, what in the dash information display people love or hate, and the reaction to sounds, messages, and controls in that space. Or the physical model of a retail space like our grocery store shows typical paths through the store, displays that prompt buying decisions, areas avoided and areas that draw traffic, good and bad signage, and how people get help from other people or from their mobile devices while shopping.

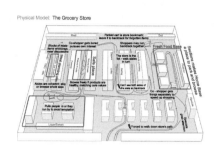

Physical Model: The Grocery Store

The Physical Model that you create for your project will be specific to your space and problem. It should reveal how the space is used, how people tailor the space, technology used in the space, the value of information and communications in the space, what support for decisions is available, challenges to the human body, and relevant collaborations. A good physical model looks across all users to raise up key stories about all these dimensions and more, depending on the insights of your team. These pictures and text chunks will invite design ideas from the multiple perspectives of the industrial designers, product designers, and other functions that may be part of creating the overall product. To walk the model, introduce it simply, focusing on its structure and some key insights. Then let people add their design ideas.

Walking the traditional models focuses the team on the details of doing the tasks, making decisions, and living in the spaces where we encounter the product. When done well they communicate life the next level down from the Experience Models and challenge the team to tune their offerings to better suit the actual use.

At the end of the Wall Walk the Visioning team will have been introduced to the different perspectives on the users' lives that were relevant to your project. They will have immersed themselves in this world and used it to generate initial design thinking. They will, through the lists, have captured the key issues that they should be addressing and initial Hot Ideas that start group ideation during Visioning. They will have tuned their inner gut feel, stimulated their design thinking, and begun informal discussion of their key insights and possible solutions. They will be ready for transformative ideation.

11

Ideation: Visioning and the Cool Drilldown

Going from user data to a design requires a creative leap, a leap from what matters to what to do about it, but getting a team to be creative is tricky. We want the team to think widely, "out of the box." Yet it's in an engineer's nature to immediately do a feasibility estimate of any idea they hear of or invent. That's why they respond so frequently, "We can't do that"—until the entire design for doing it is worked out, the idea does not seem doable. Then the same engineer who said it was impossible on Friday will announce on Monday morning that it's done. It's not possible to be creative when every idea gets immediately put to the test—and a truly creative idea may well require substantial time to investigate whether it can be done or not. We often find that the idea we thought was a pipe dream when it was first mentioned turns out to be easy when the implementation is designed. So there's no advantage to filtering ideas early.

We encourage people to think broad, wide, and radical first, without worrying about how to implement their ideas or fit them with existing products. Once you've had the radical idea, you can reduce it to its core intent, decide what's important, and scale it back to what's practical in a limited time. Following invention, the process provides many evaluation steps within the team and with users to ensure that the design works for the user and can be implemented by the people in

> *Knowing you will evaluate later sets you free to be creative*

Contextual Design. http://dx.doi.org/10.1016/B978-0-12-800894-2.00011-9

your organization. Because they know these steps are coming the team is free to step outside the bounds of what they know to be safe.

But engineers are not the only ones who can be reluctant to invent anything too radical. People worry that an idea requires data or content they don't have and can't buy or make. They worry they don't have the skill to build the solution they visioned. They worry they don't know if they can sell the new idea even if it will delight people. They stay silent because they think that their skill set—researcher, designer, or marketer—might not carry as much weight as product managers or engineers. And sometimes they worry because they fear that once they think up an idea, management will expect them to build it right away and blame them for failure if it turns out to be impossible. Unfortunately, many people have experiences in organizations which work against out of the box thinking.

So if you want to free people to think widely, make them feel secure that initial ideas will be evaluated and won't be treated as a commitment to ship. And level the organizational power in the room so everyone will participate. The best way to get a team to open up its collective mind is to put them in a defined process with clear rules of engagement so everyone knows what to do to be successful. This is the cornerstone of all our ideation techniques. To get the best thinking out of the team you have to manage the people and the process. The Wall Walk was the first of these design meetings and the precursor to all others.

A clear, facilitated process manages worries in the room

In this chapter we will describe two more design meetings of Contextual Design: Visioning and the Cool Drilldown. Following data immersion, these sessions help a team work together to generate new product concepts informed by the Cool Concepts.

Visioning follows immediately after the Wall Walk to build on the energy and ideas before people forget. Depending on the extent of the data, it may start in the afternoon of the Wall Walk or the next morning. Visioning itself will last 1–2 days depending on the scope of the project. Such a vision generally results in three to five new, high-level product concepts—significant new directions, not simple design ideas. With these in hand, the Cool Drilldown may be run the next day or later. Depending on the number of concepts to be covered it may take an additional 1–2 days, but it can be split up to cover each concept in its own meeting. The Cool Drilldown enriches the product concepts, tuning and deepening them to better support the Cool Concepts' imperatives. All three ideation meetings are linked together into a process which moves the team from data to concrete representation of their agreed upon product direction.

The Wall Walk is a good time to immerse a larger group of stakeholders in the data. But the Visioning team needs to be a smaller, cross-functional group with direct responsibility to define, design, build, and ship the resulting product. Keep your Visioning team small—if people feel that it's too hard to get their ideas on the paper, the session will be frustrating for everyone. A session of 6–10 people is plenty— more makes it hard to get air time. If you must involve more people, split into two parallel Visioning teams after the first vision, each taking up different Hot Ideas. You can bring them together in the evaluation phase.

Skilled interaction designers are a must on the Visioning team

VISIONING

Following the Wall Walk, the next step is the Visioning Session. For this, everyone must have walked the wall and you have developed your shared lists of issues and Hot Ideas. But the vision will go better if you do a quick *technology list*. Any design response uses technology to redesign the work and life of the target market. To make sure the team is aware of the technology they can use in the vision, list all the technologies they might draw on. Like the previous lists, record what anyone says with no evaluation or filtering.

The lists of issues, technologies, and Hot Ideas set focus for the vision

The technology list incorporates known technology (machine learning, screen-scraping, any content on the Web, wireless, Bluetooth, COTS products, touch screens, phone and tablet paradigms), modern design patterns or user interface approaches, specialized technology unique to the company (artificial agents, other company product capabilities, internal data and algorithms), and business conditions that the team might otherwise not think of (process design, service assumptions, business partnerships, current mission priorities). Anyone on the team who doesn't know about any of these possibilities can get a quick overview from a team member. As long as someone on the team knows the technology they can use it to invent—others simply need to know what it enables. With these three lists in hand the team has raised into their consciousness the overarching user, technical, and business context that they need to imagine a new world for the user.

A vision is the story of the new world you will invent for the user

Visioning is a grounded storytelling process based on principles of brainstorming. Brainstorming recognizes that people can't be creative if they evaluate everything they say as soon as it comes out of their mouths. So during Visioning people contribute ideas in a process that forbids judging or evaluation. The story is "grounded" because the team has steeped themselves in the user data, so their ideas are informed by that practice. But a vision is fundamentally a story of the new world you might create for your users. Participants in the vision are inventing the way the new product concept will help users achieve their intents; address their problems, challenges, and opportunities; be their best selves; and connect with the people who matter to them. Ideas might remove technology hassles or deliver a product that is direct, ready to use in moments. A vision reinvents the life of the user with technology, showing how the design will improve users' lives.

The Wall Walk stimulates design thinking— Visioning synthesizes the ideas

A Visioning Session gives a team a collaborative technique to spin out a story about the new practice transformed by technology, given a particular starting point (the Hot Idea). The story describes the new world the team envisions—without committing them to actually building it. Because the team has walked the wall, they have already started percolating on what these ideas may be. The story will just fall out without having to think explicitly about each aspect of the transformation in detail.

The rules of the meeting mirror the old game of telling ghost stories around a campfire. Someone starts the story and everyone adds on to it, continuing and building the story as it unfolds. No one is allowed to argue with the story or stop it and declare it to be a bad story—instead, they have to take it as it is and add to it however they like. Each person puts his or her ideas forward without consulting anyone else or getting agreement. The story unfolds rapidly, focused on describing how the characters in your market do your target activity in a new way. A Visioning Session will produce four to seven visions, each drawn on a flip chart page. Each vision starts from a different Hot Idea, persona, or activity. Below, we will discuss pulling specific product concepts out of your visions, but don't worry about that yet. Just let the visions explore the transformed life of the user. Identifying the product concepts is a later step. Each vision takes 20–45 minutes.

In the Visioning Session, one person (the *Pen*) stands at a flip chart, drawing the ideas as participants throw them out. The pen has two roles: encourage people to talk, but also fit their ideas into the vision as it is developing. The Pen's job is to listen, synthesize, and draw—not contribute ideas

The pen weaves the team's ideas into a story

to the vision. If the Pen starts generating design ideas he or she needs to hand the pen to someone else. Unlike a normal brainstorm, where each idea is independent, a vision session starts with one Hot Idea and incorporates the participants' ideas into a coherent story about the redesigned life. Ideas which are inconsistent with the current story are put on the Hot Ideas list for Visioning on their own later. In addition to the Pen, it's useful to have a facilitator (the *Poker*) to remind the team of the rules of Visioning and help participants pursue a thread by suggesting additional issues from the models or Affinity, additional roles or identity elements, or life situations from the Day-in-the-Life model. Together the Pen and the Poker keep the team on track and ensure everyone on the Visioning team is heard.

The core starting question for the team is "Who am I and what am I doing?" Each vision is then told from the point of view of one of the job types or personas in your market. The vision drawing shows what the new practice would be like if the vision were in place. It shows people in the roles they play or identity elements they have; the systems, products, and devices they use; how they communicate, coordinate, and relate to each other; and what data or information they can access—or is simply presented to them "automagically." It invents automation, new services, new roles in the organization; connects internal or third-party systems; assumes relationships between different parts of the company or partners; generates market messages; and shows conceptual sections of the user interface—whatever is appropriate given the project focus and scope.

Draw your visions quickly and informally to generate creativity

Vision pictures are very informal—they are drawn quickly, without a lot of structure. They tend to have lots of arrows showing communication; lots of faces showing people; and lots of boxes indicating screens, systems, or other technology components. See Fig. 11.1.

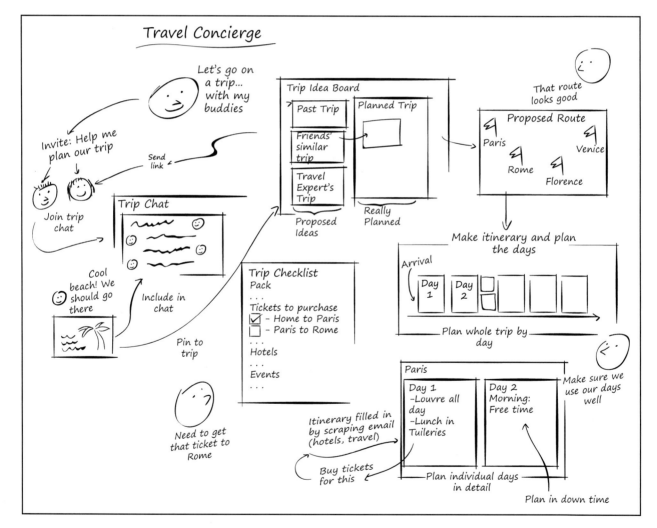

FIGURE 11.1   A vision for travel product created by a team—hand-drawn, on a flip chart. Ability to draw is not a necessary skill for the Pen.

Any vision has a thread, which starts with the initial Hot Idea and then is played out as participants expand on it:

Pen (P): *This is the Just-in-Time planning vision. So your two co-planners have middle-school kids and want to go on a trip in a few weeks to someplace where they can experience local culture. (Draws two heads.) So what happens?*

Team Member (T): *The wife gets the idea while surfing her favorite travel sites that they could spend the next long weekend in Mexico or Costa Rica and sends a link to her husband.*

P: *What is she looking at? Where is she?*

T 2: *She is at the soccer game with her phone (the Pen draws the bench and phone interface) and she saves the link to the Family Sharing Place.*

T 3: *And that place is really smart. Since there are two links for two places, our algorithms calculate the distance they want to go and add some suggestions based on knowing those links and their past trips. (Pen draws a database icon to represent the knowledge in the database).*

T1: *And the husband gets pinged that something has come up on his Travel Concierge app that says, "How about a trip?" so he opens it to see what ideas are there and right away messages his wife in the app about what weekend they are thinking about.*

In a good Visioning Session everyone feels their ideas have been heard

T 4: *And the Suggestion Engine sees the dates and starts looking for their typical hotels with a swimming pool for the kids and local arts, music, and out of the way restaurants.*

T 5: *But the kids can see it too and say what they want to do.*

T 2: *No, the co-planners don't want to get the kids involved yet because they need to have more of a plan.*

Poker: *Don't evaluate, solve the problem.*

T 4: *Maybe there is a kid app that solicits their ideas continuously...*

Follow the tread in your vision story— keep the story coherent

Pen: *Let's vision something for the kids next after we work out the co-planners. (Writes "kids' planning app" on the Hot Ideas list).*

Poker: *So what are we doing with tablets?*

T 3: *Okay, at night the pair sit down with the tablet and they can see all the links and suggestions of the Suggestion Engine for what is happening on that weekend—it makes a kind of movie of what the trip would be like in the two places and any others they select. (Pen draws the couple, the tablet, and tablet interface with movie).*

T 5: *Yeah, and they can freeze the movie to explore each place and delete it or add others... (The team continues to flesh out this plan).*

Poker: *This is a lot of up-front planning. "Just in time" means when I need it, so let's hear some support once they set out on the trip.*

T 3: *So they have the basic plan and they set out on the trip and while they are in the car...*

Pen and Poker listen for ideas which contribute to the story, postponing ideas which are too far off the main thread. When an idea conflicts with the thread the team is working on, the Pen adds it to the list of Hot Ideas—this keeps the thread coherent, while assuring the team member that his idea has been heard and will be dealt with. But if the team has two possible ideas for how to handle a situation within the story, pursue them both incorporating alternatives within thread of that story—the team and then choose to pursue one or both into design. Eventually, the team will run out of ideas that fit this thread and are ready for a new departure. Put the vision aside and start a new one. Don't duplicate ideas from vision to vision—good ideas will be recovered in the next step, so you don't need to go through them again.

Practicality is not a major consideration for a vision—remember evaluation comes later. If the team lets go of worrying about whether they can build their ideas immediately, they will be more creative and produce a vision that will account for more of the practice, more coherently. Our team above may not have the in-house skill to automate or make a movie, but working out the vision gives them a chance to explore issues of smart automation and visualization which are very likely to be part of their final design. Balance creativity against practicality—after Visioning multiple fanciful and far-reaching ideas, the team might want to vision a short-term solution. But that vision will be more creative for having opened up the thinking beforehand.

Practicality is not important during the vision—let go, be creative

Structuring Visioning as storytelling focuses the team on the coherent life of the user. Because they are telling the story of the user's new life, the team has to make that life hang together. It has to make sense—the motivations and intentions envisioned for the user have to be realistic. Events, issues, and situations from the actual data can be folded into the story so the team can explore how the new design would resolve real situations in the users' lives. Because the team is thinking about how the life hangs together, the design will be holistic and coherent. Storytelling keeps the team from brainstorming single features into a user interface framework, or simply making lists of possible small design ideas. This is the best way to ensure that the new product concepts enhance the life rather than disrupt it.

Structuring the vision as a story keeps the life coherent

A good Visioning Session is a lot of fun—everyone is tossing in ideas for what to do based on what matters in the practice—everyone's talking at once and building on each other's ideas. The major gating factor for a Visioning Session is the ability of the Pen to draw what he or she hears without a lot of filtering or explanation. You are done with Visioning when you have four to seven visions. Then you are ready to share and evaluate.

CREATING A COMMON DIRECTION THROUGH EVALUATION

Doing multiple visions lets the team consider alternatives and work out some of their implications. Each vision is built by the whole team (or subsets in parallel) and incorporates everyone's different perspective. But at the end of a Visioning Session, you have multiple visions, each suggesting a different design direction or addressing a different part of the practice. How do you choose among them?

In Contextual Design, you don't have to. Instead, you synthesize a new solution incorporating the best of the individual visions.

Creating a common vision is not a compromise

Committees have the reputation of producing mediocre designs because people compromise—instead of doing either of two reasonable designs, they settle for something halfway in-between, or they incorporate all the features of both to make everyone happy. Synthesizing a common vision is a way to avoid this. Rather than compromising on features, producing a design with a little something for everyone, the goal should be a design which is coherent and clean, and which supports the issues in the market.

The key to such a design is to treat each vision not as a monolithic block which must be accepted or rejected as a whole, but as a collection of options which can be reconfigured and redesigned into a coherent solution. If the team had to choose one option over another, they would argue—each person would have their own pref-

Find the best parts of all other visions—and fix the worst

erence as to how to trade off different issues. But it's a false choice. Every vision will have impractical or undesirable elements; most visions will have some elements you don't want to lose. Create a better solution by identifying elements that work, recombining them to preserve the best parts, and extending them to address more of the practice and overcome any defects. The individual visions become a collection of design ideas which you can draw on and recombine to come up with a better solution.[1]

---

[1] This process is based on the ideas underlying Pugh matrices (S. Pugh, *Total Design*, Addison-Wesley Publishing Limited, 1991). But where Pugh depends on individual creativity, we use the dynamics of the group to produce a single vision that incorporates everyone's perspective. This helps keep people from getting overinvested in one solution. People who feel they can't be creative in a group situation still have the option of working out a design and feeding it into the evaluation process.

We do this through a structured evaluation of each vision. There are only three valid critiques of a vision:

1. Does it fit the users' practice?
2. Is it doable technically?
3. Does it fit with the business mission and organizational skills?

Look at each vision in turn and first list the positive points. Even people who dislike the vision overall can find points about it which work—if our team has people who are particularly against a vision, we put them on the spot to identify some points they like. List each positive point on a sheet and attach it to the vision. Then list the negative points—all the reasons why it would be hard to build or would break the users' practice. People who love the vision can find a few points to dislike—it will help them to let go of an idea they might be overly attached to. List these negatives and attach them to the vision as well.

List positives and negatives for each vision in turn. While you're listing negative points people will naturally start solving them, suggesting ways that the problem can be overcome. These design ideas become important in the next step of the process, but don't let them derail you now. Write them on sticky notes and attach them to the vision to save them for later (Fig. 11.2).

The group process builds consensus and reduces overinvestment

After evaluating, look across the visions and look at the core chunks of each vision. These will define concepts, feature sets, or approaches that the team might implement. The team will be primed to do this as a result of the critique they just did. With positives and negatives in mind ask the team to decide which parts they want to keep. Put appropriate colored flags on the relevant parts of each vision.

Green Light: the parts they believe in and can do, no question

Red Light: the parts they hate, don't believe in, and want to eliminate

Yellow Light: the parts that need more exploration—keep them to explore technically, organizationally, or with users

Pluses
+ Supports the co-planner role
+ Makes suggestions for the Cultural Sponge
+ Finds information relevant to past trip criteria—fits with "think for me"
+ The movie helps visualize the trip and brings excitement
+ Having a shared space supports communication between the co-planners
+ We have in-house information about travel that we can use to make suggestions
+ Our search engine can find related information and we can scrape websites
+...

Minuses
- The movie is hard to implement—how will we hook the pieces together automatically?
- Freezing the frames during the movie will complicate the user interface
- We are partnered with only a few airlines and hotels—how can we give competing information?
- We don't have a relationship with restaurants or Yelp—where will we get these suggestions?
- The data doesn't justify having the co-planners are compete—them idea points undermines their cooperation
-...

Design Ideas
- Link to the apps on their mobile devices and grab local restaurants based on their previous suggestions
- Provide a place by place graphical reference which links to more information shown in the movie
- Use Google's engine for suggestions—don't rebuild our own
- ...

FIGURE 11.2   Positives, negatives, and design ideas for the travel vision.

This simple coding technique is easy for the team to understand and the choice is almost always easy. If there's ever an argument—one participant thinks an idea is easy while another doesn't,

A process for decision-making eliminates argument

or one sees the user value and another doesn't—by definition it needs more investigation, so make it yellow. When done, the team has a shared understanding of what to pursue and what to drop. Now you can combine the desired parts into a larger coherent vision. Usually, most of the elements of the visions don't conflict directly—because each vision took a different approach, it will be possible to bring the desired parts together without conflict. Where parts do conflict— two different ways of addressing the same problem, for example, and it doesn't make sense to do both—you'll have to choose. But now it's a very focused choice centered on that design element. If both approaches support the practice well, choose the simpler, or the easier to implement. If you aren't sure which is better, identify what the team needs to investigate to make a decision, or bring the more disruptive one to the user for further test in a paper mock-up (see Chapter 17).

This whole process is designed to bring a disparate, cross-functional team of people to consensus. If some team member is hooked on an idea, be sure to include that idea in the list of Hot Ideas. In one client team, one member was hooked on the idea of a large monitor displaying test states in a scientific lab—it had gotten to be a joke in the team that this was his solution for everything. Making the large monitor the core of a vision, and then doing positive and negative points (he had to come up with three negatives) made it clear what real advantages the large monitor offered. But comparison with other visions revealed that those same advantages could be achieved more simply in other ways. In the end, he didn't have a hard time letting go of the idea.

When the team is done they will have a high-level but coherent story of how to redesign the life of their users with new technology, informed by data immersion, and co-invented by all cross-functional team members. Hidden in this story are the product concepts we can enrich in the Cool Drilldown.

The vision produces a high-level future story, rich with new product concepts

IDENTIFYING PRODUCT CONCEPTS

The visions imply new *product concepts*. Any significant product is composed of multiple feature sets, app suites, and related services that work together to deliver value. The visions contain these concepts within a story of to-be use: what the future life might look like as transformed by technology. But they will be developed and delivered as coherent product elements which have to hang together coherently. Each product concept holds together and could (in theory) be delivered as its own product. If the team's only view of their design is as a set of scenarios, they will only see the features—they will not see how the product concepts have their own structure, relationships, and coherence. To build a product the team must alternate between story/scenario reasoning to ensure the coherence of the life of the user and structural/systems reasoning that looks at the product elements as a coherent product. Contextual Design alternates between these two processes, keeping both life and product coherent and in sync.

The final step of the Visioning Session is to identify the product concepts explicitly. Each vision suggests product concepts, but any of those product concepts may have been built up across several of the visions. The vision evaluation makes it easier to identify the coherent product concepts because the evaluation focuses on the vision elements, not the entire scenario. For example, in our travel project the team identified an *Idea Collector*, a research tool with a collection area for ideas and an app for in-the-moment research; a *Trip Planner*, a collaborative planning tool for laying out the primary activities of the trip; an *Itinerary Builder* for making sure all logistics have been handled; and a *Travel Companion*, an app for taking on the trip to record and share memorable events. These four product concepts work together as a whole solution, but each can be thought about and refined on its own.[2]

> *A product concept collects features in the vision into coherent chunks of value*

The team draws each product concept separately, pulling the individual features for that concept from all the visions where it was considered. This is the point when the design ideas people contributed to fix any negatives are considered and incorporated. The team names the product concept and shows the concept in rough wireframe sketches to reveal functions and any automation. Figs. 11.3–11.5 show three product concepts that came out of our travel vision. These are not scenarios at all—they are not stories of use.

---

[2] Identifying product concepts in this way also supports iterative development processes. It would be natural to assign each product concept to a different Scrum team, for example, and the vision elements can be quickly evolved into user stories.

Their representation is structural, suggesting screens which support the intent of the product concept. The sub-team pulling a concept together does not brainstorm new function or leave out anything from the visions. They are tasked with representing the thinking of the group as it has developed so far. The next steps of the Contextual Design process will start to add detail and depth to these ideas. Sketch the product concept as a simple wireframe.

Identifying positives and negatives encouraged the team to think of each vision not as a monolithic whole, but as a grab-bag of parts. Identifying and sketching out the product concepts helps them bring these parts back together in coherent units that can be designed and delivered together. It's likely that the final vision will describe more than can be shipped in a single version, but that's all right—it means the team will be able to plan a rollout strategy which they can use to drive delivery over several versions. Even when you are focused on a short-term deliverable—say, your next update is due to ship in 6 months—you're better off thinking and Visioning widely first. Then you can either synthesize and pick out a few good features for the deadline, or you can vision widely and then

Multiple product concepts help you define a roadmap

vision explicitly for a 6-month deliverable. You'll find you automatically pull in ideas from the wider visions to put together a coherent short-term plan once you do the inevitable trimming. And you'll know how what you do in the short term advances your long-term roadmap. In Chapter 18 we discuss prioritization and rollout.

This step results in a well-defined set of product concepts, each with a clear purpose in the user's life, delivering value to the user in a way that is within the mission of the business. These product concepts feed the next phase of ideation. This is also a good time to share the vision with management stakeholders to check direction.

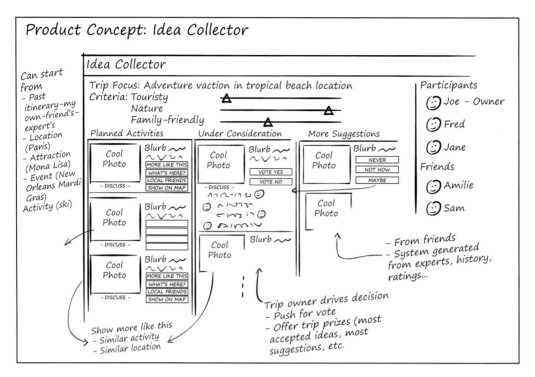

FIGURE 11.3 The "Idea Collector" product concept—a way to capture trip ideas as you stumble across them, and organize them later.

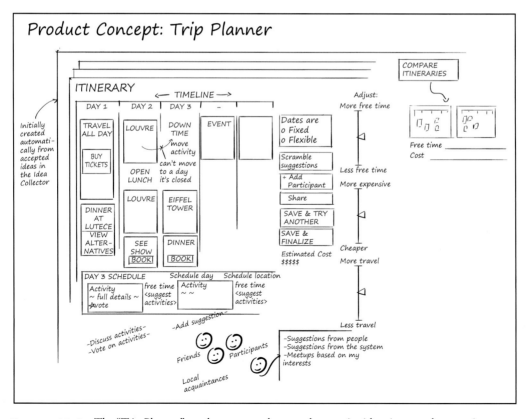

FIGURE 11.4 The "Trip Planner" product concept lets people organize ideas into a coherent trip.

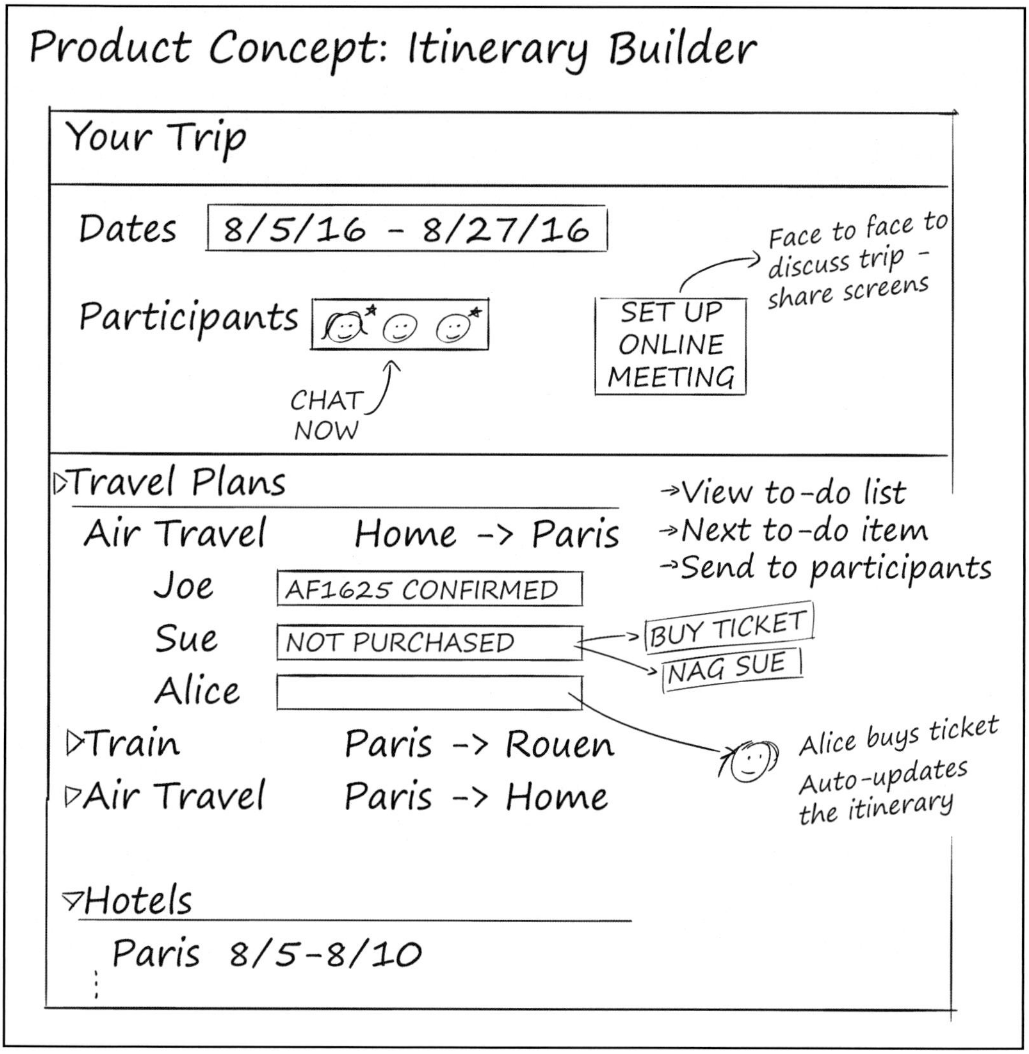

Product Concept: Itinerary Builder

Your Trip

Dates   8/5/16 – 8/27/16

Face to face to discuss trip – share screens

Participants

SET UP ONLINE MEETING

CHAT NOW

▷Travel Plans

→View to-do list
→Next to-do item
→Send to participants

Air Travel   Home –> Paris

Joe   AF1625 CONFIRMED

Sue   NOT PURCHASED

BUY TICKET
NAG SUE

Alice

▷Train   Paris –> Rouen

▷Air Travel   Paris –> Home

Alice buys ticket
Auto-updates the itinerary

▽Hotels

Paris 8/5–8/10

FIGURE 11.5   The Itinerary Builder supports the process of finalizing a trip—making sure all air tickets, hotel nights, event tickets, and other necessary logistics are taken care of.

VISIONING ON YOUR OWN

How you do Visioning when you're on your own depends on your situation. If you're in a start-up or small company so the number of people available is small but the scope is still large, do a full Visioning Session with the other stakeholders. This is your opportunity to build consensus and a shared direction, and it's worth it to bring everyone together for a half day to a day.

The catch is, Visioning works because it's based on user data in the Wall Walk. So you'll need to pull together the data you have and put it up on the wall. It doesn't have to be fancy—drawn sketches are fine, if they're neat—and you can pull together organizational knowledge as well as actual field data. Just make it clear which is which. Do the Wall Walk, Visioning, and Plusses and Minuses together—you can then clean up the vision and identify product concepts on your own, reviewing them with stakeholders afterward.

If your organization is into workshops, design sprints, or other one-half to one day events, fit Wall Walks and Visioning into the existing practice. Use the models to communicate the data and spend a little time cleaning them up, using our communication design principles—visually oriented designers *will* appreciate a well-designed model. Create an interactive event using the models to facilitate design thinking and everyone will get value out of it.

If you have a small-scoped part of a larger design, it may not make sense to do Visioning as a process. Instead, use the same process on your own or with a codesigner. Sketch options, consciously put each aside and do a different alternative. Do explicit plusses and minuses even when you're on your own. Then pull the best parts together and sketch a consolidated result. Don't worry about product concepts—you're almost certainly designing within a single concept.

Whether you do the Cool Drilldown with others depends mostly on whether you have others available who can be useful. The Cool Drilldown depends on a certain design expertise—knowledge of modern interactivity, presentation, and tools; knowledge of the ecosystem of apps and devices; and ability to design for these situations. A business-oriented product manager or tech-oriented developer is not going to be much help with this. So if that's all you have, you're on your own. But use the principles to guide your own design—systematically walk through your product ideas, enriching them one concept at a time, and then pull it all together. The process still works.

But if you're one of a few UX people on a larger project you may be able to help each other. Do the Cool Drilldown as a round robin, looking at each designer's component on a separate day. That makes addressing the Cool Concepts a whole-product effort, and means that each designer gets help on their part. And if it leads to more consistency and better coordination across the product, no one will complain.

THE COOL DRILLDOWN

The final part of ideation is the *Cool Drilldown* workshop. Design for life means designing to support all of the Cool Concepts. Designers are not used to addressing these aspects of design, so it is easy to overlook them in the Visioning Session, or simply not go deep enough. Getting these aspects of design right requires more detailed design than the quick construction of visions allows for. The Visioning Session is intentionally fast-paced—there's no time to engage in a reflective conversation exploring the implications of each Cool Concept. But once you have at least a rough idea of product direction, such

Consider each Cool Concept separately to improve the initial product concept

reflection is more focused and worthwhile. So once the Visioning Session has produced a set of clear product concepts, the team can take time to consider how to design a cool user experience.

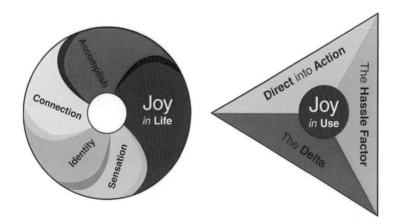

The Cool Drilldown guides designers through the implications of each Cool Concept and its associated principles for their design. Each Cool Concept focuses on a different aspect of life and implies a different design focus—what should be considered to design a transformative experience. No one person or team can reasonably consider all these dimensions simultaneously without getting overwhelmed and losing focus. So the Cool Drilldown workshop focuses the team on one new product concept and one Cool Concept at a time. The team works in small groups in parallel, so they can move very quickly. Designers become more aware of the design principles for cool and produce enriched product concepts in a reasonable length of time.

In the Cool Drilldown workshop, the team starts by identifying the product concepts they want to cover in the workshop (you might not do them all). You can cover one to two product concepts in one day with a six to eight person team (all of whom were in the vision). Taking each product concept in turn, break into sub-teams of two to four people. Each sub-team applies the principles for one Cool Concept, Accomplishment, for example, to enrich the initial product concept. Each sub-team works in parallel, optimizing the product idea by adding features or services that improve support for that Cool Concept. Review the data on the Affinity and Experience Models to feed more detailed design thinking with the actual user data; then brainstorm and sketch additions to the product concept consistent with the vision, the data, and the principles of the Cool Concept. A team can consider many important design principles, one chunk at a time.

Each sub-team does this same drilldown on a different Cool Concept in parallel, but on the same product concept. In this way, a single product concept is simultaneously enhanced to get the flow of life done better (Accomplishment), make connections to people that matter easier (Connection), support identity elements explicitly (Identity), create delightful and useful graphics and animation (Sensation), provide more direct interaction (Direct/Hassle), and eliminate learning as a task (Learning Delta).[3] Each sub-team does their drilldown independently, which means that when they're done the product concept has been changed by each group in parallel. So after the sub-teams do their work, all these independent enhancements to the product concept are brought back together in a full team review and reconciled into a single, revised design concept incorporating the best parts of all the drilldowns. The result is a redesign of the product concept that is enriched and addresses the issues raised by the Cool Concepts, making the product more effective and desirable.

Drill down in parallel teams—then combine

An alternative approach is to start each sub-team with a different product concept and then have them all focus on one Cool Concept

---

[3] See Chapter 1, p. 8 for a reminder of the Cool Concepts.

at a time, redesigning and enriching them all from a single perspective. Sharing these results in the whole team helps the team learn to think about each concept together. Then they move to the next Cool Concept and focus on enriching the product concepts from that point of view. If you move people around, reforming the sub-teams with each new round so that someone from the first team remains and someone new joins, all team members participate in enriching each product concept. This tends to keep the product concept more coherent and works well if the product concepts are very distinct and do not overlap much in function.

Whichever technique you choose, the goal is to march from Cool Concept to Cool Concept for each product concept so that every sub-team has a simple focus in each round of redesign. This way you can truly consider a large set of design principles without overwhelming the team. Start with the Cool Concepts from the Wheel of Joy in Life and then move to the concepts in the Triangle of Joy in Use—you will have a deeper understanding of the function and use before you start think-

Working in rotating small teams builds buy-in

ing about tool structure. Because everyone works on every product concept and is involved in the review and improvement cycles, you build buy-in and a shared understanding as you go.

In the Cool Drilldown you focus on the structure of the product, not on a scenario of use. It is imperative that you have trained interaction designers on the team at this point! Issues of layout and transition are critical to thinking through the implications for cool. And since you're likely to be designing multiple platforms, the team will need to think about how the product concept is represented in each. Without enough skill and knowledge of possible modern layout and design patterns the team will get bogged down in content detail, technology, or scenario-based reasoning. Having people on the design team who really know all the materials needed to design the product is critical in the Visioning team. Make sure they participate from Wall Walk onwards.

Now, with a rich set of high-level product designs in hand, the team is poised to go deeper again to design real product structure and function and create a real user interface. That will be covered in Part 4.

APPLYING THE COOL CONCEPTS IN THE COOL DRILLDOWN

Create a handout for each sub-team. Revisit the issues we listed for each Experience Model and what we have below in this overview of the focus of each Cool Concept.

Accomplishment

- Does this design support anytime, anywhere access? Where and when does the user access technology?
- What small tasks, information, or fun can fit into the small bits of available time? What useful intents can be addressed given the short time, expected interruptions, and partial attention?
- How can users start an activity on one device and then resume it later, at the same point, on another device?
- What information needs to be available to drive decisions and action—status updates, background context, relevant data? How can that information be provided in the moment—just the information needed?

Connection

- Who matters in the user's world? How can the system help users touch their people easily and often—while on the go?
- What is the user doing that they might share with others, considering both information and activities? What can you provide to help them have more things to share and talk about? Remember to support trusted advisors.
- What can you provide to help people find things to do together? How can you enhance the relationship and create trust?
- Can you support expanding a network of like people—if they are interested?

For professional connections and collaboration:

- How can you help people appear and feel professional and personal?
- How do you better support positive collaboration and sharing of real-time information on a project?
- Guard against creating online communities around products or a brand—most often, there's not a real, natural community of interest.

Identity

- What identity elements are core for this project? How can each be directly targeted with product features or information?
- Does anything in the product undermine an identity element?
- How does the product help people adopt the identity, reinforce it, and promote it?
- Are there online communities or places that will provide content to help an emerging identity, to help people decide what is "normal"?
- How does the product help the user celebrate themselves and their accomplishments relative to this identity?
- Are there competitions or fun appropriate to the identity element?

Sensation
- How can you draw people in, with color, sound, and movement? What level of stimulation is appropriate given the many contexts and cultures of use? Can you build in a "Wow!" that doesn't distract?
- How can you add a smile or a bit of play to the activity—without getting in the way of use?
- Do the graphics, movement, and interactivity support the core function?
- Is your aesthetic and industrial design modern—building on and enhancing current trends?

Direct into Action (without Hassle)
- Did you bring everything needed to fulfill an intent into one place?
- Can you get smoothly from one action to the next set of likely actions?
- Does the information needed to support a decision just appear when needed or in response to a question—how can you think for the user?
- How can you support "touch once"—never having to reenter any information?
- What can you know without asking? Do you let the user go instantly into action without fuss or hassle?
- Have you eliminated every technical hassle you can—and anything in the way of instant into action?

Watch out: It's tempting to provide in-the-moment help, preference setting, and information by putting up a screen before the user gets to the content they want. This always disrupts the experience of direct into action.

The Learning Delta
- How do you reduce what the user needs to know to zero—for the core intents, at least? What do your users already know that you can build on, including voice, touch, and other already known ways of interacting?
- Have you eliminated complexity and avoided features that the teams thinks are nice to have but aren't needed?
- Have you eliminated layers of drilldown, complex language, and anything in the way of figuring out how to use the product?
- Can you build in nudging people in the right direction in moments?
- Eliminate any need for users to read documentation—they won't anyway.

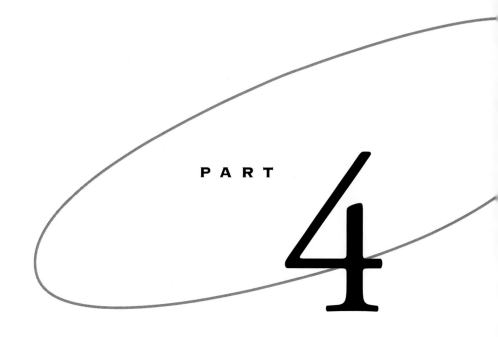

PART

4

Defining the
Product

The Challenge of Product Design

12

In prior chapters we've collected field data describing the life of the user and we've generated a high-level idea of what to build. Now we're ready to design a product that will transform that life. In this Part we describe the Contextual Design techniques used to define, design, and validate the new product concept.

Twenty-plus years ago no one talked much about design. There certainly were no Chief Design Officers. There were no specialties in interaction or visual design; information architects didn't exist. There were no mobile devices, no Web, and no Cloud. There was no business information content, or things to buy, or pictures to share. There was no social media. There was only work-oriented function that needed to be laid out reasonably across a menu bar surrounding a central area where the work of the application happened—creating a spreadsheet, document, or slideshow, or filling out a form.

This did not mean there was no design. Those of us advocating for user-centered design were focused on making the right thing and making sure that the structure, function, and flow through a single product or system was best for use. And how did we make that happen? We started by understanding the context in which the users performed tasks and ended by iterating with the users to be sure that our product design actually made sense to people.

Products have radically changed—away from monolithic applications

But as we have said, the very nature of what a product is has radically changed. With the emergence of mobile applications on

Contextual Design. http://dx.doi.org/10.1016/B978-0-12-800894-2.00012-0

multiple platforms, a simple focus on task will no longer serve us. Assigning a different product team to each mobile version and another to the main platform of a product, system, or website will confuse the user who moves from device to device throughout the day. Designers must reconceive the focus of product design away from a single task-oriented product on one platform to a whole constellation of products and apps offered by the company and by third parties, all working together to address the needs of this mobile life.

Design a suite of support for an activity across devices that keep life coherent

Therein lies the core challenge of product design: to ensure we really build a desirable, product that ensures the coherence of the user's whole life as well as the target activity with a set of apps, function sets, and products—each of which is itself coherent within the product and across a suite of offerings. In other words, how do we ensure a total positive user experience no matter what platform or physical environment users are in? This large contextual view of the user demands that we understand and design for the bigger picture of the life, use of time, physical environment, and service context that our product offerings will be part of. A myopic view on a single product feature or app will potentially lead to a myriad of disconnected parts, not an integrated, smooth, delightful offering.

In Part 4 we present the Contextual Design techniques that will help you create life and product coherence. We have already primed the team to think widely about the context and larger ecosystem within which the product will reside, with our Experience Models and Cool Concept principles. Now we must design the next layer of details in the product without losing that bigger picture—without getting lost in the low-level details of specific interfaces and features. Here we focus on techniques that will help keep life and product coherence at the heart of your design. As always, for any successful product to be produced, user researchers and designers must work closely with product management and developers. And we assume that your team includes professionals trained and experienced in interaction,

The total user experience must be delightful

visual, information, and other forms of design and in all the tools and techniques needed to design a good modern interface. The dialogue between these individuals and business functions is at the heart of deciding what to build and how it is presented and rolled out. The team-based approach used in Contextual Design will help you bring these cross-functional professionals together to ensure a successful outcome.

KEEPING LIFE COHERENT

People act throughout their days out of multiple intents[1]. Life is made up of millions of home and work tasks, all of which have to be juggled throughout the day. Fitting all of the to-dos of all of the tasks into the day, and fitting them with each other so the day works, is the continual challenge of life. Any action can fill multiple intents and fit with the rest of life in precise but unarticulated ways. And now people expect their tools and technology—apps, cars, websites, etc.—to act in concert to help us do it all without slowing us down. The principles of design for life guide a designer in understanding all these life and work intents, how they interleave throughout the day, and how to design for them so a new product fits into the moments of life on the go.

A good design is a product or set of offerings structured to allow the user to move from intent to intent, focused only on what they are trying to get done or want to experience. A good product design lets people interleave the activities of work, life,

Keep the activity coherent across products

and fun without stopping to figure, fiddle, or find. Design for life means *design for time*—for use in moments on the go, in the face of interruptions, and the users' partial attention. Good product design keeps the activity coherent within the product while also keeping life coherent as users move through their day.

---

[1] We use the word "intent" rather than "goal" because it acknowledges that not all actions are conscious, thought out, or planned. Indeed, much of daily life emerges out of an inner juggling of desires and opportunity to move forward what needs to get done in bits and pieces. This is the universe we are designing for.

Keeping the activity coherent from the user's point of view has always been the goal of good product design. The traditional challenge of design has been to keep work on a task coherent within the system. Task coherence isn't just about consistency of the user interface—a coherent product keeps the user's activities orderly and natural. When technology platforms were less flexible, task coherence sought to bring together all the function and information needed to support a target activity into one product interface. Customer Relationship Management systems, financial information applications, drawing tools, Amazon's webpage, and websites such as TripAdvisor grew up when it simply wasn't possible to do bits of a task anywhere in life—the car, the doctor's waiting room, or in a hallway between meetings.

Deliver value in bits of time across multiple platforms

To manage multiple intents and functions, these products tended to have complex menus and submenus, hierarchical information navigated by category, many tool palettes, sliding panels, pop-out windows, and more such complexity. They made everything available to the user, who then had to figure out where the functions were and how to use them. However much we tried—and we did—the burden of using a tool in this monolithic application model is entirely upon the user.

And maybe this made sense, because at the time people sat in one place, usually at a desk, and they spent long periods of time learning a product, using it, and eventually becoming experts—or, too often, becoming frustrated:

> **Financial advisor:** I rarely use my financial application— it's way too complex. I call my administrator when I'm on the road for information I need. Now I use Yahoo Finance app to continuously keep touch with the state of stocks.

> **Employee of an ERP company to a consultant:** Will you put in all the expenses for our lunch together and just bill us? Then we don't have to use our expense application—it's too hard. (This expense application was part of the suite the ERP company ships to the world.)

Customer taking to designers of a security tool: Listen to me! We don't want any more function! If you can't get our users up and running fast we will stop buying the product!

But today the Cool Concepts tell us that people will no longer tolerate highly complex applications that expect a lot of up-front learning. They want products that require no learning at all—that can be used instantly and that keep life going anytime, anywhere, in any amount of time.

How we design to support tasks and intents will continue to evolve. But no matter how it changes, as long as we're designing for life we will have to keep the intents, the tasks, the whole of life, and all supporting tools coherent and connected.

But be careful. Part of the reason we can support so much more of life, in the flow of life, is because we are creating *tiny tools*—apps that are always present and instantly available on our mobile devices. They fill the gaps in larger applications and also deliver one small part of a larger ecosystem very well. For example, applications such as TripAdvisor coexist with a myriad of mobile apps that taken together support both travel planning and the trip itself; hotel, car, and airlines apps, Yelp, Ticketmaster, and so on.

But to support an overall task, they cannot exist on their own. They have to connect to all the data and tools people need to complete the whole activity, in any location, on the go. They must provide significant sharing with others, support identity elements, and deliver joy in use. This is why the Experience Models are so critical for design. They tell you what an activity looks like in its whole life context today, so you can design a set of products to transform it tomorrow.

Monolithic applications have been supplanted by an ecosystem of support

The challenge of design is the challenge of keeping the overall life coherent—so we have to balance providing everything needed to support an intent against making the interface overly complex. Mobile apps work because they do one thing well. Focused function sets within larger applications can do the same when guided by the principles of modern design. But in larger systems, it's much more tempting to design in every function you can think of to support every case that might possibly happen. This loads these focused areas with too much function, leading to a highly complex design—the very antithesis of cool.

Scenario versus structural reasoning

The fastest path to ensuring life coherence is to design a coherent "system of support" within and across multiple products. To do that, Contextual Design techniques continuously alternate between scenario-based reasoning and structural, systems-based reasoning. We

Alternate between scenario and structural reasoning

introduced this concept in Part 3 when we talked about pulling product concepts out of a vision. Here we see how it continues to play out as we add detail to the design. Scenario-based reasoning comes easily to most team members—you just tell a story. But in our experience, structural reasoning

does not. Yet both are needed to ensure the coherence of the system and the life.

A simple example shows the power of this alternation. Consider the design of the pathways in a university quad. Students cross over the central green, sometimes on the formal paths but often not. Their intent is to get from where they are to where they want to be, in the most direct way. Each student crossing wears out the grass a little at a time, eventually producing alternative pathways ("desire lines") in addition to the pathways that were designed. Then a good groundskeeper might step back to look at the paths all together and redesign the space to fit the use. Here, where two paths run almost together, they might be merged and paved; there, where four cross, there might be a little courtyard with benches.

The people making the paths are following their everyday life activities without thinking particularly about where they walk, but following the best path for them. They are laying down a scenario of use driven by their intent. Then, having considered the set of scenarios passing through the green,

Users routinely invent new scenarios of use

the groundskeeper takes a step back to design the "system of support" for all these scenarios of use— taking good design principles and the materials of his trade into account. He then redesigns the

space, thinking structurally about what makes a good space given the demands of the scenarios of use.

Once the groundskeeper puts new physical structures in place, people discover other possibilities and build on them—perhaps the courtyard becomes a favorite spot for street musicians. When anything—space, a product, a service—is structured well, it's flexible enough to support additional scenarios of use, unforeseen by the designers.

Scenarios are the individual paths that people take to achieve a particular intent (use case)—they came in here, crossed to there, sat on the grass after that, and left over there. But each scenario can only follow a single thread. It is a view of activity over time. Each individual scenario hangs together for that person or that intent. The groundskeeper's job is to produce a coherent design for the quad that works for everyone. He doesn't look at one scenario in isolation and make structural changes for it and then look at the next scenario and make more changes. This will not lead to a nice design that works for the space as a whole. Instead the groundskeeper looks at all the patterns of use together (as recorded by worn grass) and redesigns the structure to better fit its use.

Consider all scenarios of use—then structure the product

Similarly, product designers must consider all the possible scenarios relevant to our new product concepts at once—those revealed by our user data and important to make our vision real. Then they too step back and consider the best product and user interface structure to support the new practice. They too must think of the product structurally. Scenarios keep each activity coherent; structural reason keeps the product coherent. The best way to optimize both is to continuously alternate. This is what we do in Contextual Design.

In this Part we will introduce a set of design techniques that help team alternate systematically between these two types of design thinking:

Storyboards (Chapter 13): Storyboards describe how people will do their activities with the new product we invented. Storyboards are scenarios depicting step-by-step actions, including manual steps, interaction with multiple devices, access to function, and a very preliminary user interface to accomplish an activity within the real contexts of their life and work. Storyboards allow us to redesign the practice of the user to enhance it by introducing technology support, intent by intent, or use case by use case. Storyboard design is scenario-based thinking.

User Environment Design (Chapter 14): A User Environment Design represents the structure of the product. Hidden in the storyboards are requirements on what the system needs to support to enable those scenarios. To build a User Environment Design the team must think structurally about the places in the product and what device(s) will be used to deliver that place. A User Environment Design is made up of *focus areas* which define each place and the purpose of that place. A product is defined by the places it provides to support the storyboards, the purpose of each place, the functions and content in each place and the flow between places—within one product and across devices. The User Environment Design helps the team with this high-level structural reasoning so that they can determine what the product itself will look like.

User Environment Design Validation: Once the team starts to envision the places in the product—which will turn into windows, screens, or pages—it's easy to overfocus on each space and start to "what if" into the interface. Having a specific place in the product invites the team to invent function, which usually complicates the scenarios of use we are trying to support. Checking that we don't overdesign is critical to a good user experience. In Contextual Design we run the storyboard stories, sequences from the user data, and the Day-in-the-Life stories through the User Environment Design to ensure that they are still supported coherently. This is scenario-based reasoning again.

Don't complicate the design by "what if-ing" into the product design

Interaction Patterns (Chapter 15): User interface design requires the same structural reasoning as the User Environment Design. An Interaction Pattern is a high-level structural view of the layout of function and content in the places—screen, page, window—defined in the User Environment Design. Once the places with their core function and content are designed at a high level, the team must think how to structure the places. The interaction has to work within the place to guide the user, be consistent across the product, and fit with the standards of the devices it runs on. Like the places in the User Environment Design, the Interaction Patterns also suggest new possible function. This is another opportunity to overcomplicate the design, so again we walk the new interface structure with scenarios of use to be sure that we did not lose the coherence of the practice.

Mock-up Testing and Validation (Chapter 17): User testing returns the team to scenario-based reasoning. This time, the user interacts with a paper mockup while pretending to do their own tasks or activities in the context of their own practice. We don't ask them to do planned tasks; the scenario of use comes from them. If the overall product structure is strong, it should support any new scenario the user tries; if not it will break, and the team will have to revisit their design decisions. The mock-up interview tests and validates both the product concept as a whole and our design choices of how it will work.

Iterative Testing: With feedback in hand, we return to structural reasoning as we redesign both the places in the product shown in the User Environment Design and the interface layout shown in Interaction Patterns. After a few rounds of testing—alternating between usage during testing (scenario) and redesign of the product mockup (structural)—you will have a successful high-level structure for the product and the interface that is a strong enough backbone to integrate additional function and support more detailed design.

A great product or suite of products delivering a great user experience is built upon rich user data, the principles of the Cool Concepts, and team ideation practices when team members use the modern materials of design. But to make the right thing for the user requires keeping the life, the practice, and the product coherent. The best way to ensure this—and to figure out what to build—is to alternate between scenario and structural reasoning.

Design in layers and get back to the user early and often

You need not do all the storyboards that might be relevant to a new offering before building the User Environment Design. Just focus on those that are core to the vision. With 6–10 key scenarios guided by data, you have enough to sketch out the bones of the product, define the high-level Interaction Patterns, and start testing the product concept. Let the details grow after the concept is validated; break up the validated product concept so it fits with Agile iterations (or whatever development methodology you use) and start development in parallel with working out the details. New scenarios and functional detail can follow in quick succession. Get continuous feedback from the user on how you are doing. After all, you are defining a new way of living or working—so get back to the user early and often.

DESIGN IN TEAMS

Design thinking and design decisions are hard. Unlike user data, which just needs to be collected and organized, once real invention starts there is lot of room for differing opinions. There is no one perfect design—there are many possible good design choices. In the end, the team only needs one that works. Letting the user be the final arbitrator simplifies the conversations between team members. We remind the team while they are designing that they are *on the way to test*—not on the way to shipping. This makes it easier to let go of an argument about different approaches. Nothing is final yet; they will test and then choose. Also, we provide the team with a set of design principles for structuring the User Environment Design and the Interaction Pattern. And we use the principles from the Cool Concepts to inform design thinking. Having principles encourages the team to reference them when making an argument about the design instead of simply declaring that they do or don't like a team member's design. All of this depersonalizes design decisions and helps the team move toward a common goal.

Design knowing you are on your way to test—don't overinvest

SEPARATING CONVERSATIONS

But many arguments during design occur because team members aren't really in the same conversation. They are arguing about different aspects of the problem, and they don't realize it. Contextual

Design helps the team with this by making all design conversations more tangible. When discussing how a product supports an intent or task, the team produces a storyboard. When designing product structure, the User Environment Design diagram makes it visible. Interaction Patterns represent the next layer of design as tangible artifacts and drawings of page layout. And the paper mockup of the product represents a concrete user interface for the conversation with the user.

By providing a physical representation of each point of view on design, Contextual Design helps to separate the conversations about the product structure from the redesigned task process (represented in storyboards), the page layout (represented by design patterns), and lower-level controls and layout choices in the user interface (represented in increasing detail in the prototype). If developers get involved (which we recommend), this separation of conversations helps them see that we are not talking about the internal product structure (represented by the object model) or data structures.

Separate and clarify design conversations by making them tangible

When each conversation has its own physical representation, the design discussion is easier to have. Is the team arguing about how to change the users' practice? Then they should be looking at a storyboard, changing it to reflect their thinking. Are they arguing about how to organize the product to support that practice? Then they should be modifying the User Environment design. Are they arguing about appearance and layout? Then they should be looking at the Interaction Pattern or mockups. Everyone can tell which issues to pay attention to, because that's the representation the team is pointing to and updating. Confusions among conversations are easier to avoid. Over time, teams trained in the concept of separation of conversations become self-aware; they stop in the middle of an argument to ask: What conversation are we in? What conversation *should* we be in?

This kind of clarification of conversations is especially helpful after a mock-up interview because the data may be relevant to any level of design. You may get feedback on a button style, page layout, basic function on a page, or discover a whole new way of doing a task. For a team that has learned the idea of separation of conversations and how to use the different representations, the redesign conversation will be easier too.

TEAM SIZE

We recommend that the team working on detailed design be kept small deliberately—four people are optimal. That might be one or two product managers, one or two interaction designers, and a user researcher. Other stakeholders and developers can participate in occasional interpretation sessions and reviews. Regular reviews should be scheduled when these stakeholders can participate, commenting on the feasibility of the functions the mockup represents, looking for inconsistencies, and introducing mandatory business goals. ("We must present what we are selling in the most prominent place on our home page, even if our users don't care!"). It's then up to the core team to respond to this feedback, with product changes or taking on additional test questions in future rounds. Too large a working team will require lots of time on facilitation, sharing, responding to differences of opinion, and bringing each other up to speed if they miss some sessions. A small team, trusted to do good work with a good process, is the best way to get design excellence. As we describe the techniques in Part 4, we will give strategies for getting the most out of small teams and subgroups throughout.

Design in small teams to keep the product coherent and to move fast

Storyboards   13

A storyboard is an illustrated, step-by-step presentation describing how people will perform a target activity using your new product concepts. Storyboards (see Fig. 13.1) are guided by user data, addressing the issues and situations the data reveals. Each storyboard follows a single thread, so the team draws a different storyboard for each part of the activity and each situation the user will find themselves in. Storyboards may show different points of view—the manager versus the worker or the driver versus the car dealer. The team starts by creating the core storyboards—ignoring edge cases, set-up, and less important situations of use. The team's first job is to block out the most central value of the new product showing how it will enhance life or work. These first storyboards should represent the core of the redesigned practice as impacted by your new offering. You can add more storyboards later to extend the design. Plan to do six to eight storyboards before starting work on the User Environment Design. You can do this in 2–4 days with two to three people creating storyboards in parallel.

Storyboards depict how people will live life with your product

Storyboards help the team work out how specific user activities and situations will be handled by the new design. Storyboards show how an activity will be achieved, including manual actions, interactions with existing products and your new product, and collaborations with others, across all platforms—whether you are designing a single product, a part of a larger application, a mobile app, a website, or a suite of connected products. The storyboard cells show the action:

Contextual Design. http://dx.doi.org/10.1016/B978-0-12-800894-2.00013-2

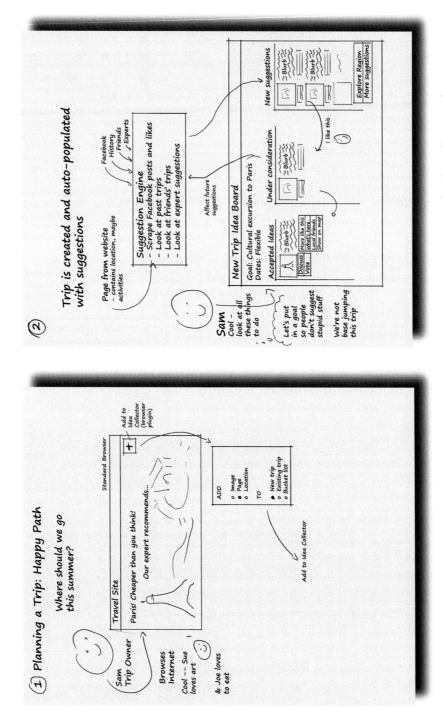

FIGURE 13.1 A storyboard showing the initial stages of travel planning, according to our vision to create the Idea Collector product concept.

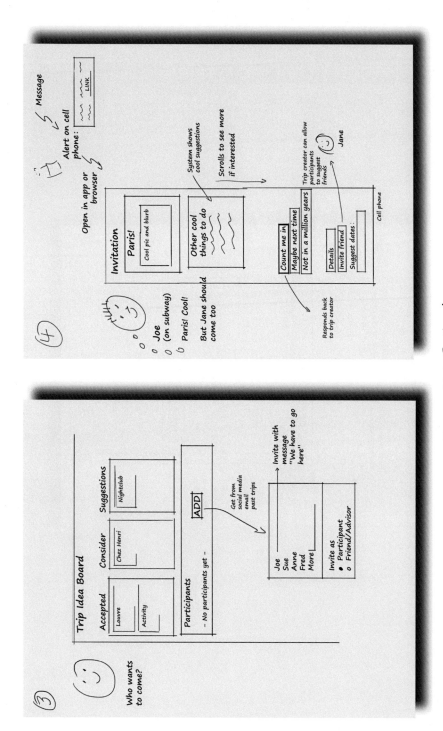

FIGURE 13.1 *Continued*

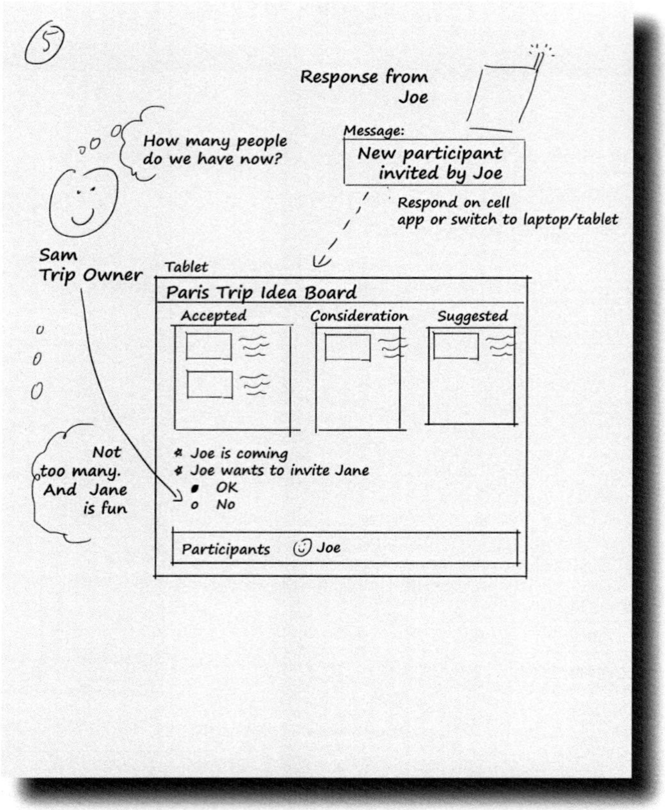

FIGURE 13.1 *Continued*

users, screens, and system actions that make it all work. They work much like storyboards for a movie, which show what happens in each scene without going into too much detail about any scene. The user interface is shown in a lightweight, very rough way as needed to illustrate the story. The context of use—physical situation and social interactions—are incorporated into the story also.

Storyboards are an intermediate step between high-level visioning and detailed design of the structure and function of the product. We build storyboards to ensure that the activities of the user hang together as coherent tasks and are supported coherently by the new product. It's easy to break the users'

Limit detail in each cell to encourage the team to start by designing the high level

existing practice by jumping from the big new idea to low-level user interface and implementation design without considering the impact it has on the flow of the user's activities. As soon as designers start focusing on technology, technology and its problems become their central design concern. Storyboards work against this tendency.

Storyboards also limit the level of detail at this point in the design process. A storyboard cell is drawn on a half sheet of 8½ × 11 paper. Each cell can only hold so much; a drawing of a user interface within a cell can only describe so much detail. This helps keep designers from diving down into the small details of their design before the overall product structure has been settled. Especially when a design addresses multiple platforms, the team needs to see the overall coherence of the activity as it moves across time, place, and platform before being caught up in the many details of each platform's user interface. Storyboards encourage the team to use scenario thinking, designing the whole flow of life to show how the user will move through time and place to get their activities done.

When the team has finished the primary scenarios of use, they create the User Environment Design from the storyboards to ensure the technology supporting the new practice hangs together as a product offering or suite. This provides an initial product structure and high-level needs for each platform; the team can then simultaneously generate more detailed storyboards for lower-level needs and start to test the product concept, structure, and initial Interaction Patterns with users. The whole product offering—even when it is a combination of a larger product and mobile apps—should be represented in the storyboards and then reflected in the User Environment Design. We wait to design the product places and the user interface until we have the core storyboards. Optimizing an interface for one scenario will not yield an optimized product or suite of apps, so it's essential to get the practice right for the core scenarios before settling on any product or user interface structure.

Storyboards are based on the vision and the product concepts, follow the structure of a consolidated sequence model or Day-in-the Life model, and pull implications from other models and the affinity as necessary. The vision produces the core product concepts to be developed and the Cool Drilldown refines them to deliver additional value. The vision defines how the users' lives are changed with that new technology; the consolidated models define the underlying structure of user actions, the strategies they use to accomplish it, and the intents that they are trying to achieve. The storyboard shows how they can achieve those intents with the new invention, extending or replacing their strategies and structure as appropriate.

Create a set of core storyboards before designing the product structure

BUILDING A STORYBOARD

The result of storyboarding is a set of drawings, but there are several steps before getting you there. The first step in building a storyboard is to make a list—as so often in Contextual Design, we use the list to organize and focus our thinking. The list you want now is a list of cases: tasks and situations to consider in your storyboards. For this list ask yourself, what are the key activities, given consolidated data and the vision? Who does them and how do they collaborate? If they are done by different people with different responsibilities in life or work, do they approach the activities differently? If you created Personas, will they behave differently? What external situations or issues might come up that have to be handled? Does time of day or being on the go change the practice? What are the real-world breakdowns that need to be addressed? Does the vision imply new activities that have to be supported? Ask these questions and list the core activities that drive value of the new product. These will need to be fleshed out in the storyboards.

1. Simple travel planning, couple going on vacation

2. Being on vacation together, modifying plans in the moment

3. Travel planning with kids. Make everyone happy, let the kids contribute.

4. Travel planning and being on vacation while one member of the group can't go.

5. Life event causes the whole trip to be put off for six months

6. Creating a record (memory) of the trip and curating it later

FIGURE 13.2   A partial list of cases to consider in storyboards. Number 4 was an actual situation from the user data and seemed to the team like an important opportunity for enhancing life. #6 suggests new work for users—but this sort of curating memories is often a valued activity for people.

The team adds to this list as you identify new situations of interest going forward, so don't be too concerned that it be absolutely complete.

Assign two to three people to each storyboard; run multiple storyboard teams in parallel if you have enough people. Assign storyboard cases to each team so they are all working on a different case.

Work on different storyboard cases in parallel small groups

The first thing each team does is set focus for their storyboard. They harvest all the data they can to support their case. Identify and walk parts of the Affinity that address issues important to the case; identify and review the parts of the consolidated models that are relevant.

Collect any sequences or parts of sequences to suggest an order for the storyboard; reference the Day-in-the-Life Model if the sequences don't cover your case. If your design envisions a new way of living or working that people don't do now with technology, you should still have data on how they do the practice manually. Our travel vision, for example, envisions an Idea Collector to collect ideas and notes about things to do—something that doesn't currently exist online. But people do make notes about events they're planning; they do research online for various purposes; they collect pictures and save stories; and many do scrapbooking in paper. Sequences describing these activities will suggest overall structure and specific issues to consider in doing the new design. Use them for storyboarding.

When collecting issues, it's most effective to give each person a model or piece of Affinity to look at and have everyone review the data in parallel, collecting issues as they go. Then the storyboard sub-team can get back together and make one list of all issues pulling together what everyone found.

Collect relevant user data to inform each case to be storyboarded

If your team is not familiar with modern inter-action designs and ways of structuring product interfaces across multiple devices, this is also a good time for them to review and learn from your interaction designers. You might look at well-designed products that support the same activity or a similar activity to learn how they are structured. (See Chapter 15 for more on how to do this.) With that knowledge in hand, the storyboards will reflect better initial design knowledge—the team will want to visualize the interface, so they should have some good examples to help them.

The next step is creating a more detailed storyboard vision focused only on the one scenario to be storyboarded. This should take 30 minutes to an hour, no more. Take the initial vision, as captured in the product concepts and elaborated in the Cool Drilldown, as a starting point. Now the sub-team creates a more detailed vision using the Visioning workshop process: talk through how users will handle the particular case the team is working on, given the new inventions from the vision. One person takes the role of pen and draws the design as the team tells the story together. Because the team is now focused on working out one particular case, the visioning is lower level and adds a lot of detail that the original vision didn't go into. It identifies and resolves problems the original vision never considered. It considers how interfaces might be structured to present function and content. So the sub-team will expand and add on to the original vision but make sure that they stay true to it. They can elaborate on it, fix problems with it, and work out the details, but they shouldn't go off and do an alternative vision of their own or make up a new product concept that the whole team hasn't bought into.

Create detailed visions of the new practice the storyboard will address

The storyboard vision should include rough sketches of user interfaces as they come up in the story—don't obsess over them, but make sure they reflect modern design approaches. If your storyboard vision is all text, you're thinking in terms of functions and lists, not in terms of holistic life practice. Or you may be listing high-level user intents that you want to support without ever saying exactly how you'll support them. Such visions will not jumpstart the structural thinking that will be needed next. But don't just draw user interfaces either—keep the people and their actions in the picture. You need to include all the human activities and their context to see how your product will fit in.

Storyboards are pictures of possible user interfaces and manual steps

You are using the user interface sketches to help drive your thinking. You are not designing the user interface at this point, but it's very hard to think about what the new practice will be without drawing out what the user will see. So assume you will be able to ship a modern interface and incorporate UI sketches as you need them, but do not try to be complete or thorough. Do not worry about consistent layout across storyboards, consistency of function, or details of interactivity. Just capture enough user interface elements to illustrate how the product supports what the user wants to do at each point. Consistency and standards conformance will come later. But you should be envisioning a specific device at each step, and you do need to consider the limitations of that platform—don't sketch a complicated user interface with lots of parts and then claim it's used on a smartphone. Make sure that it's clear what the device is on the storyboard.

Do, however, worry about consistency of action and intent. Does the user *want* to do the thing you've envisioned for them? What questions will they naturally be asking at each point? Do they know what action to take next? How? What guidance will lead them through the activity—and through the use of your product? As you go, you're likely to come up with additional scenarios that need to be worked through. Don't do it now—add them to your list of cases and deal with them on their own. It's often useful for the first storyboard you do to be the "happy path"—everything works out simply for the user. But after that, it's like any story—stories that are only happy tend to

Design the "happy path" through the product first—leave edge cases for later

be boring. Think of all the difficult, annoying problems that could occur—that you've seen in your user data. Roll those into your storyboards so that you're always working on an interesting problem.

As the team visions each scenario, they should continually refer back to their consolidated user data. Look for overall structure, distinct strategies people follow, specific situations that need to be handled, intents the user cares about, core motivations or identity elements you need to support, and breakdowns that you can overcome.

Ground your storyboard in your consolidated user data

Make sure you've thought about mobile device use and design for use in moments of time. Check the activities of the sequence—either they address a primary user intent and you should keep them coherent in the storyboard, or they are driven by current technology and you can justify taking them apart. The storyboard vision is likely to be more sequential and linear than the initial vision, and that is okay.

In practice, we find teams often forget to keep touching base with the user data. Try not to be one of these teams. It really is best if you keep yourself grounded in the real issues of the user. But if you get to the end of your storyboard vision and you've done what we said not to do, go back and use the consolidated user data as a cross-check—walk through the models looking for intents and breakdowns you missed, strategies and situations you don't support, and mismatches in how you're supporting the task and how the users think about it.

Draw storyboard cells last—create a clean neat version of your plan for the user

Once the sub-team is happy with their storyboard vision, they can draw storyboard cells on half sheets of paper. Do this in parallel, letting each sub-team member do cells for a different set of steps from the storyboard vision—all the important decisions have been made, after all.

Use the storyboard cells to illustrate the story of how this life activity is done. Each cell captures one piece of the story: an interaction with a screen of the user interface, with another person, or with a device; or it shows what the system has done for the user behind the scenes to make the next step possible. Try to fill up the storyboard cells comfortably. Cells which are stuffed with too much detail suggest you're diving down into design details prematurely. Cells which are too bare suggest you're not really spelling out (or, likely, thinking through) the real process.

Remember that being complete is not the goal at this time. You need enough storyboards to address the central cases of the system before you can start the User Environment Design. Then you will alternate between storyboarding, User Environment Design definition with associated Interaction Patterns, and iteration with the user. Working with the user may reveal more cases you must consider so just do enough at first to guide the product structure and overall approach.

THE STORYBOARD REVIEW

The last step of storyboarding is review. The pair or small team has come up with a proposal for how this activity should be accomplished which the rest of the team hasn't seen. So plan a storyboard review at which everyone shares their storyboards with the whole team. Introduce the criteria for providing feedback to focus the critique:

- Does it support the user data?
- Is it true to the vision and product concepts?
- Does it deliver on the principles of the Cool Concepts, especially considering a cross-platform mobile solution?
- Does it deliver more than the competition?
- Is it technically doable?
- Does it support a good business case?
- Is it written appropriately with the right amount of detail for a good storyboard?

In a storyboard review, each sub-team presents their storyboard in turn. This is actually the first design review in the process—and that means critique. In art or design schools critique is part of the culture, but not everyone has had that experience

Ensure buy-in and shared understanding with storyboard reviews

and we find that no one really likes the process whether or not they have that background. So the first response of the team is appreciation and applause: "Thank you for working through this problem for us!" <clap> (Yes, do this, even if it makes you feel weird.) Acknowledgment of the work helps people feel appreciated—even though they know it's part of the process. When you have worked hard—even if only

for a day—you want to be acknowledged for your effort and your good ideas. But traditionally reviews are looking for what is broken, what you don't agree with. So we build in appreciation and we teach people about the "Mom Response" (see Managing Critique with the Mom Response textbox). Anytime the team reviews each other's work, start with appreciation. And if you need it, ask for the Mom Response.

Once you acknowledge the work, run the review. One member of the sub-team stands up and talks through the storyboard, cell by cell. The rest of the team listens respectfully, asking questions, and making suggestions without a hint of judgment—a challenge for us all! Valid comments include:

"Why did you solve that problem that way?" The sub-team should be able to say what drove their decision, whether it was a technical decision or based on user data. They should have this answer on the tip of their tongue, because you'll be challenged for real down the line by product managers or engineers. Help the team get their story clean now.

"I think this direction contradicts our user data in this way." The sub-team should be able to show that it doesn't. If they can't, the issue goes on a sticky note and is stuck to the storyboard cell.

"Did you consider this user situation, strategy, or intent that we saw in our data?" The sub-team should either say yes, and how they dealt with it—or no, they didn't think about that one. If the answer is no, the question goes on a sticky note and is stuck to the storyboard.

"Did you consider this alternative design idea for handling this situation?" The answer might be yes, with an explanation of why they didn't use that idea—or no, in which case the idea goes on a sticky note and is stuck to the storyboard.

"Is that the right context for that activity?" Make sure the team is taking the context of use into account. In-depth, concentrated tasks are not likely to be done on a smartphone on the subway. Conversely, if an activity can be done throughout the day the storyboard should not envision it always on a desktop computer. If the team hasn't got a good justification for the context they've envisioned, put a sticky note on the storyboard with the issue.

The storyboard should be able to stand on its own when read by an individual without narration. Part of the review is to be sure enough drawing and information is in each cell so that when the team returns to it nothing will be forgotten. So during the review, one sub-team member narrates and one

> *Each storyboard must stand on its own without narration*

captures issues and adds detail to clarify—even noting where to add cells, if needed. But this is not the time to discuss extensive redesign or changes—write a note and send the sub-team back to resolve the issues. A storyboard review will take 20–30 minutes depending on the length of the storyboard. Remember, you are listening and writing down issues and design ideas, not discussing except for clarification.

At the end of the review, the sub-team has a storyboard covered with sticky notes. Usually, it's best to just let them go back and deal with the notes and go forward with the process without another review. But if there are a lot of significant issues, it may worthwhile for them to rework the storyboard and then bring it back to the whole team to review again. But this should be rare—beware getting yourselves caught in multiple reviews. Remember you are on the way to test. Once represented in a product mockup, you will see if your ideas work for the user, the real last word on the design.

This review is internal to the team to double-check the work and ensure an agreed-upon direction. But the storyboards, once cleaned up after the team review, are a good way to share the direction of the redesigned practice with stakeholders. This

> *Storyboard reviews with internal users root out resistance and create buy-in through listening*

is especially important when designing for internal users who want to have a say in how you are changing their lives. So do another review with stakeholders and get their feedback. This can help you anticipate resistance to change and may challenge or refocus what you are planning so that it can be more effective. Storyboard reviews are easy to do remotely by taking pictures of the cells and putting them in a slideshow. But consider your population—if presentation will matter, draw up the storyboard nicely.

Storyboards ensure the new design accounts for the context of use. But the context is not just the task being supported, or how features are structured and grouped in a product; the context that matters is the overall life of the user and the way any activity fits into that life. Storyboarding brings this context into focus for the team during the detailed design process. It lets the team work out all the scenarios, keeping them coherent with scenario-based reasoning. With core storyboards in hand we are ready to decide how to best structure the system to support them.

MANAGING CRITIQUE WITH THE MOM RESPONSE

Critique is difficult for everyone to receive. Even when a team spends only a few days creating a storyboard or design, they invest themselves in the result. And even if we all agree that we want feedback and that we are committed to creating the best product we can, hearing that someone you respect does not agree with you or that you didn't think of something important is hard to take. Simple disagreement can show up like lack of value. This is true for new people—new to the industry, the team, or to using a process. But it is also true when you've been in the field for a long time. Everyone wants to feel valued and acknowledged for their work. This is at the center of feeling connected to the team. But critique is essential to good product design. So how do you provide honest feedback and manage everyone's inevitable self-doubt?

To help we developed the Mom Response concept—a structured way to address feelings of being valued. Remember when you were young, you would come home with your art project. "Mommy, Mommy! Look at my airplane picture!" you'd say. And you'd want Mom to say, "Oh, that's beautiful! That's wonderful! You did a great job!"

This is the Mom Response—it is unconditional, uncritical, absolute celebration of the effort of another person. But what if the Mom instead said, "Oh, you colored outside the lines. Try to do better next time." The child is excited about their work and they are sharing—they want you to be excited too. But instead if Mom is critical, you are deflated. You feel that you've lost personal value. In parenting, this is a very bad thing. ⇨

It starts in childhood, but it persists into adulthood and we bring it to work—we want the people we work with to fundamentally value us. If we know they do, critiques feel more like collaboration than evaluation—like we are up to something together. But even then, sometimes we need to be told we are wonderful and terrific. And what happens if you are new to the team or a process? You feel you have to prove yourself. What happens if you are presenting to the boss, or the architect, or some other important person? You'll be nervous. Whether we like it or not, whether we admit it or not, we all need the Mom Response from the people in our world some of the time.

So this is what we teach: Anytime a team member (or subgroup) presents his or her work to a group, we remind the larger group that we have asked that subgroup to think out the problem for the larger team. So first we thank them for that effort and applaud, which is the Mom Response. We know that the work they did will help the team get to a better solution because it is easier to renovate something than do it from scratch. Having the concept of the Mom Response names the experience so everyone knows what is going on.

But then we deliberately switch to critique. We remind the subgroup that if the larger team didn't find anything to improve, they wouldn't be taking their work seriously. Change, feedback, challenge, and significant redesign are to be expected. It is the mark of collaborating professionals to give and receive critique directly and with respect. So eye rolling, argument, grandstanding, and generally rude behavior are not acceptable in any review. And as long as the sub-team or person is tasked to go back and deal with the feedback as they see fit, the larger team is still communicating value. But be careful—if you micromanage the design with many, many reviews you communicate mistrust instead.

By naming and explaining the rules of the Mom Response and Critique Response, everyone knows the rules of engagement. This frees the team to ask for the Mom Response when they just feel they need it. In our fast-paced work world we often forget to express value. So encourage people to simply ask if they feel a little beat up or undervalued. Our direct feedback can do that, whether it's intended or not. You speak as though you forgot somebody did the work; you just look at the work product and say, "That's wrong. That violates design principles. Fix this, Fix that!" The whole focus is on flaws—coloring outside the lines—ignoring what was good.

So we teach people that when you need the Mom response you say, "I need the Mom response." And then everybody comes over and says, "Oh, you did a great job!" Now, the funny part about it is, it doesn't matter that you asked. And it doesn't matter that they are making a fuss. It works anyway. And you feel better.

By the way, this is not about men versus women or other underrepresented populations. When Karen was in Germany working with an entire team of experienced, German, male developers we taught them the Mom Response—and they used it! When the project was done they told us, "The most important thing you gave us is the Mom response." We watched all these German guys, running around telling each other what a great job they did. So try it–it works! Build the Mom Response and Direct Critique into your team culture.

The User Environment Design

14

Just as storyboards keep the practice coherent, the User Environment Design keeps the product or coordinated suite of products coherent. Designers now have to consider the whole ecosystem of apps, websites, and software tools that work together across devices to support the overall intent of the user relative to the target activity. Whether you are designing one product or a larger ecosystem, designers need a way of seeing, defining, and structuring the overall product offering. When we first introduced the User Environment Design, people were mainly designing software applications and that's how we talked about it. But the basic concepts and structure of the User Environment Design are just as applicable today.

The job of the User Environment Design is to represent the overall product structure including across application boundaries. It shows the places where user interacts with the product, the function and content within those places, the way information is brought into each place, and the pathways for the user to move between places. Blocking out the overall structure of the system as a set of places, each focused on allowing the user to achieve a particular purpose, is the first challenge for the design team. The structural decisions of the User Environment Design precede decisions about the implementation or user interface. It doesn't make sense to design screen layouts until you've decided what places will be in the system and what functions the system should implement.

The User Environment Design helps teams see and design product structure

Contextual Design. http://dx.doi.org/10.1016/B978-0-12-800894-2.00014-4

In the User Environment Design, places are defined by *Focus Areas*, a core concept for structuring the user experience. Focus areas define a set of function and content all oriented toward achieving a particular purpose or user intent. A user moves from one focus area to another as needed to perform an activity. Consider this example:

> A user takes a break from a heads-down task by checking email. First she scans her messages looking for something interesting. She doesn't want work email that will draw her into another difficult task—she wants a break. So she doesn't want the whole content of the email—sender and subject line are enough to pick out something fun. Fortunately, there's an email from her husband proposing a vacation spot. Just the thing. She clicks on the email.

Up to this point this user has been in one place, the inbox, with one set of functions for reading, scanning, organizing, and deleting messages. Once she opens the message, she's in a new place. Her intent has changed; she's no longer looking for an email to read, she's focused in on the content of one email. She's reading the one message from her husband and she's got functions appropriate to that intent—read, reply, file, delete, and most importantly, click on link. Some functions were also found in the inbox; others were not. This new collection of function provided by this new place matches her new intent.

The structure of the activity drives the structure of the product

Her husband is suggesting a trip to New Zealand. Fun! She clicks the link he sent—and now she's in a new place, the vacation resort's website.

The new place has new function appropriate to her new intent (to see if she would like this resort). It was created by a different set of people, at a different time, without knowledge of her email app, but in this interconnected world, that doesn't matter. Her experience is that of moving from place to place, following her intent as that evolves given the information she takes in at each place.

Now suppose it's our goal to build a product supporting travel planning. Our user's intent, once she reaches the resort's page, is to talk about it with her husband, find additional things to do in New Zealand, forward the page to a friend who's been there for advice, and so forth. How does our new product fit into this existing ecology? Do we work with resorts to capture information from their pages, or with email providers to communicate vacation ideas between users? If that won't work for technical and business reasons, do we adopt a model like Pinterest's "Pin It" widget, an add-on that's available everywhere?

Design is about defining the places in the product so it works best for the user

Suppose we have such a browser widget. How does it work? Does it pull the user out of whatever place they were in into a new place where they can make notes and send the idea to others? That might be good—maybe commenting on the resort is sufficiently different from exploring it online that a new place will work. Or maybe it's not—maybe the user really doesn't want to lose the context of the place she's commenting on. Then how do we design our app so that the user experience is not that of leaving the place? What about other platforms—maybe users will want to do more in-depth exploration over lunch on their cell phone. Can they pick up where they left off? Is there an app on the phone and what exactly does it do?

These are the challenges of product design: create the necessary places on the right platforms to support the flexibility of the activity; design the right function into those places; and design the right access from place to place so the flow of the user's work is not interrupted. User-centered design seeks to build a structure for the overall product which supports the user's natural movement through their activities and is flexible enough that the user can invent new ways of working.

Designing product structure is designing to support the user practice as it moves through the places in the product. To design the product structure, you must be able to think about the places, their purpose, and their connection irrespective of any particular user interface or implementation. But this kind of structural thinking is hard for teams. In our early work with design teams, we found that team members tended to slide into conversations about the user interface before they were ready— before they had agreed on base structure. They were

The User Environment Design helps the team hold off on low-level detail

like architects who could only communicate by drawing pictures focused on detail inside the rooms of the proposed house instead of the overall plan for the house as a structure. "We want this function on this page," one would say, sketching a row of buttons. "The style guide says those should be side navigation," another would reply. "Do you really want to use that word?" a third would ask. When the very language you use to communicate suggests that the user interface is the topic of conversation, it's hard not to be distracted by it.

The same thing happens when developers are on the team—they want to talk about specific algorithms, data access, and whether a particular function is doable automatically. We do need to know if a technical concept is doable, but we don't need to lay the pipes and locate the electrical outlets inside the rooms of the house before knowing what the overall layout of the house will be. So we needed a way to represent the system structure directly, free of any user interface or technical implications. The User Environment Design was designed explicitly to help teams see structure and hold off on detailed design, whether it's the user interface or the technical underpinnings. And to build it we borrowed from building architecture.

Good design starts with high-level structure and fills in details later

The oldest form of design for life is in architecture—building a house. We live in the places in our house, we walk through the rooms and hallways, and we do things in those rooms. An architect of a new home would never start by choosing rugs and materials for the countertops. Instead, they start with rough sketches which they work up into a floor plan. The floor plan captures the right level of detail for talking about the structure of a house—it shows the parts and their relationships without showing how the house is decorated. The user interface of a product is equivalent to the decoration of a house—it matters, but if the structure is wrong, no user interface can fix the problems.

The User Environment Design is a floor plan for software

The pattern of use we found in software—working in a place, moving to a new location, and doing a new kind of activity based on a new intent in that place—is very much like living in a house. A person starts dinner and goes to the kitchen where the tools for cooking are located (knives, bowls, stove). A drawer sticks, and he decides to take it to the workshop and plane it down while the water boils. He takes the drawer to another place, which has the different set of tools useful for minor carpentry, and works on the drawer there. Then he goes back to finish dinner. A house consists of places to do things, functions or tools in each place which help do things, and access allowing people to move between places. The parallels between living and working in software and in houses suggested the idea of creating a system floor plan—the User Environment Design.[1]

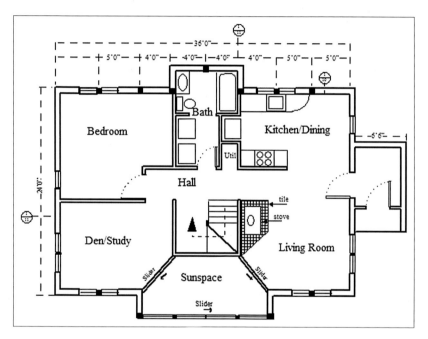

FIGURE 14.1   A floor plan. Notice how the important distinctions are immediately apparent—the relative size of the spaces and the access between them. Details which are unimportant for understanding the structure of the house—rugs, wall surface—are absent or inconspicuous. But the drawing does tie to the users' experience of moving through a house and also puts construction details in context—the *dark squares* in the walls indicate supporting posts and the numbers in circles key this diagram to cross-sections showing wall construction. This is what we need in software design—a single representation which shows how all the parts of the system relate in the users' experience.

---

[1] We're often asked if the User Environment Design is the same thing as a site map. The User Environment Design was invented before the Internet existed or the idea of information architecture were in wide use. There are similarities in that site maps show the big picture of how a site is organized, making relationships between pages, and other content components clear. But we believe the floor plan concept manifest in the User Environment Design along with its design principles does a better job of focusing the design team on keeping both the product and the user's activities coherent and so delivers user experience excellence.

A floor plan occupies a unique role in the design of a house (Fig. 14.1). It's less physical than an elevation, which shows a view of the house as though you were looking at it (an elevation is more like a user interface sketch). It doesn't show wall color or how the house is finished (which would also be more like a user interface). Yet it's not at the nuts-and-bolts level of a construction diagram (for the implementation), which might show how to put a wall together but doesn't show anything the homeowner can relate to. The floor plan selects a few of the most salient aspects of a house as it supports living and represents them: the spaces in the house, their sizes, and relationships to each other; the large things in each space which support the kind of living done there (stoves, refrigerators); and the access between spaces.

As a diagram, a floor plan supports a conversation about how well a design supports a particular style of life and allows the architect to compare that with the life the house's prospective owners want to have. Architects can walk stories of living through the floor plan to see how well it fits the homeowners. Is a room too small for the way the owners want to use it? Is it too hard to get from one room to another? Is there a lot of dead space devoted to halls or intermediate areas? The floor plan lays out all the parts of a house, letting the architect walk different cases and scenarios through it. Rules of thumb such as constraints on minimum clearances, layouts which work well, and the limitations of construction materials ensure that the resulting design is usable and implementable. Of course, once the house is built, meals may be eaten in the kitchen, and a formal dining room may be used as a music room. But this homeowner simply redefined the "place" next to the kitchen to be a "place" for music by bringing all their instruments and music into that place. The place is still coherent—it has a fundamental purpose—it's just not dining. A good structure will permit different uses which the architect never designed explicitly.

Seeing and designing structure is critical for ensuring that both the life and the product hang together to support the user. Architects

Make sure the floor plan works to support the flow of life

made a way to see the structure of their buildings when they invented floor plans. The User Environment Design represents the product structure in the same kind of way. It is built first at a high level, revealing the overall structure of the product. Then as the basic concept is validated, it becomes the specification of what needs to be built. Each place in the User Environment Design will be a screen, page, or window where the user will interact with the product. Just as a room in a house needs layout to ensure it works for the purpose of the room, a place in a software product needs layout so that the support activities can be done conveniently in that place. Interaction Patterns (discussed in Chapter 15) define the structure of each place and guide the user interface approach and architecture as a whole.

Build the User Environment Design at a high level first and validate it with users

THE USER ENVIRONMENT DESIGN ELEMENTS

In life, people move from intent to intent to get their work and life done. They engage in a variety of activities to accomplish these intents. And there's a natural flow through these activities—users will move from one activity to another, depending on what they are trying to achieve. A user-centered product, one that supports the user well, should provide direct support to help the user fulfill his or her intents by organizing the right function into coherent areas that map to specific user activities.

Every product has a User Environment Design within it

Just as any house has a floor plan, no matter how it was designed, any product has a User Environment Design implicit within it. Any product can be analyzed and its underlying User Environment Design revealed. (In fact, doing a reverse User Environment Design is one of the best ways to find the structural problems that may be plaguing your existing product.) So to illustrate the User Environment Design, we'll use an example most people are familiar with: Microsoft PowerPoint.

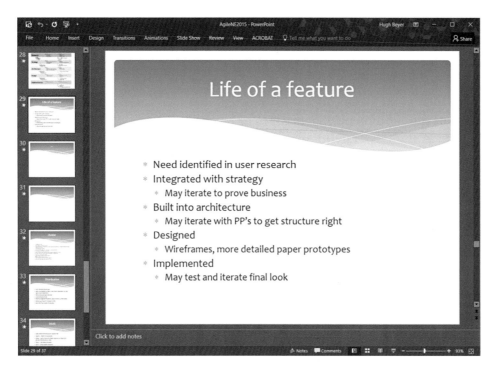

FIGURE 14.2   A screen from PowerPoint. This is the editing window, where individual slides can be designed. Note the nav bar on the left, which lets the user see the local neighborhood of the slide; and the area at the bottom for presenter notes.

---

2. Edit Slide

Purpose: Edit content of individual slide.

Functions

- System shows slide contents
- User can view and edit content of slide
- User can view and edit notes associated with the slide
- User can move to another slide
- User can bring up Slide Sorter (1)
- User can save slideshow
- …

FIGURE 14.3   The Focus Area defining the editing screen (partial). The purpose highlights the user's intent on this Focus Area; the functions list what the user can do at a high level. Further design iterations will define these functions more comple.

Fig. 14.2 shows PowerPoint's slide editing screen. The primary purpose of this place is for creating and editing the content of slides. In the User Environment Design we represent places as *Focus Areas*, where the user focuses on doing a certain kind of activity. Every Focus Area has a *purpose*: a succinct statement of the primary intent the Focus Area supports. If you can't write a single sentence which describes the purpose of the Focus Area, it's likely that the product is poorly structured, either because there are so many different functions doing different things or because the place supports no coherent activity at all (Fig. 14.3).

This window provides functions which enable doing work in the place—to put shapes, text boxes, and other slide objects on the slide, color and rotate them, and manipulate them in other ways. Functions are made available through menus, toolbars, keyboard commands, and by direct manipulation. These are alternative interaction mechanisms for performing a function; some functions can be accessed all three ways (e.g., to save the presentation, choose "Save" under the "File" menu, click the disk icon on the toolbar, or, on Windows, press ctrl-s). Which mechanism the interaction designers will choose to implement for a function matters—a poor user interface or inconvenient access to function gets in the users' way—but it doesn't change the purpose of the place or the work done there. The interaction mechanisms and screen layout are as much a distraction to understanding product structure as rug color would be on a floor plan. So we list the functions in a Focus Area once, with no indication of how they are accessed. ("Save slide show").

> *The User Environment Design focuses design on coherent activities and the functions they need*

Some functions in a Focus Area are things the underlying system does on behalf of the user: "Show slide content." Some functions can be invoked by the user: "Edit slide content". And other functions are *links*, taking the user to another place in the product: "Bring up Slide Sorter."

Functions that lead to other places in the product change the view and the function available—once the user has switched to the slide sorter Focus Area, it is no longer possible to edit the content of slides. Instead, the slide sorter supports viewing a whole presentation in order, changing the order of slides, and controlling the transition from slide to slide. Since the work which can be done is different, the slide sorter supports a new activity in a new place, and we represent it with a new Focus Area. You'd expect to find these links between Focus Areas whenever the user might need to switch between the activities they support (Fig. 14.4).

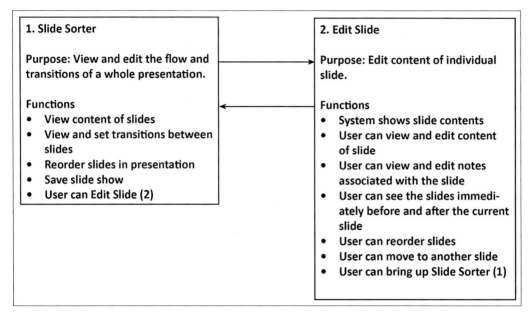

FIGURE 14.4   Links between Focus Areas. These Focus Areas support distinct but related activities. By this design, when the user is thinking about the overall flow of the presentation, she is not thinking about how to design an individual slide, so those areas can be separated. But when thinking about the slide content, she may well want to add to presenter notes, so those are naturally in the same Focus Area.

Back on the "Edit Slide" screenshot, note the list of slides in the pane on the left. This is a navigation tool, like the left navigation bars found on web pages. It's not a separate Focus Area—no independent work is done there. Instead it provides three functions: it shows where the current slide lies in the context of the slideshow, helping the user track continuity; it lets the user jump to another slide; and it lets the user do local reordering of slides via drag and drop right in that pane. But reordering slides is the primary purpose of the slide sorter Focus Area. Is this duplication of function wrong or confusing? Should there be only one place to reorder slides?

No. It's easy to start thinking logically about the design, and logic is never user centered. When a presenter is looking at a slide, it's natural to think how it flows with the slides before and after—how this piece of the presentation's story hangs together. So it's natural to rethink the ordering, and choose to rearrange slides just for this piece of the presentation. That's quite different from thinking about the overall presentation: the introduction, discussion, and wrap up. Users don't get confused when function is available in two places—they get annoyed when the function they want isn't available in the place they're in.

Navigation is not a place—no real work on the activity is done there

The presenter notes at the bottom of PowerPoint's screen are another interesting case in point. In early versions of PowerPoint, presenter notes were brought up in their own window—in a separate Focus Area. But it's common when preparing a presentation to add to the notes while editing a slide. Writing the slide content reminds the presenter of a point they want to make, so they add it to the notes. Or some content won't fit on the slide, so the presenter decides that they can just talk about that point—but they copy it to the notes so they don't forget. So there's a tight, organic interaction between slide and notes. Separating them into different Focus Areas made the work flow cumbersome. Over time, the PowerPoint team recognized the problem and merged the Focus Areas.

In PowerPoint, all the content is supplied by the user. Other products—a news site presenting stories, a shopping site presenting products, or a booking site presenting flight options—have content of their own which needs to be organized and presented. In such cases, the User Environment Design will list the content the Focus Area provides as well as the function to manipulate it.

The User Environment Design defines the function and content in the each place considering the platform

While designing Focus Areas, consider the platforms they need to support. Some will work reasonably well on any platform—they just need an appropriate user interface, which can be different on each platform. This function and content can be represented in one Focus Area with a note listing the platforms it needs to be delivered on (desktop, web, tablet, or something else). Other Focus Areas need to support users on the go, which means they must be optimized for partial attention and quick action, and functionality may be limited by screen size. These will form a mobile subsystem in the User Environment Design. Still, other Focus

Areas support heads-down, focused work and don't need to consider any mobile platform. The User Environment Design captures the whole ecosystem of support the team plans to deliver (Fig. 14.5).

Readers of the first edition of this book may notice that the formalism here is very much simplified. When the first edition came out, many formalisms were in common use and familiar to teams—RUP, object modeling, and Use Cases, to name a few. Those formalisms have

---

#. Focus Area

Collects functions and work objects into a coherent place in the system to support a particular type of work. Functions should be those necessary to do the work, not to manipulate the user interface.
*   Supports performing a coherent part of the work.
*   Named with a simple active phrase
*   Lists functions which are needed to do the work.
*   Lists content to be displayed directly in the Focus Area
*   Numbered for unambiguous references to the Focus Area. Numbers need not be sequential.

Purpose: Short description of what the Focus Area does in supporting the work.

Functions: Functions are described on the User Environment Design with a short phrase. They are written up online with a description of their behavior and justification.

*   Functions invoked by the user to do work generally start with "User can…"
*   Actions automatically undertaken by the system start with "System shows…" or "System does…"
*   Links which take the user to another Focus Area name that focus and its number ("Edit Slide (2)). Including links out to content or other applications.

Functions may be grouped under by Interaction Pattern section and component (see chapter 15) for clarity and for ease of reference when the same functions are available in multiple Focus Areas.

Avoid defining the same function twice. Name and define them in the first Focus Area that uses them and then reference the name in other Focus Areas.

Issues: Open design issues associated with this Focus Area ,user interface ideas, implementation concerns, and quality requirements

---

FIGURE 14.5 The parts of a Focus Area. The description of a Focus Area has structure so that the team can scan it easily. Initially, functions are just listed; when Interaction Patterns are defined in the next step, they are organized by sections of the Interaction Pattern.

largely fallen out of regular use and designers are much less familiar with the concept of formalisms in general. So we've simplified the presentation of the User Environment Design to be more direct and immediate.

BUILDING THE USER ENVIRONMENT DESIGN FROM STORYBOARDS

The User Environment Design is built directly from storyboards. Storyboards represent the team's plan for how people will perform their activities within the new product and ecosystem. But storyboards only consider one task at a time. Now we will review all the core tasks looking for what places, functions, content, and links they imply are needed. As we move from storyboard to storyboard, rolling in the implications of each, the team can start to see what core places are needed in the product. They may have an idea of the primary places needed, but this systematic way of pulling them out of storyboards ensures that the design provides all the functions and all the links needed to support the team's vision concepts.

Returning to our house analogy, imagine all the storyboards we might create for cooking: the quick microwaved hot dog, the Thanksgiving dinner, making kids lunches. A good place will support all these kinds of cooking, simple or complex, supporting each well. This is what a good kitchen is—everything you need to do the work of cooking from simple to complex is available conveniently, and nothing you don't need is there. We don't create a microwaving room and a separate fancy cooking room, any more than we create a refrigeration room and down the hall a food washing room. Instead, we bring all that is needed to do the work of cooking into one place. A storyboard presents the users' actions linearly but a good product will not be linear; your job is to find the implied places in the stories and assemble them and the function they need into a coherent structure. Then when you encounter the next cooking story, you first ask whether you can reuse a place you already have, maybe adding to or twisting it a bit to accommodate the new story. Need to support the microwaved hot dog in our fancy kitchen? Let's just add a microwave near the refrigerator.

Find the places in the product by walking the storyboards

Storyboards tell a single story of use: "I'm a user exploring a travel opportunity. How do I approach it? What do I do?" A scenario-based approach to design ensures the product hangs together for a single scenario of use, but it tends to hide the relationship to any other scenarios. In contrast, the User Environment Design supports structural thinking: "What's really going on in this place? Is it supporting a single, coherent activity? Does it provide everything the user needs to do that activity?" Storyboards alone can lead to a particular kind of tunnel vision—"The user is doing online purchasing? Where's the function for filtering products by price?" "Oh—our storyboard wasn't concerned with price, so we didn't think of that function." "But this is a shopping place—of course it has to have that function." Thinking about the place as a coherent whole identifies additional needs. But be careful of overcomplicating a design by brainstorming into the Focus Area. Add new function if the Focus Area makes no sense without it; otherwise, identify new storyboards and sketch out the new function in the context of the user and your data.

Don't overcomplicate the product by brainstorming function into the places identified

With storyboards and the User Environment Design working together, each focused on supporting one kind of thinking well, the conversations can be separated for the team, making them clearer and easier to have and making it easier for the team to really focus on each.

To build the User Environment Design, review the storyboards one at time, asking what place is needed to support this step of the story and what function and content is needed in that place. Storyboards implicitly define requirements for the User Environment Design; pull these implications out by walking through it cell by cell. Each cell may suggest a new Focus Area, function, content, or link in the emerging User Environment Design. The pictorial nature of storyboards help you recall the context and design implications of each cell far better than a written scenario or description. As you walk each cell, ask whether the user is in a new Focus Area, or whether you can reuse one already in the User Environment Design. Same for functions and links—has the storyboard added a new function or reused an existing function? If you are extending an existing product, start with a high-level reverse User Environment Design of the product and roll your new function into that to keep the product

The first storyboard cell defines a widget to appear in standard browser windows so the user can capture travel ideas. The user doesn't need to look at it, but the cell implies an Idea Collector Focus Area. Here is an example where the product has to interact with the ecosystem to deliver its value. So the Focus Area is the browser window—the team envisions using an extension to add function.

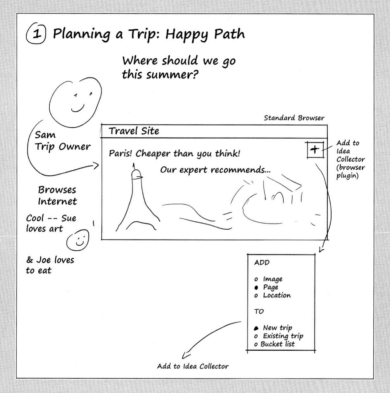

1. **Browser Window**

   Purpose: Capture interesting travel information during normal browsing.

   Function:
   • User can save a page to their Idea Collector without interrupting their browsing.

2. **Idea Collector**

   Purpose: Collect trip ideas into one place for later consideration.

   Function:
   • User can save a webpage to their Idea Collector.

Now the storyboard has the user go to the Idea Collector. This cell starts to flesh out what's there—ideas captured by the user and more generated by the product. Any thinking about product behavior (the suggestion engine) is captured with its related function.

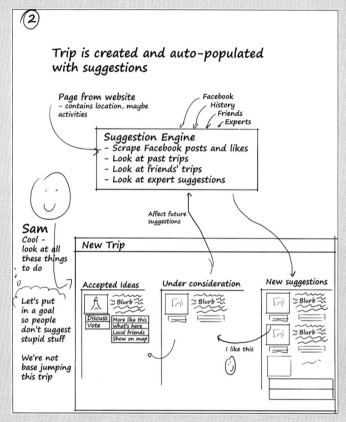

2. Idea Collector

Purpose: Collect trip ideas for later perusal and elaboration.

Function:
- User can save a webpage to his or her Idea Collector.
- System shows trip ideas (including weblinks) captured by user
- System shows related trip ideas suggested by product.
- Ideas are generated by scraping Facebook pages of the user and friends, looking at past trips, using experts' suggestions, and looking at attractions in the neighborhood of places the user found.

Now the storyboard envisions communication with others. This cell adds a way to invite participants in the Idea Collector Focus Area. The team may put in a user interface note to consider using an opening, a pane where the user can type names and choose people in place— no need for a separate window just because it is shown that way in the storyboard.

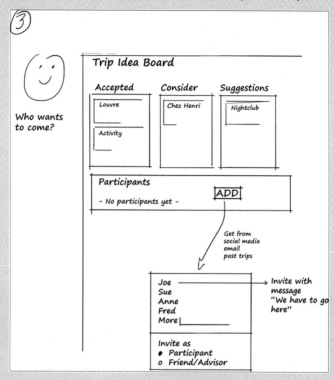

2. **Idea Collector**

- User can save a webpage to his or her Idea Collector.
- System shows trip ideas (including web links) captured by user
- System shows related trip ideas suggested by product.
- System shows participants who can see and contribute to this trip
- User can add people to the list of participants
- User can name a person to invite
- User can add a message for the invitee
- System alerts invitee on the user's invitation

Once again, the product has to reach out beyond its own borders and interact with the larger ecosystem. Here the storyboard specifies that we send an alert to another person. That creates a new Focus Area on the user's cell phone for receiving an alert. Note that we haven't made any decisions yet how that alert might happen—our own app on the cell phone, text message, Facebook message or post, or plain old email. Those decisions happen later.

The storyboard cell also introduces a new Focus Area, the Invitation. This is similar to the Idea Collector in showing basic information about the trip and some suggestions. But the purpose is very different and the context of use is different—the invitee needs to evaluate the trip and decide whether they will participate. So it's been kept as a separate place.

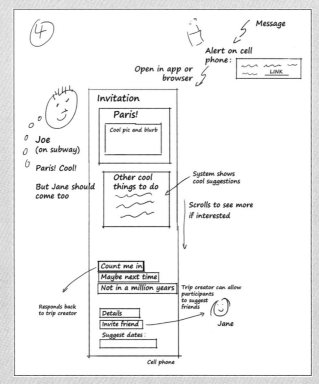

3. **New Travel Event Alert**

   Purpose: Inform people of updates in their travel community

   Function:
   - System alerts the user when new travel events happen:
   - They are invited to join a trip
   - (There will be more)

   Notes:
   - Supports any platform—phone, tablet, full computer—and uses the native alert mechanism. ➪

4. **Invitation**

Purpose: Extend an invitation to join a trip with enough attractive detail to encourage joining.
Function:
- Show inviter's message
- Show primary location and goal
- Show top-level suggestions for other things to do
- Show proposed dates for the trip
- User can accept
- User can reject this invitation
- User can reject this invitation and any similar trips
- User can suggest dates for the trip
- User can suggest friends to join the trip

coherent. Discuss these implications and revise or extend the User Environment Design to capture your decisions.

Here's how the process works in practice. Note that for brevity when we show the functions added to a Focus Area, we are just showing the additions—all prior function and purpose statements are still there.

This is the way building the User Environment Design proceeds. Each storyboard is woven into the evolving User Environment Design one cell at a time. Since the storyboards were designed individually, they may envision similar or overlapping places in the product. As the team walks through the storyboard, they determine whether a cell is envisioning a new place or can reuse an existing place, extending it as necessary. The process is exactly the same when weaving in the next storyboard—some places will already exist as Focus Areas in the product, whereas others will be newly defined. The User Environment Design will evolve to support them all. In the process, it is also likely to become overly complex—so see the section on the User Environment Design Walk-through coming up. Resist defining the user interface until you see what is needed in each place in the product.

You may build the first User Environment Design with a dedicated small team to roll in each storyboard and keep the User Environment Design reasonably coherent as they go. Most often though,

Use a small colocated team to produce the first cut of the User Environment Design

to involve the whole team and to move quickly, multiple sub-teams roll function and content definitions into a single paper User

This storyboard cell returns to the trip owner responding to the suggestion of a new participant. The main Focus Area supporting this cell is still the Idea Collector, but the cell suggests new function—the team has thought through the dates a little more, and the user can accept the new participant. System behavior is captured with the description of the function.

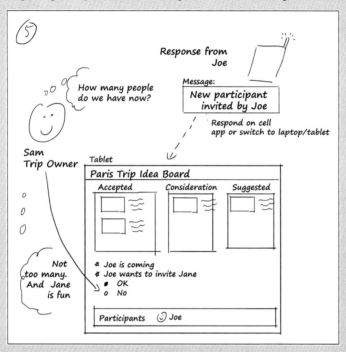

2. **Idea Collector**
   - User can save a webpage to their Idea Collector
   - System shows trip ideas (including web links) captured by user
   - System shows related trip ideas suggested by product
   - System shows participants who can see and contribute to this trip
   - User can add people to the list of participants
   - User can name a person to invite
   - User can add a message for the invitee
   - System alerts invitee on the user's invitation
   - System shows date of proposed trip, if any
   - User can mark a suggested activity as included in trip
   - User can accept a proposed invitee. System sends the invite only when accepted.

Environment Design in parallel.[2] In either case we recommend that you assign a small team to own it and be primarily responsible for its coherence. Good owners might be a designer and user researcher, or a user experience designer and a product manager. This team will oversee the structure of the product as new storyboards are rolled in. They will own the documentation and final design.

THE USER INTERFACE AND PRODUCT STRUCTURE

The User Environment Design, particularly when it is first being formed, is not influenced by any particular user interface plan or architecture. Too much focus on user interface detail at this point will get in the way of ensuring an overall good user experience. The drawings in the storyboard cells give designers a way to think in the concrete language most natural to them (user interface sketches), while still staying out of low-level user interface details as long as possible. Building a User Environment Design asks them to extract the implications from those drawings and represent them abstractly, as functions and content in places. The more the team goes back and forth between User Environment Design and storyboards, the more they start to consider the type of user interface that makes sense for presenting each Focus Area. Holding off on committing to a particular user interface structure and low-level user interface design will make for the best product design—and overall user experience.

Resist defining the user interface until you see what is needed in each place in the product

Thinking in terms of Focus Areas and links tends to keep the basic work of the Focus Area *in* the Focus Area, rather than spreading it over several places. A good Focus Area is like a well-supplied kitchen—all the tools you need are ready to hand, organized for easy access. Design focused on the user interface encourages the designer to worry about constraints of screen real estate, interactivity, and the detailed behavior of every function; it's easy to punt and decide to

---

[2] We recommend that the first User Environment Design be completed in a few days by a core team in a face-to-face meeting to ensure overall coherence. Later for reviews and changes, some members may be remote. Building a User Environment Design from storyboards with a completely remote team is challenging.

put the function on a separate screen. Design thinking with the User Environment Design takes away that excuse—if a function is part of the activities to be done in a Focus Area, it goes into the Focus Area.

Once the team has got a basic User Environment Design structure—and this will take only 2 or 3 days—they can step back and define an overall user interface approach considering the total needs of the system and the types of platforms to be supported. Then the team will define Interaction Patterns for each Focus Area considering the overall architecture. They can do this because the User Environment Design helps the team see the full structure they must design for. We discuss this in Chapter 15.

The User Environment Design promotes supporting a coherent intent in one place

Keep the user interface sketches from the different storyboard cells that contributed to a Focus Area to give user interface designers context—they show what the team was thinking about when they developed the place. Don't take the storyboard apart; take a picture of the relevant cell and save it in the User Environment Design with the Focus Area. These sketches are a starting point for designing the presentation of the Focus Area and may be testing out initial Interaction Patterns in the context of the story.

Then once the Interaction Patterns are created, you can document the User Environment Design, collecting together the sections that go together relative to the emerging user interface.

SEEING PRODUCT STRUCTURE

The challenge of building the product structure is one of continuously moving, between scenario and structural thinking. When rolling in the storyboards you are identifying functions and placing them in an emerging product structure. But even the most careful team will necessarily find that putting more function into the Focus Areas will cause it to get messy; the structure will simply not be clean enough for a good product. So the team must step back after rolling in the core storyboards and walk through the User Environment Design to improve its structure. Then they may roll in a few more storyboards and check structure again. Or better, they might go out and validate the product concept with paper prototypes (Chapter 17) and add more storyboards in the next round, while also redesigning the User Environment Design based on user feedback.

So seeing product structure is an important skill, supported by having an external representation. It's too hard to look across a whole product and decide if the parts of it are coherent if you have no physical representation. But when the product is concrete in a diagram, it's not hard to scan the purpose and existing function to find the right place for a new extension—or to decide that a new Focus Area is needed. Laying out the Focus Areas on half-sheets of paper, as in Fig. 14.6, helps you see the structure of the product.

A physical representation of the User Environment Design is easy to scan to update and review

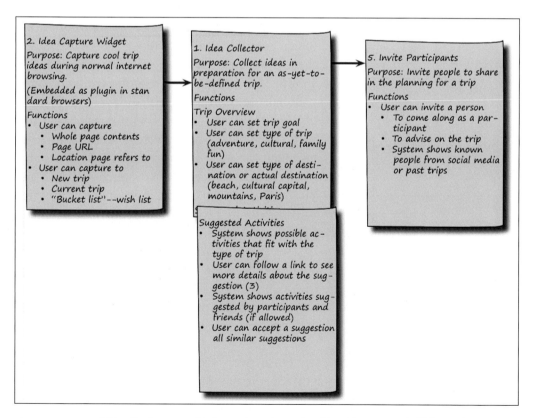

FIGURE 14.6 A User Environment Design under construction. Focus Areas are on half-sheets of paper; function is listed as it is discovered while creating the first User Environment Design. Eventually the team will capture it in a document, at which point printed sheets may be used when rolling in more storyboards. While you are rolling in, it's too hard to organize the list of functions much; do that when you enter it online.

Within each Focus Area, the list of functions, content, links, and constraints summarizes what can happen in that place. As a list, it supports checking the completeness and coherence of the Focus Area—it's easy to scan and check against the issues raised by the user data and the storyboards. When a Focus Area gets too complex, it's straightforward to review it and related Focus Areas. What types of people does the Focus Area support? What intents? For each Persona or identity element, is the Focus Area reasonable and relevant? You may have Focus Areas that support two disconnected intents—so you'll split it into two. Multiple Focus Areas may overlap in function and purpose—so you'll merge them. Through this process of examination, designers can rebalance the Focus Areas and clean up the design.

To help you see structure, be mindful of the layout of your User Environment Design (Fig. 14.7). The User Environment Design, when put online, will be a graphical model so communication design matters; the grouping of Focus Areas and their layout help the team see what the product is about. After rolling in core storyboards, organize your half-sheets of paper so you can see the sections of the product. Group Focus Areas associated with the each product concept you identified in visioning. Use the links to find Focus Areas that work together to achieve an overarching intent and put them near each other. Larger applications often have a set of Focus Areas devoted to supporting a particular intent; mobile apps tend to be more targeted to a single intent but have a larger ecosystem of apps that they are a part of.

A User Environment Design is also a model—make sure it has good communication design

Here is one way to approach the layout; start by laying the sheets on a large conference table or a wall. You will reveal the layers of the product, with entry areas at the top, shared utilities at the bottom, and groups of Focus Areas used for key tasks in the middle:

- Put any entry Focus Areas—starting points for particular intents—at the top; these are often overviews, provide quick information, or other places offering decision-making support.

- Place Focus Areas supporting the core practice below these entry Focus Areas if they don't themselves belong at the top level.

- Look for utilities—Focus Areas providing services to a group of Focus Areas. In our travel example, the "Activity Explorer" is useful whether you're first thinking about the trip, doing the logistics, or in the middle of the trip, so it is one of these. Put these beneath the Focus Areas they are supporting, creating a lower layer of supporting Focus Areas.

- If Focus Areas supporting different devices are significantly different, represent them as separate Focus Areas in their own mobile User Environment Design, particularly when they involve multiple Focus Areas to achieve the activity. Then the mobile team can see what they are building. Place this smaller User Environment Design to the side of the one for the main product. But be sure to check that common function is represented the same way and that you note how data is passed between the products. Smaller differences between platforms, often between a Web product and a tablet interface, can be captured by annotating a Focus Area with any differences in the tablet.

CREATING FOCUS AREAS

Structure into sections and components from the Interaction Pattern (once it's done)
- Sections and components can have purposes if that helps communicate.
- Functions are a simple bullet list. No special markers.

Write each function only once:
- Don't write one function to describe how something appears and another to describe how it behaves
- Don't describe what the system shows if the function implies it. (e.g., "User may choose import option from the list provided" is sufficient)

Don't create Focus Areas for small dialogues:
- Real work has to happen in the place for it to merit a Focus Area

Don't design for edge conditions:
- Write for main work practice situations and cases that came up in the user data
- Hypothesized cases can be captured as issues

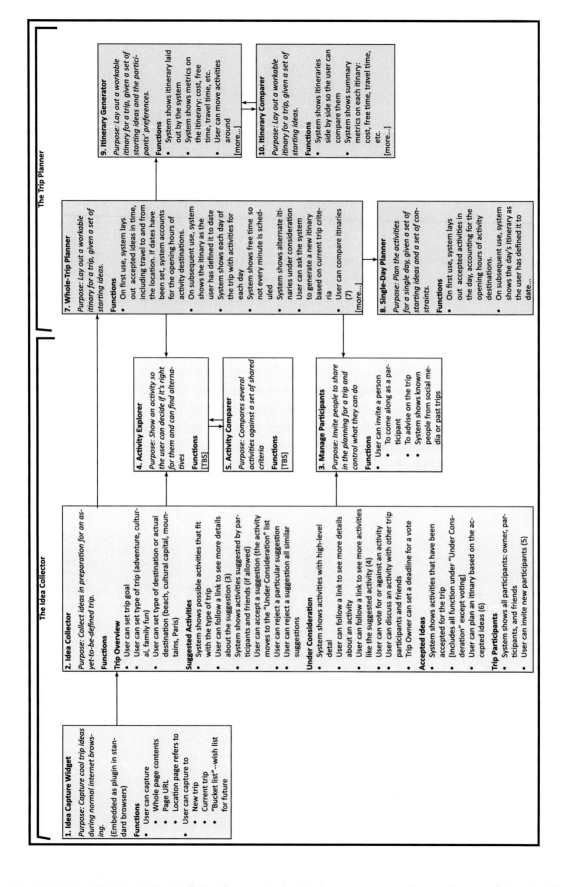

The Idea Collector

The Trip Planner

---

1. Idea Capture Widget

Purpose: Capture cool trip ideas during normal internet browsing.

(Embedded as plugin in standard internet browsers)

Functions
- User can capture
  - Whole page contents
  - Page URL
  - Location page refers to
- User can capture to
  - New trip
  - Current trip
  - "Bucket list"—wish list for future

---

2. Idea Collector

Purpose: Collect ideas in preparation for an as-yet-to-be-defined trip.

Functions

Trip Overview
- User can set trip goal
- User can set type of trip (adventure, cultural, family fun)
- User can set type of destination or actual destination (beach, cultural capital, mountains, Paris)

Suggested Activities
- System shows possible activities that fit with the type of trip
- User can follow a link to see more details about the suggestion (3)
- System shows activities suggested by participants and friends (if allowed)
- User can accept a suggestion (the activity moves to the "Under Consideration" list
- User can reject a particular suggestion
- User can reject a suggestion all similar suggestions

Under Consideration
- System shows activities with high-level detail
- User can follow a link to see more details about an activity
- User can follow a link to see more activities like the suggested activity (4)
- User can vote for or against an activity
- User can discuss an activity with other trip participants and friends
- Trip Owner can set a deadline for a vote

Accepted Ideas
- System shows activities that have been accepted for the trip
- [Includes all function under "Under Consideration" except voting]
- User can plan an itinerary based on the accepted ideas (6)

Trip Participants
- System shows all participants: owner, participants, and friends
- User can invite new participants (5)

---

4. Activity Explorer

Purpose: Show an activity so the user can decide if it's right for them and can find alternatives

Functions
[TBS]

---

5. Activity Comparer

Purpose: Compares several activities against a set of shared criteria

Functions
[TBS]

---

3. Manage Participants

Purpose: Invite people to share in the planning for a trip and control what they can do

Functions
- User can invite a person
  - To come along as a participant
  - To advise on the trip
- System shows known people from social media or past trips

---

7. Whole-Trip Planner

Purpose: Lay out a workable itinerary for a trip, given a set of starting ideas.

Functions
- On first use, system lays out accepted ideas in time, including travel to and from the location. If dates have been set, system accounts for the opening hours of activity destinations.
- On subsequent use, system shows the itinerary as the user has defined it to date
- System shows each day of the trip with activities for each day
- System shows free time so not every minute is scheduled
- System shows alternate itineraries under consideration
- User can ask the system to generate a new itinerary based on current trip criteria
- User can compare itineraries (7)

[more...]

---

8. Single-Day Planner

Purpose: Plan the activities for a single day, given a set of starting ideas and a set of constraints.

Functions
- On first use, system lays out accepted activities in the day, accounting for the opening hours of activity destinations.
- On subsequent use, system shows the day's itinerary as the user has defined it to date...

---

9. Itinerary Generator

Purpose: Lay out a workable itinerary for a trip, given a set of starting ideas and the participants' preferences.

Functions
- System shows itinerary laid out by the system
- System shows metrics on the itinerary: cost, free time, travel time, etc.
- User can move activities around

[more...]

---

10. Itinerary Comparer

Purpose: Lay out a workable itinerary for a trip, given a set of starting ideas.

Functions
- System shows itineraries side by side so the user can compare them
- System shows summary metrics on each itinerary: cost, free time, travel time, etc.

[more...]

FIGURE 14.7 Part of a full User Environment Design after the first set of storyboards have been rolled in and it's been put online. The layout and color show the different product concepts. The function has been organized by Interaction Pattern section as described in the next chapter.

The resulting User Environment Design diagram reveals the structure of the practice you will deliver across all the devices you are planning to support. This layout will let you check your links to ensure easy access between the Focus Areas that are used together. It will reveal whether you have committed any of the classic product design errors. Remember every Focus Area should fulfill a real intent, should forward the user's activities by providing content, decision support, quick updates, or something that makes spending time there worthwhile—you don't want any Focus Areas that deliver nothing except access to another Focus Area! We call that a hallway in your product. Laying out the Focus Areas in a sensible way will help you examine and normalize your product structure and sets you up for the User Environment Design Walk-through.

The User Environment Design, as the floor plan of your product, lets you see the big picture of what you are building. It shows you the places where the user will focus to achieve an intent—and

The User Environment Design lets you see the big picture of what you are building

because each place has a purpose, it encourages the team to bring together all the function and content needed for that intent. This implicitly builds in good principles of user experience design. The links make sure that a flow of action is supported by the right connections between places. Then laying out the places into coherent subsystems, each focused on supporting a coherent activity, lets the team see exactly what they are building. Taken together, the User Environment Design is the best way we have found to help teams thinks structurally about the product as a whole. So after rolling in the storyboards, the next step is doing the User Environment Design Walk-through to keep this structure coherent.

USER ENVIRONMENT DESIGN WALK-THROUGHS

You've rolled a set of storyboards into the beginnings of a User Environment Design. But as we said after four to six storyboards, your User Environment Design starts to get unwieldy. Too many individual decisions have been made without an eye to the overall coherence of the product. Perhaps any individual function in a Focus Area could be justified, but taken together they suggest a different user focus that should be separated out. Two Focus Areas that started clearly distinct will, as function is added to each, start to overlap to the point that the distinction is no longer clear. Before continuing, you must ensure that you have a good backbone product structure on which to build. So now step back to do a *User Environment Design Walk-through* to ensure coherence and consistency of the product. Never go straight from your first User Environment Design to a user interface of the product; your first cut will be both messy and incomplete, even for an initial paper prototype made only to test the concept. Doing a walk-through is part of your ongoing design process. Clean up with a walk-through after your core storyboards are rolled in, then go out and test; come back and fix the structure, perhaps roll in more storyboards, and do another walk-through; then build a new prototype and test again. Continue this cycle until you have validated and extended the product as desired.

Always walk through a User Environment Design before making any UI

You'll see additional design possibilities when you walk through your design. The design itself suggests new possibilities when you pause to inquire into it. A set of Focus Areas taken together may imply support for a whole task or additional job type like manager versus worker; three Focus Areas might be consolidated into one, addressing the fundamental intent more directly; or functions in several Focus Areas suggest an activity which could be supported directly in its own Focus Area. It's this step of rationalizing the design against the user practice that will lead to a solid, flexible base structure that supports many different uses.

Walking the User Environment Design also gets the team into position for the next phase of design. It ensures the whole team is clear on what they have chosen to put in the product and how they think it will work to support the user. It identifies *test cases*—conditions or design elements which become a focus to test with users in prototypes. In this way it becomes the preparation step necessary before iterating the design with users.

The walk-through is like the groundskeeper redesigning the quad

To run a User Environment Design Walk-through, start by laying your Focus Areas out on a wall or table as described above, so that you can see the structure explicitly. We recommend doing the first walk-through in a one or two day face-to-face meeting. Subsequent walk-throughs after the basic structure is settled may be able to be handled remotely, with good meeting tools. Or allow the User Environment Design owners to do the walk-through and fix the structure before the next mock-up testing round.

With the User Environment Design laid out, have each member of the team walk the Focus Areas and overall structure looking for issues. Here are a set of questions to ask when checking a User Environment Design—and it's no accident that they are similar to those which drove building it:

Are Focus Areas coherent? Does each Focus Area support one activity within the overall task? Is that represented by the title and purpose statement? Be suspicious of any Focus Area that has no written purpose. It's often because the team isn't clear on what the purpose is, or there are multiple activities mixed in the Focus Area. If you decide a Focus Area is too complex, split it apart to support multiple intents that may have been collected there.

Use these design principles to review the User Environment Design structure

Are Focus Areas distinct? Collect the Focus Areas which support the same part of the practice—the same activity, task, or job type—and compare them. Are they clearly distinct? Do they, taken together, provide coherent support for this part of the practice? Can they be recombined to improve the practice? Do you have Focus Areas that overlap in purpose—for example, multiple search boxes. Can merge them?

Do Focus Areas support real work? Is the Focus Area only a hallway, leading somewhere else with no real function of its own? All Focus Areas must deliver value in themselves. Look for Focus Areas which are really glorified selection boxes—the user is just making a selection, not doing any real work. Look for Focus Areas which group related function, or reveal data from the system, but which don't support a coherent activity.

Are functions and content correct? Are functions in direct support of the Focus Area's purpose? Given the practice supported in this Focus Area, are there missing functions? Is there extraneous or missing content? Is everything needed to support the intent brought into this place coherently?

Do links make sense? Do they help the user move smoothly to the next necessary action or information to support their intent? Are they missing completely, so that there is no way to get from one place to another? Do they support the activity as you designed it with storyboards?

Is your overall structure optimal? Certain patterns of links and Focus Areas always indicate trouble (see the "Classic Errors" above). Do any of these patterns appear, and do they indicate problems in the design? If you have a hard time seeing it, make a little Post-it User Environment Design with just titles, purposes, and links and look for patterns.

Is the practice supported? Finally, use the consolidated models to refresh your memory and look at the User Environment Design from the point of view of the different job types, activities, collaborations, and identity elements being supported. Does the design enhance life and work? Does the design work for each different kind of user? Does it account for the issues they care about? Run actual sequences or walk the Day-in-the-Life or Collaboration Model through the User Environment Design, asking how this user would get that real life done given the new product. See if you can make it break down.

Does the design support the Cool Concepts? Does it let the user move through their unstoppable flow of life? Will the design support accomplishing goals in small moments of time, across different devices? Which Focus Areas need to run on multiple platforms? Will they work well no matter the platform? Look back at the principles from the Cool Concepts to be sure you are supporting these core motives.

Don't get so lost in supporting a task that you forget about the Cool Concepts

After the team members identify issues individually, the User Environment Design owner or a facilitator walks the team through resolving them in a discussion with the team. Start with the high-level box structure: where might Focus Areas be combined or split up; where is the structure hierarchical, leggy, containing hallways, or otherwise bad; where are there Focus Areas without a single, clear purpose. Resolve these issues, starting with the most important and central Focus Areas and working out.

Then look at the function, links, and content of each Focus Area. Make sure everything in a Focus Area supports its overall purpose. You may choose to split out a closely related group of function at this point, or create links you didn't identify before. When you're done, the User Environment Design owners clean up and document the new structure in an editor.

Resolve the issues, redesign the User Environment Design, and get ready to test

There will be situations where the right fix to a potential problem is a judgment call. A certain design is attractive, but will it work for the users? You've split a Focus Area because you believe this part of the activity is its own concern and should be supported separately. Are you right? When you have specific questions and no data to answer them, capture a *test case*. Write it on a list and save the list for the prototype interviews. You'll look for opportunities to test these decisions directly when you're validating the design with users.

Using a walk-through this way pulls the User Environment Design back together into a structure which makes the users' practice coherent. Like a groundskeeper rethinking path layouts, the walk-through gives you a chance to step back from your design. Now you can either test it with users or extend it with more storyboards. Or, better yet, do both in parallel—the sooner you get feedback from real users on their design, the better off you are.

SEEING STRUCTURE: CLASSIC ERRORS

Exposing the database is still a problem in too many products. (In fact, frameworks such as Ruby on Rails[3] positively *encourage* putting the database in the user interface.) Instead of understanding the practice and creating a product structure to support it, product designers simply put the data tables and relationships on the screen, one table per Focus Area, requiring the user to learn and traverse the database schema. Users don't want to understand your database—they want to focus on their activities. And a hierarchical structure is prone to becoming hallways—a series of Focus Areas, each of which fulfills no real intent except to get to the next place.

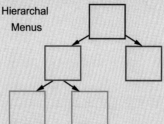

Hierarchal
Menus

One Central Place forces the user back and forth to a central place before going on to the next intent. One Focus Area becomes the central hub, whether or not it supports any real intent or needs to be in the center of the activity. What is the next likely thing a user wants to do after completing a step? Your user data will tell you. Provide function that lets the user get there without interrupting their flow of thought.

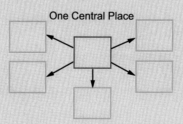

One Central Place

Legginess forces the user to traverse many places to get to the Focus Area they need. Shopping sites that move from category to category are often too leggy. Wizards can lock the user into too many steps—and are often unnecessary with proper design. Or designers, with the best of intentions, use scenario-based design and gave each task step its own Focus Area. Hierarchies can become a set of leggy hallways. Bring what the user needs into the place—don't drive them through a set of links.

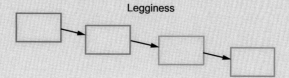

Legginess

[3] http://rubyonrails.org/.

Interaction Patterns 15

It is not our intention to describe principles and techniques of good interaction and visual design in this book. Design is now a professional activity complete with its own professional degrees and skills. Any company that wants to deliver design excellence knows it must hire trained interaction and visual designers—which is not the same as front-end design coders. To be successful with Contextual Design, you need the right skills on the team, and at this point in the process skill with user interface design is critical. But given that you have these skills available, it's helpful to have a way to go from the conceptual structure of a User Environment Design to a concrete user interface. In this chapter we describe Interaction[1] Patterns, which provide a structure for the user interface. The final step is validating and extending the design through iteration with users, which we take up in Chapter 16.

THE RIGHT TEAM

A cross-functional team is best for creating your product using contextual techniques, and this team must include skilled interaction designers. We're emphasizing the role of interaction designers because too often they are considered the last step in the process—given a list of functions and told to do a layout. But in our experience, teams without good, trained

> *Include interaction designers from the beginning of the process*

---

[1] The concepts and approach to the use of Interaction Patterns within Contextual Design emerged from our collaboration with David Rondeau, Design Director at InContext for many years. We extend special thanks for his contributions to this chapter.

Contextual Design. http://dx.doi.org/10.1016/B978-0-12-800894-2.00015-6

interaction designers always flounder. And training does matter—
that's where people learn the materials of design.

At their best, interaction designers understand how to see the
overall product structurally and how to organize function and
content coherently in any interface—whether that be a webpage,
desktop or mobile application, watch, fitness device, or any other
platform. Ideally, they will be involved throughout the process. They
should be exploring potential Interaction Patterns and approaches in
parallel—a kind of exploratory sketching and investigation of new
approaches appropriate to the team's design ideas as they come up.

Skilled interaction designers know the materials of modern design on every platform

The focus of an interaction designer is not the
visual design or what the interface looks like, it's how
the interface works. Information architects, user
researchers, visual designers, and other job types may
share this skill, but it is the explicit job of an interaction designer to know the modern tools, techniques,
and current approaches of their field—their materials of design. Only with this knowledge can they
redesign by recombining, adapting, and twisting those materials to
create a truly innovative and effective approach for the product they
are working on. And really good interaction designers know that they
must also develop a design consistent enough with the standards of
the platform so that there's nearly no Learning Delta—so people can
use the product instantly. If you do not have this skill on your team,
bring it in by the time you are ready to vision.[2]

Whatever the methodological approach, you need skilled interaction designers involved at all parts of the design process. It is best
for them to work in tight collaboration with user researchers and
product managers—this is the core of any team defining requirements and doing design. Then this core team should be closely linked
to engineers committed to a user-centered design approach. Best is
when engineers are part of the Contextual Design team as well. The
more you separate your designers from the product conceptualization

---

[2] Visual designers and to some extent Industrial designers have a focus on the aesthetics of the product. In our experience, some have an interest and affinity for all parts of Contextual Design but
others do not, preferring to sketch ideas after the basic product is conceived. The Sensation Board is
a great help to these designers.

and definition process, the less you'll be able to innovate the overall user experience. This goes for user researchers as well—their job does not stop with the research. They should be part of visioning, design, and ultimate product definition.

The importance of a truly diverse team in driving innovation cannot be too greatly emphasized. Diversity is twofold: first, getting the right skills on the team and second, making sure that the people on the team come from a mixture of gender and culture. All job types may have their particular skills and focus, but the best design comes from a tight, diverse, and collaborative cross-functional team. So get these people on your team from the beginning.

Tight cross-functional collaboration drives innovation

SEQUENTIAL VERSUS PARALLEL DESIGN PROCESS

The reality of books is that they are linear—we can only describe one Contextual Design technique at a time. This can lead to a perception that Contextual Design is a waterfall process—that each step must be done completely before starting the next, as if we gathered all user data, then organized it, then used it for ideation, and only then arrived at design. But this is not reality—data collection, design investigation, storyboarding, creating the product structure in the User Environment Design, sketching out possible Interaction Patterns, and iterative testing are expected to overlap. Initial research and visioning may be sequential but very quick, leading immediately to parallel rounds of user research, design, and development—which, in an Agile process, may overlap with development sprints. These quick iterative cycles depend on coordinated parallel activities between the cross-functional team members.

When the project is more strategic, a new market is being explored, the product is complex or brand new, or the old system is being fundamentally overhauled, a team may engage in a more lengthy and in-depth market study and planning phase. But in parallel, interaction designers—knowing the activity the product will support—can be investigating how competitive or similar products may approach design and leverage modern platforms. The team can collect data on competitors which will inform these early explorations. Then they may use all the data to generate a high-level, broad design of a suite of products which incorporates the interaction designers' early thoughts. During validation, the team tests the product concept, the user interface layout, and perhaps even mocked-up visual designs to assess branding reception. Following validation at a high level, this team may continue with a strategic user interface or they may to create a set of tactical releases—or they may do both in parallel.

Contextual Design provides a team with a set of key techniques. As long as the team is working in coordination from user data and validates with the user—either a parallel or a more sequential approach works.

Seeing interaction patterns

Once you have the right people on the team, developing Interaction Patterns aids the creation of a transformative intuitive user experience. The User Environment Design focuses the team on the overall structure of the product; it defines a set of Focus Areas and the function, content, and links within each place. It identifies utilities used across places and function available in more than one place. But it does not say how users interact with function and content, or what

the actual layout of the place might be on a screen. Interaction Patterns define the overall layout of a screen, where content and functions are accessed on the screen, how the flow of an activity traverses a screen, and navigation between screens (where a screen might be a webpage, a window, or a panel depending on the platform). Interaction Patterns

Interaction Patterns help the team think structurally about interface design

give the team a way to think structurally about the design they are creating without getting caught up in lower-level details and the graphical look.[3]

Returning to our house metaphor, once we know our house will have a kitchen we need to design the layout of that kitchen. The user experience of the kitchen depends on the location and placement of the counters, the shelving, the drawers, and everything else a kitchen should have. Kitchen layout at this level is still not equivalent to visual design. That would be low-level interior design: the paint, trim molding, or flooring materials. Instead, it blocks out the layout of the room as a whole for use, which drives and responds to the choice of furniture and fixtures. The kitchen layout helps determine where to place specific tools—the drawers, cabinets, pot rack, and so forth—as well as the larger appliances and work areas—refrigerator, sink, stove, and counters. So within a kitchen are larger structures which support the flow of work through the place and direct the location of the specific elements needed in the kitchen.

---

[3] Design patterns have been a popular concept in interface design since the profession discovered Christopher Alexander's book, *A Pattern Language*. Like others, we borrow the concept of a design pattern but our Interaction Patterns operate at a structural level. We aren't focused on solving specific interaction problems with particular widgets; we are looking at the overall structure of a screen to support the activity that takes place on that screen.

So too with a user interface. Any screen presented to the user has an Interaction Pattern placing the function and content on the screen in a way that, at best, gives the user a direct interaction experience. To reveal the idea of structure in the user interface, let's analyze Airbnb as it looks at the time of writing this book. How can we look at this webpage and reveal its structure?

We start by looking for and naming the *components* on the page. A component is a collection of content and controls that fulfills a coherent intent. Every page—any interface—is composed of a set of components which support the overarching purpose of the place. In User Environment Design terms, the purpose of this Focus Area is to help people find a place to stay. But to help people see and move through the function and content in the place, interaction designers must structure the place into a set of components. Taken together, these components define the Interaction Pattern of this place. We have overlaid some key components in Fig. 15.1.

Any product can be analyzed to find the Interaction Pattern set which structures the overall user interface—and so the user's experience. A well-designed set of Interaction Patterns helps the user get to the function and information they want directly, without hassle, and with little learning or confusion. So learning to design them and finding them when looking at your existing products, competitors, and products with reputations for good design is a skill your team should cultivate.

Let's identify the components on this Airbnb page. We'll start with the grouping of search filters at the top left of Fig. 15.1 for Dates, Room Type, and Price Range. These support the coherent intent of filtering the search results down to what is relevant for the user's situation (Fig. 15.2).

Should we include other functions in this component? We could include the Search Bar at the top of the screen, but that's really about searching to get a new pool of results, not about filtering that pool of results. What about the Filters and Sort Results buttons below? These are definitely about altering the pool of results, but a little more investigation reveals that they operate independently. On scrolling the left side of the screen, the other filters scroll out of view but these buttons are "sticky" and remain fixed at the top, just below the search bar.

Interaction Patterns define the components that deliver function and content

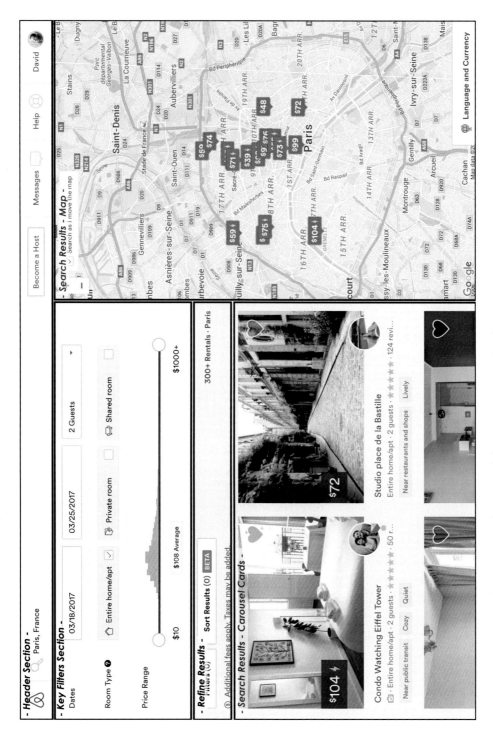

FIGURE 15.1 The Airbnb search results page with key components outlined.

FIGURE 15.2   The filter component of the Airbnb search results page—three filters working together to limit the results to the ones that are useful.

The designers seem to believe that Date, Room Type, and Price Range are the filters that are used the most often and that people don't usually change them after setting them. So it's not a problem if they scroll out of view when the user starts examining the search results. This helps us clarify the intent of the component we identified. It's not just search result filters, it's the filters most people will use first to refine their results. Clicking on the Filters button reveals a set of additional filters that slides down below Price Range. These are clearly secondary filters that people use less often than the others. They are not visible, but they are always a click away.

This helps us name the component with Dates, Room Type, and Price Range. Let's call it *Primary Filters*. When naming components, try to come up with something that describes the intent, but is generic enough that we could imagine using it in any product. Don't name it something literal, like Travel Filters because that obscures how this might be used in other domains. Don't name it something too ambiguous either, like Search Results Filter, because that hides the intent, which is what makes this component interesting. From the name and a short description of the intent it supports, you can easily imagine other search products where this type of a component might be useful—and they have nothing to do with travel.

Every component supports a coherent intent

FIGURE 15.3   A *Carousel Card* in the search results.

FIGURE 15.4   A *Carousel Card* that only appears on clicking a flag on the map.

Looking at the rest of the screen, there are obvious components, such as Search Results. But it's not a standard list of search results. The results are displayed as tiles or cards, each card with an image and some key information (Fig. 15.3). So we'll reflect that in our name: *Search Results—Carousel Cards*. We've added *Carousel* to the name because each image acts like a carousel. When you hover over the image, controls appear.

When analyzing components of a screen, don't worry about the amount of content or the number of controls. Some components may have only one control, whereas others have many. What matters is that it supports a coherent intent.

As you sketch out the components, you can draw components that are not immediately visible, such as the *Search Result–Carousel Card* that appears when you click a search result on the map (Fig. 15.4). Other hidden components may be too large to capture in the same sketch, such as the *Secondary Filter* that covers the left side of the screen when it appears (see Fig. 15.5). In this case, just sketch the pattern again showing the change of state.

Also notice the level of detail that matters when identifying structure at this level. When we identify the *Primary Filters component*, we don't have to indicate the exact filters used, the types of controls used, how those controls work, or even how many filters there are. That level of detail doesn't matter. What matters is that the intent of the component is clear and that all the elements in the component support that intent.

Some components may be hidden until the user interacts with the screen

Fig. 15.6 shows what Airbnb's Interaction Pattern looks like for this page after we sketch out and identify all the components.

But if we take only a component view, we miss the higher-level structure of the screen. Good designers don't just randomly place components on a screen; they are organized to enable use. The next step is to analyze how the components are organized into *sections*. A section is a collection of components that fulfills a coherent higher-level intent. Look across the screen and identify the components that are working together to accomplish a higher-level intent. Because

Components are collected into Sections that define the screen structure

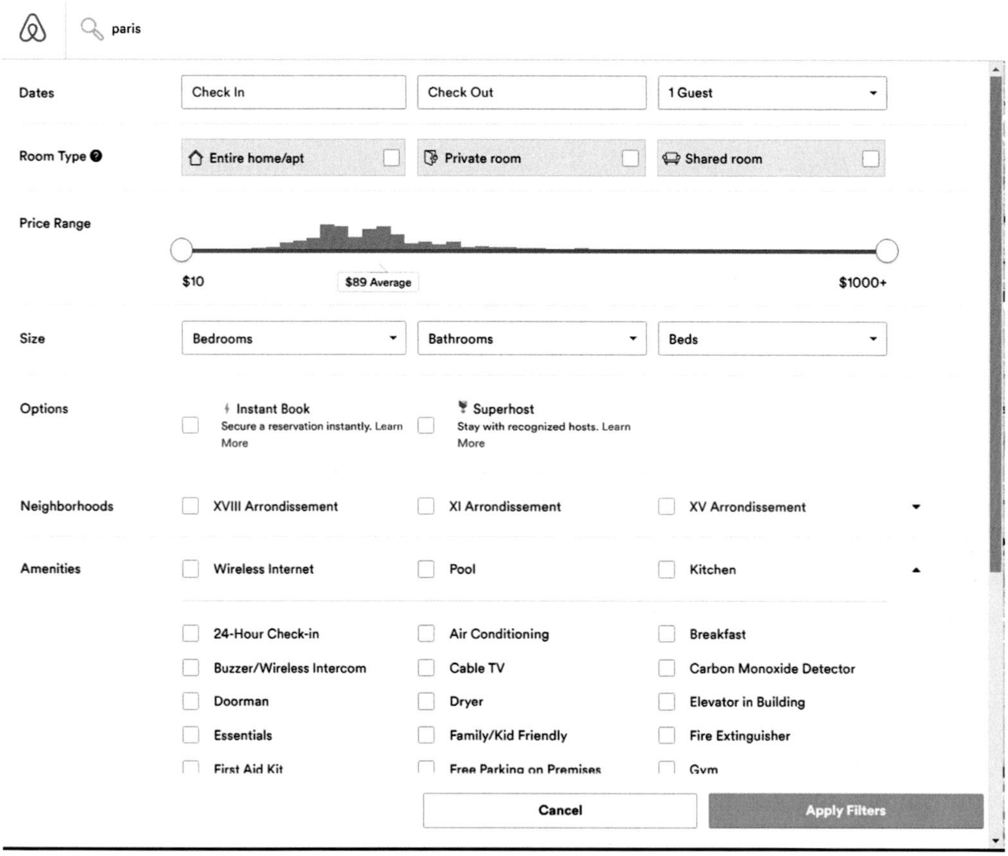

paris

| Dates | Check In | Check Out | 1 Guest ▾ |

Room Type ❷ ⌂ Entire home/apt ☐ 🗋 Private room ☐ 🛋 Shared room ☐

Price Range

$10 $89 Average $1000+

Size   Bedrooms ▾   Bathrooms ▾   Beds ▾

Options ☐ ⚡ Instant Book
Secure a reservation instantly. Learn More
☐ ♟ Superhost
Stay with recognized hosts. Learn More

Neighborhoods ☐ XVIII Arrondissement   ☐ XI Arrondissement   ☐ XV Arrondissement ▾

Amenities ☐ Wireless Internet   ☐ Pool   ☐ Kitchen ▲

☐ 24-Hour Check-in   ☐ Air Conditioning   ☐ Breakfast
☐ Buzzer/Wireless Intercom ☐ Cable TV   ☐ Carbon Monoxide Detector
☐ Doorman   ☐ Dryer   ☐ Elevator in Building
☐ Essentials   ☐ Family/Kid Friendly   ☐ Fire Extinguisher
☐ First Aid Kit   ☐ Free Parking on Premises ☐ Gym

Cancel   Apply Filters

FIGURE 15.5 The same screen as above with the secondary filters expanded, taking over the left side of the screen.

this is an analysis of the UI, the components have to be grouped together on the screen to be part of the same section. Using the same criteria that we used for naming components, name the sections you identify. As with naming components, try to pick something that communicates the higher-level intent without being too literal or too ambiguous.

From our analysis, we identify three sections: the *Header, Search Results–Scrolling* and *Search Results-Static*. We named the two search results area this way because they work together to create a more direct experience for the user. The section on the left scrolls, allowing

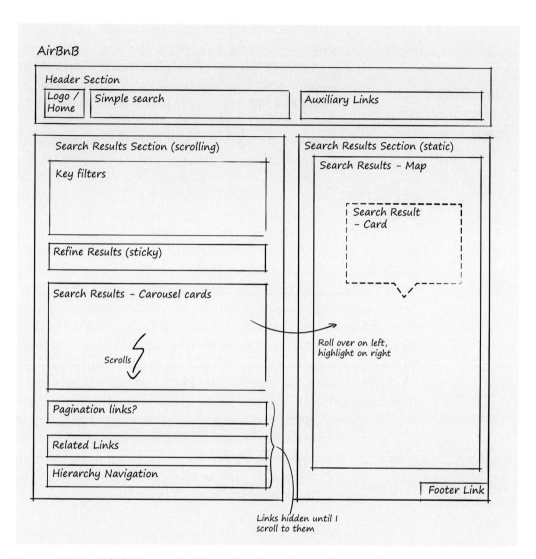

FIGURE 15.6 Airbnb's Interaction Pattern showing sections and components.

the user to view and browse lots of search results, while the section on the right remains static, not moving when the user scrolls. The left side contains more results, with more information, that must be scrolled through to see it all. As you roll over each result on the left, it's highlighted on the right side, showing its location—which is why that section is static and doesn't scroll.

You'll notice that the section names don't contain the words *card* or *map*. That's because the form the data takes within the section doesn't matter in this case. What's interesting is the way sections work together—scroll through items in one to see new information about each result in the other.

Name sections and components to reflect their intent

In most applications and certainly in most web pages, there are standard sections that appear frequently. They are sections that have become almost universal, such as a *Header* or a *Footer* section. In cases like this, it's fine to just give it the name that everyone recognizes. Trying to name it something else will only cause confusion.

You may have noticed that the screen itself is another level of the interaction pattern. A screen is a collection of sections (and components) that fulfills a coherent, even higher-level intent. We use the same naming rules as before. In this case, we've called this screen pattern *Dual-Context Search Results*. Different screen patterns can then be combined to create a subsystem that supports a coherent intent and subsystems can be combined to form large, complex systems. For the purposes of this book, we're going to focus on screen patterns, sections, and components.

Keep in mind that there is no right or wrong way to identify interaction patterns. There isn't one "right" name for that component or section and there isn't one "right" way to organize the content and function on your screen. Just focus on the distinctions that matter to your project. As long as you stay out of the weeds and think structurally, you'll be on the right track.

Analyzing products for their Interaction Patterns teaches structural design

Analyzing the structure of this interface reveals sections which in turn contain components—all laid out intentionally to encourage easy scanning and Direct-into-Action use. When you are designing the interface for your product, you need to define the Interaction Patterns which will work best given the purpose, function, and content of each place—and they need to be consistent with modern practices of the moment. Doing an analysis of well-designed products will help your team learn to think structurally, which makes them more likely to design a coherent system and user experience. Defining Interaction Patterns as the first step of UI design forces the team to think structurally and create a solid foundation for their designs. Specifying all the low-level details of the actual interface can be done later, or in parallel.

BENEFITS OF ANALYZING INTERACTION PATTERNS

- Great for encouraging interaction designers and the whole team to design structure before detail
- Helps people who are not interaction designers think beyond widgets and low-level controls
- Helps teams that are entrenched in their thinking to get "unstuck" and become more innovative
- Helps teams analyze new interaction paradigms or particularly well-designed interfaces to understand what to adapt for your project and why
- Help the team see problems in your existing product or your competitor's
- Gives the team a common language, improving the efficiency and quality of design discussions

Every Focus Area in the User Environment Design will be associated with a particular Interaction Pattern appropriate for it. Focus Areas that need to interact with the user in the same way should use the same Interaction Pattern. So if we decide to use the above Interaction Pattern for search, every place in the product which lists options for trip activities should use it. Similarly for other types of places—

Every Focus Area presenting content and function in a similar way should use the same Interaction Pattern type

if we create a trip dashboard, every dashboard should use the same Interaction Pattern. You can and should reuse Interaction Pattern at the section and component level as well. If we have voting, all the voting should use the same components. If a trip activity uses the above component, you had to better have a very good reason for using a different one elsewhere in the user interface.

Note that what matters in choosing your Interaction Pattern is the type of interaction that needs to be provided. The content does not matter. Airbnb is searching for accommodations, but it would be interesting to think about using the same interaction for other types of content—anything where it's useful to see the search results in a two-dimensional layout as well as in a list.

Only if the user intent or the interaction required of the user is entirely different, should you use a different Interaction Pattern— for example, the initial intent of the *Carousel Card* (which Airbnb addresses) is to decide whether this is the right accommodation for me. The component is intended to sell the accommodation. Later, once it's part of my itinerary, there's no need to sell it anymore—in

> *The set of Interaction Patterns you design for your product are your UI architecture*

fact, that would be annoying and distracting. So then you'd need a new component. Or if you're addressing a very different job type or person—maybe you're sending the trip information to a local friend so they'll know your schedule—you may need a different component or a whole different Interaction Pattern to address their different intent.

When you have defined Interaction Patterns for every Focus Area and ensured that any Focus Area with the same intent uses the same pattern, you will have defined your user interface architecture. This will guide your choices for any new Focus Area that might be added to the product—simply reuse the appropriate screen pattern, section, or components. Fig. 15.7 shows an example of a set of patterns working together for a whole product.

INNOVATION AND INTERACTION PATTERNS

The challenge for the team is to create the best interaction design they can for their users. But the right design is contextualized by the state of the technology, the current expectations of what constitutes good, modern design, the need for continuity within a platform, and the expectations that users have about how to interact with products. It also, of course, has to deliver the features and content as defined by the User Environment Design you created. So what does innovation look like in this context?

Not every kitchen looks the same, even though most kitchens have the same high-level requirements. Kitchen designs may vary the layout to deliver particular benefits or deliver a particular aesthetic. The large kitchen table was a standard in the 19th and early 20th centuries; in the 1950s it was considered old-fashioned and in the way; since the 1980s it has returned as the central island where you can cook or gather round for informal snacks. Similarly, the sections in an Interaction Pattern and components within those sections may be laid out differently, but any layout is constrained by all the expectations placed on the design.

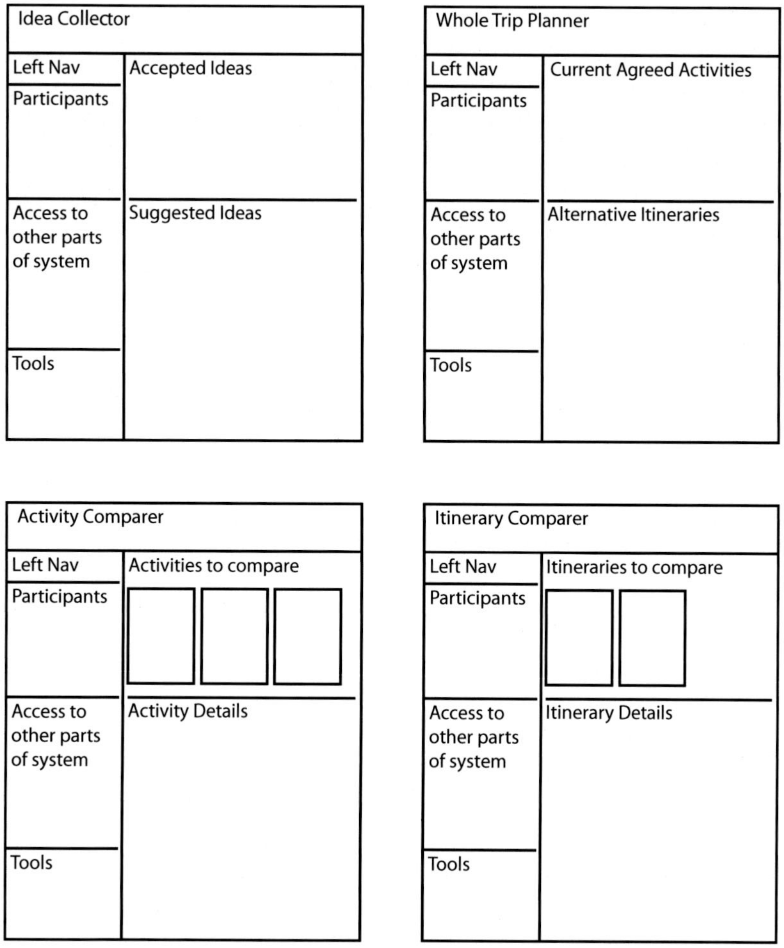

FIGURE 15.7 A set of Interaction Patterns that work together in a product to support a high-level user intent.

Designers can change their Interaction Patterns to increase the cool factors defined by the Triangle of Joy in Use: Direct-into-Action, the Hassle Factor, and the Learning Delta. (The cool factors of Accomplishment, Connection, and Identity should have already been dealt with during ideation and storyboarding. Sensation for most products is part of visual design.) With function and content defined, the interaction design focuses on the overall principles of good design, augmented by principles from

Build in delight—design for the Cool Concepts in the Triangle of Joy in Use

the Triangle of Joy in Use. But what does that mean? Innovation rarely starts from nothing; innovation is mostly the recombination of known parts, adapting them to deliver new, desirable experiences. This is the space where interaction design innovation lives.

So how does the team get started? Where do those "known parts" come from? As suggested above, the interaction designers on the team may investigate possible user interface approaches in parallel to the team's work. They may educate themselves on modern design principles and on what competitive products are doing. This can include as much of the whole team as you like and will inform the team's design work from visioning forward.

To encourage our teams to think widely we often start by investigating existing Interaction Patterns to familiarize the whole team with the materials of interaction design, to ensure everyone starts to think structurally, and to push them to begin the exploration of possible Interaction Patterns for the product. Start by looking at other products which are similar in task, intent, or purpose. Don't restrict yourself to your own domain. Looking in your own domain will show you what your competitors are doing and what your users may expect, but if that's all you do, you'll just be playing catch-up. You won't see new possibilities that way. Look also at similar activity structure outside your own domain and see what you can adapt.

Find possible Interaction Patterns to use and reinvent

For example, part of trip planning is to sell activities—to make immediately clear why they might be fun or desirable. In what other domains does content have to sell itself quickly? This is very like a shopping problem, only the user is shopping for trip activities. So what do good shopping sites provide as fodder to the travel designers? They let you compare products side-by-side, filter by price, and other characteristics (some of which *will* be unique to the domain), save good possibilities for later, and so on. Draw high-level Interaction Patterns of a few good sites to see their structure and what function they offer. This begins your collection of materials to use in your own design.

Look at consumer products that are popular and cool, even when they are quite different in domain. They may suggest ways of interacting in the product that can be adapted to your purpose. Today, consumer products are setting the standard for delivering the cool user experience, so business products will want to steal and adapt elements for their design. This is not mere copying—this analysis jump-starts the designers' own creativity by giving them a set of options and a starting point. And since most designers are visual thinkers, having such a visual representation is an important aid to creativity.

Steal ideas from consumer products or whatever is the talk of the town

The goal here is twofold: make sure you understand the expectations that have been created in the market which your product will have to meet and expand your ideas about the Interaction Patterns which are now being used so that you may adapt them for your own purposes. Innovation comes by stealing and twisting design elements—and sometimes even function— to provide better support for your users. For our Travel Concierge product, we want users to be able to compare activities in the Activity Explorer. Maybe we should take the side-by-side comparison that many shopping sites provide and twist them to our purpose.

And for standard types of interactions where you aren't looking for much change—simply borrow the best patterns out there. That is what makes you modern. If every major shopping site on the internet lets the user sort by price and brand, your travel product will probably have to support sorting by price and vendor.

To define preliminary Interaction Patterns, identify 2–4 existing products to analyze, assigning each to a pair of team members. Find the sections and components used in these products and draw the Interaction Pattern for each primary interface you care about, writing in the primary

Borrow the best Interaction Patterns in use for standard interactions

function in each section. That will help you see what you might want to borrow. Look across all these approaches and choose a preliminary approach for your product—then let the needs of the User Environment Design and validation with the user iterate your design. A forward-thinking company can also decide to push the boundaries of design—to try to go after a really new approach to supporting the practice. This must be defined early in the project as part of your project scope and will guide what the team tries out in early prototype tests (see Chapter 19 for a discussion of defining project scope).

Expect the dialogue about the best design to continue throughout the process from the Vision forward and to include all members of the team. As early as the product concept drawings from visioning, the team can step back and see the types of places that your product will need: entry screens that might be dashboards; content screens for reading information in depth; list panes for traversing items; forms for gathering information; and more.

Innovation is the recombination of known parts with the right twist for your product

You may identify a need for a new type of place and go on a hunt to see if it's been done before and if so how designers dealt with its unique challenges. Each of these types of screens will have Interaction Patterns associated with them, and where they exist in other products already you can choose to match the existing paradigm—or deliberately break it.

Once we have some concept of what the places in the product might be, and the purpose of those places, we can start to imagine possible ways to present function and content in that place.

If interesting high-level Interaction Patterns are identified early on in the project, the team can try them out in storyboards. This allows the team to play with various presentations at a high level before committing. The storyboards sketches are a way to explore different Interaction Patterns along the way. Since designers (and everyone, really) do better if they can imagine some sort of user interface when storyboarding and creating the User Environment Design, sketching Interaction Patterns early informs the reinvention of the work—as long as the team does not constrain the activities they invent to make them fit existing patterns.

Over the years the manifestation of place in products has changed. Once it was a hardly noticeable command line, then it was a green screen form, next a WISYWIG interface, then a window with dialogue boxes. Now a

As long as users interact with places, they will need structural design

place is a webpage, a screen on phones, tablets, and watches, or a display on a kiosk. Gameboards, the television screen, and walls of museums are all display places where people interact—and in the future we expect more interaction with signs in the street, walls in the home, and whatever else we invent! Whatever the realization of a place is, the Interaction Pattern will be needed to help designers think about how to design that place structurally.

So what makes for a good place structure? It has to work for the activities of the user, but also address the Cool Concepts and fit modern user interface standards of the moment. All the products in a user's life set their expectation for how products are structured and how they will behave. Violate these expectations at your peril— in rare cases it may be worth it, if differentiating your product has value and the users can adapt (and want to!). Much more often, you should fit with and build on existing paradigms so that users don't need to do work to understand your product. So to create a modern user experience, the team needs to have a command of the Interaction Patterns in current widespread use.

BUILDING INTERACTION PATTERNS FROM THE USER ENVIRONMENT DESIGN

The User Environment Design collects all the product requirements from all of the storyboards and organized them into coherent areas, each focused on its core intent. Now it's up to the interaction designer to figure out creative ways of making the function and content available in one coherent place in the interface. The sketches from the storyboards offer suggestions for the user interface design and show the concepts the storyboard designers intended to reveal. But the interaction designer now has to decide, for all the storyboards collected into this place, for all the types of people and activities the place might support, and for all the devices where it must be available, what is the best user interface to deliver?

In our travel storyboard example, the Idea Collector starts out as the area where the trip owner organizes their ideas. But then it becomes the place where a newly invited participant can find out what's going on and whether they want to be involved. Will the design for the first user group also work

Design a set of Interaction Pattern's to deliver the best overall user experience

for the second? A Focus Area collects information from *all* of the storyboards. So no single storyboard represents everything that has to be thought about when designing the interaction with a place. With all requirements collected in a Focus Area, the interaction designer can consider all of the function and content together when designing the interface. If the team has been trying out multiple Interaction Patterns the designer can look at the sketches and decide what worked and what did not. They now know what types of places are truly in the product and so what Interaction Patterns they will need.

To start, the team looks across the User Environment Design to identify the types of places they need Interaction Patterns for. Once they agree and design the Interaction Patterns, they can map function and content into them. These patterns are a hypothesis—they will adapt as more function and content are rolled in from the different Focus Areas. The initial Interaction Pattern set will be reexamined and normalized after initial design and then again after it is tested with users in the validation pass. Eventually a full set of Interaction Patterns will be specified for the whole product.

The team creates an Interaction Pattern for each major Focus Area in the User Environment Design. They ensure that Focus Areas supporting the same style of interaction use the same Interaction Pattern. Appropriate Interaction Patterns depend on the platform (phone, tablet, desktop, or other)—if you're supporting multiple platforms, create a pattern for each platform. The team also needs a concept of how screens might work on a touch versus mouse interface—and if interactions such as disclosure of hidden content will operate by different mechanisms on different devices. Each platform has its own interaction standards to take into consideration. When complete, the set of Interaction Patterns operate as the user interface architecture.

Start with a preliminary set of Interaction Patterns for your core places and platform

With the Interaction Pattern as a starting point, the team creates a user interface for each Focus Area. Choose the most central and most difficult areas to do first—in a perfect world you might produce an Interaction Pattern for them all, but your time is generally too limited for that, and simple Focus Areas don't need this level of analysis anyway. The purpose, functions, and content defined by each Focus Area provide the requirements for the Interaction Pattern: it needs to provide a place

Design clusters of Focus Areas that go together—together

for each function, making it ready to hand when needed and only when needed, in a structure that allows for easy scanning, access to content, and clear interaction. Design clusters of Focus Areas that go together to achieve an intent, together—then check that you use the same approach for other Focus Areas of the same page type elsewhere in the User Environment Design. This is particularly important if parallel subteams are working on different clusters in parallel. Collect the sketches for the Focus Area from the storyboards for inspiration.

Fig. 15.8 shows an Interaction Pattern for collection of research results. This Interaction Pattern was created for another project

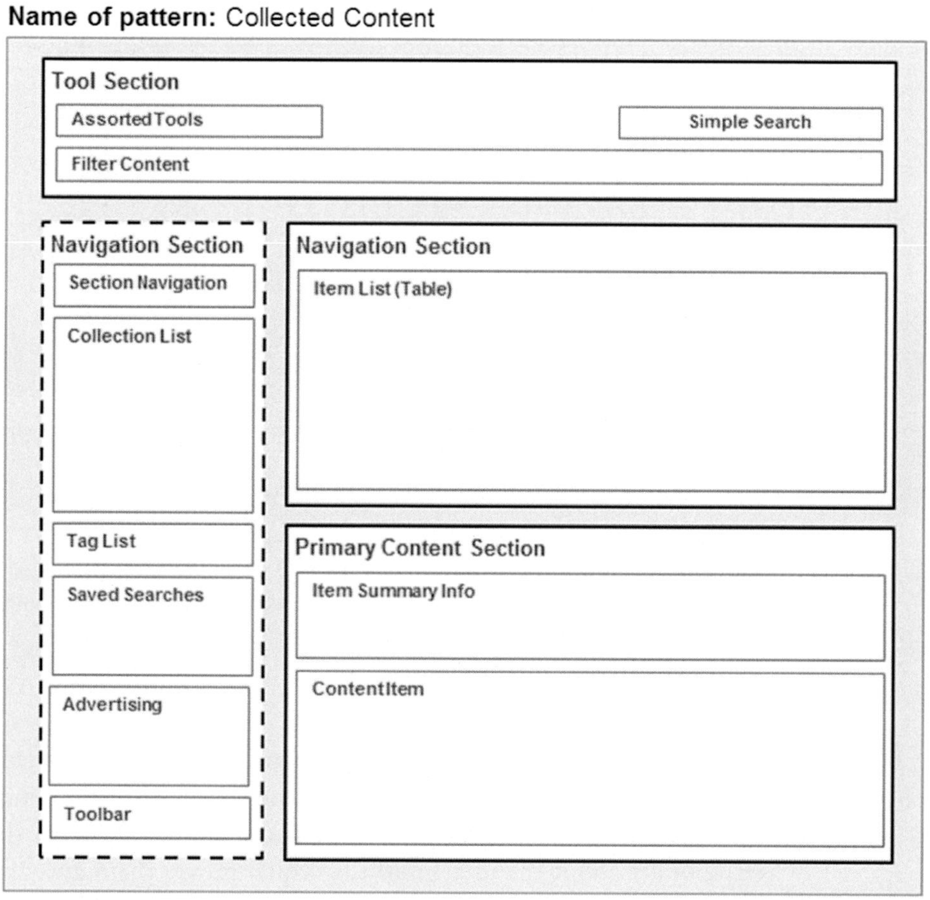

Name of pattern: Collected Content

FIGURE 15.8 A generic Interaction Pattern for collecting content across the Web, showing the primary screen areas that support the overall task.

and used as the basis of the Idea Collector for our trip application (Fig. 15.9). The actual functions, content and intent reshape the Interaction Pattern to make it appropriate to the product it is being used for. Generic Interaction Patterns are useful to make sure users can get up and running in your product right away—they will be familiar with the current user interaction approaches. Build on and twist them enough to make them familiar while adding new value as we did in (Fig. 15.9).

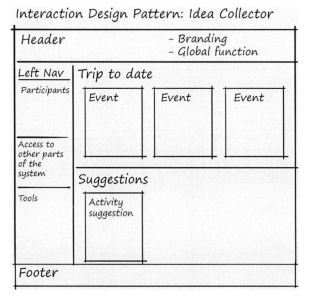

FIGURE 15.9   A preliminary Interaction Pattern for the Idea Collector. The layout shows ideas that have been provisionally accepted for the trip as well as suggestions from the system and other people. Collecting ideas for a trip is similar to collecting content during research (Fig. 15.8)—this design adapts the overall structure for picking and choosing trip events.

Interaction Patterns act as a framework for designers, focusing them on the structure of the page and the structure of the product from a user interface perspective. The patterns help the team think structurally about the user interface, which moves them away from thinking only about functions or look of the page. Pushing the team to think structurally ensures greater consistency within and across the product. And by starting the team with analysis of existing products, the team is encouraged to use modern design approaches and principles while they are reinventing the practice. We don't address the whole field of user interface design here, but Box 15.1 lists the main principles we use to ensure the team produces a high-quality user experience.

Interaction Patterns ensures cross-product consistency

The layers of design, from storyboard to User Environment Design to Interaction Pattern, all

BOX 15.1 THE KEY PRINCIPLES WE CONSIDER DURING USER INTERFACE DESIGN

User Interface Design Principles

User Environment Design

1. Purpose/intent of the place is clear
2. Purpose/intent of each component in the relevant Interaction Pattern is clear
3. Everything you need to achieve the intent is in the place--and nothing more
4. Navigation to the next reasonable action is apparent and in the place
5. Needed content is instantly available and in the right chunks for quick consumption; the next needed content is clearly available

User Interface

6. Prominence: Most important elements to the intent take the most space/central to the eye
7. Relationship: Page elements are visually related to one another to achieve the overall intent
8. Visual Flow: The eye has a clear starting place and path to follow that supports the intent
9. Interaction Flow: Moving from one step of a task to the next is obvious and easy
10. Clarity: It's apparent what can be done and how to do it, and the results are clear
11. Simplicity: There's one place to achieve each intent; there's no unnecessary complexity on the screen

Cool

12. Direct Into Action: immediate and actionable support for actions, decision-making, and instant results
13. Hassle is reduced at every level
14. No learning is needed to interact with the product
15. Sensation and animation are used sparingly to complement functionality or bring a smile without distraction
16. Modern Interaction Patterns are used everywhere

inform each other. Seeing and designing structure at the screen level is an essential skill in the design process. The initial Interaction Patterns will change as the team works through the low-level

Interaction Patterns evolve with addition of function and iteration

design, but they provide a concrete starting point. Harvesting known Interaction Patterns introduces less experienced teams to design possibilities already out in the world, which they can use as is or revise for their own purposes. Experienced teams use them to think about what they will add to push the envelope.

With an initial set of Interaction Patterns in hand and understanding how function and content will map to them, the team is ready to find out how their design will be received by users. Validation and iteration are essential for a transformative user experience, and we will take this up in Part 5.

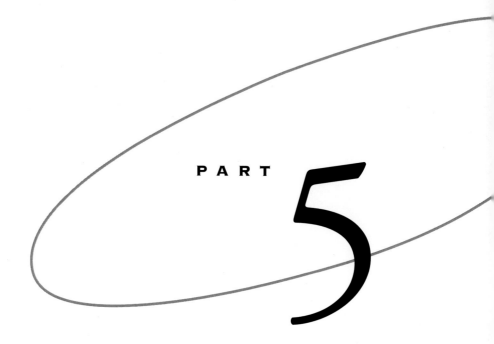

Making It Real

Making It Real 16

At this point, by using contextual techniques we've understood the people in our target market, developed a product concept, fleshed it out with storyboards, and defined a basic product with a user interface structure. Making this product concept real involves three main steps: validating and extending the design through iteration with users (Chapter 17), prioritizing and scoping what can really be shipped (Chapter 18), and planning and staffing the project in the first place (Chapter 19). This part considers these key areas.

Contextual Design is a user-centered process, but it's been quite a few chapters since talking to users was the main activity. It's now time to ensure people want the product by validating it with users. Also testing and iteration helps refine the high-level product concept by adding function and detail to the user interface. Prototyping is the final *immersion* process in Contextual Design. Returning to

Shipping on time means managing the project work and decisions about what to ship

the field with prototype in hand returns designers to the context of the user. This reimmersion reminds them of the problems they set out to solve, and the rich environment and user interaction provides many insights for improving the design. Also, interviewing new users with prototypes expands the number of people you touch.[1] This gives you the confidence that you are indeed designing a product that addresses a market, not only a few individuals.

If the users don't think your product delivers value, you have no business case to build it; if they won't spend money on it or recommend it you won't be able to sell it. So you need evidence that your

---

[1] Some business IT projects are creating support for a small set of specialized user roles within their organization. In this case, of course, you return to those users to iterate the final design.

Contextual Design. http://dx.doi.org/10.1016/B978-0-12-800894-2.00016-8

product concept will be well received to justify doing more detailed design and planning a rollout. Roll-out planning needs to be based on a stable product concept, even if it's high level. In Contextual Design that means going back to the user for several rounds of testing and using this feedback to design in real customer value. That means testing the business case as well. So find out if you are going in the right direction before investing more and more effort in a concept that doesn't work.

At the core of the Contextual Design process is the principle of using reliable data about people's real lives as the basis of decision making. Data and immersion in data drives requirements, design, and business choices. It is the reliable ground that the team can stand on when interacting with each other and with stakeholders. It levels the playing field between people with different organizational roles and power. And it keeps the team on track. At this point in the product development process, the best way to stay on track, ship on time, and ensure you are building the right thing is to let the user arbitrate your design discussions. Teams can get lost in their own opinions of what they think is best; they can get attached to their favorite design ideas; they can put in way too much detailed function or user interface elements, and so they can take way too long to agree on a design. Teams that get bogged down in design are usually those which have lost touch with their users—they aren't going back out to interview or test prototypes on a regular basis. Talking to the actual users of the product or product suite is the single most effective way to influence these conversations both within the team and with management. So get back to the user quickly and often.

Users are the final arbiters of the goodness of your product

Finally, no project really works without the right people on the team and significant planning and project management. One of our greatest lessons has been that even with great design techniques, even with a reliable and repeatable process such as Contextual Design, if you do not have a clear project scope and a person skilled at project leading to keep the team on track, the project will simply not move forward smoothly. If you are trying to introduce user-centered techniques to an organization—or simply continuously show their value—you can't afford any kind of failure or churn in the team. We wrap up the book talking about these issues.

VALIDATING WITH USERS

When you create a design captured in a User Environment Design and a set of Interaction Patterns, this design is really a claim about what will work for the target user. Your claim is that this particular product simplifies the users' work, enhances their lives, overcomes pain, delivers delight, and otherwise enables them to live a better life. This is what it means to deliver value. So, how do we test this claim? How do we find out where the design falls short and how to improve it? How do we communicate the design to users in a form which they can respond to—in a form which helps the team see the consequences of different design decisions and react to them clearly?

Most of the approaches commonly used to communicate a new design to users don't seem to recognize how difficult a task this is. One typical way to get feedback is to do a demo to potential customers in a conference room or at a conference. Certainly the customer will tell you something—but is it reliable? You're asking people to view the product's user interface, and understand from screen images and your verbal description. You are asking them to imagine how that product as presented might impact their lives—which, as we said in Chapter 2, they are not aware of. You are asking them to envision how their practice and life will change when they have the new product concept—and then come up with alternatives when it doesn't work! The task is overwhelming—it's no wonder most people in a demo situation just complain about an icon that confuses them, comment on the color, or ask about one or two key features they care about.

The challenge of validation is how to help the user experience a new product

Requirements specifications as a communication device fare no better. Most are text; most break the product down into categories that relate to the technical system, not the user (all reliability requirements together, for example). Even when the first level of organization is by UI component, their textual and list-based nature tends to present features in isolation. Agile methods break functionality into user stories, which are supposed to address user value but are so fine-grained that they make it hard to see the product structure.

It's hard even for designers to see how a feature relates to other parts of the design; users reading the requirements find it even harder. Requirements specifications are less approachable than a demo, and make it no easier to imagine the impact the proposed product will have on users' world. They have their place in development by specifying exactly what's in the product, but they aren't a good way to communicate a design.

Scenarios test the customer's response to the story—not the product design

Other forms of communication such as use cases, scenarios, or our own storyboards attempt to communicate more context of use. These methods tell stories of how people will work in the new product, so they communicate better than a model or specification. However, each scenario can only tell one story out of the many the product must support. And they all suffer from the same basic drawback: users have only an unarticulated knowledge of their own practice and cannot check a proposed design against their own experience unaided. They can react to such a story at the level of "I hate that" or "I love that"—so scenarios can help test the marketing pitch. They'll help answer the question "what matters to the user" but not "how should the product be structured for them."

To get actionable, reliable feedback users need not just an artifact, but a process which will allow them to live their own lives in the new product and articulate the issues they identify.[2] Without such a process it doesn't matter how many signatures are on the requirements document—there's no guarantee that the specified product will solve any real problems or put an end to the continuous shifting of requirements. Prototype testing is the best way to immerse the user in the product and the target activity at the same time. How do we help users be codesigners so that together we can understand their world and the product impact?

Because no one articulates their own practice as an ordinary thing, the obstacles to making users effective codesigners are real and have to be faced head-on. It would be nice if the users could

---

[2] This is, of course, the core insight of Participatory Design practice, and much of Participatory Design research is looking for better ways to make "living their own lives" more real.

give concrete reasons why a design should be changed; usually they can only say that the design just feels wrong. The design process needs to create a way of interacting which helps them articulate the issues. Second, users have not spent time studying the whole user population for the proposed product, as the team has. What this means is that any user testing a prototype can only respond to it from their own point of view. Third, users aren't technologists—they don't know the range of possibilities that technology can support. They may be either too far fetched and unrealistic in their ideas or excessively cautious. Finally, they don't know what it takes to make a design hang together. And why should they, after all? It's their job to do their job, not design products.[3]

Prototyping helps users really imagine working in the product

And yet it's absolutely critical that these users, steeped in their own lives, be made a powerful partner with the design team, so they have real influence over the design. It's the users who will have to live with the new product. If it's an internal system, they have a right to say how the work they do will change. If it's a commercial app or product, it won't be bought if it doesn't fit their needs and lives. So the challenge for design is to include users in the process to iterate, refine, and extend the initial design concept put together by the team.

How do we get the best feedback and make customers strong codesigners?

We have found—as is now well accepted in the overall UX field—that users can respond to mockups of the proposed solution. Prototypes act as a bridge for communicating between user and designer. A prototype enables users to interact with the proposed product as they would with any product. "I think *this* should happen when I touch *here*," they say, unaware that they have just redesigned a focus area in the User Environment Design—but the designer can tell, because they can see how the comment relates to the User Environment Design and Interaction Pattern structure.

---

[3] For a discussion of these issues and a range of techniques for overcoming them, see D. Wixon and J. Ramey (Eds.), *Field Methods Case Book for Product Design*. John Wiley & Sons, Inc., New York, NY, 1996.

They can investigate the issue further if it challenges fundamental assumptions and value of the design.

So once you have a product concept and initial design built about a deep understanding of the users' world, a prototype field interview is the best method for gathering feedback from the target population.

DRIVING DESIGN CONVERSATIONS WITH USERS

In Contextual Design, we borrow the idea of rough mockups from Participatory Design[4] by using rough paper prototypes to start the codesign with users. The goal of the prototype is not to provide a demo; prototypes are a prop in a contextual interview, enabling the user to play out the experience of living with the new product. By acting out their own activities in the prototype, users can make their unarticulated knowledge explicit. Fleshing

Paper prototypes help the user focus on product structure

out the prototype with the users' own data, tasks, and life situations gives them the touchstones they need to put them into the experience of doing the work. Here we *immerse* the user in their own context so that they can really immerse themselves in the new tool well enough to imagine what using it will be like.

Through their interaction with the designer/interviewer, users can explore different technical and design possibilities. The designer knows technology and provides options which the user considers, matches to their experience of the moment, and discusses why one alternative fits and another doesn't. It's another application of Contextual Inquiry—using the prototype in the *context* of the real practice to ground the discussion. The *partnership* within the interview leads to codesign, and together user and designer *interpret* the implications of issues as they come up. The prototype itself gives the interview *focus*.

---

[4] D. Schuler and A. Namioka (Eds.), *Participatory Design: Perspectives on Systems Design*, N.J.: Lawrence Erlbaum Associates, 1993.

To look at product structure, the first prototypes are always paper (Fig. 16.1). Paper is eminently practical and meets the primary need: it makes it possible to express the structure of the design in a way users can understand, and it makes it hard to overfocus on low-level user interface detail. When a screen is drawn by hand, it's pretty clear that icon design and fancy direct manipulation are not the important points. When users interact with paper, they aren't distracted by the detailed UI and graphics; they have to focus on structure of the product and the page layout. They know by the rough format of the prototype that we aren't talking about every low-level function, its placement, interaction, and all the other things that will eventually be added to a fully specified product. It's easier to talk about the overall impact on life when the stimulus is bare bones. Even

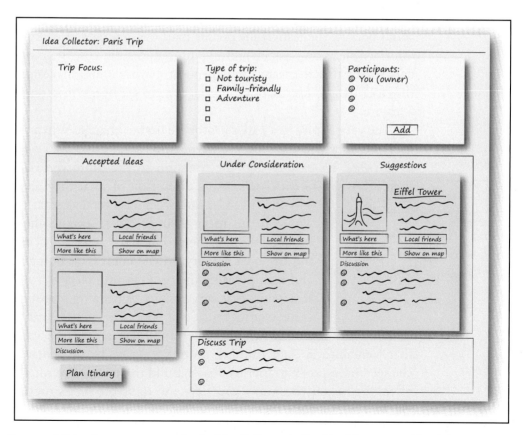

FIGURE 16.1 A paper prototype for the Idea Collector, built with sticky notes and hand drawn.

building architects, who aren't constrained by writing code, often prefer to communicate their first ideas to clients as sketches rather than finished drawings.

Because paper prototypes are so quick to build and test, they help the team make decisions and avoid getting too invested in their favorite solutions. We regularly mock up a design alternative in paper on 1 day and test it with users on the next day. We have results and are ready to rethink the design within 2 days. It's possible to go through multiple iterations, trying out many different ideas, in the course of a week. There's no time for people to get overly invested in one design alternative, and no reason to argue for any length of time over two alternatives. It's almost always faster to take the alternatives to users and try them out. Most arguments in a design team come about because the team really doesn't have the user data to make an informed decision—paper prototyping reduces the cost of getting data so low that the team can depend on having it and makes getting user data so fast that no one has time to get overly invested in a feature.

Prototype testing helps drive design decisions within the team

The very nature of a paper prototype invites change. When the user gets to a screen in the prototype and says, "But now I need to do *this*," it's easy to add the function to the prototype right then. It's easy to invite users into a discussion of what they need, why they need it, and which of several alternatives would better meet their need. It's easy to move into codesign of the product. The user is discussing her own activity, in the context of doing it, and manipulating the product interfaces planned to support that very activity. A running prototype is necessarily more complete and prettier, which inhibits user feedback—they don't want to disregard the work that went into it. And running prototypes can't be immediately changed in response to user feedback. Build them after two rounds of testing, when you know you have the right product structure and Interaction Patterns.

Paper prototypes invite codesign—they are quick to change on the fly

Because they are easily portable and can be used in any environment, paper prototypes also helps the team *design for life.*

Test how well you support the *unstoppable momentum of life* by joining your user at breakfast and accompanying them on their morning commute or while they run errands. Talk about dead time, and prompt them to use your design as a way of filling in time that would otherwise be wasted. At the office or the return home, look at switching to a desktop or tablet to continue the task. Test identity elements with users who exhibit those attributes and see if your design excites them. Watch to see whether the people who are collaborating feel more connected. And iterate Joy in Use: sensory stimulation, directness in the interactions, hassles, and learning can be explored on running prototypes after iteration in paper. Add the visual design, animation, and interactivity and compare alternatives to get further feedback.

Paper prototypes help you design for life—make them mobile

In addition to making sure that the product fits into and adds value to the user's life, paper prototyping help identify detailed requirements which users simply can't communicate except when experiencing an actual design. It's natural to develop requirements in layers, just as an architect works out the overall layout of the house before deciding where the closets go. The vision was the first layer of design; then the Cool Drilldown filled in more detail. Next we designed more detail in storyboarding, and more again with the User Environment Design and Interaction Pattern. Now we need an additional level of detailed user data to work out exactly what will happen in each focus area and exactly how each function will behave.

Prototypes help flesh out requirements and detailed design

For example, we designed the Idea Collector to include suggestions from the system, based on the users' interests. But how will this work, really? What suggestions might be more useful—similar activities, or complementary activities? Same price level, or a big blowout event? A complete specification of all this detail cannot really be based on the user data, which didn't address these questions. The only way to get this level of specification right is to work it out with the user in the context of the specific design. Prototyping in paper lets the team complete the detailed design without committing anything to code or detailed UI design prematurely.

And because of immersion in the prototype and in life, it becomes possible to see new innovations the team never talked about. When a product supports practice in a significantly new way, putting it in place will change the users' world in unpredictable ways. Once in place, users will shift their own practice in response. These *emergent practices* can be seen during prototype testing—and so, new requirements are identified.

Prototypes reveal future possibilities resulting from the new product

Way back in the 1990's, before instant messaging or texting, we designed an office support system that we tested with an executive secretary. "Oh, I'd never interrupt my boss when he's in a meeting," she said. "That simply wouldn't do." We walked her through a paper prototype which included an instant messaging function. "When he's in a meeting, this message just appears on his screen?" she asked. "No one else can see it? I'd use this all day."

If you can immerse the user in the experience of the life you're proposing, they'll be able to tell you how their own attitudes and practices will change. Recognize the emergent work practice yourself, before your competition does, and you can leapfrog a whole generation of products.

Contextual Design mandates continuous iteration and extension

Working through a prototype of the new product, pretending to do real activities, and discussing the interaction of the product with the practice reveals issues that would otherwise remain invisible. Starting with paper gets the basic structure and function right—then moving online gets the details of UI and interaction right. Together, user and designer can explore how the product will impact the practice and how practice is likely to change in the future as a result.

Contextual Design prototyping and other methods

Prototype testing within Contextual Design can look similar to other practices that bring mockups and prototypes to the user. Rapid prototyping, usability tests, and A/B testing all place a version of the product before people and ask for feedback. What is the difference? At its core Contextual Design is generative—its goal is to drive invention. It asks the question, "What should we be making?" We drive the answer to that question first, by being sure that the initial product concept is informed by immersion in rich user data. Second, validation testing ensures we are going in the right direction. With paper and then online prototype testing, we simultaneously ensure we have the right product concept with the right user experience presentation, fill in requirements, and build in usability.

Contextual Design drives generative innovation— not just iteration

Rapid Prototyping is a separate discipline heavily used in Participatory Design, which seeks to develop effective systems by iterating and prototyping with the user. Unlike Contextual Design, there's no up-front process of research, consolidation, and Visioning; the goal is to do those steps directly with the user. There is a lot of synergy between the Rapid Prototyping approach and our own. The big difference is where that initial concept comes from. Any prototyping process starts from *some* initial concept, which designer and user refine together. It's always easier for the user to renovate an existing design than to start from a totally blank slate. But because prototyping is iterative, it's hard to make fundamental change to the initial product concept, so you want to be sure the first cut addresses the right issues. In Contextual Design, we generate the initial product concepts from data in Visioning. In this way we ensure that our solution responds to, fits in with, and enlivens the user's life. Iterating after that hones the idea that we know will deliver value.

In usability testing and A/B testing the tester is given a product design, but the process is not generative. The intention is to test the existing design, not invent a new one. Classic usability tests measure users' performance on set tasks, often to ensure they meet metrics defined in advance. Today companies may bring people into the lab as part of concept testing or to see if certain detailed function is correct. The more you can get the user's real world into the lab, the more reliable the outcome—at least, pick test scenarios based on field data. Usability tests are also an iterative process that hones a design and helps make choices between different approaches within the framework of the product concept. And they are great for ensuring that all the UI nits are dealt with before shipping. They tune a user interface to clean up any rough edges or unnecessary difficulty in understanding or interacting with the interface.

Usability and A/B testing can't challenge the product concept

Usability professionals who can't participate in developing the product concept are constantly frustrated at being asked to fix major structural problems through last-minute Band-Aids. By the tail end of the design process, it's simply too late to decide your product addresses the wrong problem. This is the very reason Contextual Design was invented in the first place!

Finally, A/B testing, website analytics, and other "big data" methods are currently popular ways of comparing design alternatives and finding problems. When the product is delivered over the web, these methods are easy to implement and therefore enticing. Particularly for high-volume products such as websites, they can be very valuable—if you're Amazon, a 1% increase in conversion rate can equate to millions of dollars.

Use Contextual Design to come up with product concepts—then A/B test alternatives

But like usability testing, A/B testing must come after a concept has been generated so it's no substitute for a generative, user-centered design process. And A/B testing depends on having alternatives to compare—generally multiple ways of achieving the same intent. Building those alternatives requires a design process that incorporates user-centered thinking. Use Contextual Design techniques to come up with your alternatives—then, if your product has enough volume of users for this testing process to make sense, use A/B testing to evaluate which is better.

In the end, if you want a process to help determine what to build and how to structure it so that it is desired and valued by your target population, the product concept needs to emerge from a deep understanding of the lives in that population. And if you want users to give feedback on that product concept—and not focus on small details of the user interface, visual design, or incompatibility with existing tools—start in paper and interview in person. Hold off getting online feedback until you know you are moving in the right direction.

PROTOTYPING AS A BUSINESS TECHNIQUE

As a design team, you have to be prepared to talk not only about why your design will work for the user, but how your business will make or save money on it. Prototyping techniques dovetail with quantitative techniques and with business intelligence to validate the business model. Prototyping won't tell you how big your market is, or how much people are spending on the type of product you are building. But it will tell you how excited people are once they see the design and understand the impact.

Prototype interviews can also help quantify your value proposition. At the end of a mock-up interview, we explicitly ask what the user valued most—what they would be willing to pay for the product if they are the buyer, or whether they would recommend the product to the buyer. One

Prototyping can get feedback for the business model and marketing

customer said she would pay three times the price the marketing group thought was possible, because she understood the potential impact on her practice. Of course, there is a risk that the opposite can happen. One client believed they had a $2000 product, but prototype users said they would pay $500. So checking with the users during prototype interviews is just good business sense.

Another aspect of the value proposition is the cost savings you may introduce, and you can test that as well. For example, if you're designing a troubleshooter, measure how long it currently takes to deal with problems. Go through a number of instances to see the range. Then, after the user has interacted with the prototype, get their estimate of the time savings, reduced rework, and other value your system provides. If it looks good, later you can measure the result. Having experienced the product and, in "let's pretend" mode, actually experienced the savings, their estimate will be better than anyone else's at this point.

It goes the other way, too. Your business model might tell you that IT organizations will spend a few billion on "virtualization" in the next year—but what do they think they are getting when they ask for virtualization? What are the key drivers and the expected value? How is this saving them money or protecting them from risk? Your field research on this starts to flesh out the market need and, if it is there, your prototype testing lets you assess if your product concept is of enough value that it will bring in revenue. Prototype testing will give you a gut feel—later you can use real market research for pricing and business planning. Similarly, if you interviewed customers of your competitors in Contextual Interviews, then your product should reflect value above the competition. Take your prototypes out to users of the competitive product and find out how you did. Talk about the benefits and disadvantages of each and look for where your product can differentiate itself. This feeds your market message as well if the results are positive.

Prototyping is important for internal projects as well. By prototyping with users within your organization, an IT team can build trust and excitement. When designing IT systems for the business, employees who will use the new IT system can see progress, they can talk directly to designers, and they can see how their responses shape the design. It's immediately clear that the design team is listening. Many teams also use their storyboards to communicate what the new work will look like as employees often fear what technology will do to their job. Both tools can support conversations with people who are affected by the new technology and help gather feedback on what will work and what may not. And both tools help employees know that technology and business managers are listening to them.

Prototyping helps buy-in and trust of an IT application within an organization.

This can cause its own problems—one team generated so much interest and excitement with their user interviews that they had to ensure every user in their organization was included. Another team had to hold many, many feedback sessions, sharing storyboards and building consensus on the definition of a work week before they could agree on an implementation. But surely these are better problems to have than mistrust and contempt. The interest and involvement generated by the sessions lead to easier acceptance and adoption of the IT system when it comes time to roll it out. And it creates good will.

Data goes a long way to facilitating business conversations and decision making. So be sure to validate your product concept and get the feedback you need not only on the design, but on the business issues as well.

PRODUCT PLANNING AND STRATEGY

The last part of making a design real is all about shipping. We won't get into implementation in this book, but we do need to discuss how to make the step from your validated design to a product roadmap. Any Contextual Design project will nearly always constitute more than you can ship in a single release. Prioritization always matters—even picking features off of an enhancement database is a process of making decisions on what to ship now and what to hold back. In Chapter 18 we will talk about how to use the User Environment Design and your user data to help you make decisions and cross this last bridge to a successful solution.

A strategic Contextual Design project—exploring a new market, designing a new product or significant addition to an existing product, or a suite of apps to interact with a larger product offering—helps the team (and the company) see the scope of what may be delivered over a series of releases. Many of our projects of this nature have supported product rollout over 2–5 years. But even a fast Agile project with limited scope addressing a single job type can result in more function than can be shipped in a single release or by a single team.

> *Good user-centered design produces more ideas than you can ship in one release*

Instead, the data and the product concept feed a series of releases or a set of parallel Agile teams. So knowing how to segment and prioritize the validated design is an important part of ensuring you both support the business and deliver something of value to the user *with each release*.

Over the years that we've been actively developing, promoting, and using Contextual Design ourselves, more than a few development methodologies have come and gone.[5] As of this writing, Agile methods have peaked, but we are already starting to see people looking ahead toward methods that might overcome some of Agile methods' limitations.[6] So in this discussion, we'll talk more about the principles of prioritizing and shipping than about specific methods, except as examples.

Prioritization generally happens at two levels. First, a full Contextual Design process nearly always produces a solution that's too big to ship as one release. Not only will it take too long to build the whole thing, but you don't even want to—you want to get out in the market with a useful solution and enhance it over a series of releases. As a business you want to start earning revenue as soon as possible, and the act of putting a release in the market will change the market in ways you cannot predict. So better to be at least a bit agile rather than think in terms of one monolithic solution.

Get the first release out fast but be sure it delivers value and has great user experience

A popular buzzword of the moment is "Minimum Viable Product."[7] Ship only the essential function first, then iterate from there. It's a powerful concept, but be careful of it—in practice, it's easy for "minimum viable" to translate into "the least we can get away with...with no real commitment to quality or true value." Agile development only exacerbates the problem. If in one sprint the team ships a story that addresses the need and allows the user to do a task, even if it's clumsy and ugly, where's the justification for improving on that feature rather than working on new functionality in the next sprint? The pull of new function is hard to resist.

[5] From the beginning of our career using Contextual Design, we have adapted and coordinated our work with companies using waterfall method, RUP, JAD sessions in IT shops, rapid prototyping approaches, scenario-based design, business process reengineering, Six Sigma techniques, Agile, start-up cultures, and more.

[6] Ladas, Corey. *Scrumban: Essays on Kanban Systems for Lean Software Development.* Modus Cooperandi Press. 2009.
Beyer, Hugh. *User-Centered Agile Methods.* Morgan & Claypool Publishers, 2010.

[7] Ries, Eric. *The lean startup: how today's entrepreneurs use continuous innovation to create radically successful businesses.* Crown Publishing, 2011.

So take a page from Scrum's, Definition of Done where a feature isn't done if it has no test cases.[8] It's not done if the code is hacked together and buggy. "Done" means done with full quality and a complete test suite. Teams need the same discipline on the UX side. Done means with a high-quality UI, all the interactivity a modern UI needs, a design that delivers direct into action, no hassle, no learning burden, and appropriate use of animation and a modern aesthetic as defined by the Cool Principles. Otherwise you'll always feel like you're not shipping a quality product.

But why are we developing a design with "more than needed" in the first place? Isn't it at the core of Agile and other rapid development approaches to do only what's required at each point? Let's turn to an artist metaphor. A painter has a concept that is very loose; she wants to create a picture of a person standing in front of a fence before a field of wheat. She knows the person will have a hand, a face, and more; the fence will have posts; the field will have wheat and sky—but how exactly will it hang together? The artist starts by sketching the large elements of the drawing so she can see the structure of the painting and the proportions of the elements. The artist does not start painting all the detail of the hand or face—each layer of detail is added all over the painting simultaneously. The painting emerges from the artist's dialogue with the canvas—ideas once thought essential change by seeing the parts grow up in relationship to each other.

So too with designing products. It is natural for any requirements process to generate more to ship than can be done in any one release. But knowing the full scope of the possible elements of the product informs the designer of each part—just like the sketch of the bigger picture informs the artist. A

The full scope of the design guides and focuses each subsequent release

user-centered process such as Contextual Design delivers a broad, validated design direction. Then subsequent choices of what to ship are guided both by the overall larger product concept and by the user's response to each release. Like the artist we shift, change, and deepen the design as we see what emerges. But the direction is set by

---

[8] https://www.scrum.org/resources/scrum-guide.

having a larger validated vision and high-level design of the product scope as laid out in a User Environment Design. Having a validated big picture of direction serves us well—we see where we are going, whether through multiple releases or parallel releases. Then we tune each release with continuous user feedback. Operating with one eye on the horizon and one eye on the path in front of us is the best route to success.

A tight cross-functional partnership during the project makes consensus on a release easy

A tight partnership between UX, product management, and engineering is critical. By acting as a team you can make the best tradeoffs for the implementation, the user, and the business. In the end, whatever you ship must work for all three every time. So take key engineers along on initial customer visits and make sure they participate in ideation sessions, including walking the user data. You need to create advocates within every job function involved in shipping the product to ensure the whole team knows how the product direction is guided by the voice of the real customer.

SHIP THEMES SUPPORTING AN INTENT

The first challenge of roll-out planning is to divide your overall concept into large chunks that can be shipped in a series of releases. Each chunk should have a focus and a theme so that you have a coherent market message when you release. What's more compelling: "Version 2 of Travel Planner with 100 new features!" Or, "Version 2 of Travel Planner, now with the Travel Buddy, your on-the-road assistant!" Many products seem to adopt the first strategy. We recommend the second.

Themes focus the developer on user intent—not a list of features to implement

Organize your releases around themes even if you're in a technical situation that allows you to deliver iteratively—if your product runs on the cloud, for example, and you can release a tweak whenever you like. When major new functionality comes along, you still want to make a market splash and you still want your users to focus on the new features so they adopt them. That's easy to do if you have a coherent theme you can talk about. Themes also help parallel teams know what the intent of their part is about—they're not just implementing a list of features unrelated to each other. This way the developers, particularly with access to user data, can think about what they are really delivering to the user.

The product concepts we identified during Visioning and the Cool Drilldown will usually be your starting point for these themes. Each product concept intentionally pulled together a coherent set of functionality that addressed a particular user intent. A product concept that supports a coherent activity can be shipped independently of the rest, and much of the design and development can be independent as well. (Check against the User Environment Design and the user data to make sure that's the case.) Although a product concept is smaller and more focused than the whole vision, it's still likely to represent more functionality than you want to ship in a single release, and it will include optional, nice-to-have functionality in addition to the core functionality, which you may not want to delay the whole release for.

The second layer of prioritization is within a release. Within a release, the functionality envisioned in the User Environment Design needs to be communicated to development in small, actionable units, whether those are individual requirements from a requirements specification, user stories in an Agile process, or something else. And as long and bitter experience teaches, however carefully we plan

Prioritize in layers—break the design into coherent chunks then prioritize function within it

and schedule, it is likely that we will have to slip functionality to future releases as we get close to the end of development. Knowing the theme and the core value to be delivered allows us to focus on what is core to achieving that intent and be sure to get it built.

Prioritization within a release should follow Agile principles: organize development to get to a usable product as quickly as possible and grow from there; develop core functionality first and then do the more optional features; work closely in parallel with the development team to ensure that they know exactly what to do, and when changes inevitably have to be made, they are made in ways that protect the user experience. Making sure that developers have relevant storyboards, the Interaction Pattern, and the detailed design will help them gauge the impact of any changes and point them back to the UX team for consultation.

Where development of a Contextual Design project will differ from classic Agile projects is in iteration during development. A Contextual Design project has already tested the concepts, the fit with user practice, and the rough UI with fast, paper prototypes. Sometimes this is called a "Phase 0," where the requirements are worked out—it's a separate activity that precedes Agile Development. You won't need to research, design, and iterate those aspects of the product during development. You will be able to focus your efforts on detailed UI design, which can happen in parallel with development, working with engineers, and testing preliminary code versions with users as they become available.

Contextual Design delivers a validated product concept into an Agile process

Knowing how to prioritize your design into business-viable shipments means that anything you ship delivers clear value to the customer and also revenue to the business; that the product's great user experience enhances the corporate brand perception; that the robust core function can be built by the development team in a timely way; and that the sales story over multiple releases shows that the company is marching toward an even more powerful set of function. The User Environment Design structure and the contextual data help with this thinking—along with real communication and collaboration across your cross-functional product team.

PROJECT PLANNING AND EXECUTION

"What are we supposed to do," an engineer asked us once, "Knock on people's doors, asking them to let us watch them use our product?" The real answer to that question is, "Yes—do that." Not without setting up the visit ahead of time of course, and there's some planning to do, but in the end it all comes down to showing up and watching. Sometimes the most difficult barrier to introducing a new way of working is people's assumptions about what is or is not "done."

Once people accept the idea that they are going to try a user-centered design process, they need to know exactly what steps to follow. Otherwise no real action can take place. Often the resistance people put up against new ways of working is that they simply can't imagine themselves working that way—of course, because it's new. So it's important to have clear, concrete actions which will enable a Contextual Design project to get started. So in Chapter 19, we will discuss setting the focus for a project, how to plan who to talk to, variations on the data gathering process that may be required by different problems, and team formation.

The team organization and project plan needs to fit the problem and your business. Explicitly defining the scope of the project and the project focus is a crucial first step. This becomes the guiding light of every decision made thereafter. If a company is only willing to consider fixes to an existing product—if all they want is a few new features—you will just be frustrated if you plan for a wide project scope that seeks to fundamentally change or challenge the current approach. If your company is asking for fundamental, serious innovation, is exploring a new market, or is looking for adjacent products, then looking for a few new feature sets, modernizing the UI or making a list of quick fixes is exactly the wrong approach—now you need to look widely and have real skill on the team to meet the challenge. But make sure you understand what the real goals are. Companies will often *say* they want innovation but really only want a few new features—they will say they want to take a new direction, but in reality be unable to sell or execute on anything that is too far afield from their core mission. So to be successful, the first step is to look past what the stakeholders tell you to what is really possible in the current business environment.

A clear project scope and focus is fundamental to a successful project result

You also have to find the practice you are addressing. Remember beneath every product design—even for a project which is only dong usability fixes—is the target activity you are addressing and the people doing the relevant activities. Companies are notorious for framing project as about "porting to a new technology" or "getting a great new modern interface." This frame focuses the team on technology and design, not on supporting the user. So never think of your project as fixing a product—it is always about redesigning the practice of the user to improve it with technology.

With the scope, target task, and job types clearly defined you can start to plan what data to collect from the field and how. There's no one-size-fits-all Contextual Design process; the nature of the product, your company, what they want you to deliver, and the nature of the practice you plan to support will change how to gather user data, what user data to gather, and how to deal with it. And you will need to fit within the methodology and timeframe your company has chosen. A successful Contextual Design project has to execute in a timely, organized way that fits with the lives of the team and the company.

Treat a Contextual Design project like any other— project manage it well!

Contextual Design provides a set of techniques which form a backbone for a user-centered design process of any scope and size. It can deliver value in a few weeks or handle a more strategic process in a few months. How long or short it takes is all in the planning of the steps necessary to achieve your project focus, understand the target task, work with the people you have available for the team, and schedule users and team members to do the work and more. Without real project management at every level the work is likely to wander, become unfocused, take too long, and be put aside for corporate fires—like any other project. So here's some guidance on how to manage a Contextual Design project.[9]

Make customer-visit setup as smooth as you can

Companies that have the right infrastructure to support user-centered design have an easier time. The two most important elements are helping in setting up visits and organizing so the team can really collaborate. If you have a user research team or usability group, good—you can work with them to get your field visits set up. But many organizations don't have the procedures in place to make scheduling these interviews easy.

---

[9] See also *Rapid Contextual Design* Karen Holtzblatt et al; December 2004 Morgan Kaufman. This book was written as a handbook for many of the key steps of Contextual Design. It is a good reference for anyone managing your project.

In these organizations, work with people who are in contact with customers—the product manager, the services organization, or the sales force. You may find that these people are reluctant—they may be suspicious of letting engineers talk directly to customers. But customer reactions to the visits are nearly always enthusiastic. One customer was so excited to be included in the process that she had her internal company newsletter do a piece on how well their vendor was listening. When users feel like they are being listened to for the first time, the sales force and marketing soon come to recognize the benefits. And when the users are internal, they feel like they have control over the new system being built.

In this world of distributed teams, it may be heresy to talk about face-to-face meetings. But we must deal with the fact that being together, working together, and building the initial consolidated models and design together will deliver a much better result. Throughout the book we have indi-

Let the team work in face-to-face meetings for a better result

cated when it is important to be together and when you can do things remotely. When the team is starting the project, when they are first working together and forming into a team, when they are first understanding the data, when they are thinking through the storyboards and the design—when all the truly generative work is being done, do your best to bring your core team together. This is the best way to create a shared understanding of the user and the solution. So fly people in and go together to the customer. Book conference rooms for consecutive days. Order in food. You are trying to build a working team. Face-to-face work can be interspersed with remote work—as long as you have a good project manager and a core team of a few people to hold it altogether.

Try to create a team room located near the core team, who (best case) are colocated. A lot of the work in Contextual Design meetings produces artifacts to focus thinking; a team room lets you hang them on the wall so they're always in sight. A room

Get a dedicated space for your team to work together

invites the whole team to sketch visions together and even when working in parallel sub-teams, work in the same space so they can talk to each other and reference the data—which is on the wall.

When that room has good remote meeting tools, remote members can easily be brought into the conversation. Dedicating a room for the team for the life of the project—even if it is short—also provides a place for the stakeholders to go see what is going on in real time. Anyone who wants to catch up can browse the walls on their own, or another team member can use the walls to see what has happened. One manager told us he prefers to use the room to find out how the team is doing—he found it more immediate and more real than a status report or presentation. And a team room is a great ad to other teams for user-centered techniques. They can see the data and the design thinking and invariably, they start talking about wanting a project like that too. So don't just give the team a drive to store documents and pictures online—give them a place to collaborate.

Pick and manage the people with care—and they will perform

Last, the success or failure of any project is squarely in the hands, personalities, cognitive style, and idiosyncrasies of the team member. Pick the right people both for their technical skills and their interpersonal skills, help them become a well-functioning team by using our techniques to manage their differences, and find a truly organized project leader. You'll be guaranteed a great result.

Validating the Design

17

In Contextual Design, we use validation with paper prototypes to get user feedback quickly. Iterating with prototypes is a design tool, and testing early keeps the design on track. We like to get back into the field quickly after the vision. So keep the time from the beginning of consolidation to the first prototype interview short: 1–2 weeks for a small project or 3–4 weeks for something more complex. Even if you need to gather additional interviews to fill gaps in your knowledge, you can fit them into this timeframe. And that's when you're doing a full design process for the first time. Once the team has developed their basic product and UI structure, Contextual Design moves into a continuous process of extending and iterating the design with user feedback—a process which is likely to continue across several releases.

> *Get back to the user within weeks—don't get lost in design discussions*

If you take longer than that, either you are working out more detail than you need or you are bogged down in arguing about the design. All design work after the vision is *on the way to test*. It is not on the way to implementation. Performing product concept and structure validation before further specification can help the team let go of the need for every detail to be finalized. The quicker you get back into the field, the less the team will get attached to any part of the design.

Testing with paper prototypes validates not only the structure and preliminary user interface of the product, but it also is another way to run scenarios of use through the product to make sure it will work for the user. But in this case these scenarios come straight

Contextual Design. http://dx.doi.org/10.1016/B978-0-12-800894-2.00017-X

from the users—they use their own work or life activities and interact with the mocked-up product as though it was real. Then the designers can see where function and links need to be added and if the Interaction Patterns guide the user to the function and content they are looking for. In this way we not only test the product structure but we also give the users an experience with the proposed product that is immediately relevant to their life. They either get excited by this or not. This is the best way to find out early if the new product concept is worth building and get feedback to build a business case.

Don't worry about being perfect—you are on the way to test not ship

This iterative testing starts with rough mockups built using ordinary stationery supplies (Fig. 17.1). These prototypes are quick to build, focus the user on the product concept and structure, and invite the user to codesign. The original work on low-fidelity mockups was done at Aarhus University as part of their research into Participatory Design.[1] Karen Holtzblatt adapted these methods to software in her early work on Contextual Design.[2] Since then, the technique has been widely popularized.[3,4] We'll describe our approach in a minute, but as you read it, keep your focus on the primary value we see in paper prototyping: the ability to use the prototype to foster a design conversation, not a demo. It's the interactivity of the prototyping session, where the user is placed in his or her own context, can interact with the prototype like it's real, and can make changes in real time that gives prototype iterations their power.

Paper fosters a "let's pretend" situation for the user to try out the product

---

[1] P. Ehn and M. Kyng, "Cardboard Computers: Mocking-it-up or Hands-on the Future," in *Design at Work*, J. Greenbaum and M. Kyng (Eds.), p. 169. Hillsdale, NJ: Lawrence Earlbaum Pub. (1991).

[2] Holtzblatt, Karen, Jones, Sandra (1993): Contextual Inquiry: A Participatory Technique for System Design. In: Participatory Design: Principles and Practice, edited by Douglas Schuler and Aki Namioka. Lawrence Erlbaum Associates, Inc. Hillsdale, NJ. 1993. pages 205–206. This article mentions our use of paper prototyping—we adapted the participatory techniques at the same time as Ehn and Kyng were publishing their book.

[3] "PICTIVE—An exploration in participatory design," in *Human Factors in Computing Products CHI '91 Conference Proceedings*, 1991, pp. 225–231.

[4] Snyder, Carolyn. Paper Prototyping 2003 Morgan Kaufman.

The prototype is built so that it tests the most important issues of the design.[5] If the design is to run on mobile devices, the prototype may be implemented as smartphone-sized cards to test whether it can be useful in that size and in real life contexts (Fig. 17.2). We validate these designs with people while they are on the go, not just in their homes or offices. If the product collects and presents information, as many task support products do, real content is developed and embedded in the prototype so that users can experience having such content available at the moment of need. This helps us test content tone, length, clarity, and structure. And it lets us test how the overall product works across platforms.

Build paper mockups for every platform you will deliver the product upon

The interview is designed to mimic as closely as possible the context of real use. For example, when making new interfaces for automobiles, one team puts mockups on the dashboard of the users' own car and played prerecorded audio from an iPod and mini speaker. In the test, they drove with users in their cars, imitating the verbal and visual messages of the new system. In this way the design team saw the user's actual response in their car while driving. They discussed the user's reaction with them and, codesigning, determined the best way to communicate to a driver. In the same way, mockups for mobile devices can be presented as cards on the target device itself, so designers can see how the device affects user interaction.

The design should be tested with three to six users in a round before redesigning based on the feedback. The number of users in a round depends on the scope of the project, but you never need more than six in a round. Multiple rounds of mockup interviews and iteration allow design and testing in increasing levels of detail. Over the course of the rounds of prototype interviews, the team moves from rough representations to wireframes with increasing detail, to online clickable prototypes—possibly with a visual design treatment so that can be tested as well.

Test users in rounds alternating between test and redesign

---

[5] Lean UX embodies the same philosophy: identify and test critical points early.

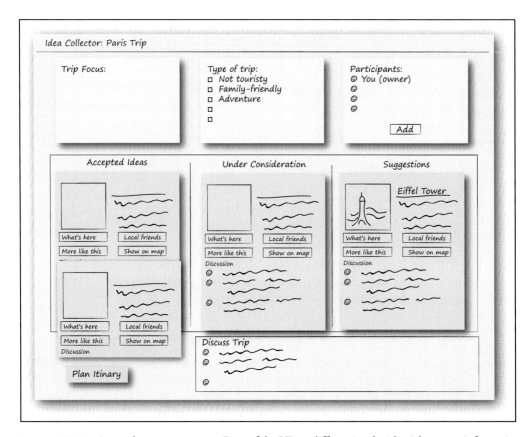

FIGURE 17.1   A sample paper prototype. Parts of the UI are differentiated with sticky notes; information is handwritten so it can be added to or changed with users on the fly. Each trip activity is on a standard-sized Post-it so that they can be manipulated individually, and new ones can easily be added in the interview. The Interaction Pattern for this page is the *Dashboard*, which is also being tested.

The Contextual Design process for prototyping is: walk through the User Environment Design to ensure it's consistent; design a wireframe-level UI using your Interaction Pattern that represents the User Environment Design and mock it up in paper; interview users using the paper mockup in their own life or work context; interpret those interviews in the design team; make changes to the User Environment Design and UI to respond to the issues; and repeat until the design stabilizes. Three rounds of testing is enough to validate the product concept, work out all the issues, finalize the product and UI structure, and build in usability. Add visual treatment in the third round or add a fourth round to test the aesthetic design and branding. In an Agile process, stories can be written and sprints started after the first round or two, with subsequent design iterations happening in parallel with development sprints.

FIGURE 17.2 A mockup of a cell phone interface, designed before touch screens became common. The prototype mimics the size of the target devices; each screen of the product is on its own card and fits into the shell so the user has the experience of seeing the information in the actual size.

BUILDING A PAPER PROTOTYPE

A primary requirement of the prototyping process is ease and speed of building. Remember that part of the goal is to make it easy to try out design options with users—if it's too hard to build the prototype, people will be less willing to use them as design tools. Off-the-shelf stationary supplies, especially sticky notes in all their varieties, are the basic components of a paper prototype.

Rapid prototyping tools[6] are so easy to use these days that it's very tempting to build with them right from the start. Resist that temptation. Even if they were as fast as paper, they won't support the same kind of codesign conversation you'll get in paper. If you're skeptical, try two or three in paper, and a few using your tool of choice. Then, you decide.

The key for a successful prototype is to put everything that might have to move during the interview on its own sticky note.

A good paper prototype is clean but looks like it can be changed

This includes pull-down menus, accordion boxes, and the objects of a direct-manipulation interface. (Anything you can drag-and-drop should be a sticky note that you can literally drag-and-drop.) The interviewer will fill in the content of the interface with the user's own data during the interview, so leave room for that. If your system is presenting content, you need to provide it written exactly as called for in the design. Print it and put it in the right place in the mockup. Take extra copies of UI elements, both to write the user's content on and so they can try out different things over the course of the interview.

If the product combines hardware and software (Fig. 17.3), use other kinds of props in addition to the paper mockup. Pens make good bar-code scanners; pen boxes make good handheld devices; and stationary boxes make good tablets. Excellent low-fidelity devices can be built with foam core. Sticky notes can be stuck to the user's own phone or tablet to test interfaces in the places and contexts of use for those devices.

The paper prototype represents the structure and the behavior of the proposed user interface. It's rough and handwritten, but neat and legible—the user needs to be able to read it. If you need to go out before all focus areas have been designed, the ones you didn't get to can be represented as a blank sticky note with a title bar—this gives enough structure to discuss the place with the user, should it be wanted. Organize the paper so that all the

---

[6] Balsamiq and Axure are two.

parts for a screen are together, with extra parts that appear on demand on a separate sheet. Put the screens in order of expected use. Make a copy of the final prototype and all its pieces for every user to be interviewed—you can copy the parts and cut them into pieces. You are pulling together a little interviewing packet complete with extra supplies for changes. Now you're ready for an interview.

Create a complete interview packet for each user—they write on the prototype!

FIGURE 17.3   A prototype for a scanning device. The foam core prototype mimics size and weight of the actual device; the picture on the top represents a small view screen for an embedded camera.

BUILDING A PAPER PROTOTYPE

The screen: Use a sheet of card stock as the background to represent the screen, in whatever size fits your platform. This gives you a stiffer base to the prototype, which is useful when manipulating the parts during the interview.

Windows and panes: Use a sheet of paper or a large sticky note of about the same size as the card you're using for a screen. In the interview, watch for issues caused by multiple overlapping windows, if you're on a desktop, or for users getting lost in multiple panes, on a touch screen.

Decorate windows with a title bar and any permanent contents. Draw a menu bar and write in the names of pull-down menus. Draw scroll bars if any.

Tables and textual content: Often useful to have this on its own piece of paper. That makes it more convenient to swap in and out, and to replace with the user's own content. Bring extra to every interview.

Pull-down menus, including hamburger menus: The name of the pull-down menu goes on the window because it's always visible. The contents of the menu go on a smaller sticky note. Write the name of the pull-down menu at the top. In the interview, keep the menu to one side and put it on the window when the user clicks on pull-down icon to simulate pulling it down.

Tool pallets and button bars: If they are permanent, draw the space for them on the window but put each tool or button icon on its own sticky note (cut these small by hand). In the interview, you'll want to talk about what needs to go on the bar or pallet and having them on their own note makes it easier to reconfigure them. It also makes them appear more manipulable and inviting to press.

If you're designing a floating pallet, put the whole thing on its own sticky note. Either draw the tools on it directly or put them on their own small notes, if you want to design exactly what goes on the pallet.

Radio buttons, check boxes, controls: Draw directly on the screen. Use highlighter if you want them to stand out.

Dialog boxes, pop-up boxes: Use smaller-sized sticky notes for these. Draw permanent content directly; use separate notes for things that may change.

Special techniques: The more interactive your design is, the more you'll want to extend these basic techniques to represent your design. Drag-and-drop is easy if you put the element you want to drag on its own sticky note, so the user can pick it up and move it. If you want to represent an overlay of information—such as annotations on a document—use clear plastic and put sticky notes on it. If you're designing a tabbed interface, use flags to represent the tabs. Play with the medium—anything that represents your intent and isn't too complicated to create or use is fair game.

RUNNING A PROTOTYPE INTERVIEW

A paper prototype interview is run by two people, one who runs the interview and moves the parts of the prototype around and a second who silently takes handwritten notes to track what is said and what is moved. Conducting the interview is very similar to a contextual interview in attitude but very different logistically. The mechanics of handling the paper prototype make it a little more complex to run. But like a contextual interview, the attitude is one of inquiry, probing into the reasons for the user's actions and generating a sense of shared discovery, cointerpretation, and codesign. The same principles that guide Contextual Inquiry guide a prototyping interview:

Context: In a contextual interview, you stay grounded by staying close to the on-going actions and real past events of when the user was performing the target activity. You can't do real "work" in a paper prototype, but you can stay grounded in real events. Either pretend to do the user's activity of the day or replay a real past event. You can also alternate between doing a real task and replaying it in the prototype:

> *Don't do a demo—work through the user's real activities*

> **User (U):** *Well you know, I'd never use your product. I run across fun destinations when I'm just browsing around the web. I wouldn't use a special tool.*

> **Designer (D):** *[Knows that their design integrates with the user's regular browser, but doesn't need to say so yet.] So show me. When was the last time you ran across an interesting site?*

> **U:** *We're planning a trip to Paris, so I'm keeping an eye out for interesting things to do. Here's one site I like a lot because they talk about nontouristy things to do. See—here's riding bicycles in the Bois du Boulogne. [Clicks link]*

> **D:** *Is this something you might do? What makes it attractive? [Writes key information for this activity onto a "browser window" sheet that's part of the prototype.]*

U: *It's outdoors, it's not typically touristy, and we all like to bike.*

D: *So, let's say this is your browser. [Puts the page representing the browser window in front of the user. Page has the plug-in widget for capturing activities.]*

U: *Okay. What's this? [Points to the widget.]*

D: *Why not try it and see?*

U: *[Touches the widget. Designer puts the sticky note representing the dialogue to capture an activity on the browser window.] You mean I can save the page right from here? Cool! [User touches the button for saving the page.]*

U: *What do I do now?*

D: *What do you want to do? Keep browsing around?*

U: *Really, I want to share this with my husband right away. If he's not up for it, there's no point in even saving the idea.*

D: *Okay, we'll let you do that. [Writes a new link, "Share…" onto the sticky note.] How about that?*

U: *That's good. What happens when I touch it?*

D: *Hmm… Maybe this. [Pulls a "trip activity" sticky note off the Idea Collector part of the prototype, puts it on a larger sticky note, writes "Share Trip Idea" across the top, and puts them in front of the user.]*

U: *That's good. So they can see what the idea is? Nice. But I want to be able to write a note too…*

The designer writes new data into the prototype to show how the interface would look with the user's own data in it. This keeps users interacting with the prototype, either touching and changing it themselves or telling the designer how to manipulate it. Don't let users drift into generalities—if they start talking about what they would like in a product, pursue a real story to see how the changes would play out. As they act out the story, invent fixes to the product to support them better. One design team working on a portable device well before smartphones were invented drove around with their user. When she bought gas, she said, "And now, I pay for it with this thing"—and she pretended to plug it into the pump. Having the device in her hand, it was easy to invent new uses for it.

Codesign depends on the user touching and interacting with the prototype

Partnership: The partnership between user and designer is around codesign of the prototype. As the user interacts with the prototype, both user and designer will discover problems. When the user raises problems or suggests different ways to do things, the designer modifies the prototype to represent the suggestion. The designer also gives the user design options by suggesting several alternative solutions to a problem they've run into.

There will often be points where the user's expectations don't match what the designer intended: "So clicking on the widget will bring up user reviews of this activity, right?" In such cases, always pursue the user's interpretation first: "Right, how should that look?" Start codesigning this new possibility immediately. You're not committed to the design you and the user come up with, but by exploring it you can find out what they are thinking. You may discover a whole new issue or approach that you hadn't thought

Pursue the user's ideas so they can see how it plays out—then show them the idea you designed in

of before. You'll take the design you work out back to the team and integrate it properly later—or at least incorporate the ideas underlying the changes. In the interview, once you've explored this other avenue with your user and come to a natural stopping point, you can return to the prototype you designed: "That was interesting. But remember back here, when you first saw these photos? Suppose I told you it just captured the idea without interrupting your browsing?" This is also a good way to handle the user's design ideas. If they are limited by their experience or skills—if their idea is just what they are used to on current websites or apps—pursue their idea until you see what they are trying to get at. Then you can draw on your wider range of options to come up with cleaner or more inventive solutions. In this way, you'll see both what the user had in mind and, when you share them, his reaction to your ideas. You'll also give the users more technology ideas they can incorporate and apply themselves.

Focus on feedback about the product and interface structure—why your design worked or didn't

Interpretation: When the user reacts to some aspect of the prototype or to the designer's ideas, the goal is to find out what they expected and why the prototype or suggestion doesn't match. It's okay to discuss their ideas—it's important to understand what they want and why, not just the specific idea they propose. Remember, just because they suggest a design change or idea doesn't mean you have to implement it—it is just another way of getting information about their intent.

In every case, you're looking to understand the structure of the user's practice and whether it matches the prototype, but you'll be talking in the language of the UI. So in this example, designer and user talk about the browser widget and the dialogue it pops up. But the solution they settle on is the one that matches the practice. The data the designer will take home is structural— do the places and functions really support the user's intent? Do the Interaction Patterns help the user see what is presented and know how to act in each place? The particular presentation might work, or might be replaced by a better mechanism that the team invents once feedback is collected. As long as the user's intent is met, the UI designer is free to redesign the structure and details of the interface.

Nonverbal reactions reveal complexity, overwhelm, and frustration

It's important that you stay open to the user's reaction (verbal *and* nonverbal), and that you be willing to respond by changing the prototype promptly. One designer took out a prototype with two alternative interfaces, one of which (her favorite) merged two focus areas in the User Environment design and was based on a calendar. When that one was placed in front of the first user, she visibly recoiled. Her reaction was clear even before she said, "Oh no, I don't want that—that's much too complicated."

Focus: As we discussed above, the User Environment Design represents the team's claim that this product will improve the users' practice. The focus of a prototyping interview is to test that claim, and fix the product when it's wrong.

Keeping to this focus is hard, because it's easier for people to assimilate changes and see them as a minor adjustment than to recognize a challenge to the basic structure or assumptions of the product. It's important for the designer to be looking not for validation, but for the ways in which the product fails. Taking this attitude makes it more likely that designers will recognize a fundamental challenge.

The User Environment Design gives designers a way to listen, which also makes it easier to break existing assumptions. With the structure of the User Environment Design supporting them, designers can tell whether a suggested change affects only the UI, the Interaction Pattern, or whether it's really challenging the structure of the product. When the User Environment Design was created and when the prototype was reviewed, designers identified specific tests to check for during the interview (we'll discuss this more below). Where the team considered alternative designs, the prototype tests the chosen option; if the user has problems with it, the designer can introduce the alternative design on the fly and see if it fares better.

Focus on how the product fails to support the intent—not just validation

Finally, focus keeps the conversation on the right level of design. Early in the process the prototypes test the structure of the User Environment Design and the Interaction Pattern, not the UI details. If the user suggests changes to low-level UI detail—a new icon, a different word—the designer just writes them in. They don't need to be discussed—they aren't in the focus—but the user does need to be heard, so write it down. Later, when the prototypes are intended to test the specific Interaction Pattern and UI detail, the designer will discuss and suggest alternative UI mechanisms. The same is true if the entire focus of the project is to clean up an existing product's UI—the prototyping interviews will focus on UI issues from the beginning.

THE STRUCTURE OF AN INTERVIEW

Interviewing around a paper prototype has very much the same structure as a normal contextual interview. The difference is that after the initial discussion, you move to working with the prototype. The interview goes as follows:

Setup.   Prototype interviews, like any Contextual Inquiry, need to be set up in advance so that everyone knows what to expect. Users can be people the team has talked to already, or entirely new users—new users have the advantage of expanding your user pool. In this way, some large projects have worked with 40–60 users over all the iterations they did in the course of the project. Interview three to six users with a prototype, then review the feedback from them and redesign the prototype before going out again.

Don't do an interview with people who don't do the activity supported in the prototype

It's especially important to make sure a prototype interview is set up with people who actually do the activities the prototype supports. The user needs to have current or recent examples of doing the activity they can replay in the product, or there's no way to test the prototype with them. In setting up the interviews, find out what the users are doing and make sure the activities you care about are covered.

And set the expectation that you'll run the interview in the location where they do the activity—work, home, or on the go. The context and information or artifacts in that location will stimulate a more realistic use of the prototype.

For the team, the designers who will run the interviews need to be familiar with the User Environment Design and the paper prototypes. Review the prototype as a team and identify additional tests—issues which the prototype will test because of the way the prototype was designed. Perhaps the designer put lots of buttons and other interface components on the screen—then you'll find out if the user is prone to overwhelm. Perhaps the designer added a strong visual element that separates what should be one focus area in two— then you'll test whether dividing the focus areas. Whatever the issues are, note them along with the design choices you decided to test in developing the User Environment Design. These will refine your focus for the interviews.

Introduction.   Start by introducing yourself and the focus of your design, including the kind of activities the design supports. It's not necessary to describe the design itself at this point. You just want to start the user thinking about the kind of activity you'll want him to do.

Then find out about the user, how the target activity is part of their work or life, and the particular relevant tasks they have to do or have done recently. At this point you're looking for a *hook* to get you into the prototype. You're looking for all the different situations, current or in the recent past, which your product would support. You may not find one; it's possible that this person simply isn't doing the activity you support right now. But that's rare if the interviews are well set up. Usually, you'll find a couple of situations which are good candidates for recreating or doing for the first time in the prototype.

The paper prototyping situation: let's pretend

Transition.   Once you've found a set of appropriate situations to recreate, choose one to start with and transition to the prototype interview. Bring out the prototype and introduce it. Give a brief summary of the screen they start with: "Here's an app that lets you collect ideas for a vacation trip." Do *not* do a whole walk-through of the prototype. As you introduce it, write in the specific data for the user—if they're in the middle of planning for a trip then write in places they are considering. If not, write in places from their last trip—or leave it blank and start planning a new trip. In any case the UI should show what the user would see at that point in the process.

Don't walk through the product in detail—jump into the part relevant to this user

The amount of discussion needed to introduce the product depends on how much change you're introducing to the practice—if it's small, you can go right into the prototype; if large, you'll have to introduce your approach. "This product organizes your travel planning by giving you a place to collect ideas and then turn them into a concrete plan for the trip." That would be sufficient to introduce the user to our Travel Concierge.

The interview.   Once you have the prototype out and ready, move the user into interacting with it. If you're reproducing a recent event, suggest that he replay his actions in the prototype and you'll play computer, making the product work like it should. Or get him to start interacting with the prototype by inviting him to explore, describing what he sees and what he thinks it will do. You might run the real task in parallel in the old or a competitive product—then switch back to the prototype to show how the new product will work. If the product is supposed to show data or content, using the content from doing the real task.

If the product doesn't work, start redesigning alternatives with the user

Give the user a pen so he can modify parts of the prototype as you go. Some users will dive right into doing their activity; others will want to poke around and explore the different parts of the product. Let them follow whichever style is natural for them.

If the user asks for an explanation of some part of the product, you can give them a one- or two-sentence description. This is an important place to listen for the "no." If you get a blank stare, and have to keep elaborating on the explanation in hopes that they will get it, you have a concept that doesn't work. If your user can't figure out what an "idea collector" is, or can't understand how they might use it to capture ideas while browsing, it's too big a mismatch with their current practice to be useful. Using the product will require huge amounts of retraining. Don't try to force it to work—start looking for alternatives.

Run paper prototype interviews in pairs

Always run prototype interviews in pairs; it's too hard to try and manage the prototype, interact with the user, and keep notes at the same time. The notes of a prototype interview are critical to reconstructing it with the team later—it will be hard to recover the sequence of events from just the prototype, and an audiotape misses too much. It usually works best to assign one person to be notetaker, who writes down what is happening and does not interact with the user. The interviewer runs the interview and manipulates the prototype. It's usually not necessary to videotape the interview. Video can be valuable if you are communicating back to a design team that is not going on their own user interviews and doesn't really understand them. Video can also be critical if you are looking at problems in the detailed interaction with the UI. Otherwise, we've found the extra effort of videotaping gets in the way of rapid and frequent prototyping.

While running the interview, if you're replaying a past event, keep referring to that event to keep the interview grounded. Ask how the user how the product should respond, and when she says something you don't expect, design on the fly, extending the design you have and pulling in parts from other focus areas in the prototype when they're useful.

In our example above, the user suggested something the designers hadn't thought of—sharing an activity idea immediately before even saving it to the Idea Collector. So the designer follows the idea by adapting and repurposing elements of the design. The design already had a way to summarize an activity, so the designer reused it. User and designer pursue the direction the user proposed, sharing the idea. This is a challenge to the User Environment Design and to the flow of the activity, but that's for later—after the interview is being interpreted the team can think about User Environment Design implications and redesign as necessary. The designer can also return to the question later in the interview, if that makes sense:

Ground the interview by replaying specific events— codesign to make it work

D: *So now you've seen this whole Idea Collector piece…*

U: *Yeah, it's good. I like that.*

D: *But look, remember how we started with sharing the bicycling idea with your husband? Let's say you've done that, but he hasn't responded. That shouldn't show up here yet, right?*

U: *No, I'm going to want to see it. I want to know that I suggested it and he hasn't responded.*

D: *So where should that go?*

U: *Let's see… probably here in the "Under Consideration" section. We are considering it, after all, until he shoots it down.*

The user returned to the original design idea when she added a new intent. Once she had a chance to work through using the product in a pretend situation, she could look back, see the implications of her original suggestion, and provide further feedback.

Wrap-up. The final wrap-up of a prototype interview starts with a simple summary of the key points that came up during the interview. Summarize the points, and if it's useful summarize any parts of the prototype you didn't get to, for a quick reaction. But this won't be contextual data, so don't spend a lot of time on it.

Check the value explicitly—and find out what to ship first

Finally, check the emotional response to the product and the sales point. Ask, "Do you like this product? Will you buy or recommend it? How much will you pay for it?" You're not looking for a real, committed figure here. You're looking for a sense of how valuable and exciting they think the product really is. And you can uncover their expectations and threshold figures for cost. You can also ask them for the top three features they think are the most important—now that they used the product they can tell you from experience. Then say, "If the team can only implement one which should it be?" Now the user is helping you prioritize. At the end of the interview, you'll get a response based on experience with the product, influenced by excitement generated by the interview. In this way, the response is better grounded than you can get from a focus group or demo.

This is the general pattern of a prototype interview. If you're tracking an ongoing task rather than replaying an old one, the user will alternate between doing some real tasks and then redoing it in the prototype; if you're replaying past activity you'll be repeating all steps of the activity in the mockup. Just like in a retrospective field interview, look for any artifacts (like receipts of air tickets or hotel reservations) to help the user remember what they were doing. Designer and user discuss the prototype, using real interactions relevant to activities that matter to the user to drive the conversation. From time to time they invent some alternative, elaborate it for a while, then come back to the prototype as designed. The designer uses her knowledge of the User Environment Design, Interaction Pattern, and technology to drive the interview—if you can recognize when the user is challenging some aspect of the overall design you can probe for details immediately, instead of having to wait for another interview.

Later in the design process, when you trust the structure of the product represented in the prototype, concentrate more on the specific Interaction Pattern and UI elements and on enforcing the limits of a real product. When the user tries to do something the design doesn't allow, instead of taking it as an opportunity for codesign, act like a real CPU: beep at him or her. See if he or she can figure out how to make the product work given the limitations you're building in.

Exercise different parts of the prototype by switching activities. Follow the task the user is doing or recreating until it's done or has moved beyond the scope covered by the prototype. Then choose another situation to follow that will exercise any parts of the prototype that haven't been touched yet. Usually, you won't get to all the parts of the prototype in a single interview and that's okay; end the interview after 2 hours and save the rest of the prototype for the next user.

Going online.   The first two rounds of prototyping should be in paper and in person, for all the reasons we listed above. But after the basic structure has been stabilized you'll start to be interested in details of the interaction and UI that are hard to reveal in paper. With modern prototyping tools—and modern tools for building real UIs—it soon gets simpler to model these interactions in working code than in paper. By this point you've seen the users in their own contexts many times, so you have a good understanding of it—and the issues you're looking at depend less on context anyway. This is a good time to start testing your visual design—if you want to test more than one look you can do two versions and get feedback on the look as well.

Create an online prototype when product structure and UI architecture stabilize

You may use your online prototype in person or, if it is a web-based product, you may run a remote interview. At this point your product structure, Interaction Patterns, and basic content and function are set. So the focus of these interviews is more on visual design and low-level user interface elements. For elements of the design that run on mobile devices, you'll do best to run at least some of the interviews in person with running prototypes on the device. That way you'll get a better feel for how the user interacts not just with the screen, but with the whole device. You'll also be able to better see device-specific issues—use of screen real estate, touch versus mouse, swiping, and all the rest.

The prototype you test may range from pure images to working code, and you'll adapt the interview accordingly. At the beginning, you may have UI images in Adobe Illustrator or a similar product, and you just screenshare with the user, showing the UI by turning layers on or off. You may use a prototyping tool that implements some of the interactivity, in which case you might prefer to give the user control and watch as they use the prototype. Especially in an Agile context, you may have working code which can access real content, in which case you'll definitely want to let them run the interaction. In any case, tailor the prototype to your user's interests if you can—if you found out when setting up the interview that they are interested in a Caribbean vacation, don't show them a prototype full of European cathedrals.

An in-person interview using an online prototype is run like a paper prototype session. For a remote interview, use a screen-sharing session so you can both see the same thing. It's possible but harder to host the prototype on a web server and look at it together without sharing screens—only do that if screen sharing is impossible.

Test remotely if you don't need to watch interaction with the device

For the introduction, get the user to tell you what they're doing and look for a current or recent task that you can replay in your prototype. You usually won't be able to actually change the content, but you'll continually refer back to their actual tasks as examples. Get the user to bring up and show examples of what they do.

When you're ready for the transition, bring up your prototype. Let them tell you what it does and what they see. If they want to explore, either give them control or tell them you are their cursor and have them tell you what to click on.

Then follow a task. As each screen comes up, let them react to it and describe how they would use it. As necessary make the connection to their data and your prototype by saying things such as, "The main area there where you're seeing beaches would be full of snorkeling tours, since that's what you're looking for right now."

Since your focus is on the UI and visual design, now probe for responses to layout, color, and imagery. Listen for the emotional reaction caused by UI choices: "Sounds like you're finding this screen a bit stressful or confusing. Do you think all the red is making that worse?" Listen for places where the interactivity of the UI is causing confusion—controls that only appear on hover, accordion folds that aren't obviously able to open, trays that are nearly invisible when shut. Do not jump in quickly with explanations, or you'll never find out about these issues.

Focus the last rounds of interviews on lower-level UI and the visual design

Wrap up as for any other prototype interview.

THE INTERPRETATION SESSION

The last part of a prototype interview process is the same as for a contextual interview: the interviewers bring the data—their own and the notetaker's handwritten notes and the marked up paper prototype—back to a design team and replay the interview for them so that everyone can see what happened and offer their different perspectives. This Interpretation Session is focused narrowly on identifying the issues raised by the interview.

Prototype Interpretation Sessions are run like contextual interview Interpretation Session

Issues are captured as notes by a notetaker, but in general we don't build an affinity from these notes. Most of them are about specific issues in the interface, so a general technique like an Affinity isn't needed. Instead, capture them in a spreadsheet, associating each note with the focus area and section it relates to. See Fig. 17.4.

Round	Note#	User	Interp Note	Note Type	Focus Area	Section or Component	Resolution Type	Decisions/actions taken
1	1	U2	V: Likes the idea of the "capture an idea" widget embedded in the browser	UE	Browser Widget		No change	
1	2	U2	Wants to be able to share an idea immediately from the browser widget	UE	Browser Widget		Modify-UE and UI	Add function to allow this
1	3	U2	Wants to jump immediately from the browser widget to the Idea Collector	UE	Browser Widget		Modify-UE and UI	Add function to allow this
1	4	U2	DI: Change the widget from a simple "capture this" to an ever-present representation of the Idea Collector	DI	Browser Widget		Not enough Info-keep testing	Requires a redesign, and more users want to work
1	5	U2	V: Didn't get why the there are multiple columns for ideas at first, but liked it once we worked through it	UI	Idea Collector		Change-UI only	Put some labels in the UI

FIGURE 17.4   Notes captured during a paper prototype Interpretation Session. The columns show: which round of interviews the note came from; user; the note itself ("V" means it's a validation of the design); whether the note introduces new practice, or addresses the User Environment Design or UI; the focus area affected; the section or component of the Interaction Pattern affected, if any; and how the issue will be resolved.

Most of the data from an early prototype interviews will be structural issues for the User Environment Design. Capture these and tag them with the Focus Area they relate to. Do the same for reactions to content. You may also get feedback on the Interaction Pattern used for layout and lower-level detail of the user interface, even though this is not the primary focus of the first round of testing—capture them and tag them with the User Environment Design focus area and section. They will be dealt with after the User Environment Design structural issues are refined. Any issue that has to do with layout, presentation, graphic elements, interactivity, or wording is a UI issue. There will also be some issues, which describe aspects of the user's practice or raise new issues that weren't seen before but aren't directly related to the prototype. Flag these with "UP" for user practice, but don't try to resolve them in the meeting. Afterward, you can add them to the affinity or update an Experience Model as necessary to capture the new practice elements. If there's any disagreement about where an issue goes, move it upstream—put it on the User Environment Design in preference to the UI, and flag it as user practice in preference to either. This whole session is good practice in separating conversations, as each conversation has its own model and its own place on the wall.

Separate your conversations by sorting feedback into the diagram they are about

Throughout the Interpretation Session, the primary task is to see behind the user's reaction to the UI to understand the underlying issue. If the user was overwhelmed, was that because the focus area wasn't clean, the design didn't match his approach, or was the UI for that part of the product unnecessarily complex? Examine the user's actions and words to understand what his reaction meant to the design. After multiple iterations, the product structure stabilizes and the interviews will focus more on the Interaction Pattern and UI and finally, visual design. In these Interpretation Sessions you will see User Environment Design issues drop off and an increase in feedback on the layer of the design being tested.

DESIGN ITERATION

When a design has been tested with three to four users, it's time to iterate. The issues raised by the users are grouped in the Interpretation Session so related issues can be addressed together. Changes to Contextual Design Models may affect the User Environment Design, and changes to the User Environment Design may affect the Interaction Pattern and user interface detail. No one wants to spend hours on some aspect of the user interface only to discover later that a change to the User Environment Design obviates that whole part of the interface. So the first issues to deal with are those related to the models—look those over and decide whether any of the new practice poses a sufficiently serious challenge to your design that you should do new storyboards. (If you did your initial research well, this should be rare.)

For the models, collect the issues from all users for each type of model. Organize them to see what they imply for the model. Extend it with any new aspects of user practice: new activities in the Day in the Life, new or expanded identities, new relationships, or collaboration strategies. If

Address practice issues first, then product structure and then UI

this new data affects the focus of the design, you'll deal with it as part of addressing the User Environment Design; otherwise, it becomes part of your permanent representation of your user population.

Then turn to the User Environment Design. First consider whether any of the model changes affect the design, and if so identify which parts they affect. Then look across the data from all the users and ask what the primary structural issues are. Look for ways to redesign the overall product to address these issues. Then start working on sets of issues part by part, starting with the parts that are involved in the most important and far-reaching issues. Collect the issues across all users for each of those parts, and consider how to redesign them to address the issues and the new information from the models. Use quick storyboards, if necessary, to help you think through particular activities in the changed product. Go on from section to section of the User Environment Design until you've addressed all the issues you need to. You may decide that some issues are at too low a level of detail to bother with yet, or affect some part of the product which is too peripheral. There's no point in spending a lot of time to get a part of the design right if it's only going to be cut later. Work to get the core product stable, then prioritize what to ship, and then do the details.

Add storyboards and restructure the User Environment Design as part of the redesign

If you build the first prototype on the core storyboards only, you may have additional storyboards to roll into the product for your second round. Do so at this time and restructure the User Environment Design so that any new function, content, and changes to the Interaction Patterns are incorporated. Restructuring the product tends to pull apart the design, so finish with a User Environment Design Walk-through to pull it back together again. Check the Interaction Pattern for implied changes too. Clean up the loose ends and make sure the design is reasonably clean.

Now, roll the User Environment Design changes forward into a redesign of the Interaction Patterns, including any changes needed based on user feedback at that level. First look for broad issues that affect the Interaction Pattern architecture as it was designed. Did the base structure work? Did your Interaction Patterns guide users through each place? Did you achieve overall consistency? If you need to change the base metaphor or redesign Interaction Patterns, do those first, before addressing any of the lower-level UI issues.

Finally, collect the lower-level user interface feedback and redesign all aspects of the prototype. Review the new design together, and mock the whole thing up in paper. Do a second round of testing, review, and redesign. Your third round of testing can have a more detailed UI and, if you choose, a visual design. At this point you may put the prototype online. This round may be run in parallel with your first development sprint in an Agile process.

COMPLETING THE DESIGN

This is the iterative, user-centered process of Contextual Design. As you expand your design to address more and more of your vision, the product will change and flex to accommodate new issues. The core design may be quite stable, but when you move to address a new area of practice, you'll collect more user data—though it's likely to be tightly focused on just the aspect you want to address. You may set up interviews to capture data for an activity you were never able to observe until this point. Or you may discover the opportunity to get this data in the middle of a prototype interview. If it's important, set the prototype aside for a bit and do a regular Contextual Interview to get the data you need. Then return the interview to the prototype. Later, in the Interpretation Session, move to capturing Contextual Inquiry-style notes when you hit that part of the interview. You may choose to add them to your Affinity or consolidated models later.

Throughout these iterations, you're always using the prototype to drive user visits and keep the team grounded in real user data. Returning to the user every 10 days to 2 weeks keeps the team focused and moving forward; in our experience lack of regular contact with users is a primary reason teams lose focus and break into arguments with each other. A prototyping approach to design keeps you going.

Return to the user every 10–14 days to keep yourselves moving forward

This iterative design process continues until the team is sure it has a workable design. Usually after two to three iterations of a part of the User Environment Design with users, that part is pretty stable. The number of structural issues fall off and UI issues start to predominate. This is your signal that the structure is pretty much right. The same thing happens with the UI architecture—after a round or two, the basic set of Interaction Patterns should be stable. With the product and layout structure stabilized you can concentrate on UI details. And if you are presenting content, you keep iterating its structure and tone. With each iteration you can extend the prototype to test the structure of another part of the product while getting detailed feedback on more stable parts as well. The part that has stabilized can also be moved simultaneously to implementation design and code. Prioritize what parts of the product to deliver, as we describe in Chapter 18, and build a shipping User Environment Design and set of Interaction Patterns for the next release. This becomes your working requirements specification.

An iterative design process easily merges with an iterative implementation process

When you move through a design in this way you can be confident that you've understood the requirements and have designed the appropriate product structure. Development of the product can proceed through the implementation and testing of running code in much the same way that we've tested prototypes. This maintains the user contact while implementation progresses. The iterative prototyping process merges with an iterative implementation process that coordinates all the parts of the team to deliver on the vision.

PROTOTYPING ON YOUR OWN

Prototyping is a key design skill no matter your situation. When you're working on an existing product, it's likely to be the first technique you use. No matter how big or small your design, it's easy to mock it up in paper and take it out to test. But when you're not prototyping as part of a full Contextual Design process, some things will change.

Most importantly, a prototype that isn't based on the full Contextual Design process will uncover more fundamental problems than we lead you to expect here. Rather than predominantly identifying UX and UI issues, you may find there are fundamental mismatches between your product and the practice. You'll want to capture this information—even if you can't use it right away, your product isn't going anywhere. You'll want the information when the next major version comes along.

So organize your prototyping interviews with the intention of gathering user practice data as well as prototype feedback. During the introduction, look for tasks relevant to your part of the process, and then do some inquiry into those activities, either as retrospective accounts or ongoing work. Look for mismatches between the assumptions built into your prototype and what your user is trying to do. Explore these with the user; talk about the mismatch and what the user will have to do to get any value out of your design while looking at the prototype. Modify the prototype as usual, looking both for what will really solve the problem and for solutions that fit with your scope.

Afterward share the feedback with the larger organization. Talk to your Product Manager and others who set overall product direction about the problems you see. Don't just present problems—talk about possible solutions too, especially solutions you worked out with the user. Then, in the short term, do the best you can with the part of the product you do control. You are planting seeds that come from user data suggesting that a redesign should be on the roadmap. Don't nag or evangelize—just share data continuously. They may eventually invite you to lead the redesign.

Another change from the full Contextual Design process is that you're more likely to have running code that provides a framework for your prototype and assets that make it easy to produce a prototype that incorporates the final look. When you're doing a small modification to a larger product, it's fine to start with a more detailed prototype—you're looking for feedback on user interface and interaction right from the start. But print it and take it out in paper, even if an online prototype is possible. You want to be able to modify it in the moment. And take out sticky notes, flags, and the rest of your prototyping kit—if you discover a big mismatch, you'll want to fall back on less detailed prototyping and sketch solutions with the user.

Prioritization and Rollout

18

Just about any Contextual Design project needs to do a prioritization step. User practice is seamless and complete, and we seek to make our design for that practice seamless and complete—which means it's nearly always larger than we can ship in a single version. Fortunately, all the work done by the team to this point means that prioritization and rollout, like all the rest of the project, can be based on user data.

Choosing what to put in each release is a team and communication challenge. It requires your interdisciplinary team to agree with each other and with your stakeholders on what's important. But this is the same challenge we have been dealing with throughout the book. We've talked about how a team needs to work together and built consensus on what the user issues are and what the design response should be. We will depend on that consensus now as we move to ship. Without it, the teams argue right up to the ship date about what should be in or out; individuals slip in things they think are important; UX and engineering argue over what makes a good user experience—balancing technical constraints against real support for the user's intent. Product management has one mandate, user experience another, and engineering yet a third. But all product choices depend on three things: what will work for the user; what is technically possible in a reasonable time frame; and what is good for the business. The business will only support products that are

> *Prioritization is a people problem: all relevant players must agree*

Contextual Design. http://dx.doi.org/10.1016/B978-0-12-800894-2.00018-1

consistent with its core mission, able to make money now and into the future, and forward the business's market message. All the players must work together to get the right product out the door. So any prioritization session must create agreement between product management, UX, and engineering.

Many methodologies have been tried over the years to aid this conversation, but there's no way out of it.[1] In our experience, the best way to ensure that requirements are correct is to use a user-centered process such as Contextual Design because it focuses the cross-functional team on making decisions with data, not opinion. With data in hand, much conflict is avoided because the user need is clear, the business value is explored, and engineering is involved at least from visioning forward, so nothing proposed is totally impossible to implement. But now we must be very practical and focused on the short term. Given the current constraints of technology, time, and platform, and given the product design as we envisioned and tested it, what is the best first release? What will deliver value, make money, and can be built in a reasonable time?

In Contextual Design we plan our rollout based on the product concepts we identified after visioning, as enriched during the Cool Drilldown, worked out with storyboarding, captured in the User Environment Design and Interaction Patterns and refined through iterative prototyping. The resulting User Environment Design now represents the full product concept, based on the team's understanding of the users' world. It is the

Be a data-driven organization—choose informed by user data

basis for breaking down the overall concept into parts which can be shipped in a series of releases or divided among teams or individuals for parallel development. Because the User Environment Design shows all parts of the product (or suite of apps and products) in relationship to each other, it's a basis for planning as well as a basis for design. It also has the Interaction Patterns and example interfaces from the prototypes available to help envision how the defined function should be laid out. Together these artifacts act as a high-level requirements document appropriate for guiding planning. Recognizing that the team was likely to produce more than

---

[1] Even Agile methods don't get you out of the prioritization conversation. Agile depends on a prioritized backlog of user stories. But how did those stories get prioritized?

could be shipped in a single release, the team did not need to specify every detail of the design. So the User Environment Design is at the correct level of definition to be used as a planning tool.

Not only will most products need to be delivered over a series of releases, most products don't stand alone. They work together with other products or underlying systems to support a whole activity, work task, or business process. Even small apps will share data with other apps and plug into all the mechanisms of the host platform—messaging, alerts, sharing, and so forth. And companies don't care only about individual applications or products—they're often looking for ways to tie their different products together into a unified strategy for supporting their target market or business. This suite constitutes their larger market message, inviting customers to sign up to their overall branding vision. So any release must be thought of as a collection of products which taken together supports a coherent part of life.

The User Environment Design is a planning tool

The challenge for the team is to define releases that keep the users' practice coherent and can be implemented by the people available in reasonable time. It's easier to keep releases coherent with the User Environment Design, which shows the subsystems, their parts, and their relationships. The User Environment Design guides planning by breaking the design into natural product chunks, relevant to the user, which can be considered independently. Whether each chunk represents a small part of a single product or a complete application in its own right, the User Environment Design shows what's going on in that part and how it relates to the rest of the system. Based on this, a team can organize and plan their development approach.

Define a release to be delivered in a reasonable time that keeps the users' practice coherent

PLANNING A SERIES OF RELEASES

These days, customers won't wait years to see a first version of a product—or even a much-anticipated update. Businesses will have found other vendors, or their needs will have changed so much that the product will no longer be useful. Consumers have come to expect continuous updates of their web and mobile applications. With the ability to release over the cloud, customers expect delivery on a promise in a timely way. Once they might not have been happy to be pushed multiple releases a month, continuously disrupting their user experience—but Facebook, Adobe, Amazon, and every cloud-enabled service out there has trained them to expect it. They surely aren't interested in struggling along with a product that is not up to modern standards. All software—consumer, business, and internal—has to respond to the new standards set by modern tools and the way they embody the Cool Concepts. So any release must not only provide value to the user but also meet modern expectations for the user experience.

All customers want quick product releases—no one is willing to wait years

It's not even good engineering to spend years producing the maximal solution—any product will miss the mark to some degree. The sooner there's a version out there, the sooner the team can correct their mistakes and build on the new practice that users will invent around the new product. So taking a long time to ship is not good business and it's not good for the user, either. But what is the correct size and scope of a release? What is too big to deliver in a reasonable time? What is too little and uninteresting to be worth it—an annoying upgrade taking over your mobile device and slowing down your users? Getting the release right-sized is the goal of any planning session.

It's a good goal to have a first release out in under a year, even for significant projects. This release sets the users' first impression of the product and the organization that delivered it. The product should make a splash in the market or make a significant contribution to the users' practice. But it also needs to hang together as a coherent way of working. Every function interacts with other functions in the design—it's a waste to do large amounts of work to ship a function and none to ship the other parts of the system that make it useful. The last-minute sessions to decide exactly what will make it into a particular version are the most painful—what are the criteria for choosing what to cut? The last feedback from a user group? The most recent customer to call his or her account representative on the carpet? Whoever shouts loudest on the engineering team? Teams need a process for deciding what functions are most important for the work of the user and how to deliver them in chunks that keep the work coherent.

With the right User Environment Design, you have the bigger picture of what you want your product to deliver to the user. This gives you a goal to strive for and a direction to your development. It helps you define a series of releases, each leading you closer to the vision, and each deliverable in a reasonable time frame. For product companies, creating a larger vision and delivering to it over a series of releases means you have a coherent market message. Reveal the vision as your strategic direction, and then each release is not only useful in its own right but is also another down payment toward your commitment to the market. Instead of selling individual features, you can sell product directions that address problems people experience in their work. Everyone—marketing, sales, services, and development—can push their work in this common direction.

The User Environment Design shows the full product concept and helps you carve it up

Fig. 18.1 shows a User Environment Design for the Travel Concierge design we visioned in Chapter 8. The layout, reinforced with the top brackets, shows two of the four product concepts we identified at that point—the Trip Planner and the Idea Collector. But since this is a User Environment Design laying out the structure of the product, not just a set of concepts, it's also identified the Activity Explorer Focus Area as a utility component that supports both the Travel Companion and the Trip Planner.

Focus areas work together to support tasks or roles— ship them together

So a User Environment Design is comprised of a set of product concepts, each organizing a set of Focus Areas relevant to the product concept. Each of these concepts identifies as a coherent set of function that could be shipped together to address a primary user intent. But within each product concept, some aspects are more critical than others. Some function is core—drop that and you might as well not ship the concept at all. Other function is good to have, but can be considered an add-on. In Fig. 18.1, for example, the Itinerary Comparer is certainly good to have, since the design

1. Idea Capture Widget

Purpose: Capture cool trip ideas during normal internet browsing.

(Embedded as plugin in standard internet browsers.)

Functions

- User can capture
  - Whole page contents
  - Page URL
  - Location page refers to
- User can capture to
  - New trip
  - Current trip
  - "Bucket list"—wish list for future

2. Idea Collector

Purpose: Collect ideas in preparation for an as-yet-to-be-defined trip.

Functions

Trip Overview

- User can set trip goal
- User can set type of trip (adventure, cultural, family fun)
- User can set type of destination or actual destination (beach, cultural capital, mountains, Paris)

Suggested Activities

- System shows possible activities that fit with the type of trip
- User can follow a link to see more details about the suggestion (3)
- System shows activities suggested by participants and friends (if allowed)
- User can accept a suggestion (the activity moves to the "Under Consideration" list
- User can reject a particular suggestion
- User can reject a suggestion all similar suggestions

Under Consideration

- System shows activities with high-level detail
- User can follow a link to see more details about an activity
- User can follow a link to see more activities like the suggested activity (4)
- User can vote for or against an activity
- User can discuss an activity with other trip participants and friends
- Trip Owner can set a deadline for a vote

Accepted Ideas

- System shows activities that have been accepted for the trip
- [Includes all function under "Under Consideration" except voting]
- User can plan an itinary based on the accepted ideas (6)

Trip Participants

- System shows all participants: owner, participants, and friends
- User can invite new participants (5)

3. Manage Participants

Purpose: Invite people to share in the planning for a trip and control what they can do

Functions

- User can invite a person
  - To come along as a participant
  - To advise on the trip
- System shows known people from social media or past trips

4. Activity Explorer

Purpose: Show an activity so the user can decide if it's right for them and can find alternatives

Functions

[TBS]

5. Activity Comparer

Purpose: Compares several activities against a set of shared criteria

Functions

[TBS]

7. Whole-Trip Planner

Purpose: Lay out a workable itinary for a trip, given a set of starting ideas.

Functions

- On first use, system lays out accepted ideas in time, including travel to and from the location. If dates have been set, system accounts for the opening hours of activity destinations.
- On subsequent use, system shows the itinary as the user has defined it to date
- System shows each day of the trip with activities for each day
- System shows free time so not every minute is scheduled
- System shows alternate itineraries under consideration
- User can ask the system to generate a new itinary based on current trip criteria
- User can compare itineraries (7) [more...]

8. Single-Day Planner

Purpose: Plan the activities for a single day, given a set of starting ideas and a set of constraints.

Functions

- On first use, system lays out accepted activities in the day, accounting for the opening hours of activity destinations.
- On subsequent use, system shows the day's itinerary as the user has defined it to date...

9. Itinerary Generator

Purpose: Lay out a workable itinary for a trip, given a set of starting ideas and the participants' preferences.

Functions

- System shows itinerary laid out by the system
- System shows metrics on the itinerary: cost, free time, travel time, etc.
- User can move activities around [more...]

10. Itinerary Comparer

Purpose: Lay out a workable itinary for a trip, given a set of starting ideas.

Functions

- System shows itineraries side by side so the user can compare them
- System shows summary metrics on each itinerary: cost, free time, travel time, etc. [more...]

Figure 18.1 A User Environment Design for the Trip Travel Concierge, showing two of the product concepts. Before storyboarding, the team decided this was the most important part of the product to ship first and focused all their design effort here.

lets the user set up multiple alternative itineraries—but it's not a must-have. The user could simply look from one to the other if we don't provide it.

Having structured the User Environment Design into coherent parts relevant to supporting the user, we can use its structure to engage everyone in a conversation about what should be in a release.

Ship the core first—nice to have functions can be shipped later

We can look at the User Environment Design from a marketing point of view, asking what kind of package would make a market splash. So The Trip Planner is a coherent product concept, but will shipping it, by itself, have much impact? It's just another organization tool. And thinking about the Cool Concepts, does it really address them in any interesting way?

But add the Idea Suggester and we have added the Direct-into-Action principle of "think for me": a way of suggesting activities and locations that fit the users' interests without having to ask. Those interests also reflect and reinforce the user's identity by suggesting activities that support their core identity elements. Now we have a smart app that helps the user explore, not just an organization tool. So adding the core function of the Idea Suggester to the Trip Planner *might* make a splash in the market—and that might be a better first product than the Planner on its own.

Another way to prioritize a product is to deliver coherent support for a role, job type, responsibility, or task. Once we've shipped our V1, we might notice that we've done little to support the Cool Concept of Connection. So we might choose to add the roles of coplanner and trip participant, turning trip planning into a collaborative activity. That might be a good V2. Note that adding collaboration and connection will augment functionality of each of our product concepts—the Trip Planner (many people can view and add), the Idea Suggester (people can suggest, and vote or comment on other suggestions), and the Travel Companion (adding ideas, photos, and updates during the trip). When designing a release to support a new role, look across the whole User Environment Design to identify function that supports that role, wherever it may be.

Because the User Environment Design represents the system structurally, it helps the team see the parts of the system that

THE USER ENVIRONMENT DESIGN AND COTS PRODUCTS: SUPPORTING IT BUSINESS DECISIONS

Not only can the User Environment Design identify the parts you will build, but also the parts you want to buy from vendors as commercial off-the-shelf (COTS) products or as 3rd party components of your final solution. The User Environment Design defines requirements for the acquisition, showing what it must do, how it must be structured, and how it must fit with the other parts of your system. Sharing the storyboards helps your vendors see the motivation behind your requirements. These scenarios may have been central to internal buy-in—so you violate them at your peril!

In one case, an IT shop designed its desired solution directly from a vision and storyboards, representing it in a User Environment Design. Then they brought vendors in, showed them the User Environment Design, and invited them to bid on delivering it using their products. The vendors had to prove they could customize their system to support the structure and functions specified in the User Environment Design. They chose the vendor who was most successful at showing that, with reasonable modifications, they could support the most of the design the team had specified.

In this case the Interaction Design Patterns remained very rough since the team knew that they would have little influence on the overall UX of the bought application—unless they required the vendor to customize that too. But rough Interaction Design Patterns still show how to group function in a place. This provides more information for evaluating the vendors under consideration. Does their built-in user experience structure the layout of the screen in reasonable ways? If not, you might consider another vendor.

might become reasonable releases. But there are many ways to cut a system—by product concept, by role, by intent, and more. The team needs to be in a dialog about the different ways to break up the User Environment Design. This will be affected by whether or not the User Environment Design represents a suite of mobile and desktop products, additions to a larger desktop product or something else. The corporate business strategy may guide these decisions. And they will be affected by the development method, which may be more or less friendly to small, quick releases. And of course there will be more factors. But because the User Environment Design lays out a coherent system structure based

Think of shipping additional support for a role or new task for the next release

on and validated by user data, the odds of producing an incoherent release are much lower.

Once the team has identified a set of possible ways to slice up the system for release, the team can decide which to start with for the biggest impact and how to roll out from there. This should inform your product road map. As UX professionals, we have real user data and articulated design principles from the Cool Concepts which we can use to participate in the conversation about what to release. Developers can look at the function and automation required in each release and decide whether it can

Check your release concept and market message with customers to help you choose

be implemented in the desired time frame. And because there is a user interface associated with the Focus Areas relevant to each release, marketing and product management can easily illustrate the product release concept sufficiently to hold focus group sessions to determine its "wow" factor. Presenting the release concepts to prospective buyers helps determine the sales potential of each alternative, and engaging customers in a discussion of price point helps project business value. And of course, it's possible to put the ideas up in an online survey to get feedback from the larger market.

Once everyone can see exactly what is involved in each release alternative they can use the tools of their profession and their knowledge to assess the viability of the product release concept. And because there is a tangible representation of each concept in the User Environment Design, all the members of the team no matter their function can understand and see the implications of the conversation. The User Environment Design is a design artifact which can support this difficult conversation—and which embodies the commitment to making decisions based on actual data—from the user, from product management, marketing, and from engineering time estimates. It supports the team in their journey to finding the right release concept to ship.

Once your team decides what the next release will look like, you should make a *shipping User Environment Design* showing just those Focus Areas and functions that are to be part of this release. This shipping design, when all Focus Areas and functions are fully specified, forms the core of the requirements specification for this release. Then look at the impact on the overall Interaction Pattern architecture and user interface. Designers may need to make adjustments to ensure the interaction design still works based on UI principles. The larger Interaction Pattern architecture also guides these

Capture a release in a shipping User Environment Design

decisions; designers may need to simplify but they will simplify in a direction that allows for additional function to be shipped in the future without disrupting the user experience. New Interaction Patterns should be designed so they can grow up into the planned Interaction Patterns.

The decision of what to cut is also an engineering trade-off which has to account for implementation difficulty. So, the UX team may need to consider alternative presentations of a function or Focus Area in the UI for the first version. The UI can make the function easy or complicated to implement. For those functions core to a Focus Area or to a role, it may be worth designing a sophisticated UI which makes the operation of the function smooth and easy. But for less cen-tral functions (which are nonetheless needed to support the work) a bare-bones UI approach

Simplify the shipping UI but ensure it can expand to planned Interaction Patterns

may be sufficient. Everyone on the team needs to flex to the real-ity of real-world product development constraints.

So by extracting and redesigning the subset of the strategic User Environment Design you intend to ship and representing it as a shipping User Environment Design, the team can see whether that subset stands on its own as a self-contained product support-ing coherent practice. They can validate it, run scenarios through it, prototype it, and test it with users. They can find out both whether it works as a coherent product and whether it works as an interesting release—whether it provides enough to make customers interested in adopting it.

Note that if the focus of your release is to provide function for a new role or job type, the support for that role needs to be complete and interesting enough in itself to capture the interest of people performing the role. For example, if all a user can do as a trip participant is vote on suggested activities, it's of limited value to them. Everything they do is in service to the main organizer of the trip. But let them also make suggestions of their own, comment on each other's suggestions, and conduct a conversation about the trip, and they become true participants. They start to have a real stake in the outcome. That's what you'll need

Ship the functions needed by the role or task you intend to support

to hook their interest. So during prototyping of the larger product, probe for users' overall reaction to a pared-down product—but be sure to find people who really are currently performing the role, or your results won't be valid. Add or tune function to make the pared-down system work in this release for the target population.

Once you know you have a viable release you are ready to specify each screen and move into development. And you will also know what you intend to build next—though that will change, depending on the reception of the first release.

All these ways of looking at how to prioritize a release depend on being able to articulate the core innovation of the new product. What is the one key change in people's prac-

Identify your core contribution to your customers and ship that

tice which the product introduces? Don't look for a feature, look for the key way in which the proposed product release improves the life. Look for the key differentiator your product offers over the competition, or the core way your product helps your customer advance their goals. Once you've identified the key differentiator, ask: What's the minimum subset of the product necessary to introduce that change? The User Environment Design helps to maximize the impact of a new product by showing what part of the product will implement the core innovation coherently.

THE RELATIONSHIP BETWEEN UX AND PRODUCT MANAGEMENT

Our discussion at this point may seem to cross over into the responsibility of the Product Management organization. That is true, and it is unavoidable. The UX designer is responsible for the whole user experience, including product functionality, product structure, and interaction design. Ideally, they base their decisions on detailed knowledge of the customer. The Product Manager is responsible for the product, including requirements, rollout plan, and ensuring everyone works together to meet the schedule. They base their decisions on market research (which rarely includes contextual data as we understand it) and the needs of the business.

So there's an inherent overlap in responsibilities. Product Managers typically operate without the deep user insight generated from contextual inquiry—so we recommend you include them in customer visits and interpretation sessions from the beginning. Traditional techniques on their side include market research and voice of the customer initiatives, which too often only focus on what customer executives say about their needs. These methods don't capture detailed user practice, but you need that perspective to design well—so you need to be working closely with them throughout the project. For this reason, we like to put the product manager on the core team of a Contextual Design project. In many cases they are the owner and initiator of the project.

Having them on the team helps develop a shared understanding of direction and so reduces potential conflict. This conflict often emerges when designing rollout strategies—requirements driven by the business may not reflect end-users' needs. And feedback from the business and customer management (the buyer) may or may not match with the end-users' needs either. In rollout and prioritization discussions, make sure the data you have collected is present and visible and use it to justify any position you take. If others take positions you think are wrong, show the consequences using your data.

And remember that there are times when the business arguments *should* win. If customer management won't buy the "right" solution because they are focused on other issues, then that's not the right thing to sell. And any business has a focus—you can only sell what your business thinks is within its mission and is organized to sell. When the product manager is a partner, together you can negotiate these constraints. Then you can balance overall needs of your company, the customer buyer, and the user.

PARTITIONING A RELEASE FOR IMPLEMENTATION

Real products are not built by a single person—they are built by teams working together. So the design is inevitably partitioned among team members for development, and every developer must be able to focus on his or her own part independent of the others. But any requirements document has holes—developers in front of their machines at 2:00 a.m. have to make decisions that affect the users' experience. With the User Environment Design, those decisions can be made with the knowledge of how it affects the overall design and other design teams. The shipping User Environment Design organizes requirements to show how the product release is structured for the customer. But the User Environment Design also helps manage a project by showing how it can be split up for implementation by teams or individuals working in parallel.

The concepts of the User Environment Design can help a team keep the coherence of user practice during implementation. If you assign work purely based on technology or implementation considerations, each developer may not have a coherent piece of the user value to code. That will lead developers to lose the focus on the user. They can't see how the work is supposed to hang together, so they have no way of knowing if a decision they make to fill holes disrupts the user's flow of or supports it. This is one key value of the Agile user story—each story is intended to capture not just a piece of system functionality, but a piece of user value.

The User Environment Design maintains coherence of user activity during implementation

The User Environment Design and associated Interaction Patterns will guide you in breaking up work while keeping the user experience coherent. If one release includes several product concepts, they can naturally be handled by entirely separate teams. Each Focus Area represents a coherent intent of the user, so that's another chunk of work that can be assigned independently. If the team is using Agile, a whole Focus Area is usually too large for a single story, so it's likely to become an epic.[2] Then functions or closely related groups of functions that together address a user intent can be captured in a user story. In this way, each user story, though stand-alone, ties back into the overall structure of the shipping User Environment Design and into the reinvented practice it supports, as captured in storyboards.

---

[2] An epic is a large user story capturing more work than can be done in a single sprint. It is made up of smaller user stories (or smaller epics) for implementation. It may take several sprints to complete an epic. An epic can span more than one project, if multiple projects are included in the board to which the epic belongs.

So the developer is never left on her own—she's always got the larger context to reference in making those 2:00 a.m. decisions.

For any product to work, the teams focused on implementation components need to understand how they relate to user-visible behavior. The team or developer working on the Suggestion Engine in our travel example has to go deep in the technology of recommendation engines, algorithms to determine similarity between two activities, and all the machinery that makes for useful suggestions. But they can't just live in the world of technology. They have to understand the user context and the relevant identity elements to understand why some dimensions of similarity matter and others don't. Having access to the user data, a shipping User Environment Design, and the tested Interaction Patterns keeps the developer situated in the structure of the overall system and the context of use. This keeps them focused on the best overall outcome during lower-level decision making.

The Interaction Pattern architecture maintains UX coherence during implementation

The User Environment Design also reveals how utility components support different Focus Areas or subsystems. That helps the implementation team figure out who needs to work with whom. Our Idea Suggester will serve during idea collection, trip planning, and evolving plans while actually on the trip—so anyone working on it needs to work closely with the teams responsible for those product concepts. They all have a stake in the design, and the UI will have to be coherent across all three. The User Environment Design reveals all the players who are concerned so they can agree. And it shows where you'll want to assign the UI design to one person or to people who coordinate closely. And the overall Interaction Pattern architecture keeps the UX designers and the developers focused on ensuring an overall coherent user experience. In this way, the whole team—even those working on internals—stays grounded in the users' practice. The User Environment Design and Interaction Pattern architecture provides a map of which development teams and UI designers need to work together.

The User Environment Design helps see how implementation teams need to coordinate

Links between Focus Areas assigned to different teams show additional points of integration that also have to be coordinated within the implementation team. A link shows that one part of the product needs to provide access (and perhaps data) to another part and that the activity flows from one part to the other. The parts need to connect technically, so some kind of call or invocation mechanism needs to be provided. This might be through the underlying platform (moving a cursor from one screen to another), by using standard application integration mechanisms appropriate to the platform or through special APIs. Not only do the software components need to access each other, but the user also needs to feel like it's one consistent product as they move from place to place. It's important that the product have consistent appearance and behavior across the Focus Areas that are linked and used by the same people. The links identify additional areas where the UX designers need to coordinate, using the Interaction Pattern architecture as their guide to consistency.

So the User Environment Design keeps teams from becoming myopic and overfocusing on any one situation or part of the system.

The User Environment Design helps developers working on a part see their place in the whole

The Idea Collector focus area is used by the primary trip planner, by participants, and by friends. But the primary planner has much more of an intentional focus on the trip than any of the other roles—trip planners will be much more tolerant of interrupting their work and thinking about the suggestion than other roles. The User Environment Design helps the design team think about all the different users of a part of the product and makes sure it supports them all well.

Taken together the User Environment Design and Interaction Pattern structure provides a map to the implementation and interaction designers alike. The User Environment Design supports a conversation between the owners of the different parts of an implementation team about how to deliver the product. And just as the floor plan shows the layout of that bathroom—where the shower, toilet, and vanity will be—the Interaction Pattern shows how the parts of the Focus Area are shown and interact.

The line between a large application with many parts and many apps that coordinate to accomplish a larger activity is becoming blurred—with the tendency being toward many small apps on mobile platforms supporting a larger desktop application. Taken together, these apps have to act like a larger system, seamlessly supporting the flow of action across the suite of apps to accomplish the target activity. A User Environment Design representing the overall system and associated Interaction Patterns with UI designs for every platform help all the teams working in parallel communicate. With a clear map of what is being built that each team member had a hand in creating, the teams will be able to make decisions more quickly and with less contention—and that overcomes the biggest challenge to shipping on time.

A physical representation of the shipping product focuses redesign conversations

DRIVING CONCURRENT IMPLEMENTATION

Using the User Environment Design and Interaction Patterns, the team can determine exactly what to ship and move themselves into the next level of specification for shipping a real product. But the plan also guides the other functional members of the team and other groups in the company in what they need to do. And they can start these activities in parallel with implementation:

User interface design. Armed with the validated Interaction Patterns and the shipping User Environment Design, the interface designers can get down to the work of designing and iterating the actual UI to be shipped with the product. This is the time when the user researcher, interaction designer, product manager, and developers must work very closely together to make sure everything works for the user, the implementation, and the overall design and branding. But each role will have its own skills and deliverable expectations which can now work in parallel, coordinating continuously. Toward the end of development, user research and UI professionals may start working on the detailed design for the next release or sprint while development is finishing up the previous one. That way they can be one step ahead, ready to "feed the developers" with a consistent, compelling, and validated design.

Product management.   Product management has the key coordination role across all aspects of delivery—software implementation, services, support, marketing, and the rest. When the chips are down, it's up to them to ensure the final user experience in all its aspects is coherent and attractive. They have rollout plans, road maps, and Gantt charts, but few representations that help maintain coherence. Certainly working with development in terms of user stories is no help—user stories are *designed* to break the user experience into tiny, independent chunks. For them, the User Environment Design and Interaction Pattern are like the construction plans for a construction project manager—they show the system as a coherent whole and allow progress at any point to be mapped against the plan.

A tight partnership between cross-functions is essential throughout implementation

Marketing.   With the plans for what will be shipped in hand—and a visual representation of it—marketing can start developing their own communication plan for rolling out the new product or version. They know what will be there and the value proposition taken directly from the results of prototype interviews and any focus groups or surveys done to choose the release. They may still need to set the overall message or nail down the pricing in coordination with the product manager and business manager. But with a clear idea of what will be shipped they can now start their own work with confidence. We often invite marketing professionals to walk the wall during the vision to begin to give them an idea of the customer needs. This helps them get ready even earlier.

Planning services and support.   Designing a product which is itself a service means the whole Contextual Design effort needs to focus on and design the service elements intentionally (see Box Service and UX Design, Two Practices on a Collision Course, Chapter 19). Much of the development work for these products isn't software at all—it's defining business processes, physical layouts, the behavior of service providers and so forth. But even when you're not designing a service, many business products involve a significant service or on-boarding component. Once the team defines the shipping product, the groups responsible for these processes have a clear specification for what the product will do and what they have to support. They can start gearing up for this support in parallel with development, using the User Environment Design and prototypes as a reference.

Planning business processes. If the shipping User Environment Design represents a business support system, it's supporting specific business processes. If the design team doesn't include people responsible for business process design, they'll need to coordinate with those mapping and redesigning the process. Changes for employees will likely be a combination of changes in technology support and changes in roles, responsibilities, and policies. The best outcome is when the whole effort is coordinated and work together—then each discipline can complement the other. If the process people design the process without a deep understanding of how technology might support the employees, they will likely create unnecessary or unwieldy changes that might have been handled elegantly with technology. But if technology proceeds without understanding possible changes to the organization, they cannot gather the right field data to inform both the process redesign and the technology solution. So add business analysts to the cross-functional team and coordinate the whole effort to get the best result.

In our experience, Six Sigma and process professionals are surprised at how fast Contextual Design can identify the issues that need to be addressed in any process that needs optimization. So starting together and co-creating the technology support informed by possible process changes keep the whole effort on track. Once the User Environment Design is in place, the business process can be designed with the knowledge of the technical support that

Don't redesign the process independent of the technology—and vice versa

will be available. This can occur in parallel while the design team is building the release or evaluating COTS products. The process team can walk through the system to see how it supports the anticipated process, tuning both as they go.

Software implementation.   Since the User Environment Design specifies behavior without specifying the user interaction mechanisms, an implementation based on the User Environment Design function description can be developed free of UI code so that the UI can be updated without changing the underlying implementation. Then the detailed UI is hooked to the underlying implementation so that there's a clean separation between the UI-specific code and the code that implements behavior. This kind of implementation is not only cleanly layered, but it also maps easily to modern SaaS (software as a service) frameworks. As an additional guide to the implementation, annotate the User Environment Design with implementation constraints—for example, the required speed of following a link, or the constraints on size or access time of a Focus Area.

Infrastructure development.   Particularly when you're delivering a SaaS product, but also any time you have significant backend support, you'll need to plan how that infrastructure will be structured and deployed. The User Environment Design provides the requirements for the backend, including the communications between subsystems that the backend may need to support and the storage requirements for shared data. Harvest these implications from the User Environment Design and use them to drive your planning.

Because the User Environment Design is focused on the structure of the product as experienced by the user, it gives a way to structure and think about the overall system, whether delivered as a single product, a suite including apps, or a business IT system. It helps the team keep the user practice coherent by guiding communications within the team, with the implementers, and across other groups needed to deliver a product.

Implementation has its own coherence, which will come later and which may be represented in object models and other development artifacts. But the structure of an implementation is less useful for planning a user-centered project than the User Environment Design and Interaction Pattern architectures. Thinking about the User Environment Design ensures that the parts of the product and the components that are delivered are coherent from the user's point of view. That's the key value of the User Environment Design and Interaction Patterns in planning: they ensure you don't lose coherence for the user in the turmoil of getting the implementation out the door.

The User Environment Design puts the user experience in the center of development

As such, it's a natural structure for presenting product requirements to all involved. It is a good basis for creating slides and demos of possible products to be delivered now and in future releases. It forms the basis for real cross-functional communication and coordination. Finally, if a team adopts this approach, they will be rewarded with clarity around what they are designing and delivering—and they will have a physical artifact to support clear conversations with others involved in the whole product shipping process. This is the way Contextual Design puts the needs of the user in the center of the development discussion.

Project Planning and Execution

19

We've now walked through the entire Contextual Design process. You know how to run an interview, build models, vision, identify new product concepts, refine, and test the design. Along the way we've talked about how to run a design team in the context of Contextual Design, using our principles of immersion and design for life to keep the team focused and on track. We have emphasized the role of a collaborating cross-functional team and discussed how to manage different interpersonal styles. Now we step back and briefly discuss key aspects of planning and organizing a Contextual Design project. We cannot emphasize more the value of a person skilled at project leading who can keep the team organized and moving forward, and who can corral partici-pation from whoever is needed. Without that person, nothing gets done. Planning, keeping all the details and people organized, and being very clear on the goals and focus of the project to make sure it stays on track—these are all must-have skills for any Contextual Design team. In this chapter we go over key aspects of organizing the project. These planning aspects are less exciting, perhaps, than the process itself but they can sink a project if not handled well.

Don't neglect planning if you want to be successful

Contextual Design. http://dx.doi.org/10.1016/B978-0-12-800894-2.00019-3

FORMING THE CROSS-FUNCTIONAL TEAM

The Contextual Design team needs a mix of knowledge, skills, and personality types to be successful. It should consist of a core team, who are on the project essentially full time. For them, this is their primary job—this is what they are measured on. They are not only the primary workers on the project, but they are the drivers—they make sure it happens to a defined schedule. They may have helpers to set up visits with users, get conference rooms, and the rest, but these helpers support the team who owns the design. The team needs to be managed and run by the people who are tasked with delivering the solution.

The core team consists of two to four people from the key functions of your company for this project. The best core team consists of a user researcher, interaction designer, product manager (or equivalent in a business), and an engineer who knows the technology. These people must have enough stature in the organization that the work that comes out of the team will be respected. If you are serious about user-centered design you want your best people involved, not just those who have time on their hands. Brand new people are also problematic—they don't know your company or culture so they will have a harder time managing the organization.

Put your best people on the team—not those who are "available"

And make sure that one of these core team members is a *Ducks-in-a-Row planner*. Every team needs someone who likes being organized. They're the people who ask what the interviewing schedule is 2 weeks from now, because if we don't start setting up those interviews now they won't happen. They're the people who lay out the plan for a week and realize that you've asked an interviewer to get from Cleveland to Seattle over lunch. A good ducks-in-a-row person is the most critical differentiator between a team that runs smoothly and one that doesn't. This seems to be a personality characteristic which not all product managers or project leaders have. So don't assume anyone with the job title can fill the role—you are looking for a very organized person who can get people to do things for the project.

We have also noticed that good teams are often led informally by partners working together to move the team forward:

The Gas is the energetic, lively, charismatic person that keeps everyone going. They feed energy into the team. They make team design fun by their enthusiasm; they keep sessions from bogging down; they insure the team keeps moving forward. They push.

Be mindful of the characteristics of the people on the team when forming it

The Oil keeps an eye on everyone else. A team that's all gas can burn up, feel dismissed, overworked, and even ignored; the Oil watches when people are emotional, sees who is getting stepped on during lively team meetings, and makes sure that those emotions are handled. The Oil modulates the Gas.

Knowing the people who might be on the team, consider their personality characteristics as well. Who will be your Gas and Oil, who will bog down the conversation, who is open to new ideas, and who might be threatened? Choose as well as you can, and then manage the team you get. To ship the product you must deal with the human beings who have the responsibility to design and deliver. But Contextual Design has built managing people into the process, as we have described all along.

If you cannot get a full-time commitment from all four of the job types we called out, make sure that they are at least *adjunct team members*. You will need their knowledge and buy-in to move forward. Adjuncts do the same work as the core team but they participate less often and they are not expected to drive the project. They might be content creators, developers, product managers, UX people, or business process reengineering professionals. Adjunct team members might do one or two interviews, assist in interpretation sessions 2 hours at a time, and help build the affinity for a half a day or

Involve everyone who feels ownership of the product appropriate to their role and time

two. If they have key skills, they should be in the Vision and Cool Drilldown to drive the product concept. You must have good interaction designers and technologists available. Interaction designers are critical starting with the vision through validating the design. During the detailed design phase if you do not have a technologist on the team you will need one to review your assumptions and ensure the design you are creating is doable. Expect adjunct team members to devote 25–40% of their time to the project. Managers are not team members unless they want to do hands-on work—and in our experience, even if they *say* they want to be hands-on, you'd better not plan on it. They may own the project but they are stakeholders, not members of the team doing the work.

Identify and name your stakeholders: the people that care about and will be evaluating the outcome. Stakeholders may be members of other projects dependent on this project, content creators and editors, marketing who will create the market message, those that will design services, industrial designers who will design the physical product, and more. You know which people and groups are needed to get the product out the door—these are your stakeholders.

Plan in regular communication with your stakeholders

Stakeholders will help kick off the project by sharing what they and the business really cares about; they want regular status updates and to hear about your cool insights or transformative design ideas. Pull them into the Wall Walk and even Visioning. Plan regular updates for stakeholders on progress and to walk the data, the models, the storyboards, and the prototypes. These can be formal or informal interactions; they can be to a group of stakeholders or handled one at a time. Keeping the stakeholders in the loop and responding to any requests to communicate to the broader organization is part of the job of the core team.

Getting the right business functions involved in the project is critical to successful innovation. Design your team intentionally, just as you design everything else. When everybody works together as an equal, participating in all aspects of Contextual Design, they are immersed in the same customer data and work out product direction through structured activities. Through working together day in and day out they magically take on each other's point of view while collectively developing a shared understanding of the customer, the opportunity, and the direction for the product. Then, armed with a common direction, they can act independently in their job role guided by the same user and product assumptions. The team itself is your premier design tool. It pays to spend some time on it.

SETTING PROJECT SCOPE

To start your project, you need to set scope and focus. Only then can you determine how to plan your field study. Typically, a project's mission is defined in terms of the solution it will deliver: "A cool phone app to promote travel sites," "The next version of product X," "An electronic clipboard for doctor's offices," "Get the old product on to the new platform." This is the kind of problem statement that is usually given to the project team by the business or marketing—it sets a desired deliverable, often with a time frame but it does not define the right solution. So to do the right thing for the company, to have a successful project, and to get the right user data to guide your design, you need to better define your team's challenge.

Start by asking what the business is looking for. You must align yourself with the business goals—or, if it's really worth it, fight to change them. If the goals are not clear at the beginning of the project and agreed to by all stakeholders, you are asking for disappointment and conflict. Your

Determine your project's tolerance for real innovation and change

narrowest scope is "looking for fixes," whether this is a usability improvement release or finding one good feature improvement to ship or fix. This focus tells you that you are looking at current users of the existing product or section of the product. A scope this narrow is not intended to be transformative, it is not trying to deliver an overall cool user experience, and unless you fixed every usability nit in the system you are not going to make a splash in the market. This is iterative improvement, which may be very important, but it's a step-wise change. Collect data, organize it with an Affinity Diagram and perhaps a sequence model or two, then vision short-term fixes.

For any wider scope, you project will benefit from using a set of the Contextual Design models to characterize your user's world. Such a project is no longer focused on the tool itself—it focuses on improving the practice of the people engaged in a target activity. So the next level of impact is when the project wants to add a significant new feature to an existing product or system or determine what to build in the next version that will be impactful. Whenever you are adding something to an existing offering—whether it's new features, an associated app, a section of a website, a new job type to be supported—you are constrained by the existing design and system capability. This tells you that you are not utterly reinventing the user interface, that you must rely on the capability of the existing technology, and that your solution must fit within the current product.

Wider still is when the company knows that it needs to revamp the whole user interface or indicates that it is truly open to significant

> *The wider the scope, the greater innovation and change to the product and for users*

redesign. Sometimes, to make this clear, we ask directly "Can we rip off the whole top and reorganize everything in it?" If they say yes, we know that we may be constrained by what content or data they can access but that really thinking about how to reinvent the user's world is part of the goal.

We and they know that we won't ship it all right away—but by letting the design range widely, the team can invent a direction and then pull back to a practical subset for the shipping release. And for this, often we can encourage the company to think widely about a suite of offerings including companion mobile apps at the same time. Now the team knows they have permission to change the product in significant ways.

Finally, you may have the opportunity to create really new products. The company may be exploring a completely new market to see what might be good for them; they may be looking for adjacencies to understand what else they might be offered to existing customers; or they may have decided that a particular activity or job type is what they are going to go after next. They may have an existing or new technology they hope will support this population, so your project will need to understand and be thinking about that, but for the most part this is an exploration trying to answer the questions: "Can we expand into this area?" or, "How do we support this population or activity we know nothing about?" This is a very wide scope—and a big responsibility for the team. They will need to understand the potential customer, invent a solution, and build a business case before the business will give the green light. Start-ups who use customer data are in a similar situation.

Service and UX Design, Two Practices on a Collision Course

John Zimmerman
HCI Institute, Carnegie Mellon University

Service designers design services, from banks to hotels to health care to travel to retail. Over the last 30 years, this design practice emerged from marketing and operations departments as they reacted to businesses' transition away from manufacturing and toward delivering services. UX and service grew up side by side, and today they increasingly must work together.

Delivering services is different from selling products. When customers purchase products, they exchange money for ownership of a thing. When customers purchase a service, they receive a valuable performance; however, customers do not own anything. A coffee shop provides a good example of a product–service system. Customers purchase and own a cup of coffee; the product. They use the service, the coffee shop, which includes the environment, the hours of operation, the offerings, the workers and equipment to produce the coffee on demand, and the behavior of the employees. The distinction between products and services is mostly economic.

Service and UX design can appear surprisingly similar. Both have a strong focus on experience: user experience in UX design and customer experience in service. Both follow a human-centered design process to understand needs. Both engage in codesign to better envision possible futures people want and will accept. And both prototype to investigate and assess if they are making the right thing. Two important distinctions include project scope and output. UX generally focuses on making a technical system that people want to use; outputting a prototype that captures the intended user experience. Service designers more holistically address all aspects of a service including a services' physical environment, service worker policies and roles, branding and marketing, and supply management. Service designers typically output a strategy describing how to transition from current service delivery to an envisioned future service.

Technology and economic changes keep bringing UX and service design together. Services increasingly deploy self-service tools ranging from ATMs, to transit kiosks, to self-checkout at stores. They also routinely create websites and apps as new service channels. More recently, they began investigating digital interactions in physical service scapes, making apps customers use while in stores. They need UX designers who know how to work with technology. At the same time, UX designers now mostly design services and not products. For example, free mobile apps and online tools mean the user is not the customer—not the one who pays. Peer economy services and social computing services also benefit from a service perspective that addresses the flow of value across many stakeholders in an ecology. Today most UX projects benefit from team members who focus on the economic issues and how the new technology integrates across all aspects of a service.

Contextual Design, a design method used by both UX and service designers, provides a perfect space for these two practices to work together. UX designers bring expertise in envisioning new technical systems and understanding what digital materials can do. Service designers bring expertise in how services generate value for themselves and a set of stakeholders including users and customers. Contextual Design helps the design team visualize the entire system to discover where new technology can produce value, and it can reveal the best opportunities for a service to innovate.[1]

---

[1] For more on service design see Andy Polaine, Lavrans Løvile, and Ben Reason (2013) Service Design: From Insights to Implementation. Rosenfeld Media.
Service Design Network: https://www.service-design-network.org/.

SETTING PROJECT FOCUS

Once you know exactly what challenge you are taking on, you can start to plan your Contextual Design project. You need to define the problem you intend to solve in terms of the user practice you plan to support, not in terms of the technology. Once your scope is wider than a focus on tool use—which must always be considered in design, no matter the project—you need to figure out how to see the target activity in the whole life or work context that surrounds it. You need to determine what your interviews will focus on to get the best data, given the project scope. So ask yourself these questions:

Project scope determines project focus

> **What activities** will the new product support? What key user intents will they enable or improve? This is the user practice you need to find out about.

> **What roles** both at in life or work or types of people engage in these activities? Does age, type of industry, or other demographics significantly change the practice? If so, you need to plan how many of these roles and contexts you will sample.

Agree on exactly who doing what, when, and where you will interview

> **Who do these people interact with**, formally and informally? How do other people contribute? Who provides inputs—information or guidance—and who consumes the results? Do you need to interview the whole collaborative group, or can find out enough from the users you do talk to?

> **What life context** do those activities take place in? Home, work, car, hospital, school, leisure location? What geographic locations matter? When does the activity happen—in summer or winter, morning or evening, daily or intermittently? You will need to set up interviews in these different places and times.

> **What platforms** are available in those contexts? Desktop, tablet, smartphone, wearable? You will need to sample people using multiple platforms.

What tasks or key intents matter to the project, given your target activity? If the target activity is traveling then travel planning, booking all arrangements, and doing the activities on the trip are all part of what you may focus on during the interview—or may decide to prioritize some of these out.

Who are the competitors? If there are significant competitors in the market, examine any marketing data to determine your advantages and disadvantages. This will help you define activities worth looking at while in the field—and consider interviewing users of competitive products directly.

These questions help you figure out the kinds of people and situations you need to understand. Don't fool yourself into thinking that your product is so innovative there's no user data that's relevant. Anytime you think you are inventing something that has never been seen before, you are on rocky ground. There is always data to be collected to inform your design direction. If you're automating a new practice (as in the way the fitness industry transformed exercising) or introducing new technology (such as cloud computing), you may not have an existing product to use as a guide. But even though the practice will be changed, there's still a way to study it. Before spreadsheets were invented, people did the work—they used paper ledgers to chart their accounts. Before cell phones were invented people did the work— they used phone booths. Define the practice or experience your new product will replace, and study it to learn what matters and how it is structured.

There is always a way to collect field data for your project—no matter what you are making

This way you can be sure people can make a smooth transition to your new products. And it will not stifle any innovation! Both the first spreadsheets and the first word processors were developed through detailed understanding of the people in their prospective markets. Look for analogs of the technology and see how they are used in the real world. If you are automating something that already exists, such as sound or text-to-speech, look for places in everyday life where sound or speech is already used effectively. Look at the context—what else happens when people talk, such as eye contact and nonverbal cues? When is silence important? Look at what the new technology replaces—for example, Bluetooth replaces signal-carrying wires, so where are wires used? There is always data on human behavior and experience which can inform the direction of your project's work.

When your project scope is very broad, you may find that the target activity has multiple significant parts and it's hard to cover it all. It is possible to simply collect your data and design in layers. But in a fast-paced world, consider starting with a broad and shallow study looking across all the key tasks and contexts—maybe three interviews for each part of the activity—so that you can see the way the practice hangs together. Use this for initial design thinking and to determine where to dive in deeper.

Finally consider which Contextual Design models are appropriate for your project. After you review the nature of your target activity, roles, and contexts, choose which models you will use (in addition to the Affinity Diagram, which is always important). Refer to Chapter 7 to be reminded about when to use each model. Each model can only be built if you collect data relevant to it, so be sure to plan for collecting that data in your interview. For example, if you are going to build a Day-in-the-Life model, plan to do a retrospective account of the days before the interview, investigating how an activity moves across time, place, and platform.

The data you collect determines what you will design—choose wisely

These considerations will guide you in determining who to interview and how to set up and run the interviews—both the initial Contextual Inquiries and the later prototype interviews. And it will clarify further what the project is really trying to address. If you decide that you are only going to focus on travel planning and booking, you know that you are not visioning solutions to support people during the trip. And it goes the other way too—the data you collect limits what you can design.

The project scope and focus set up what to pay attention to and what to ignore. They keep the team on track and help them meet business expectations. To be successful, you need to plan the project so you get the data you need to meet your business goal. This is why knowing very explicitly the project scope and focus is so critical.

DETERMINE THE INTERVIEWING SITUATION

Your initial inquiry into the practice gave you a focus for the project, revealed some characteristics of the domain, and told you what tasks and situations you need to observe. Exactly how you will set up the interviews is driven by the nature of these tasks. So now you need to consider the constraints on the interview situation, given its context. Consider the practicalities (construction equipment may not have a second seat for an interviewer) and cultural impediments (interrupting a meeting or a surgery to offer an interpretation is highly disruptive). So how do you need to set up the interview situation to get the best data?

The key questions for defining the interviewing situation are always: How do I get close to the work? How close can I get? How do I create a shared interpretation with the user? Here are some ideas:

Normal. A normal task can be planned, is performed in a reasonably continuous session, and can be interrupted by the interviewer. Writing a letter, nearly all enterprise worker activity, driving, installing software, shopping, and any type of service are all normal tasks. The

> *Tailor the interview to the constraints of the work you observe*

interviewer can plan to be present to observe a normal task and can interrupt (mostly) at will to understand it. Normal tasks can be studied through a standard contextual interview. It may be useful to ask the customer to save activities of the sort you want to study to do during the interview; for example, when studying an ordering process, we asked the user to save up what they needed to order so we could watch them do it in the interview. This does alter the normal flow of life, but very minimally, and the increase in relevant data makes it worth it. Seasonal work is still normal—you just have to schedule interviews at the right time of year!

Intermittent. An intermittent task happens at rare intervals over the course of a day. It cannot be scheduled and does not last long. It's so infrequent that the chances of observing it during a standard contextual interview are low—you'd spend hours to get 5 minutes of data. Looking something up on Google with a smartphone and recovering from a system crash are intermittent tasks. The key to learning about them is to create a trail that will enable the user to recreate a retrospective account of the event. For in-the-moment information lookup you could give users a diary and have them make a note whenever they go to Google—but since Google has a history, it might be better to use the history as the log. Walk through each entry from the beginning of the day talking about why the user went to that site and what they did there.

Uninterruptible.   Some tasks simply cannot be interrupted to do the interpretation. A surgical operation, a high-level management meeting, and a sales call are all situations which cannot be stopped to talk about what is going on. In these situations, you want to capture the events clearly enough that you can recall all the details later. So start with the usual overview to introduce the project and find out what they plan to do that day, and uncover any entering issues you might look out for. Then let them do the activity while you watch. You might plan interruptions, such as providing for regular 15-minute breaks in a long meeting where participants can discuss what happened in the part of the meeting just concluded. When the meeting, class, or medical procedure is over, share your observations and interpretations with the user. Be sure to keep good notes to review.

Observe and interpret with the user afterwards if interrupting isn't practical

Or you might videotape the event, and then review the videotape with the user, stopping to discuss events as they occur. This is how we handled the situation of interviewing construction equipment operators; we instrumented the cab for 20 minutes while we watched from outside. Then, standing by the equipment at the construction site, we reviewed the video together, looking into the cab for reference. The video gave us a better retrospective than we could have otherwise since we weren't in the cab. Do not interpret the videotape on your own. You lose too much insight and cannot be sure of your interpretations if you review the tape alone later.

Extremely long and complex.   Some tasks take weeks, months, or even years to complete; some are business processes that involve multiple people coordinating. Insurance claims, developing a new drug, and building a 747 are all tasks which take substantially longer than the two to 3 hours of a typical contextual interview and involve many people to get the job done. To understand tasks of this sort, take a cross-sectional and cross-role approach. For a long process, interview a wide range of users at different points in the process. This cross-section of time can be gathered simultaneously and then built together to see what is happening in the whole process. Alternatively or in addition, segment the work by roles: focus on the job of the insurance agent, then the claims

Take a cross-sectional and cross-role approach to deal with complex situations

officer, and then the financial back end. Always include the key workgroup of each—including the customer. Each user will tell you about the role of others. Taken together, you will see the whole process. And if you are collaborating with process reengineers, your data can help ground some of the data they are collecting in conference rooms.

Extremely mobile.   Sometimes the person is a sales person, an auditor working in multiple locations, a partner in a firm, someone delivering services or goods in trucks. Whether they are always on the move or sometimes in different locations, the answer is the same. Go along on any trips or for the entire service day. If you want to see the use of devices during commute time, for example, you need to be in the car during the commute. Get home by public transit or have a team member follow in another car. If the user works in multiple places plan to collect some data in each of the key places and do retrospective accounts of recent activity in the other locations. Almost any project these days should be including data collection on people on the move!

Extremely focused.   Sometimes the problem is so focused on the minutia of a person's actions that it's too hard to run a standard interview. You might be polishing the detailed interaction of a computer user with an application's UI, or studying the details of how a craftsman manipulates his tools. You would miss too much if you depended on unaided observation and would get in the way of the work too much if you interrupted every moment. This is a case where videotape can be useful. It will capture the details you would

> *There is always a way to gather reliable data for your project*

miss, and you can run it discussing it with the user until you understand a particular interaction. Again, you are using the video as a better capture of a retrospective account and again, interaction with the user is critical. Another option is to use the techniques of the uninterruptible situation and agree on periodic interruptions every 20 minutes or so to discuss what you are seeing.

Internal.   Sometimes the inquiry needs to focus on internal mental processes, such as how decisions are made—how a travel planner trades off the interests of different participants, for example. In this case, the interviewer must be present when the mental process is happening—there's no way to recover enough in a retrospective account. You may need to create events which will cause the mental process to happen so that you can be present. Then interrupt a lot; make a lot of hypotheses about what the user is taking into account in their thinking. Warn them this will be very disruptive, but as long as the user has agreed to do the interview they will keep working through it and you will learn something about how they do it.

There are of course many more situations we could list. The main message is that if your goal is to get as close to the ongoing practice as possible, there is always a way to gather reliable, true-to-life data on your target activity.

DECIDING WHO TO INTERVIEW

At this point you have analyzed your interviewing situation and defined who you want to interview and their context. Now you need to get real about what you can do in the time you have available. You may need to break the project into several parts

or run parallel teams to get the work done on time. Setting up a
matrix like the one below may help you choose.
Remember, either you can cover the space the
project is to address or you will need to scope the
project back.

The scope of your project may change once you look at how many interviews it implies

We use a simple matrix to help us figure it out.
Here is an example of what a team might start with
to study travel, using a few of the relevant variables—
there may be more in actuality. Make sure each vari-
able really matters—that it will change the users' strategies, values,
activities, intensions, or identify elements. In this matrix, you see that
we just assume that we need a mix of gender and age range; we work
out the rest by what the team thinks will change the travel experience.

INTERVIEWEES: MEN AND WOMEN AGES 25–55	TRAVEL PLANNER: BIG VACATION	TRAVEL PLANNER: FAMILY TRIP	TRAVEL TO VACATION HOME	ON THE TRIP	TOTAL KINDS OF TRAVELER
Single	1		1	2	4
Married/part-nered, no kids	1		1	2	4
Married/part-nered small kids	1	2	1	2	6
Married/ partnered kids over age 12	1	2	1	2	6
Empty nesters	1		1	2	4
Total lifestyles	5	4	5	10	24

In general, you want to interview three to four people in each role or
context you identified as important to the focus. In our travel matrix each
column is one important role/context combination; you can see from
the totals in the bottom row that this scope means you have to interview 24 people to get at least four in each of those boxes. Other demographic differences—geography, economic income, education—are

varied in each context or ignored if not relevant. A typical project may have 8–12 interviews for a small project, 15–24 interviews for a larger one, or as much as 25–30 interviews for something really big. Anything more than that is unwieldy both for managing the interviews and managing the team. And for almost any project real knowledge can be had with 18–24 people. If your project is addressing only one role in one context interview five to six people, but most projects—even the most focused—involve more than one role and one context.

18–24 interviews are enough for even a large scope—6 for a small one

But what if you need to scale back? If you were on the travel project and it needed to be done more quickly, you might reduce scope. You might decide that supporting the trip itself would be a later project and for now you'll focus on travel planning. That removes a whole column with 10 interviews from the matrix. If you can't reduce scope, consider focusing on just the most important demographic. For travel, you might make your initial focus people with no children, in which case the matrix will look like this:

INTERVIEWEES: MEN AND WOMEN AGES 25–55	TRAVEL PLANNER: BIG VACATION	TRAVEL TO VACATION HOME	ON THE TRIP	TOTAL KINDS OF TRAVELER
Single	1 or 2	1 or 2	2	4/6
Married, no kids	1	1	2	4
Empty nesters	1	1	2	4
Total lifestyles	3 or 4	3 or 4	6	12–14

Or you could go the other way and only interview family with children. How to decide? Look at your market data—who has the most money and biggest population? Start there. When you change the focus and the plan like this, double-check your numbers to make sure you still believe in the data. Above, we added more singles to balance the number of married people.

Even a fairly contained focus for travel planning can blow up into a huge project including business travel, trips overseas, in national parks, with planned groups, etc. So be clear on the most important contexts for your project—and what maps best to your business mission. Nearly any project will look at different roles and contexts in multiple passes rather than trying to do it all at once. This makes the project more Agile friendly, but it was true even before Agile came along.

Collect data in layers— expanding what you cover iteratively

If you are making business software, you want to go to at least four to six businesses to see variety. In choosing sites and individuals, go for diversity in work practice. You are looking for the common underlying structure that cuts across your customer base—you will do this best by studying very different users, rather than studying similar users to confirm what you learned. Underlying work structure is common, so you will check your knowledge just as well with a very different user as with one who is similar.

And remember market segments identified by marketing are not the same as differences in the practice. Financial institutions, high-tech, and retail may be different market segments, but office work is done very similarly in any modern corporation. These different types of companies will not give you substantially different perspectives. (Office work is so similar

Interview users whose work is as different as possible

it is actually hard to get a different perspective. In an effort to find cultures which would be substantially different, one design team studied the military and Japanese companies. They found little that was new.) Every time our clients insist on expanding the numbers of people to interview to match the way marketing thinks about the customer population, they get lots of data overlap and redundancy. This is frustrating to the team and not helpful to the design. But if you need to do it to keep the business happy, just do it. Then they can see the overlap too. Just start the project sampling the key different contexts and consolidate your models after 15 interviews— then roll all the rest of the data into that structure.

Focuses on differences in practice not differences in market segments

To find different practices, look for different underlying strategies, e.g., doing work as a business for hire as opposed to doing it as a department in a large company. Look for work culture differences, e.g., a trucking company versus a high-tech company. Look for different physical situations, e.g., a company distributed across several states versus a company that only operates in a single state. Look for differences of scale, e.g., a small business versus a large corporation.

When you finish this analysis you will have further scoped your project and you will know who to interview. And it's okay to be smart when choosing—include the important client whom Sales wants to keep bought in. Finally focus on customers from the key markets you think are most likely to spend money—don't go universities just because it is easy to set up visits, if they won't buy the product.

Expect setting up user visits to take 2–4 weeks depending on whether you have good vendors or internal processes to get to them. If you have to work through your sales people and send out emails to entice your users, it will always take longer. It is best to set up an organization to handle customer visit setup; if you can't do that, make it one person's job. It is all part of the challenge of any user-centered design process. Finding the right person to interview, talking to all the people in the company or at the customer site who have to approve, and setting everyone's expectations correctly simply takes time.

Initial visit setup simply takes time; make sure it's someone's job

However, don't get too far ahead in lining up the visits. As you study the data, you will change your idea of what to find out about next. The Travel Planning team wouldn't want to be locked in to interviewing 10 people going to their vacation homes after they've studied three and discovered that they all barely prepare because they have done it so often. And don't forget to confirm the interview the day before you go. Make sure you talk to the people you will interview individually in advance and that they understand what will happen.

SETTING THE INTERVIEW FOCUS

You now know exactly who to interview, where they will be, and what they will be doing. Your interview focus starts with what matters for your project, but how that plays out depends on who you are interviewing. Contextual Inquiry does not define a common protocol to be used with everyone. Go into an interview with nothing but a focus statement at the top of your notebook page. Any field interview can go in many directions, so you need to know what to pursue and when you have gone off track. So for each interview, set your own focus: boil it down to a short statement of the key tasks to watch for that person. This statement can be written by interviewers in their notebook, and will keep them on track during an interview. A focus for the main travel planner of the family might be: Look at how they track their plan, get information, share it, collaborate on a decision, and choose where they stay and how they get there. Such a focus suggests how to guide the interview and what to pay attention to during it. Focus statements are best when they use simple language. People looking for "where people stay" will think more broadly about the user's intent than if they write down "choosing a hotel."—so write down what reflects the scope of your project best.

During the interview, follow the overall focus and interview structure, gather the data you need for the Contextual Design Models you have selected, and pay attention to tool use. The initial focus will be revised and expanded through inquiry into the practice, with the user and during the interpretation session.

Focus evolves as you learn about the work

PLANNING THE SCHEDULE

As soon as you are ready to set up visits the need for real planning and project management kick in. Nothing is more frustrating for team members than not knowing what the plan is—even if it changes. People feel out of control if they don't have all the information they need for the interview, the date, place and time for subsequent interpretation sessions and design meetings, and who to call if there is a problem at the visit.

Scheduling your project on a day-to-day level is about making trade-offs to get the work completed. Depending on the project, the number of team members, the number of interviews, and the project length there are an endless number of possible schedules. The goal is to make sure that you don't overextend the team by stacking too many interviews on top of each other. Interviews should be interpreted within 48 hours, so you need to space them out.

Schedule your project in a day-by-day plan and invite everyone who has to be there

If you have the budget and can get a group of interviews scheduled in one physical location, you can have the whole team travel out and perform interviews and interpretation sessions off-site. This can be a good team-building activity for a new group—start with an intensive field trip together, focused on the design problem. Then you can work well in small groups or remotely. The following considerations will help you develop a workable schedule.

Train the team. If you have one or two untrained members, bring them up to speed on Contextual Inquiry before the project starts, including some practice interviews. Then train them in each process as you go. Go on the first set of customer interviews shortly after the training to solidify team members' new knowledge.

Start with a few interviews. Interview a few people at a time. Starting with two to three key interviews and interpreting them right away means that you can start to learn the users and the data. Remember that the interpretation session helps reset your interview focus—you do better interviews after you start interpreting.

Conduct weekly Process Checks to manage emerging issues

Create a day-by-day plan. If you plan your week well, everyone will know where they are supposed to be and can plan accordingly. Day-by-day schedules structure your time and set expectations for how long things will take—you will know when you are falling behind and be able to adjust.

Conduct weekly process checks. At the end of each week (or more often) gather the team and do Plusses and Minuses on your process. Say what is working well in the process, the schedule, and the team dynamics, and say what needs to be improved. Brainstorm fixes for the problems and try them out the next week. This is about airing issues in the project and making sure resentments don't build up.

Respect the home/work balance. No one can work all the time—down time is important not only for family life but simply to stay sharp. Contextual Design is mentally demanding (that's what makes it fun). A Contextual Design project is intense because people are working together all the time collecting, interpreting, and thinking about the data and the design. So plan in down time.

Do your scheduling at the level of the week and at the level of the day. You are coordinating a whole team of people whose activities have to interlock closely—it's a much more intricate problem than most team scheduling. Here's how you might think about the weeks for a medium-size project with18 interviews doing all parts of Contextual Design with a 4-person team—two core people and two adjuncts.

Week 1	6–8 contextual field interviews and interpretation sessions
Week 2	4–6 more interviews and interpretation sessions; build preliminary Affinity at end of week (invite helpers!)
Week 3	Refocus and do the last 6 interviews and interpretation sessions; get ready to consolidate
Week 4	Rebuild the Affinity and consolidate 2–3 target Contextual Design models (everyone works this week pretty full time)
Week 5	Clean up the models, get them online, and make them graphically enticing (use your helpers). Get ready for visioning; invite the larger visioning team. Invite the stakeholders to see the data on day 1 of the vision. (Remember to invite them far enough out to get on their calendar.)
Week 6 (or when you are ready)	Vision for 2–3 days identifying product concepts, and do a cool drilldown on 2–3 concepts the last 2 days (or drilldown the next week.); this can be done in a four-day workshop. (Everyone works this week pretty full time)
Week 7	Storyboard for 3 days; build the first cut of the user environment design
Week 8	Validate user environment design, do interaction Patterns, start sketching the UI for the prototype
Week 9	Finish UIs and create paper prototypes (including making copies). (Make sure someone is setting up prototype visits!)
Week 10	Conduct first round of 3–4 prototype interviews and interpret; redesign the paper prototypes
Week 11	Conduct second round of 3–4 prototype interviews and interpret; redesign the paper prototypes

At this point you are ready to move into Agile planning, do a visual design and test it, get the mock-up online or otherwise move into detailed design and implementation. The key is to plan out the process and stick to the schedule.

Plan the process, invite the people, stick to the schedule

A smaller project can be much faster:

Week 1	6–8 contextual field interviews and interpretation sessions, optional preliminary affinity
Week 2	4–6 more interviews and interpretations sessions; build and finish affinity at end of week. (Invite helpers!)
Week 3	Consolidate two Contextual Design models and get them online and printed. (Invite helpers!)
Week 4	Vision, identify product concepts, and do a Cool Drilldown on two concepts. Don't forget to invite stakeholders and the team! (You might stop here to rescope to a potential deliverable and proceed with a more constrained plan that will be closer to the shipping product.)
Week 5	Storyboard for 3 days; build the user environment design
Week 6	Validate the user environment design, do interaction Patterns, do the UI for the prototype.
Week 7	Create paper mockups and do the first round of testing with 3 interviews and interpretation sessions; redesign the paper prototype
Week 8	Conduct second round of 3 prototype interviews and interpretation sessions; redesign the paper prototypes

Then move into Agile, visual design, and all other activities.

Finally, here's how you might think about the structure of the interviewing week, ending with a preliminary affinity. If you travel you'll leave Sunday and come home before you start the affinity on Friday at home. Or you will stay and collect eight interviews in this week and not build an affinity.

Do a day-by-day detailed schedule and publish it

MONDAY	TUESDAY	WEDNESDAY	THURSDAY	FRIDAY
AM Interview in parallel at 2 locations; each person conducts 2 interviews.	**All day** Complete 4 interpretations in back-to-back sessions. Capture chosen models Include a 3rd or 4th person to help in interpretations if possible. They can be conducted remotely.	**AM** 2 parallel customer interviews Return immediately for interpretation sessions.	**Option 1: All day** Build preliminary affinity of approximately 300–400 affinity notes. Include at 2–4 more people to help. With no helpers, 2 people will need Friday to finish. **Option 2:** Collect more data to complete 8 this week, building the affinity on Friday.	**All day** *Option 1* Clean-up affinity. Check affinity, identifying holes for subsequent interviews. Reset focus for next round of interviews. Take the rest of the day off.
PM Second interview		**PM** 2 back-to-back interpretation sessions. Include with helpers.		

Plan out all your weeks this way for the duration of the project. You'll be glad you did, and everyone will know what they are doing and when they are needed.

With a clear project scope and focus you can pick the right variant of Contextual Design and the Contextual Design models for your project. With the right people in place you will have the skill to invent. With a cross-functional team you get the skill and the buy-in you need—and they will understand and believe in the project outcome and be poised for parallel work after the project. Then it's all execution—setting up the visits, making the schedule work for everyone on the team, lining up the people, places, and conference rooms—and of course the users. Contextual Design tells you what to do to make transformative

Success is truly dependent on execution excellence

products—the Cool Concepts help you see, understand and support our core human motives. Contextual Design organizes a project by laying out a series of activities which help teams collect, interpret, synthesize, and use data about their target population and then to use it to drive design thinking. From there Contextual Design guides a team to design the structure of the product and the user experience and then returns to the user to iterate the ideas. But without good project execution nothing will happen. So let the activities we discuss here guide you to success.

MANAGING THE TEAM

Finally, we return to the third core principle in Contextual Design: team design. Emerging research highlights the power of diversity to enhance innovation, and we hope the next years will see a significant increase in women and other underrepresented populations on our teams. But diversity has always been a challenge when people are brought together to design and build products. It takes many job functions to build a product, each with their own skills and experiences—and each of these people come with different interpersonal and cognitive styles. So Contextual Design has always had to help diverse people work together to come to a shared understanding around what to design and build. Once you accept that working with other people is at the crux of what gets in the way of shipping innovative products on-time, the need for techniques to help real working design meetings becomes apparent. We have introduced these throughout the book and pointed out issues in managing the team given each step in Contextual Design.

Diversity on the team promotes innovation in the product

To make a team work, provide all the key components needed to help them work well: a clear shared goal, determined by setting project scope and focus; an agreed-upon process including specific steps, models, and a schedule. Get the right roles and skills on the team not only to get the job done—such as cross-functional skills—but also skills to keep the team moving forward—such as a natural project leader and a bit of *Gas* and *Oil*.

But even with that, the team still needs to manage itself and deal with individual differences in personality and cognition to be a truly creative team. And this only gets harder if you are trying a new process with skills you aren't expert at and traveling to get to the users. Success comes when the team can take advantage of each person's best skills. So we provide techniques and suggestions to help with this specific to each process, such as dealing with overwhelm during the

Manage the interpersonal tone of your team explicitly

affinity, differences between convergent and divergent thinkers, or cognitive style. (See section Cognitive style and working teams below). We have moderators to help some people speak up and others stop dominating conversations. We have techniques to tune the process, such as the end-of-week process check—which also lets people say honestly what isn't working for them so that they are heard and helped along. Importantly, we ask everyone to buy into managing the interpersonal tone of the room and valuing every teammate; we expect each member to understand and modulate their own style. And we help them figure out how—by naming a cognitive style so it is known, by creating the *Mom Response* concept to ask for positive feedback by writing down what everyone says so they are heard, and so forth.

Contextual Design has often been called a backbone process; it includes everything you need to do from understanding the user to designing a successful product and user experience. Any group or company may decide to slide additional processes into the backbone; they may use only some of the steps or some of the models; or they may replace our design processes with their own. But the most important thing for any team is to have *an articulated and agreed way of working and roles* to make the work.

With that in place, leadership and innovation emerge out of the combined skills and creativity of a diverse team—diverse in skill, background, gender, and ethnicity. In Contextual Design we trust in the knowledge of the team. We build on the skills of each person brought into the room not only because all these people are needed to ship a product but because we believe that many minds, well orchestrated, within a user-centered design process will deliver the best result.

But that means accepting the idiosyncratic differences between people, building on their strengths and working around their weaknesses.

Observe your people closely and leverage their strengths

A team does not need everyone to be a good notetaker in an interpretation session—but two is nice; not everyone has to be great field interviewers—as long as you have enough to get the data, with others helping to capture the data or concepts; we don't all need to know about technology, interaction design, how to understand people, or the needs of the business. But if we put all these people together and give them a way to work, user data to arbitrate decisions, and a way to get along, we can lean on all of these strengths. Then, when you are not the one with that key skill at that point in the process, because you believe in the team you will support the result. No one person is enough to make a great product—but a well-functioning team can be.

Contextual Design creates a new team culture and way of working—committed to using data about people's real lives to drive requirements and design. And embedded in each step is a set of values, clear roles, decision-making processes, and a commitment to manage interpersonal differences. We don't promise that you will be comfortable with every step of Contextual Design or that you will be skilled in every activity. But you will be great at some and good enough at others to help the team along. Together you can create great products and services—and have a little fun!

COGNITIVE STYLE AND WORKING TEAMS

Over the years, we have found that cognitive style affects relationships between team members more than any other kind of individual difference. When people must really collaborate to create a vision, storyboard, or UI design together, we find that people with different cognitive styles can easily rub each other the wrong way. When people clash we need to intervene to help them deal with it. But cognitive styles are often complementary. Cognitive style is something you are born with. There is no better or worse style—and intelligence or creativity has nothing to do with it. So be happy with what you have been given and learn to manage it in yourself and others.

To help we have named some of the styles that manifest themselves in design sessions. Here are some differences we have found useful:

The Cloud: The Cloud is a web thinker. They connect and integrate everything into a web of relationships. They can see how the data in the Contextual Design Models builds a bigger and bigger picture of the problem, and this lets them generate a wider and more complex response. Because they are carrying this thread of integration in their mind, they don't like to be interrupted during a Wall Walk. But their design ideas are very high level and "cloudy." They are terrific in generating overarching product concepts but much less interested in the lower-level details of exactly how something works. Every project needs at least one Cloud, but more than two and they will never ship a product. They'll just keep generating more and more high-level ideas without ever bringing it down to something concrete.

The Brick: Every Cloud needs and often finds a partner who is a Brick. As the Cloud on a team generates more and more ideas others (and even the Cloud) get frustrated because they are all overwhelmed with the output. But a good Brick starts to see how the parts of the Cloud's ideas may be brought together into shippable or at least structured product concepts. The Brick says "I could take this and this and this together and we could make this." And the team says, "Really?" And the Brick says, "Yes!" and starts structuring a product concept with enough detail (not too much) to give it bones. Then when they need some new ideas the Brick calls the Cloud over and says, "Give us some more ideas on this"—until there are enough. In a good partnership, the Brick helps the Cloud manage their output and make something real. The Brick helps the team take action. But a team of all Bricks is much less creative. Find your Cloud and Brick partnership and you are golden.

The Popper: The Cloud connects every idea together; the Popper connects nothing. Every piece of data is a new stimulus for a new design idea. The Popper is a divergent thinker; there is no attempt to connect ideas while in dialogue with the data. So the Popper pushes the teams thinking wider. They come at the problem from many points of view. This too can frustrate the team because the Popper keeps throwing out new, disconnected ideas when everyone else is trying to focus. But the divergent ideas bring in creativity, and if you also have a Cloud these new ideas will be woven into the thread and make the overall result better. More people are Poppers than Clouds or Bricks. Use them well, but don't let them tear your direction or design apart.

The Christmas Lights Thinker.   The old Christmas lights were linked bulbs; if one bulb went off the whole string went dark. Nothing could happen until the one failing bulb was found and replaced. The Christmas Lights Thinker is a person whose brain and creativity is linear. They remember all the facts, and associated dates, and all the names of the presidents in order. They use their orderly mind to line everything up—all the details in a Vision or Storyboard or any design. They'll see that all the parts are present and complete and hook to other parts. But if anything is missing—no matter how small—their whole string of lights goes down and they can't move forward. And they stop the team from moving on until the hole is dealt with and their bulb is relit. They will not—they cannot—take a step if they miss a piece of the story or if something isn't correct. They will insist that you fill the hole, look up the fact, or fill in the missing step in the design before considering anything that comes after.

Imagine a Cloud working with a Christmas Lights Thinker—not a good partnership. The Cloud ignores details and the Christmas Lights Thinker won't move on without detail. They can frustrate each other so much that it may be best if we simply don't team them. But if both can modulate their style and increase their patience, we will get a better result. One team member was a Christmas Lights Thinker so we gave her that concept and told her to tell us when she needed a fact. Once she knew what was going on she could declare it. "Wait! My light bulb went out! Just give me a minute or can you fill in the blanks for me." If she and we know what's going on we can find a way to move on and improve the design—because often the hole really does matter. And sometimes we ask them to write it down—put in a "placeholder" in her mind—until later when we need the detail. This works too.

The Diver: The Diver is much like the Christmas Lights Thinker and frustrates and holds up the team in much the same way. But the Diver—often a technologist, sometimes a UI designer—wants to prematurely jump all the way down from a very loose product concept to the lowest-level details of the code, implementation, or UI. When we are trying to identify high-level product concepts or redesign the user's practice in Storyboards, working out the implementation is simply not relevant—storyboards are in effect developing requirements for the implementation. The Diver stops the action until they can understand how the code will work. And if the Diver is a project manager, they won't move on until every last detail of the task is laid out—which just frustrates the people they're managing.

So we tell the Diver what they are doing so they know, and then we offer a challenge: "Can you dive across the surface instead of down deep? Can you look for the holes at the level of the design we are dealing with (redesigning the practice) instead of jumping down to the implementation?" If they know they are being disruptive but will later be important when we need all those deep holes filled, they try to modulate their behavior. And over time we have seen these folks learn to focus on higher-level issues!

These are the main cognitive styles that we have seen clashing—and helping each other on a team. In the end, you can't change what you are but you can learn to recognize when you're stuck. You can learn to recognize that it's just a clash of cognitive style. You can learn to declare that you're stuck and get help—and you can all learn patience once you see the value of the other styles. Then you see that the problem is not that "annoying person"—it is simply our individual differences! These differences help get us to success.

Conclusion 20

In this book, we've introduced Contextual Design 2.0—a 25-year-old method reinvented for the modern age of pervasive, always-on technology, and for the emergence of design as a real discipline. Though the techniques of Contextual Design can stand alone, they build on each other to make a comprehensive method covering the ground from user research through front-end design. This means that development has a stable ground on which to start coding, with enough validation and product definition to ensure the user is still supported when all is said and done. Each Contextual Design technique is strong on its own, being carefully crafted to perform one part of the design task well. Put together, they are even stronger, ensuring that the user voice stays strong and clear throughout the process.

As we presented and dissected each technique in depth, it may have been easy to lose track of the principles driving the process. We listed three in the Introduction for special attention: Design for Life, Immersion, and Design in Teams. We added the idea of scenario and structural design thinking as we explored how to get the best product for the user and the business. It is worth revisiting these and highlighting additional principles before we close. So we'll wrap up here with a reminder of these principles, calling out just how we've used them:

> *Everything starts and ends with the user*

User-centered design. Everything we do starts with the user and ends with user validation. We form our understanding through field research, talking to users where they live and work, while they do

Contextual Design. http://dx.doi.org/10.1016/B978-0-12-800894-2.00020-X

the activities we are designing for. We may augment field visits with market research, surveys, or other techniques but we never substitute these other techniques for going to the field. The data is richer and generates more insight than any other; we never trade this off.

The user focus permeates Contextual Design. We start, of course with user research. But every technique between research and validation also puts the user in the center. Consolidation lets the team see the structure and pattern of the users' life, across all users, from multiple points of view. Visioning tells the users' story as they live their lives and do their activities, using technology as they go. The storyboards tell the story again, cleaned up, in detail, and focused on one particular chain of events. The User Environment Design shows the structure of the system as the user experiences it, and the Interaction Patterns show the structure of the UI as the user interacts with it. Finally, of course, paper prototype interviews close the loop, validating our direction and fleshing out the detailed requirements.

Design for life.   User data is a given, but core insight of the Cool Project was that design for life is not the same as design for task or design of technology. Products today allow people to mix their lives and work to a greater degree than ever, and however much we

Lives have no boundaries. Neither should products

all joke and complain about it, we like it. We like being able to settle a work crisis while at our child's baseball game; we like cruising vacation sites during a break at work. Any design has to consider the whole of life if it's going to fit into life—if it's going to be a product or a service people call cool.

We start our focus on design for life in the interviews themselves, through the specific interviewing techniques we discussed in Chapter 3. We carry that focus forward through the Experience Models, maintain it in Visioning, and then take it as our primary focus in the Cool Drilldown. Storyboards show the new design being used in all the places and situations of life; then the User Environment Design and Interaction Patterns reveal how it shows up on different platforms. Through the use of device-specific prototypes, the fit to life is tested during the mockup rounds.

Immersion.   Hearing about the user is one thing; understanding and embodying knowledge about the user at a gut level is another. Because people are people, just telling them information about the user doesn't really communicate—not at the level necessary for design. So we design immersion experiences throughout the process in which team members experience the lives of their users over and over. Whether it's participating in an interview, hearing the story in an Interpretation Session, doing or walking a consolidated model, or testing a design, we constantly bring designers face-to-face with the world of their users in ways that make it impossible to ignore. And this immersion naturally tunes the "gut feel" of the team so they naturally become user-centered designers.

Help the team become natural user-centered designers

Take multiple perspectives on a problem.   There's rarely only one useful way to look at a problem and in Contextual Design we rarely look at a problem in one way. We take notes of an interview—and build models. We don't build one—each different model gives a different perspective. Capturing issues in a Wall Walk, we are perfectly happy to capture contradictory issues if people are seeing different things in the data. We don't do one vision—we do several, and there's no need for them to be compatible.

Alternating scenario and structural thinking throughout the design phase is another way of changing perspective. First look at the design from the point of view of a thread of use—then switch and look at the structure of the thing itself. Each point of view gives insight and informs the other.

Design by humans.   It's a core principle of all our techniques that we have to work with the strengths and limitations of being human rather than against them. Some methods require huge amounts of slow meticulous tracking or thought, the original Quality Function Deployment process, for example; we find that few people can stick with that level of detail. If people don't want to use the process, no matter how

Release the power of the people on your team

valuable it is, it won't be used. Similarly it's usual to assume that writing up a report or sending a memo will communicate; we don't depend on it. Some data gathering methods ask for total objectivity from the interviewer; we don't think that's possible and use the interviewer's subjectivity instead. Nearly every organization acts as though people can truly participate by sitting still in a meeting and listening passively; we find that people invariably zone out in such situations.

Instead, we define techniques that draw on people's strengths. Field research is hard—but sitting with someone side-by-side and talking with them about what they're doing is easy. We can all do that. Paying attention for long periods while sitting still is hard; instead, in our meetings we give everyone an interactive task to do which they have to pay attention to; the work gets done and everyone stays hooked in.

It's tempting to demand people be better. Better people would follow every detail. Better people would never zone out. There's an analog to design: "Better people would read the documentation, including that footnote on page 45". But that never works and isn't necessary. Instead, we take the approach that people are just fine the way they are—awesome, in fact—it's just our responsibility to set up the situation so that that awesomeness is released.

Design by teams.   Techniques for managing teams are never an afterthought in Contextual Design. Every piece of the method has been developed with the understanding that it will be performed by a group of people working together, rather than by an individual. Certainly you can do every step as an individual, but that's not how we developed or thought about the process. Nor is that the typical way of working in most companies.

Manage the team to harvest creativity

Design by team means that making the team work together is a core concern. At the very heart of Contextual Design is the philosophy that if you tell the team what to do and how to do it, they can be successful. So for each step of Contextual Design we define the process, the roles or jobs that need to be done, what constitutes a quality result, how to critique effectively, and how to tune the process to fit their needs. Given the diverse nature of people and the skills we gather to do the work, we have found that clear structure and rules of engagement ensure a successful product design and a good working team.

Yet even with a clear, well-structured process, teams are still composed of people. So we build team-management techniques right into the process. These techniques repeat across the steps of Contextual Design:

Externalize conversations. Every team conversation in Contextual Design has an externalized form. The discussion about implications of an interview are captured in notes and models in the Interpretation Session. The vision is captured on flip charts. The User Environment Design is captured in a diagram. And so for every step—there's always a way to put the conversation on a piece of paper (or an online document) and in front of the eyes of the team, even if that's just a simple list.

Externalizing the conversation is valuable in itself. It makes the discussion easier to have because you can see what you're talking about. But also there's wisdom in the old rule from Robert's Rules of Order that speakers address the Chair, not each other. Disagreements and discussions are about the data or the design, not about the annoying person who is disagreeing with you. Like speaking to the Chair, speaking to a model, a sketch, or a list of plusses and minuses orients the participants toward the thing they should be paying attention to, not the person who is across from them.

Name what you want to control.   Throughout the process, one key technique for managing teams is to name the concepts we want teams to manage. We start by naming roles: the moderator, the notetaker, the modeler. Names bestow power—the moderator is allowed to tell one person to stop talking so another can make their point; the notetaker is allowed to rephrase a point in a succinct and direct way (and the rest of the team is allowed to push back if they don't think the phrasing reflects their intent). But this power is not an imposition on others—this is

> *Naming gives you a lever to manage yourself and others*

power given freely so that the rest of the team is free not to worry about these concerns.

Naming design from the "I," a rat hole (Chapter 4) or the Mom Response (ref) takes problematic team behavior out of the realm of interpersonal conflict and personal limitations and puts it into the realm of shared experience that can be discussed openly without embarrassment. Calling something a rat hole adds a dimension of humor to a reminder to stay on topic. Names come with rules of how to deal with the named behavior—which we discuss and which become team norms. It's hard to say, "I feel beat up and vulnerable, so how about some affirmation now." It's much easier to say, "Hey! Where's my Mom Response?"

In the same way we name personal differences that affect how the team operates. The Gas and Oil help the team work well; the Cloud, Brick, Diver, and the rest name cognitive styles and also come with tips for how to handle those behaviors. Naming increases awareness, tells people they come by potentially difficult behavior honestly, and externalizes the characteristics that will show up in team interactions. Naming makes them fair game for discussion and strategizing. Rather than being annoyed with Jim, the engineer who gets stuck on technical details, another team member can say, "Jim! Stop diving now, it's not time for it. Why don't you dive across the solution for a bit, at least while we're visioning?"

The user is the arbiter.   We end this list of principles where we began: with the user. Throughout Contextual Design, we never forget that the user is the only real measure of the design. Before visioning, the user is the only authority about what is true in their lives, what they're trying to accomplish, and how they want to accomplish it. After Visioning, the user is the only measure for whether any design idea is any good. Prototyping isn't just a nice-to-have failsafe to make sure that your design is good. Prototyping is an integral part of the design process. If you're arguing about what to ship stakes are high and, probably, so are emotions. If you're arguing about what to test, stakes are much lower. User data and user tests are the ground on which your design

Let the user level the power field on the team

rests—and no one really wants to argue with the ground. Becoming a data-based organization means that you have the user data you need to make arbitration possible. And looking to external data to help decision making is another way to remove interpersonal friction and level power. With data, power is in the user value—not the opinion of the smartest, loudest, or most important person in the room.

In addition to the above principles, there are a few more keys to success to keep in mind. You need your project driver, the person who can keep ducks in a row, who likes to line up ducks, and who can't help but line up the ducks if he or she finds them wandering. Find this person and cherish him or her, wherever they are in the organization and whatever their role. If they don't have the formal role to order everyone around, give them the role informally—use names to make it legitimate. Give them a scepter and call them Queen of the Schedule if you have to—just make sure that they exist and they are listened to.

And make sure you have decent designers on your team, as we discussed in Chapter 19. Design is a skill that needs to be trained; it doesn't happen by accident. If you're fortunate enough to be in a company that values design, there will be plenty around. But many companies in established industries still see design as an afterthought. You'll need to work to find people who can carry this part of the task.

Cherish your project drivers and designers

Finally, let us conclude this book by talking briefly about organizational culture. When the first edition came out, user-centered design was new and radical; now user research and user experience design are a standard practice. But a truly user-centered organization is still a rare thing. True, UX designers have a place in many organizations—but many organizations still treat them as less powerful than developers. Sometimes they are seen as usability testers providing a compiling operation to get out the nits in the UI. Or they may be used as the designers of buttons and layout of preexisting function—rather than being charged with understanding the market, or with finding, defining,

The mission of user-centered design is not over

and designing the right product for your business. A real equal partnership between user research, design, and product management
and a deep respect for UX professionals and their function by development is critical for true user-centered design. So we have come a
long way, but the organizational change mission of our work—and
yours too—is not over.

If you're in this situation, you'll have to do what you can. You
will be at the forefront of showing, bit by bit, the value of the work
we do. We hope the *On Your Own* boxes throughout this book have
given you ideas for how to implement some of the techniques when
you don't have the whole organization behind you. Try them out,
talk about some of the ideas from this book—but don't get strident.
Don't run around telling everyone how they're wrong—even when
they are. Do what you can and share what you do—promote the
results, not the process. Let people see the value. Then, when they
ask, "How did you do that?" you can answer, "Well, there's this cool
process, see…"

Index

'*Note:* Page numbers followed by "f" indicate figures, "t" indicate tables and "b" indicates boxes.'

Printed in the United States
by Baker & Taylor Publisher Services